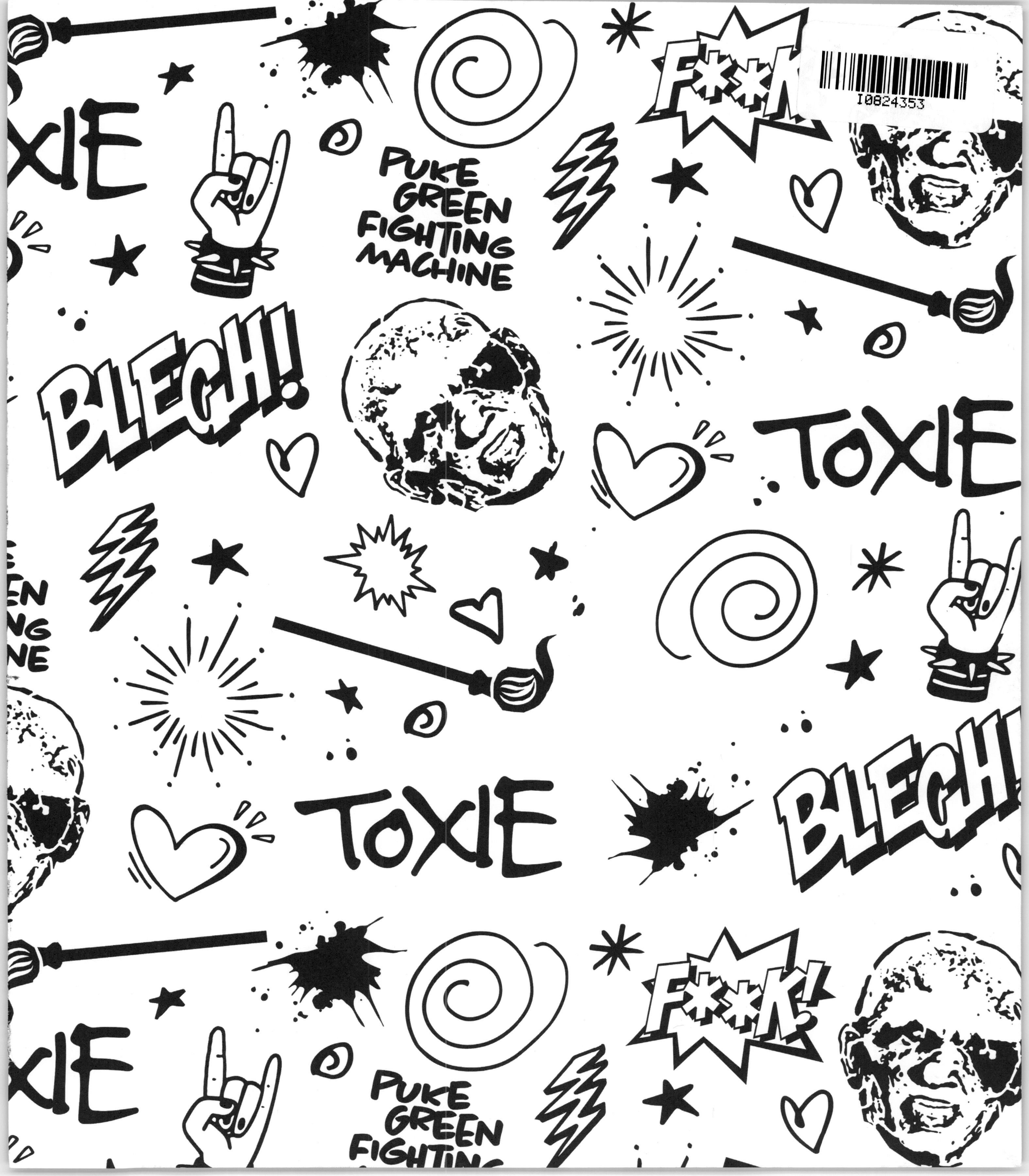
TOXIE
PUKE GREEN FIGHTING MACHINE
BLECH!
F**K!

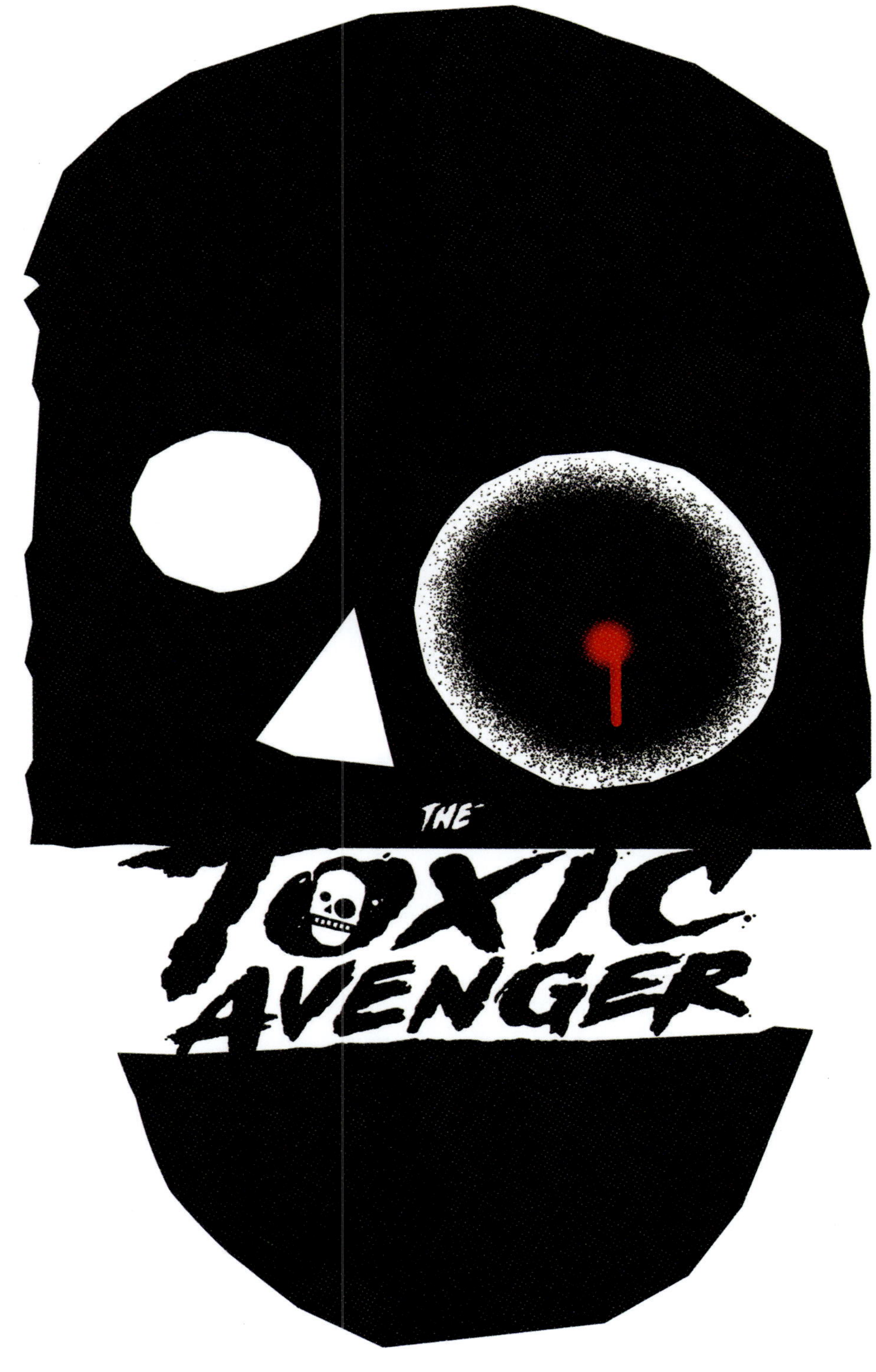
THE
TOXIC
AVENGER

ISBN: 9781789099904

Published by Titan Books
A division of Titan Publishing Group Ltd.
144 Southwark St.
London
SE1 0UP

FIRST EDITION: September 2025
10 9 8 7 6 5 4 3 2 1

EU RP (for authorities only)
eucomply OÜ Pärnu mnt 139b-14 11317
Talinn, Estonia
hello@eucompliancepartner.com
+3375690241

DID YOU ENJOY THIS BOOK?
We love to hear from our readers.
Please e-mail us at: readerfeedback@titanemail.com or write to Reader Feedback at the above address.
To receive advance information, news, competitions, and exclusive offers online, please sign up for the Titan newsletter on our website: www.titanbooks.com

A CIP catalogue record for this title is available from the British Library.

Printed and bound in China.

THE TOXIC AVENGER

WRITTEN BY DAN JOLIN

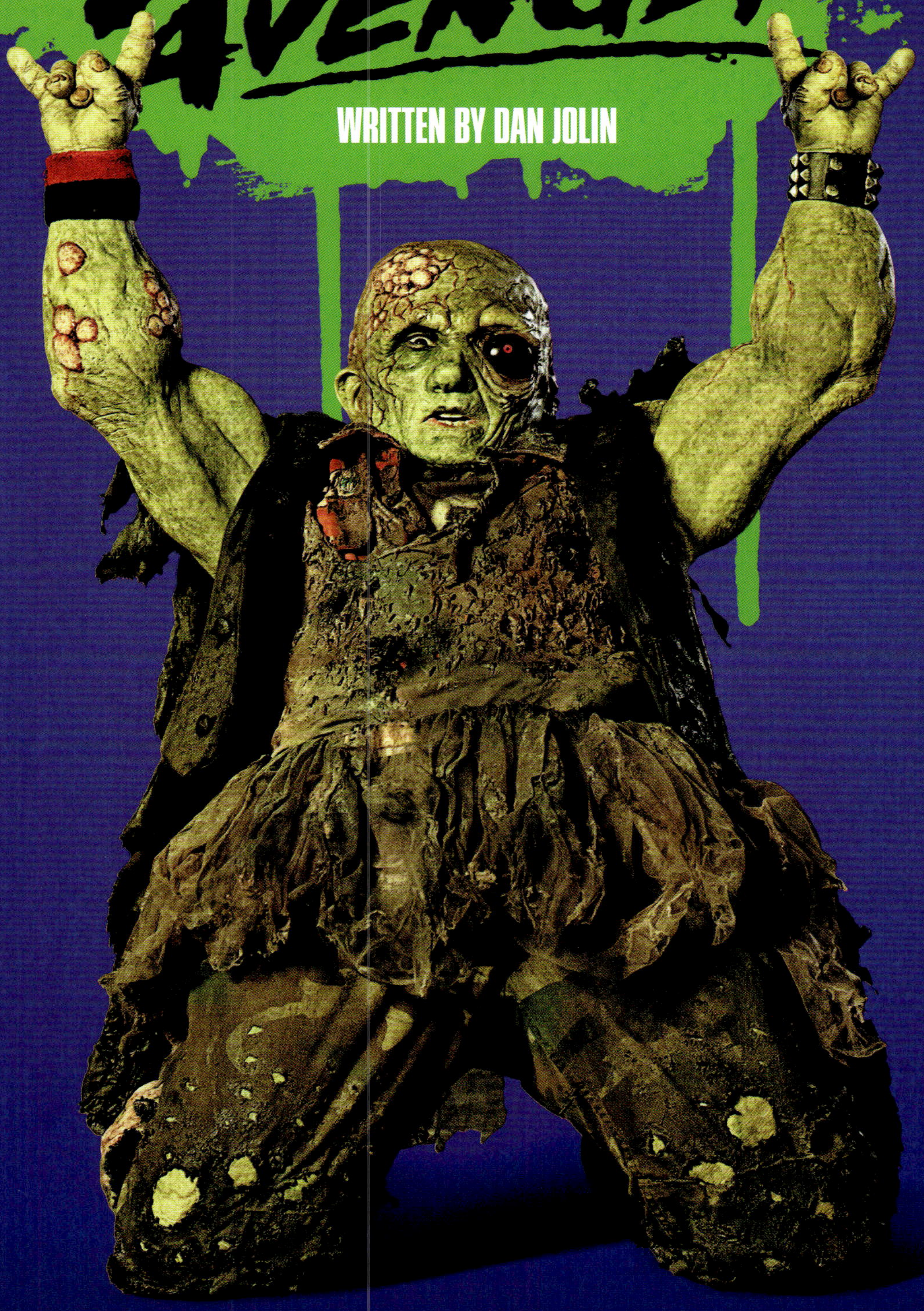

TITAN BOOKS

Contents

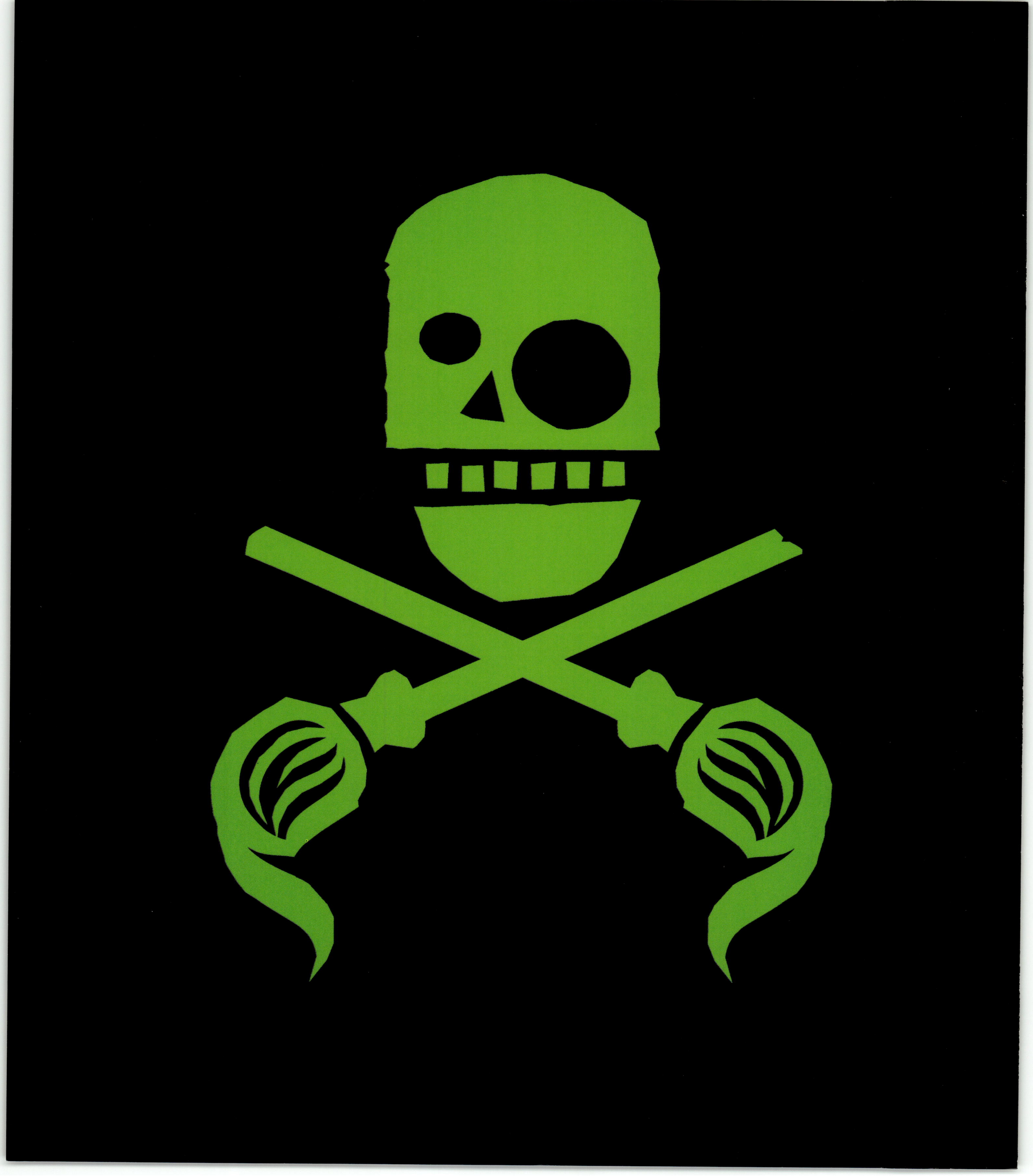

"If you know the enemy and know yourself, you need not fear the results of a hundred battles."

— SUN TZU

"I am as I am. Whether hideous or handsome depends on who is made judge."

— HERMAN MELVILLE

"If this is gonna be that kind of party, I'm gonna stick my dick in the mashed potatoes."

— MANTAN MORELAND

Introduction

"A mutation? An infection? An... *evolution*?"

— BOB GARBINGER

It is hard to think of a cult classic that's more cult than *The Toxic Avenger*. Released in 1984 and directed by indie moguls Lloyd Kaufman and Michael Herz, it was an ultra-low budget, gore-spattered "live-action cartoon"[1] that merrily, messily blended slapstick comedy, horror, superheroics and anti-corporate satire. Its protagonist was a violent, hulking "hideously deformed creature of superhuman size and strength," which came into being when a bullied health club mop boy named Melvin Ferd Junko fell into a barrel of toxic waste. He wore a singed tutu and used a weaponized mop to brutally murder the bad guys of his New Jersey hometown, Tromaville ("Toxic waste capital of the world"). Opening with a warning of "scenes of extreme violence," *The Toxic Avenger* featured its "Monster Hero" cooking a criminal's hands in a deep-fat fryer; a 12-year-old kid getting his head crushed by a car; and the remorseless execution of a guide dog (this final scene yielded the highest volume of hate mail). All "violence as good, clean fun,"[2] to quote Kaufman, who has always been as much of a showman as he is a studio head.

This was the tenth film from Kaufman and Herz's independent, New York-based studio Troma Entertainment, whose mission statement Kaufman summed up as "actively trying to do exactly what we aren't supposed to do. We hate the status quo and we like to shake things up.[3]" Previously, he and Herz had purveyed exclamation-pointed "sexy comedies" like *Squeeze Play!* and *The First Turn-On!*, but with *The Toxic Avenger* they contrarily shifted to horror after reading a *Weekly Variety* headline announcing, "The Horror Film Is Dead." Since then, they've overseen such memorably titled splatterthons as *Chopper Chicks in Zombietown*, *Fat Guy Goes Nutzoid!!* and *Poultrygeist: Night of the Chicken Dead*. Kaufman once described much of Troma's output as "goat shit… but goat shit for which we have lots of affection."[4]

In the case of *The Toxic Avenger*, that affection spread fast and far. A midnight movie hit at Greenwich Village's Bleecker Street Cinema, it's since spawned not only three sequels, but also a Marvel comic, a Broadway musical, a board game, an adult colouring book and even, in 1991, an environmentally aware kids' TV cartoon, *Toxic Crusaders*, in which a freakish supergroup battled evil alien polluters. The eponymous hero, affectionately known as Toxie, has become Troma's Mickey Mouse. He is often seen marching in the Macy's Thanksgiving Day parade.

"We had no money to advertize," says Kaufman, now in his mid-seventies, sitting in an office that's proudly wallpapered with *Toxic* posters and paraphernalia. "Word of mouth and the fans—that's Troma's secret sauce. And yes, we're a cult. We're like Hammer. Probably more like a screwdriver. Or a Bloody Mary. But you can't buy that. Rupert Murdoch cannot buy that. No way!"

It didn't take long before Hollywood took note of Toxie's huge underground following and came knocking at Troma's door, apparently keen to bring him into the cinematic mainstream. "He's the ultimate underdog," says Kaufman, explaining the character's essential and commercially translatable appeal. "You feel sorry for

[1] Lloyd Kaufman and James Gunn, *All I Need To Know About Filmmaking I Learned From The Toxic Avenger*, p. 175

[2] ibid.

[3] ibid. p. 159

[4] ibid. p. 6

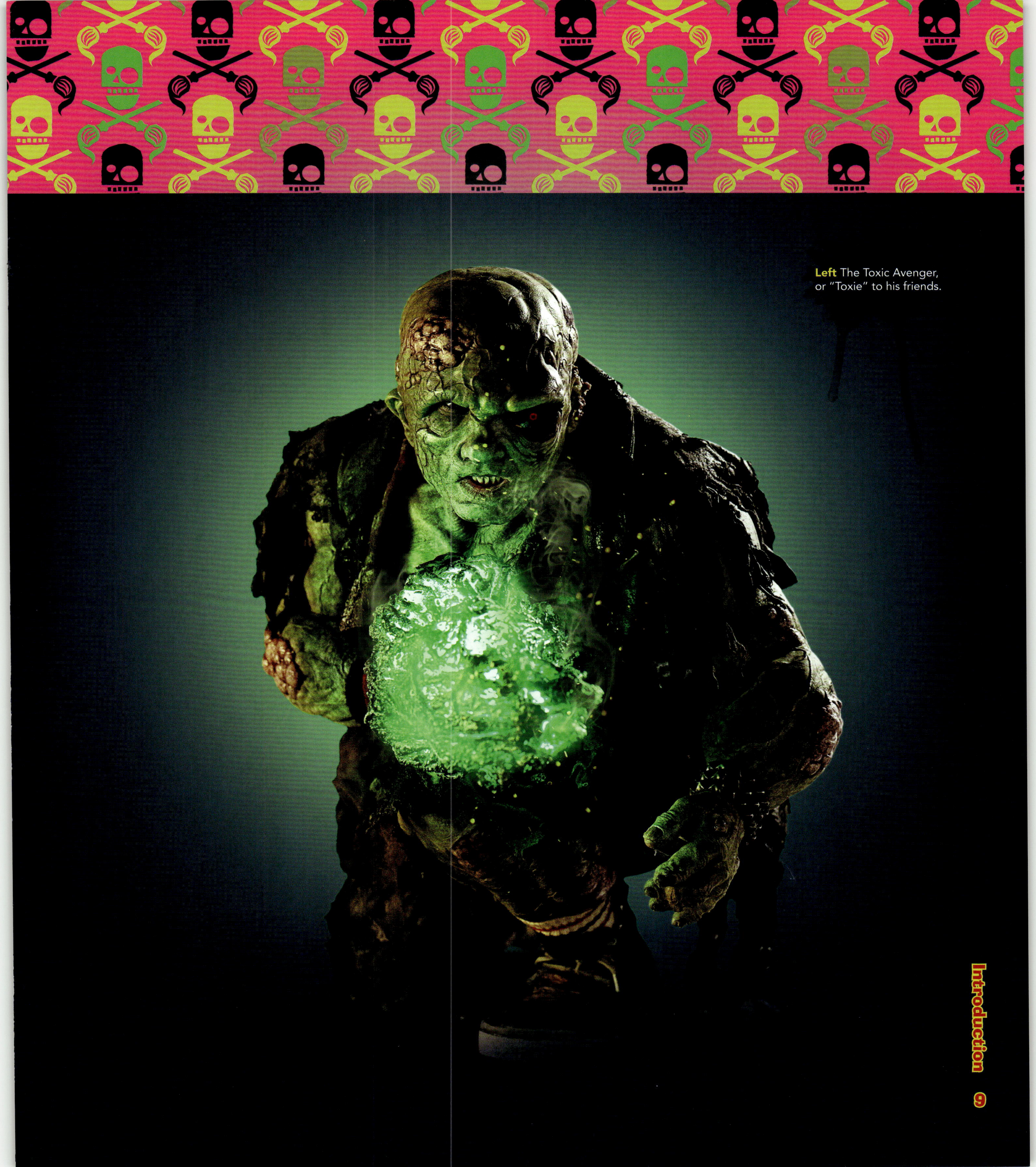

Left The Toxic Avenger, or "Toxie" to his friends.

"It felt like there was a real opportunity to do something that could resonate in a more prominent way, while still having all the fun and wackiness of the original."

– ALEX GARCIA,
Producer

the guy. You relate to him. I remember my stepmother took a supreme court judge from Germany to our first investor screening. She wept! So it really has pathos."

However, early efforts to reinvent *The Toxic Avenger* withered on the vine. In the early '90s, it looked like New Line, the studio behind the *Teenage Mutant Ninja Turtles* movies (and later Peter Jackson's *The Lord of the Rings*) would produce a big-budget *Toxic Crusaders* adaptation, but the project was ultimately never greenlit. More recently, in 2013, *Hot Tub Time Machine* director Steve Pink co-wrote a family-friendly action-adventure remake that, for a time, had Arnold Schwarzenegger attached (although not, reportedly, in the title role). But Schwarzenegger withdrew and, after another attempt failed in 2016, the chances of a Toxie multiplex movie seemingly evaporated. Fortunately for Troma, one of the original film's fans would grow up to become a producer at Hollywood studio Legendary Entertainment.

"I first saw *The Toxic Avenger* sometime in the late '80s when I was still too young to be seeing it," says Alex Garcia. "It's one of those films that, as a kid especially, makes your brain explode." It was also, he now believes, "ahead of its time in many ways. Even given all the gonzo elements and the way it pushed the violence and the gore, there were great ideas at the core of it: the put-upon guy who takes back the power, and the environmental themes that are layered within it—which, sadly, are even more prominent today."

For Garcia, the time has never been riper for a fresh *Toxic Avenger*. "We live in an age of increasing pessimism about the world around us," he says. "It felt like there was a real opportunity to do something that could resonate in a more prominent way, while still having all the fun and wackiness of the original. The key thing we look for at Legendary is material that feels compelling and distinctive. It felt like Toxie, with the right filmmaker, could be that."

Over the years, *The Toxic Avenger* would occasionally pop back into Garcia's mind as a potential project. Fortuitously, in late 2018, just before he started shooting *Godzilla vs. Kong*, it popped loud when Garcia met up with a good friend, musician and composer Seth Persons, and discovered he'd recently worked with Kaufman and Herz.

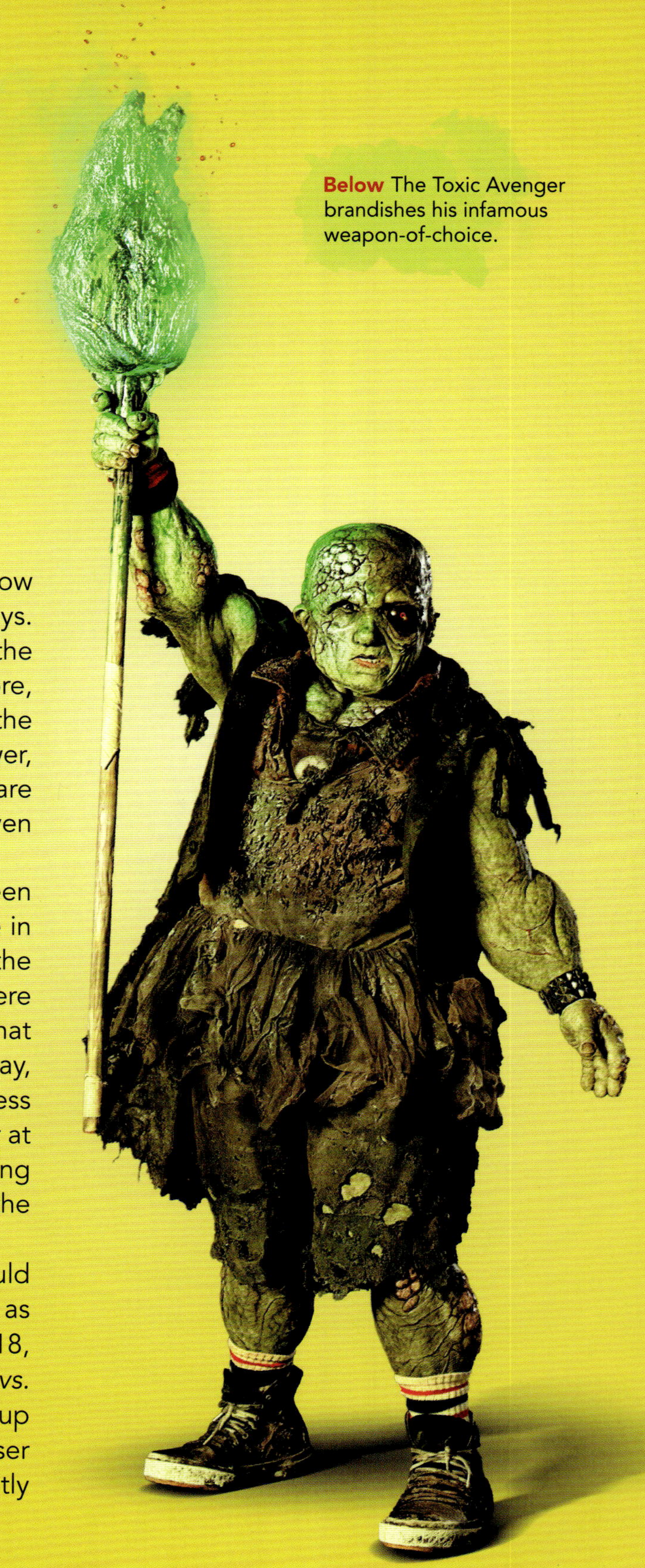

Below The Toxic Avenger brandishes his infamous weapon-of-choice.

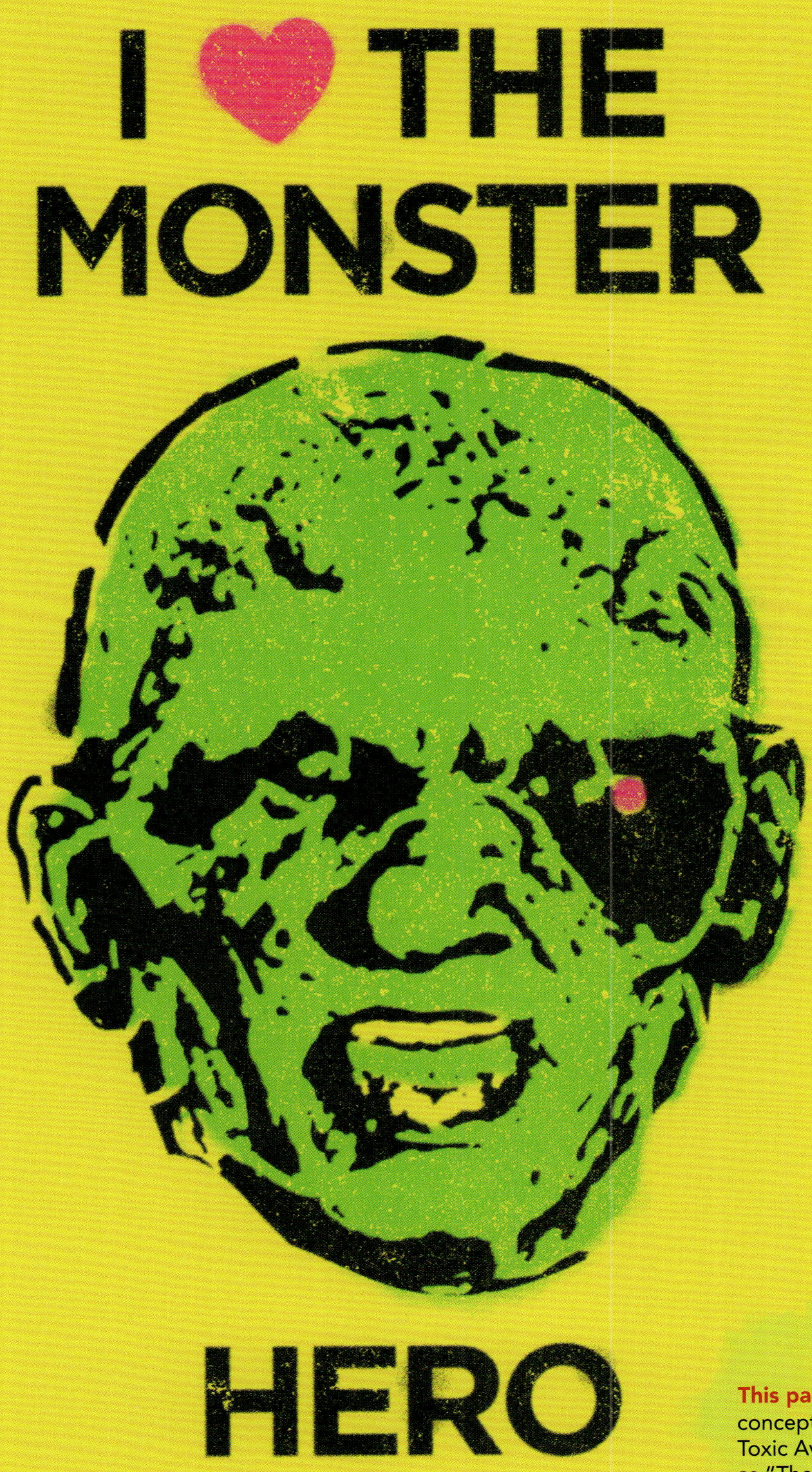

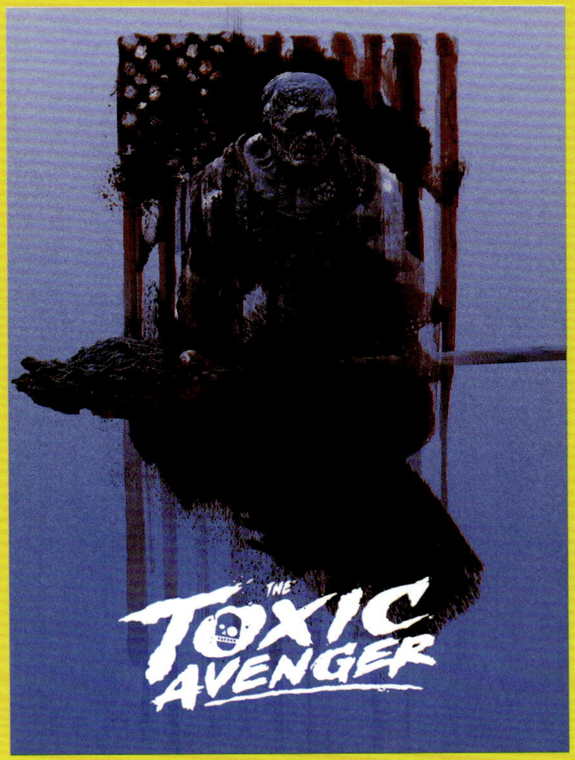

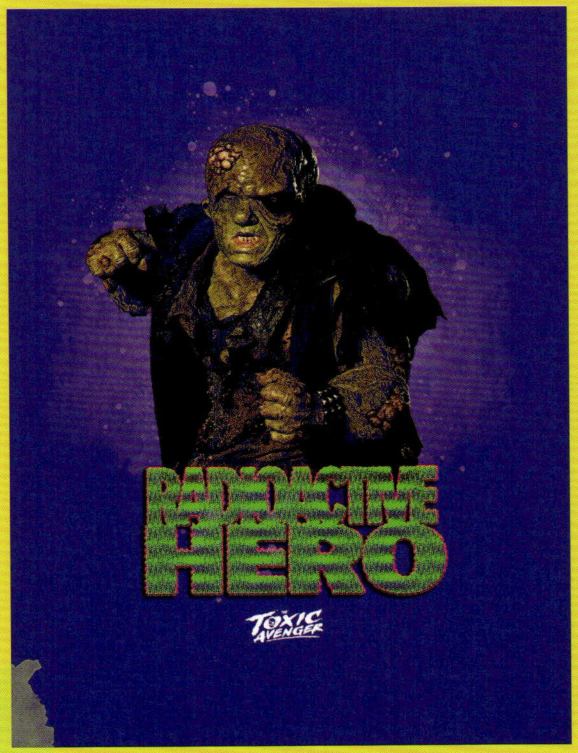

This page Poster concepts for the all-new Toxic Avenger, also known as "The Monster Hero".

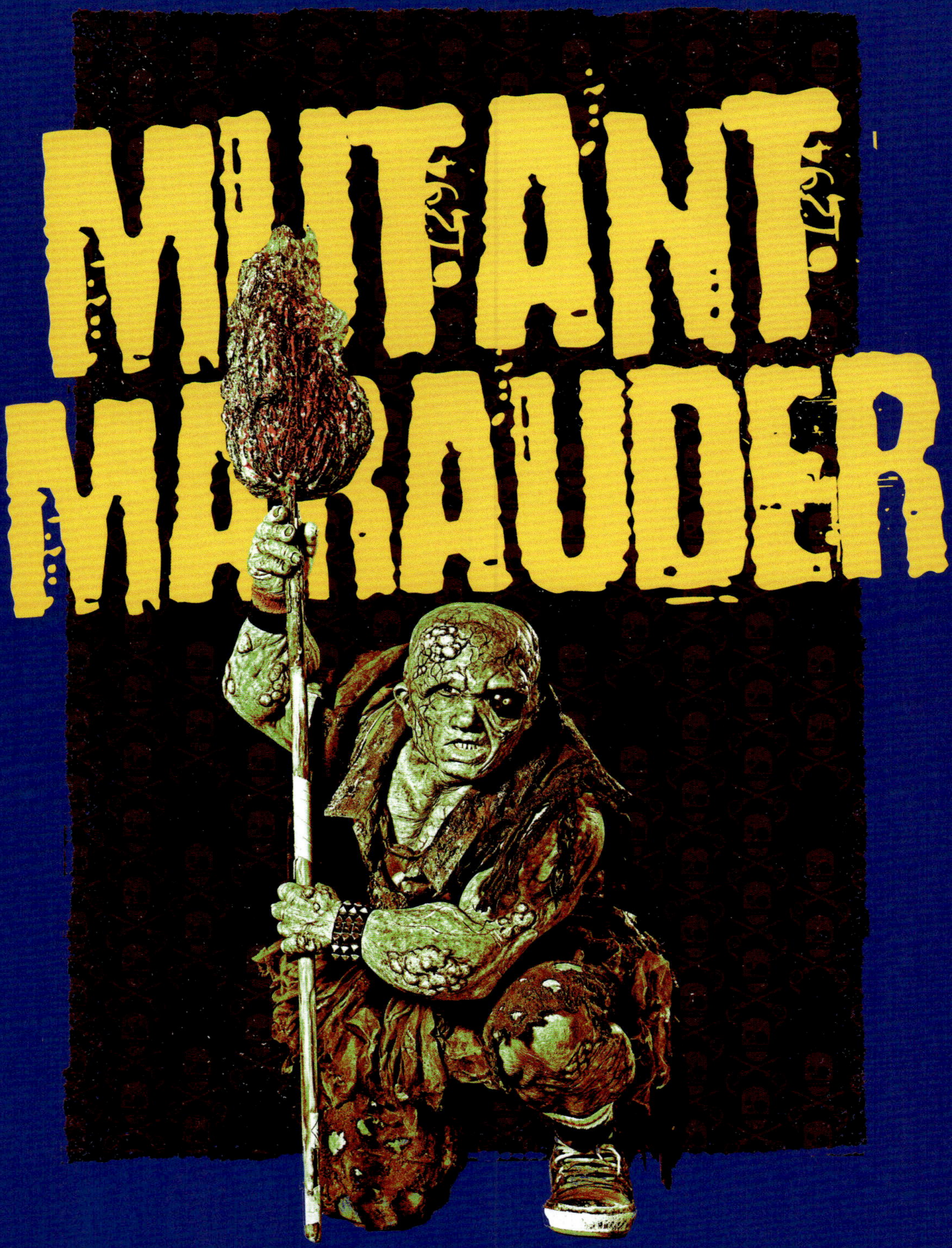

"We have open calls where anyone can come in," explains Kaufman, who at the time was prepping his latest movie *Shakespeare's Shitstorm* (a "Tromatic" adaptation of *The Tempest*). "This guy brought in his mandolin and he played a wonderful melody, and I fell in love with it. It turned out he is good friends with Alex Garcia, and mentioned this wonderful project he'd been on with Troma."

Garcia wondered aloud whether the rights to *The Toxic Avenger* were currently available, and Persons put him together with the Troma bosses, who revealed the rights *were* available. Herz and Kaufman were impressed by Garcia's genuine enthusiasm for the film and his pitch to do something fresh with the title without sacrificing its spirit and ethos. "I think both Lloyd and Michael understood that we wanted to do something that would respect what they've done as independent filmmakers, while creating something new," says Garcia. After just a few conversations, they sealed the deal.

Another filmmaker who'd grown up loving *The Toxic Avenger* was Macon Blair, star of Jeremy Saulnier's offbeat revenge thriller *Blue Ruin*, and writer-director of sharp-witted Sundance Film Festival-winning black comedy *I Don't Feel at Home in This World Anymore*, featuring Melanie Lynskey and Elijah Wood. Blair recalls first seeing Kaufman and Herz's trash hit during sixth grade at school, in his hometown of Alexandria, Virginia. An older brother of a friend had lent him a VHS tape of the film, and the young Blair was indelibly impressed. "It was just so over-the-top and ridiculous and berserk," he says. "You could tell that, as haphazard and wild as it was, they were working overtime to try and entertain the viewer."

It was "the perfect time" for him to discover Toxie, as Blair and his friends (including a young Saulnier) had recently obtained a VHS camcorder and were still figuring out how to make their own home-made movies. "I would say it was pretty influential. It made us ask, 'How can we push the envelope and be as gross and silly as possible?'"

Both Garcia and Chairman of Worldwide Production & Television for Legendary Entertainment Mary Parent were deeply impressed by *I Don't Feel at Home in This World Anymore*, particularly its idiosyncratic sense of humour, and the way it mixed a witch's brew of heart and violence. So, when they started discussing writers and directors for their *Toxic Avenger*, Blair was at the top of the list.

Blair, however, was initially nonplussed. The whole appeal of the original, he reasoned, was its "shoestring charm" and its "deliberately bad taste." So how would that work at the studio level? Were they intending to do a "serious, *Dark Knight* version" of it? Or a "PG family version?" Either way, he couldn't see it working. So, he told his agent he wasn't interested and hit the hay.

But Blair awoke the next morning realizing his error. For the longest time, he'd been toying with the idea of making an original monster movie that would be "gleefully silly and noisy and very rated-R, but at the same time very sweet and heartfelt and warm." However, the creature-effects element meant it wasn't financially viable, and he'd instead funnelled some of his ideas into his comic-book writing. But now it occurred to him: "If there was ever gonna be a studio-backed IP that demanded that type of silliness, that demanded monsters, that demanded blood and gore and slime, but could also be emotional and kind of like a *Rocky* underdog-type story, *Toxie* was the only one that fit the bill." He very quickly called his agent and said, "Actually…"

Fortunately for Blair, his approach was exactly the one Legendary favoured. Not a watered-down *Toxic Avenger*, nor one which tried to rationalize its subject matter or bleach its lurid palette, but one which revelled in the original's splattershot buffoonery, while grounding it in emotional authenticity. After a single conference call confirmed Garcia and Blair's shared passion and definition of what the film could be, Blair was on board. And he received the Lloyd Kaufman seal of approval, too.

"They selected a director who's terrific," says Kaufman. "He loves Toxie, he loves the Troma movies, he wants to keep the Troma spirit and flavour. Other than giving some notes—and he has accepted some of them—I leave him alone. This is his Toxie. He's made it totally his own. It's a film by Macon Blair of Lloyd Kaufman's *Toxic Avenger*. He has a lot of guts. He loves cinema. He's not out in LA, he's in Austin, Texas, with the cowboys and sharpshooters and he-men!"

Blair immediately knew he had to change and personalize the original film's setting and characters. The '84 *Toxic Avenger*'s action kicked off in a health club—mainly because, while working as a location scout on John G. Avildsen's

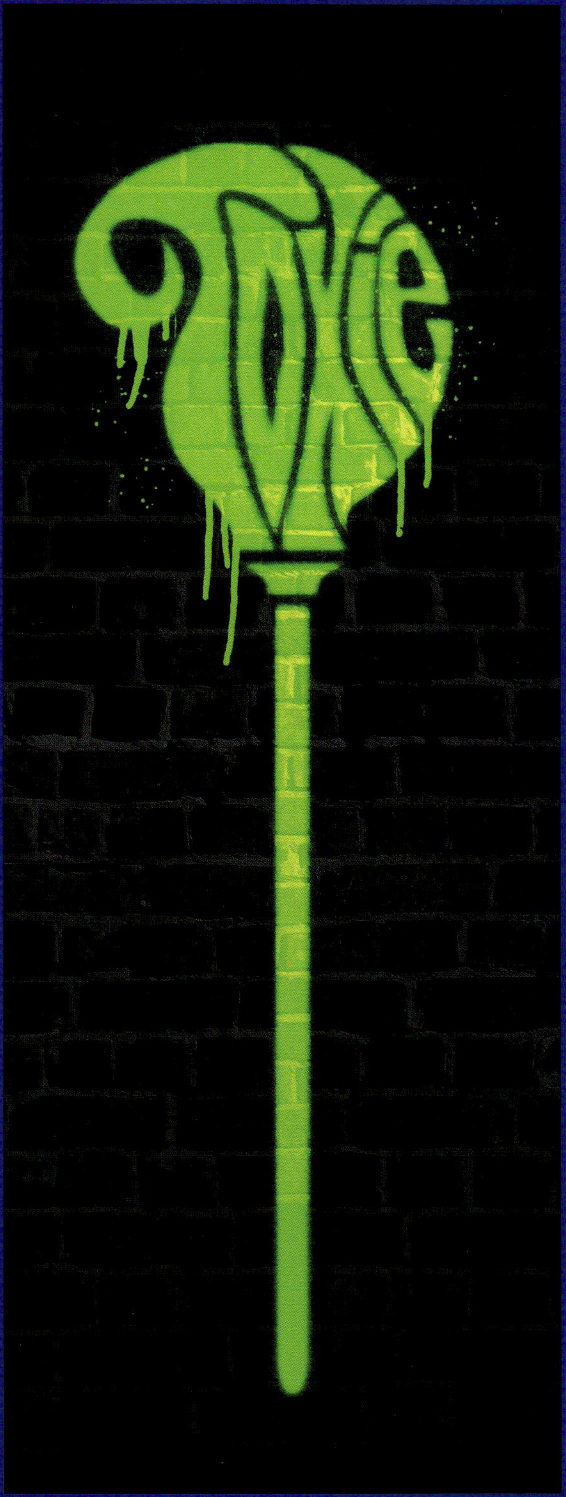

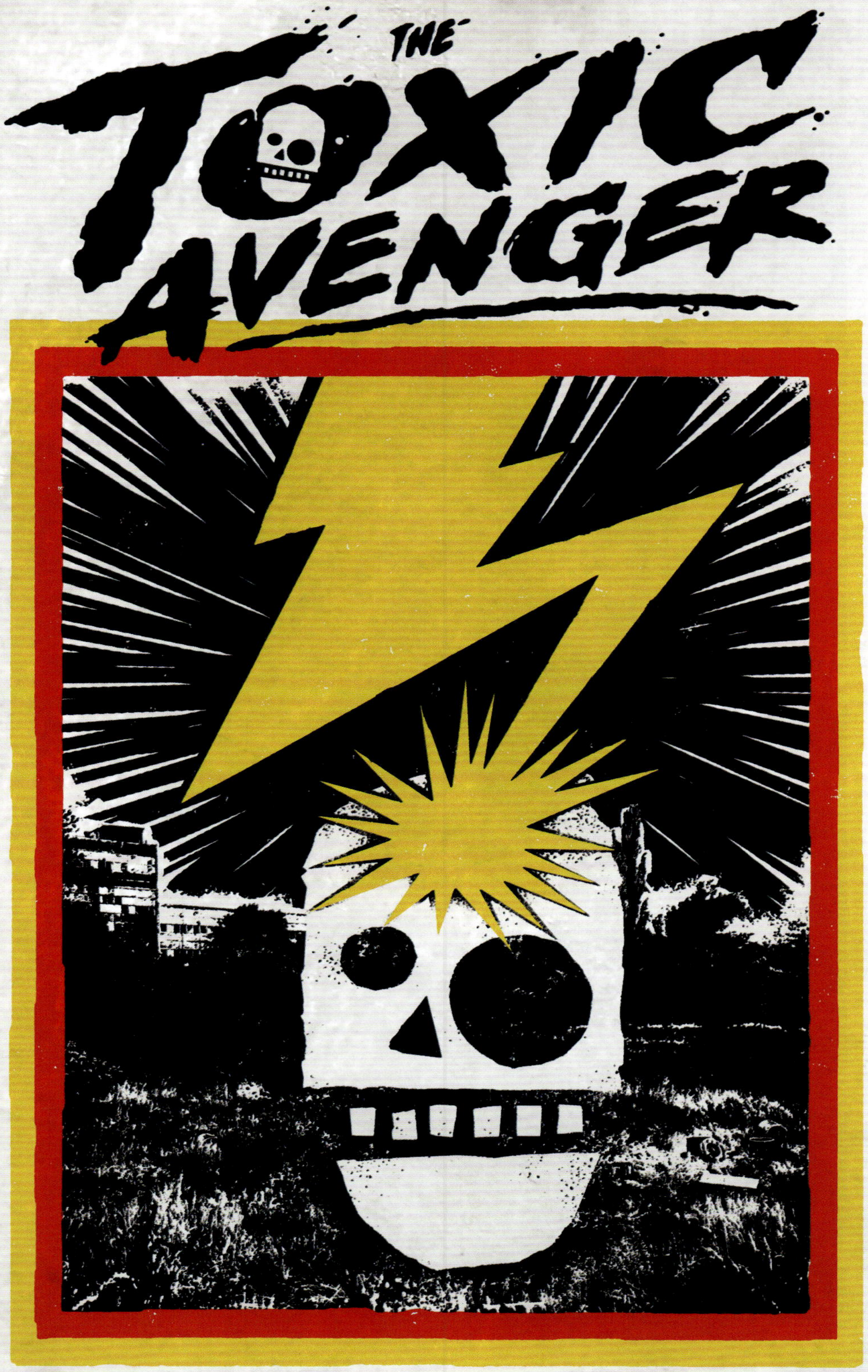

Oscar®-winning *Rocky* during his pre-Troma days, Kaufman had imagined some great ways gym equipment could be used to horribly dismember people. Meanwhile, its hero's everyday-guy incarnation, Melvin (memorably if bizarrely portrayed by Mark Torgl) is an awkward, horny teen who's rejected and abused by all the buff-bodied cool kids in Tromaville. After he mutates into Toxie as the accidental result of a horrible prank, he uncovers a conspiracy involving the town's corpulent mayor (Pat Ryan Jr.) and its criminal gangs, while falling in love with a visually impaired woman named Sarah (Andree Maranda), ultimately becoming accepted by the people of Tromaville as their grungy saviour.

In Blair's version, the health club has become a major healthcare company named B.T.H. (Body Talk Healthstyle), under the dominion of amoral factory owner Bob Garbinger (Kevin Bacon). B.T.H. has pervaded the community of St. Roma's Village (which, with a few letters knocked off the town sign, becomes "Tromaville"), and among its many downtrodden employees is middle-aged janitor Winston Gooze, a very different kind of underdog to Melvin Junko.

"I didn't want to do another version of the same story, meaning a teenager working at a health club," says Blair. "You still have an outsider who is going to stick it to The Man and dismantle the corrupt system, but instead of it being a young kid who the cool kids are mean to, it's a stepdad who's having a hard time connecting with his stepson." Blair puts this shift down to his own age. "I'm old now, and that's what I tend to think about. It felt natural that the personal ingredients I'd add would come from that. As opposed to 'Who am I gonna ask to the prom?' or 'How can I get a date?' it's, 'Why won't my kid talk to me?'"

Winston, played by *Game of Thrones* star Peter Dinklage, has not been dealt the greatest hand in life. He's lost his wife, Shelly (Rebecca O'Mara), leaving her anxiety-ridden teenage son Wade (Jacob Tremblay) in his care. Furthermore, he is diagnosed with a potentially terminal illness which, conveniently and ironically, is not covered by B.T.H.'s healthcare insurance. During a drunken attempt to rob the company's factory and a mix-up with a vigilante environmentalist named J.J. Doherty (Taylour Paige), Winston is mortally wounded by Garbinger's crazed hit squad The Killer Nutz and tossed into the factory's toxic waste—transforming him into Toxie (physically performed by Luisa Guerreiro). Not only must he step up and, with J.J.'s help, release Garbinger's stranglehold on his community, but he must also overcome his uncanny grotesqueness and make things right with his stepson.

Kaufman's one big note to Blair was to ensure the movie had all the poignancy of the original, and Blair certainly did that. In fact, that's what really stood out to Legendary. "The thing that got us most excited by his take was the heart," says Garcia. "The story of the single stepfather who's struggling to make a dent in the world and who, through this journey, really learns to connect with his stepson. He becomes a happier version of himself by becoming a mutant freak."

Throughout the development and production process, Blair also kept a laser-sharp focus on giving his *Toxic Avenger* a distinct visual approach. Aside

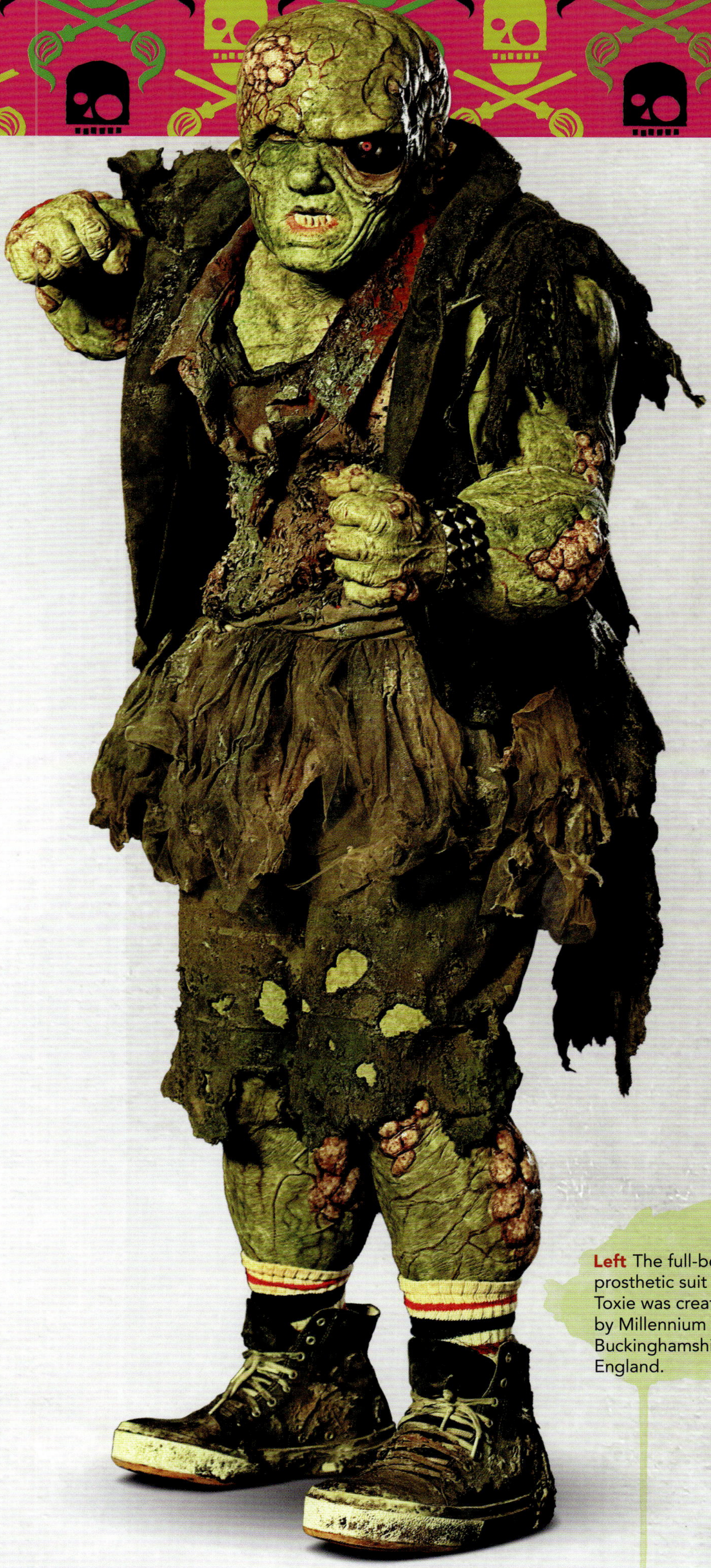

Left The full-body prosthetic suit for Toxie was created by Millennium FX in Buckinghamshire, England.

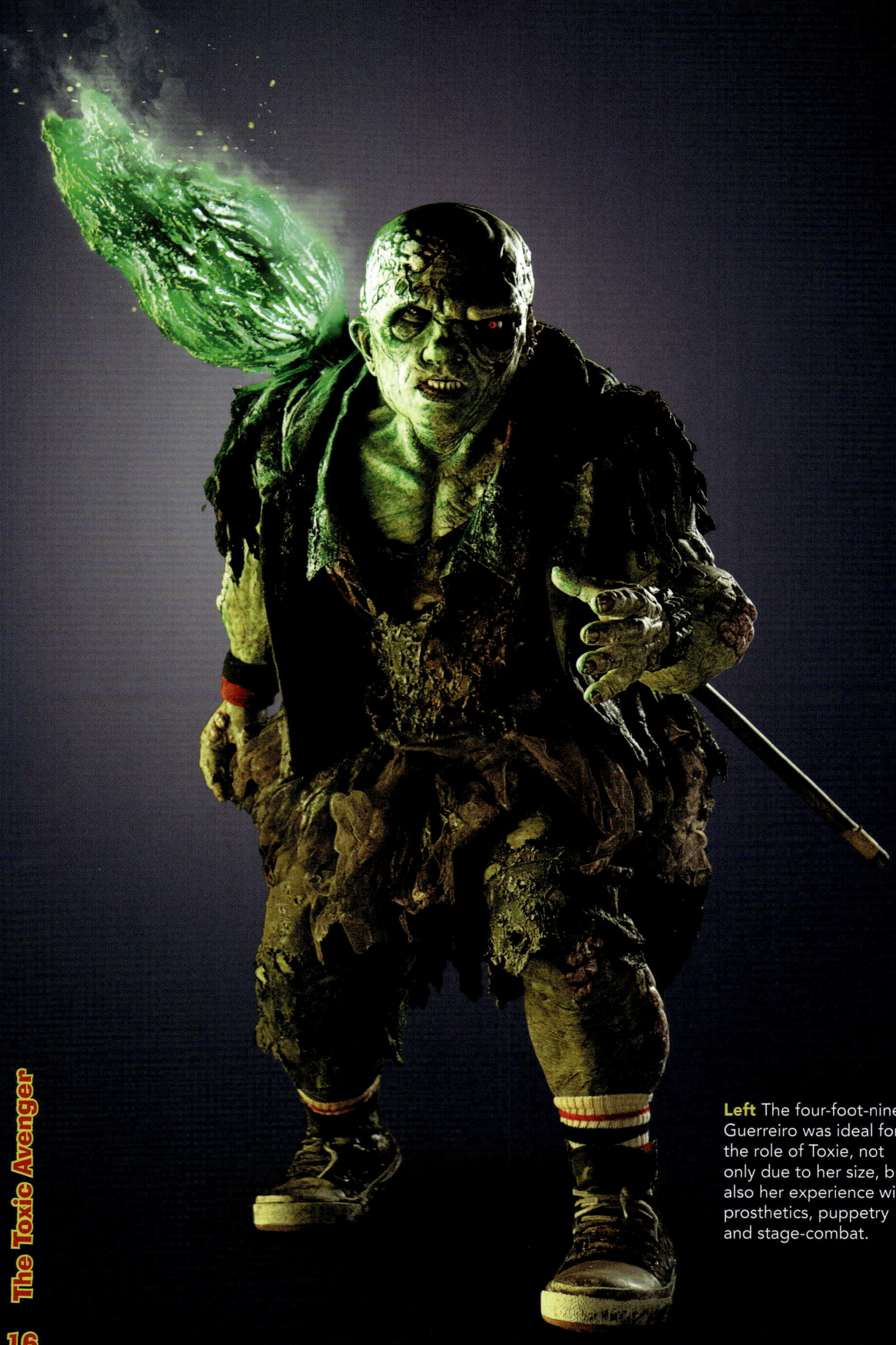

Left The four-foot-nine Guerreiro was ideal for the role of Toxie, not only due to her size, but also her experience with prosthetics, puppetry and stage-combat.

from obvious narrative influences like Paul Verhoeven's *RoboCop*, Tim Burton's *Batman Returns* and, like the original, James Whale's *Frankenstein* ("as soon as we started talking about this movie, I said, 'Toxie needs to be chased by a mob with torches!'") he also settled on the punk sci-fi estrangement of Alex Cox's *Repo Man*—another 1984 cult classic—which was shot by Dutch cinematographer Robby Müller. This in turn led Blair and his director of photography Dana Gonzales (whose work includes TV shows *Legion* and *Fargo*) to draw inspiration from a number of other beloved films in Müller's canon: Barbet Schroeder's *Barfly*, William Friedkin's *To Live and Die in L.A.*, and, most significantly, Wim Wenders' stark, striking 1977 neo-noir *The American Friend*.

"There's a lot of green lighting in that movie," says Gonzales, "so that became a staple of *The Toxic Avenger's* aesthetic, with all these green hues—as well as just stripping things back and making it more like a single-camera, foreign-film narrative. We could have gone the other way and made it comic-booky and glossy and as structured as you can humanly make it, but Macon didn't want to do that."

Interestingly, as they started scouting locations around Sofia, Bulgaria (where Blair's crew refitted the same studio backlot as Legendary's previous production, *The Texas Chainsaw Massacre*) another inspiration hit them. "We were in some very architecturally grand buildings with these big marble staircases and big, echoey hallways, and we'd say, 'Oh, this is just like *The Conformist!*'" Gonzales is referring to Bernardo Bertolucci's 1970 political drama, set amid the imposing decor of '30s, fascist-era Italy, and that film primarily influenced the scenes concerning Garbinger and his power-hungry cronies. "To me, this film feels a little bit like *Kick-Ass* meets *The Conformist*," laughs the cinematographer.

Blair's final inspiration isn't visual at all. "This might have been confusing to people, but in early conceptual meetings I would say: the Ramones," he reveals. This New York power-pop punk act formed in 1974 (the year of Blair's birth) and, with just a few frenetically strummed chords, shocked new life into the US rock scene. "We've got a movie here where there's a magic serum that an evil company is developing, and it transforms a guy and gives him powers, and there's an Excalibur-esque weapon in

"If we're true to the first film's spirit, go-for-broke entertainment value and sense of rock 'n' roll, then hopefully we'll please as many Troma fans as we can."

– MACON BLAIR,
Director

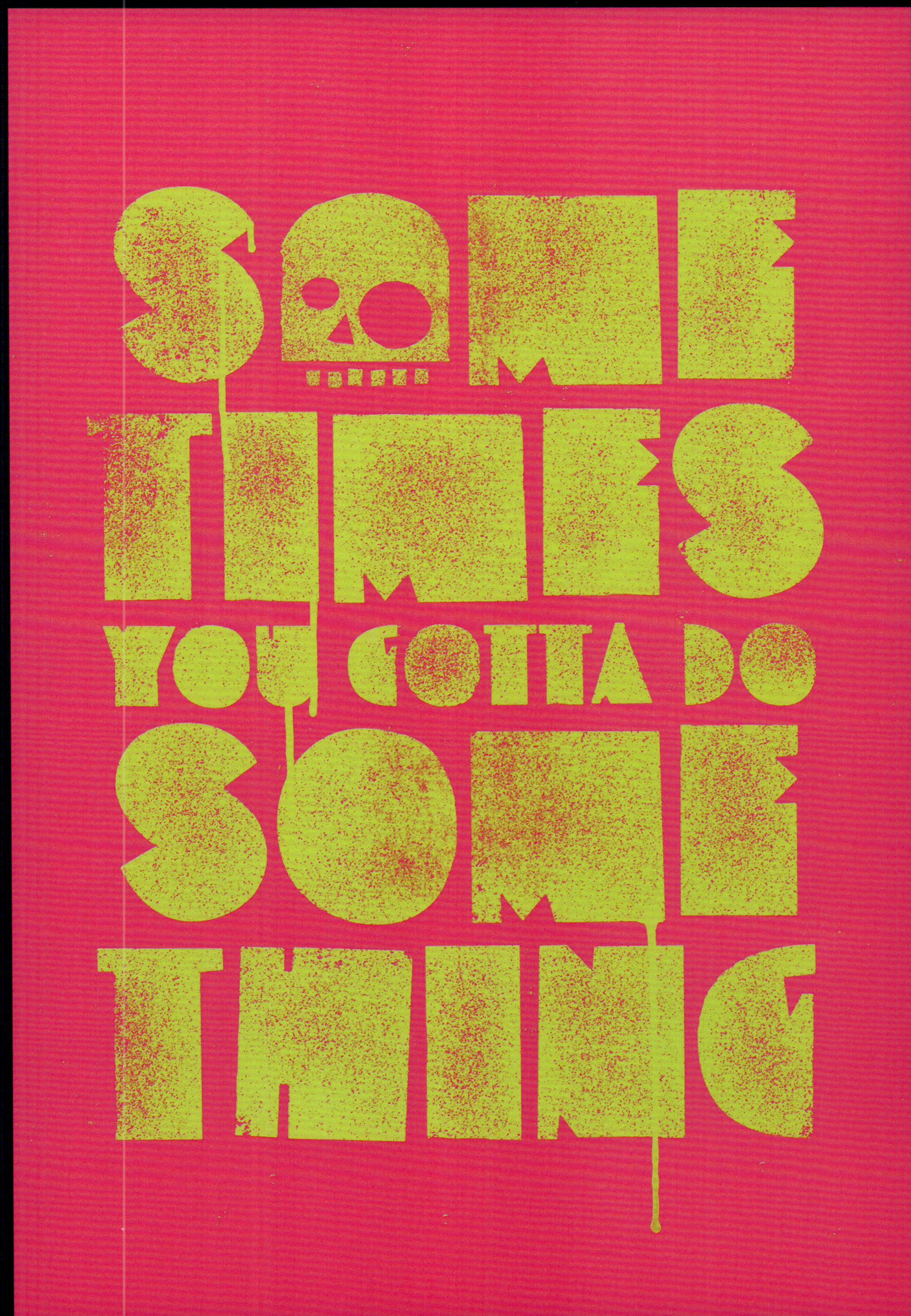

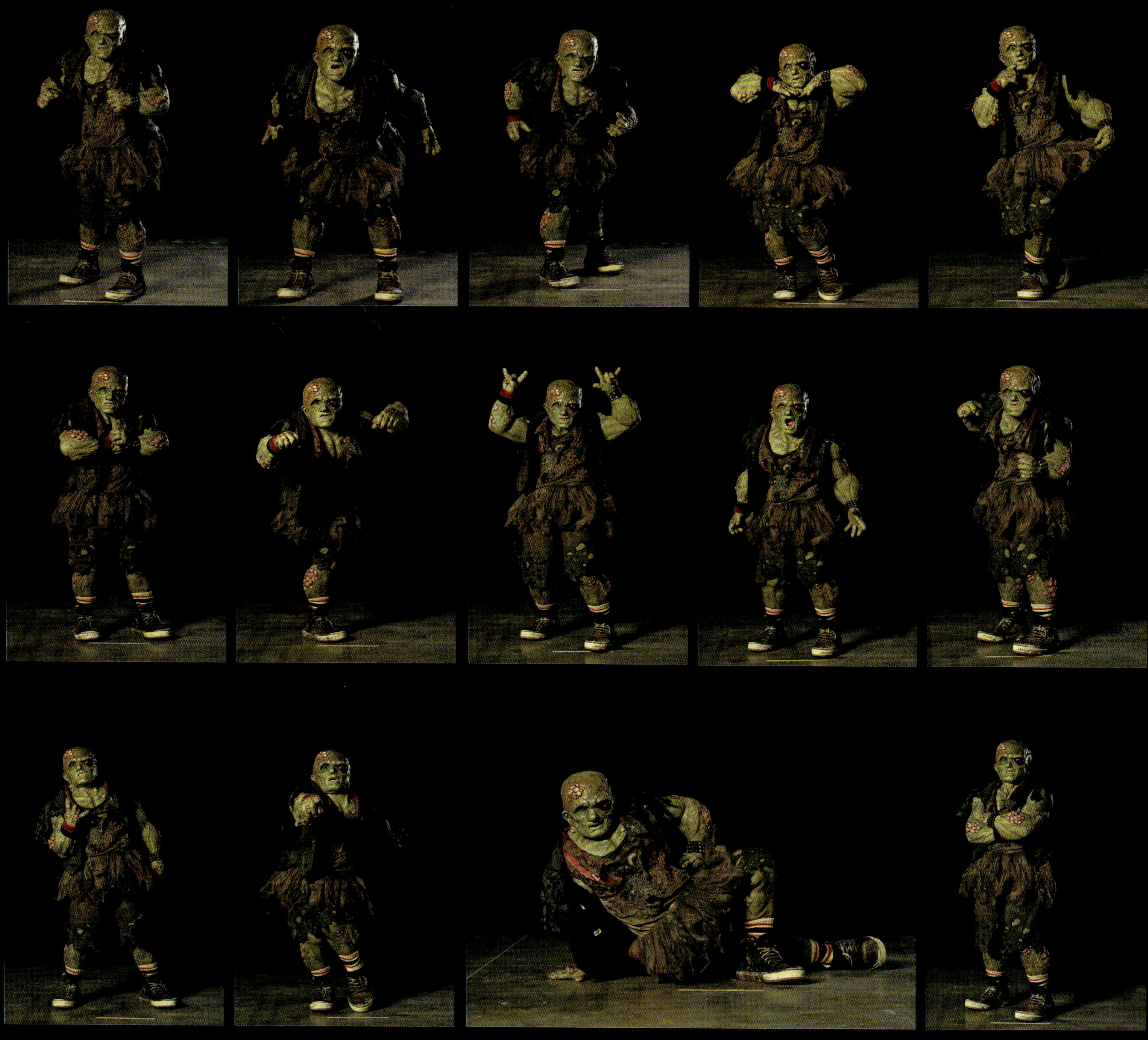

Toxie's mop. There's all these very familiar genre tropes that we've seen a thousand times. But we've done it deliberately. Like, 'Yes, you have seen it a thousand times. That's why it's comfortable. We know what we're doing here.' But we're playing it fast and with attitude and with our hearts on our sleeves. To me, that felt like the Ramones, where it's the same chords, the same simple song structures that you've heard versions of before, but it feels unique because of *how* they played it. They just did their own thing with it. It's familiar, but new."

Which brings us to Blair's greatest challenge in rebooting *The Toxic Avenger*: how to make it something the original's hardcore fans will embrace, while also, frankly, making it palatable to a mainstream audience.

"Holy shit, that was like the biggest math equation that constantly needed to be solved," says Blair. "I think, if we're true to the first film's spirit, go-for-broke entertainment value and sense of rock 'n' roll, then hopefully we'll please as many Troma fans as we can. For the larger audience, if you treat the emotion really honestly, then by the time this book comes out, my fondest hope is that, even after seeing all these people getting their faces exploded and the fart jokes and everything, people will get kind of choked up and feel really energized by it."

Blair and his team have themselves invested a lot of energy and feeling into crafting this new vision of Toxie and Tromaville. It has certainly impressed their creator. "The script's great and Macon is a real filmmaker," says Lloyd Kaufman. "I think the world is going to be very happy with this movie."

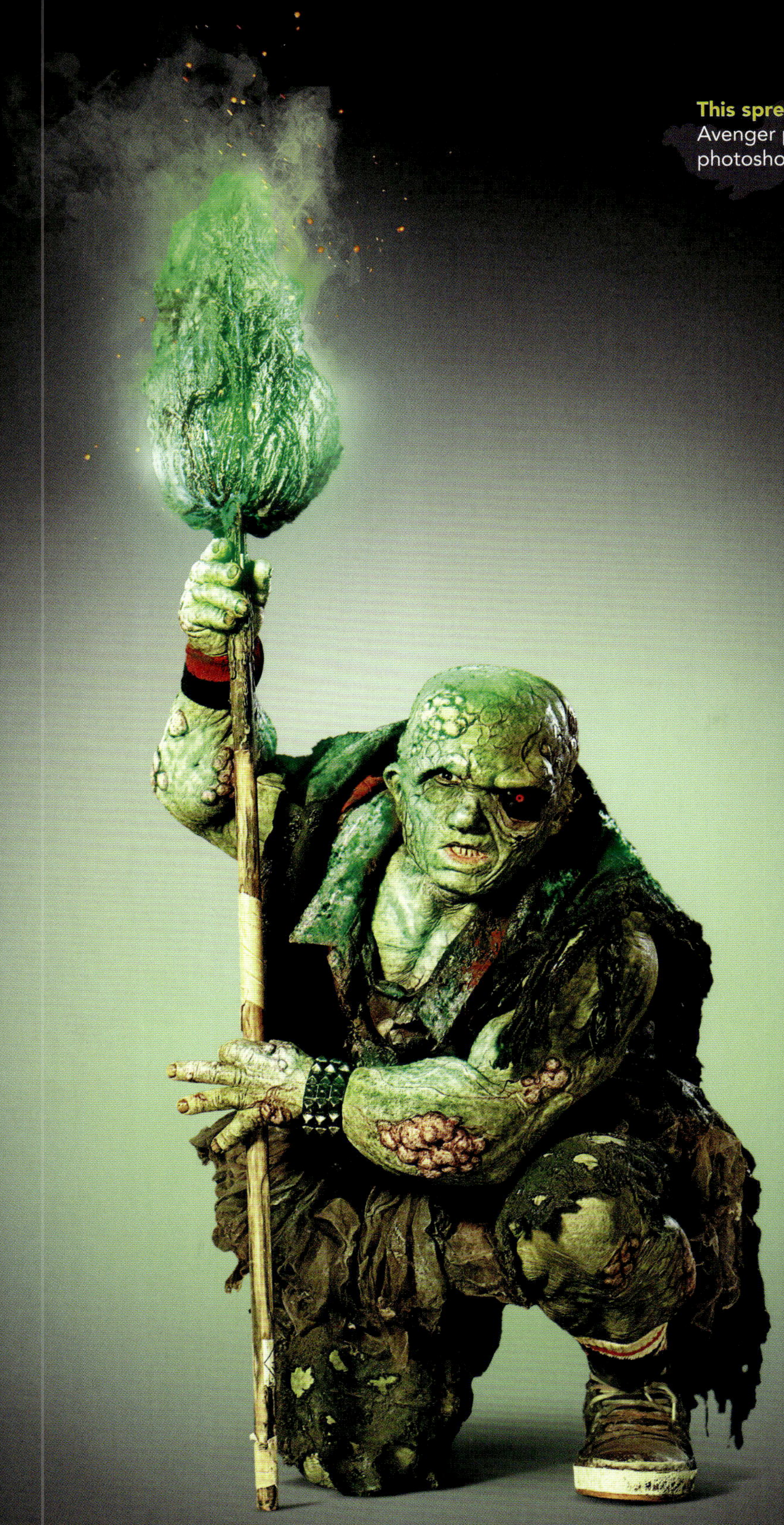

This spread The Toxic Avenger poses for a photoshoot.

WINSTON GOOZE

PLAYED BY PETER DINKLAGE

As a former Manhattanite, Peter Dinklage was aware of Troma Entertainment. Every time he strolled through Midtown, he'd pass their Hell's Kitchen office, its location vividly marked by a poster for *The Toxic Avenger*. Looking up at that image of the grimacing (or possibly grinning) mutant hero, with his deadly mop in hand, it could never have occurred to Dinklage that one day he'd be playing him.

Or, to be more specific, that he'd be playing the guy who transforms into Toxie. Not the gawky teenager Melvin Junko from the original, but an entirely new alter ego: Winston Gooze, a former metalhead widower whose factory-janitor job barely enables him to support his teenage stepson, Wade (Jacob Tremblay). And to make things worse, shortly after the film begins, Winston is diagnosed with a terminal illness.

"He's a sad sack of a guy," says Dinklage. "Life is really knocking him down. He's sweet and gullible, but unfortunately because of his sweetness and gullibility, he's pushed around by the world."

Finding the right person to play Winston was one of Blair's biggest casting challenges. "You need an actor of a certain calibre and visibility to justify the budget," he says, "but who are you going to offer it to? It's a strange movie on the page. I totally get you could read it and think, 'This kind of seems dumb. Are they serious about this?'" He had a few phone conversations with some potential Winstons where he'd try to assure them, "It's dumb on purpose, in a way that its purposeful dumbness is meant to be smart. Does that make sense?"

Evidently, it didn't. But luckily it made sense to Dinklage, whom Blair had befriended in early 2017, when the former was on the judge's panel at the Sundance Film Festival and awarded Blair's debut *I Don't Feel at Home in This World Anymore* the Grand Jury Prize. ("I sort of bribed him to be my friend," Dinklage jokes.) But it took Blair a while to realize how great Dinklage would be in the role. After all, as great as Dinklage is, in everything from indie comedy *Living in Oblivion* to game-changing TV fantasy phenomenon *Game of Thrones*, at four-foot-five he wouldn't be anyone's first thought for a character repeatedly described as being "of superhuman size and strength."

The pair were in the midst of discussing another project when it suddenly hit Blair: "There's no reason at all that Toxie needs to be eight feet tall. All we need is for Toxie to be the same height as Winston. With the original character, there's only a slight height increase. He's mutated. He gets muscles. That's it."

That was when he knew: "It's Peter." An actor who, with only around 30 minutes of screen time, would be able to forge a connection with the audience, before going unseen for the rest of the movie. "He has the gravitas, but also a quiet type of comedy, and I don't know if it's because of *Game of Thrones*, but everybody loves him and you're just instantly on his side when he shows up in movies," Blair says.

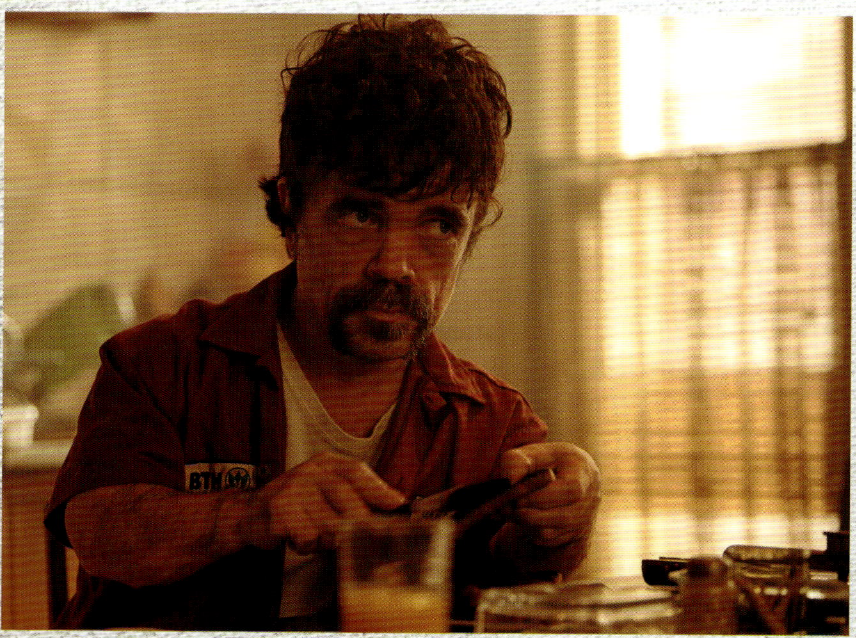

Left Peter Dinklage as "sad sack of a guy" Winston Gooze.

Below Winston Gooze, beer in hand, wanders the streets of Tromaville.

Right Winston with the mop that will become Toxie's weapon of choice.

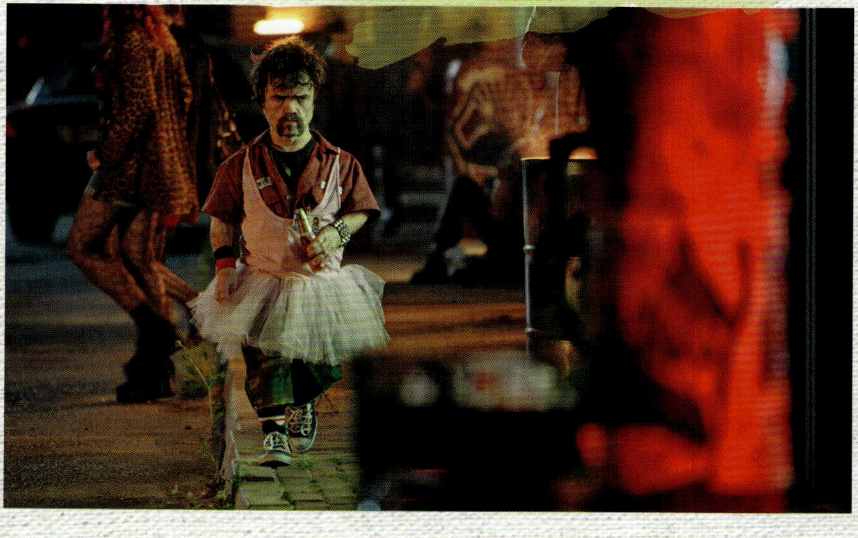

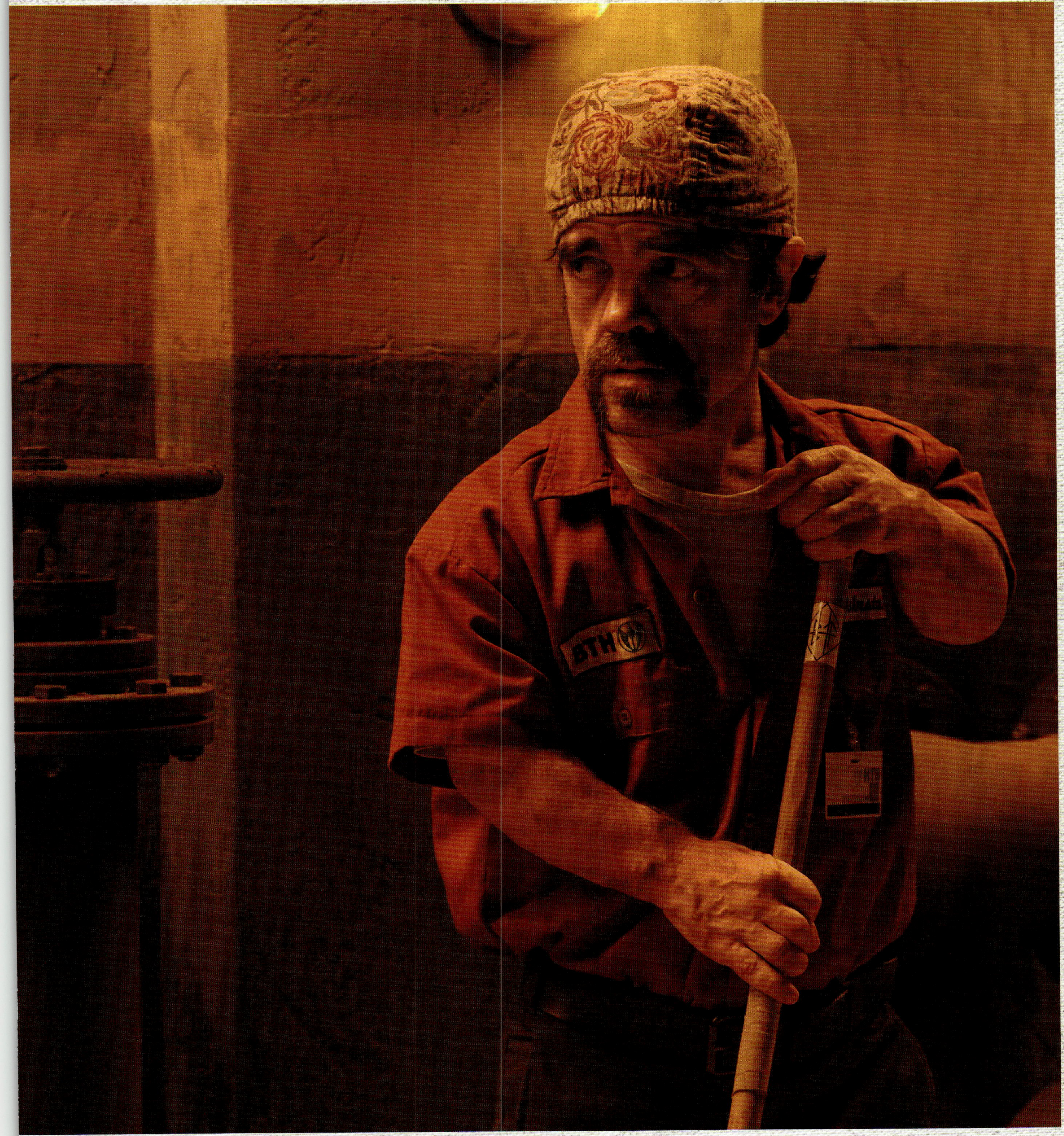
BTH

"The tutu is everything. I loved the combination of a tutu and heavy metal gear, the contradiction of looks. It's brilliant."

– PETER DINKLAGE,
Actor

Kaufman heartily approved of the decision. "That takes guts, right? Most people are going to expect to see 'a hideously deformed creature of superhuman size and strength,' and they've got Peter Dinklage, which is a wonderful new spin on that."

Dinklage was game, based firstly on his respect and affection for Blair, but also on the fact that he'd never played anybody like Winston before. "Most of the characters I'm asked to play are very intelligent, well-spoken people who maybe have a darker element to them and manipulate people, perhaps in not-so-healthy ways," he says. "I thought Winston would be a really nice change of pace." In addition, he appreciated the father-son relationship that Blair had crafted at the script's heart, with its added layers of complication: firstly, that Winston is a stepfather, making it a more "uncomfortable relationship" with Wade, and secondly that he transforms into a "literal monster" while struggling to maintain that relationship. "It really takes mature themes and turns them on their head and has some fun with them. But much of it is played straight. My scenes with Jacob have an emotional weight to them and we didn't shy away from that."

The only thing that gave Dinklage pause was the fact that Blair wanted to realize Toxie using prosthetics and animatronics, rather than digital effects. "I've done prosthetics before, and I've loved the process, but Bulgaria in the summertime? With six hours of prosthetic makeup on? I hesitated." But before he'd even had a chance to voice his concern, Blair assured him that he wouldn't need to wear all the makeup himself. Part of the concept, he told Dinklage, was that another actor would be playing Toxie, just as Mitch Cohen was the original film's alter ego to Mark Torgl's Melvin. "That made my decision much easier," says Dinklage.

Winston's pre-Toxiefication look wasn't

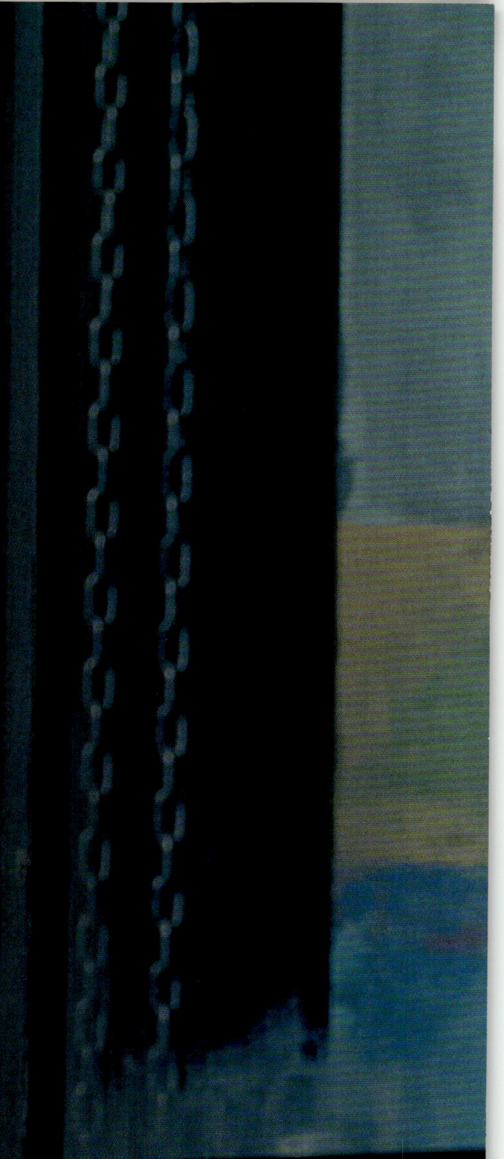

Below left Winston dons a pink tutu in a failed attempt to connect with his stepson Wade.

Below and right Winston's odd ensemble comes to include a mask and tuxedo jacket after he sneaks into a swanky party as a waiter.

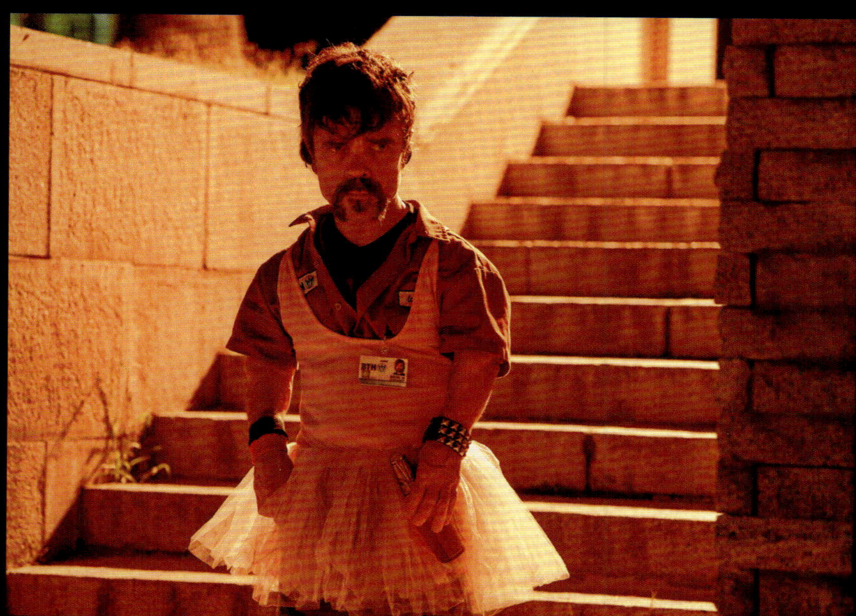

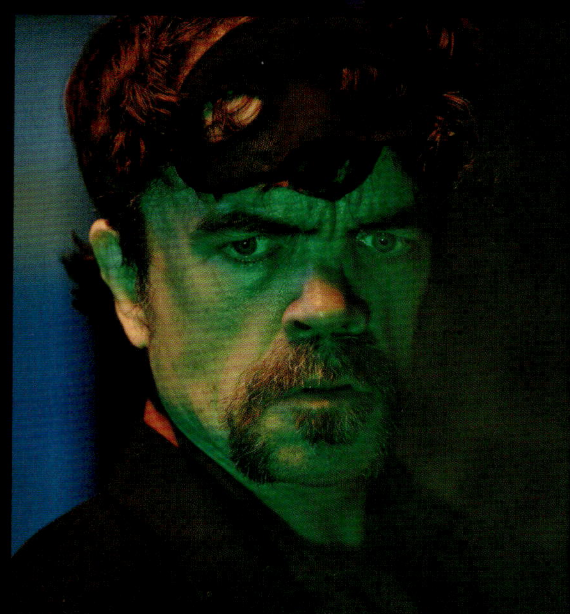

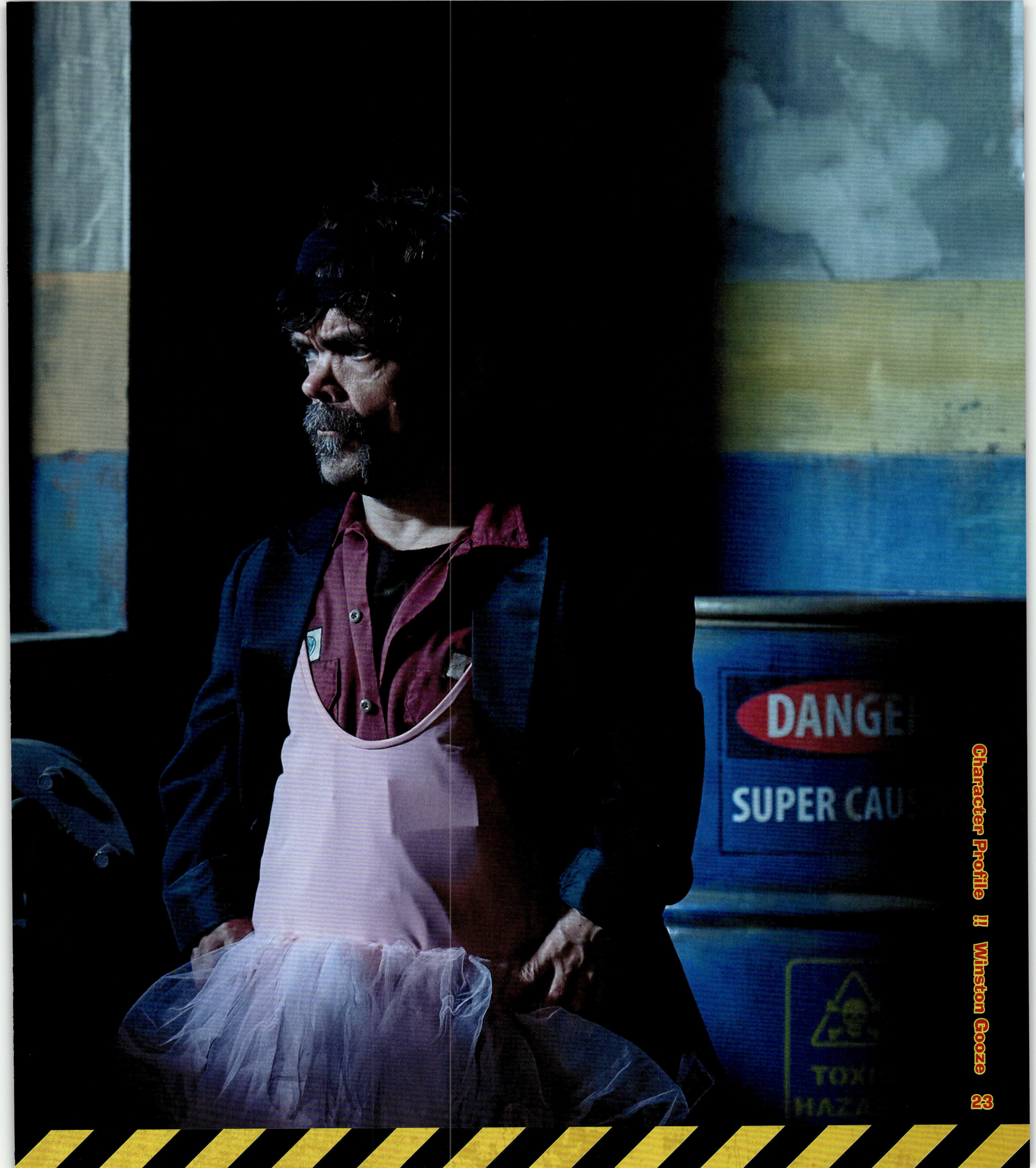
DANGE
SUPER CAU

exactly hard to wear. "He's got an ageing rocker vibe," explains New York-based costume designer Vanessa Porter, whose previous projects include Brawl in *Cell Block 99* and *The Farewell*. "He used to be a groupie for his wife's rock band, so we gave him a metal T-shirt and camo shorts and Converse sneakers."

As someone who grew up in New Jersey during the '80s, it all felt very natural to Dinklage. "The mullet came easy," he laughs. "You know, everything cut off, the tube socks... it's sort of this awesome throwback to '80s fashion. I had a lot of fun with the design team, right down to the fake tattoos—but not *so* many. Because a guy like Winston doesn't really have the courage to get covered in tattoos, right?"

He also had a lot of fun with the tutu. In the original, Melvin is forced to wear Toxie's signature piece of clothing as part of the cruel prank that leads to his transformation. Here, it forms a touching callback to a happier moment in Winston and Wade's life, where they wore tutus for Halloween. In a drunken attempt to connect with Wade—starting the long night that will lead to his 'death' and rebirth as Toxie—Winston pulls it on over his usual attire and clumsily twirls around his apartment.

"The tutu is everything," says Dinklage. "I put it on to entertain my stepson, but he's not having much of my shenanigans. It was fantastic. I loved the combination of a tutu and heavy metal gear, the contradiction of looks. It's brilliant."

The role came to fit Dinklage so well, Blair still can't believe he didn't think of him right away. "It's one of those things where in retrospect you realize, 'Oh, we could have saved a year if we'd just asked him in the first place.'" But he sees a parallel in the way that Indiana Jones was originally going to be played by Tom Selleck, before a scheduling conflict forced a pivot to Harrison Ford. "Now it's like, who else is Indiana Jones? It can only be Harrison Ford! So I really believe that, in almost every case, whoever ends up playing the part is who the universe always intended to play that part. It sounds hippy dippy, but I really believe that's true."

Below left Blair, while wearing a face mask, shares his thoughts with Dinklage in Winston's apartment.

Bottom left Blair and Dinklage talk between takes on the set of the B.T.H. Factory.

Bottom centre Dinklage listens intently to Blair, as the director reflects.

Below Winston Gooze in his apartment.

Bottom right Winston on his laptop in his apartment.

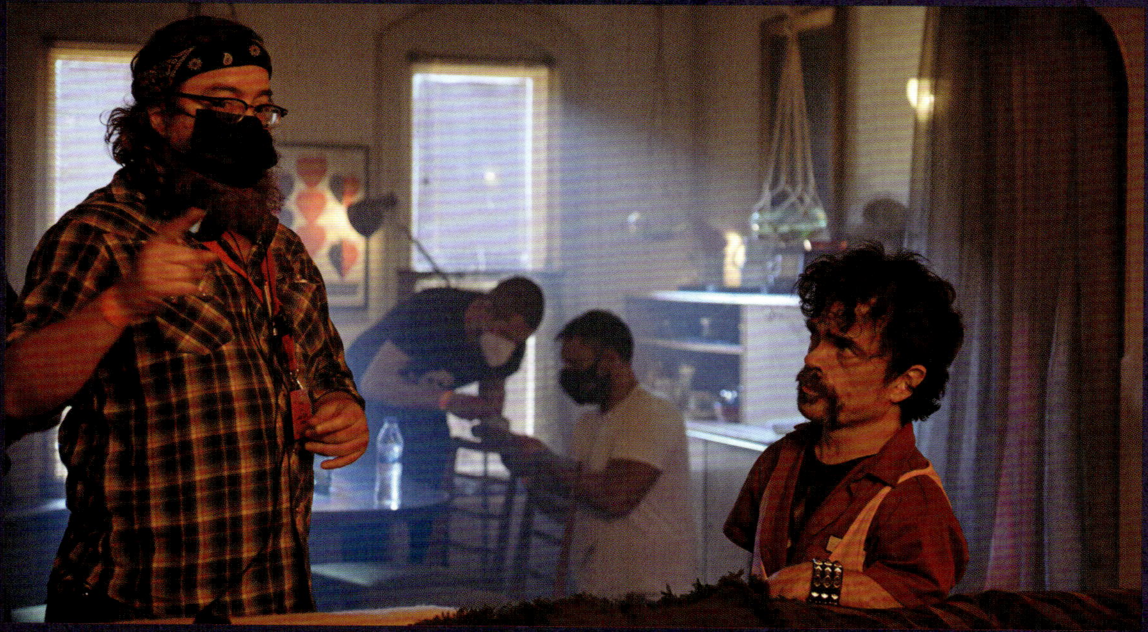

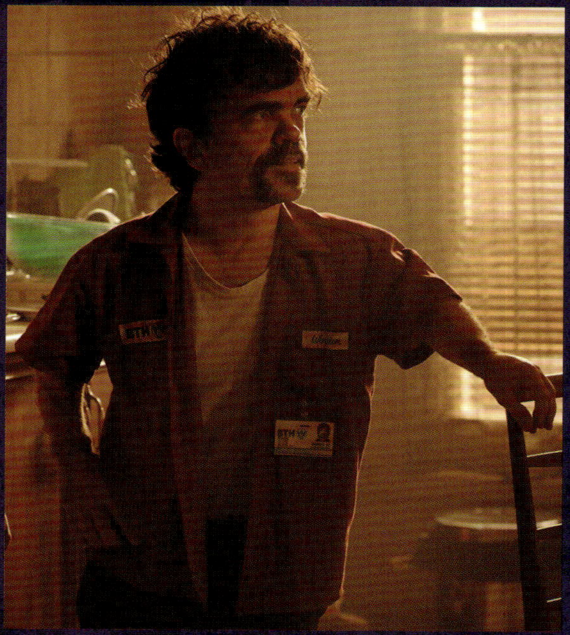

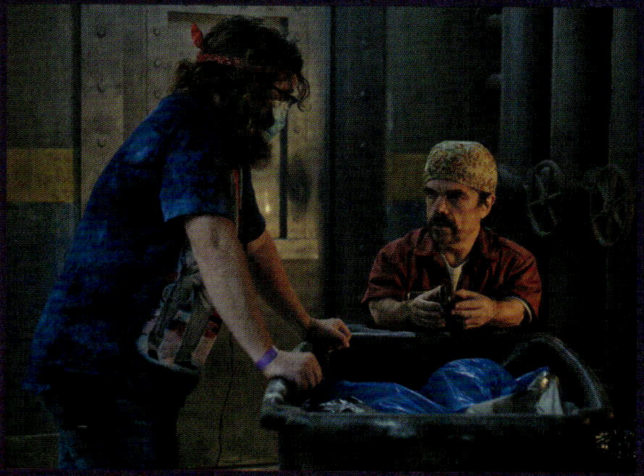

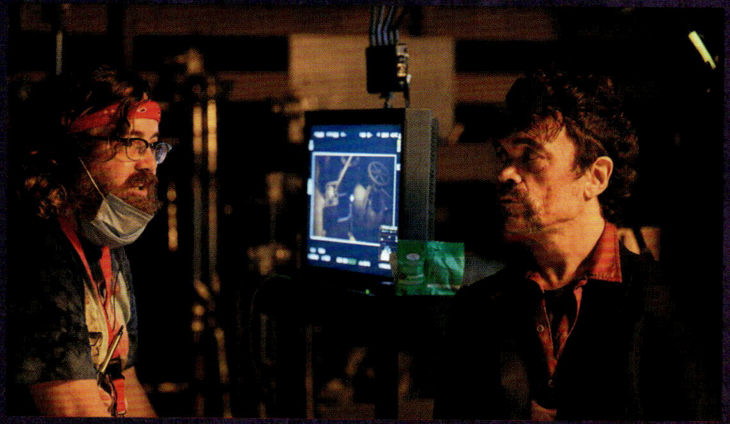

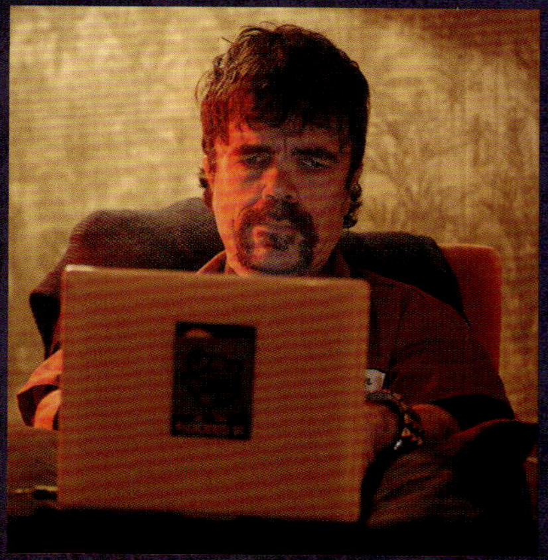

Guardian Angel

Meet Shelly, the lost love of Winston's life

The primary reason that Winston is so adrift in the world is that he's never fully recovered from the death of his rock-singer wife, Shelly, played by Irish actor Rebecca O'Mara (*Herself*). As well as being spotted in Gooze family photos, Shelly also appears in a Heavenly dream sequence (that did not make the final cut) during the climactic battle; an important, deep-breath moment that brings a sliver of peace and affection amid all the extreme, monster-driven mayhem.

"I don't think she's literally a spirit," says Blair. "It's more like a memory or something that's going on inside Winston's head. But it is a ghostly type of character, let's say, so she needed to have a warmth and familiarity—like, 'Oh, this is the person Winston's been missing this whole movie'—while also having this otherworldly vibe, so it doesn't feel completely realistic or natural."

During auditions, O'Mara immediately struck Blair as someone who could pull off this balance of "heart-breaking energy" and a slightly disorientating "unblinking texture." She was, he says, "able to straddle those two tones simultaneously, in a really interesting way."

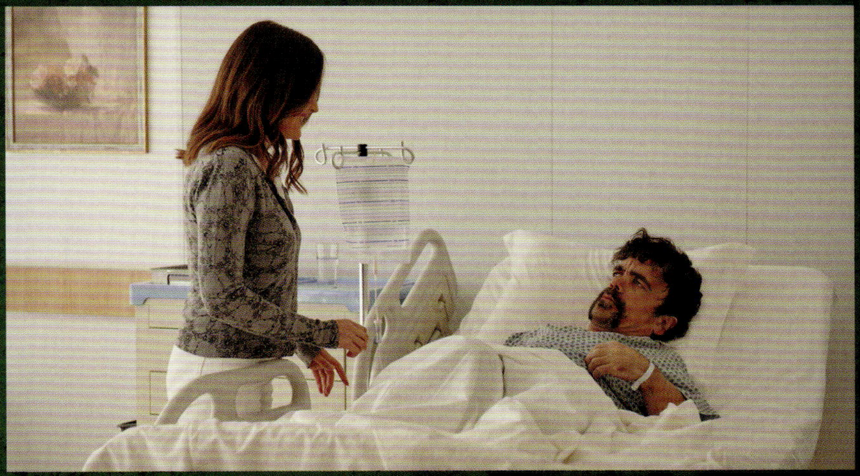

This page Towards the end of the movie, Toxie has a vision of himself as Winston again in which he reunites with his late wife Shelly.

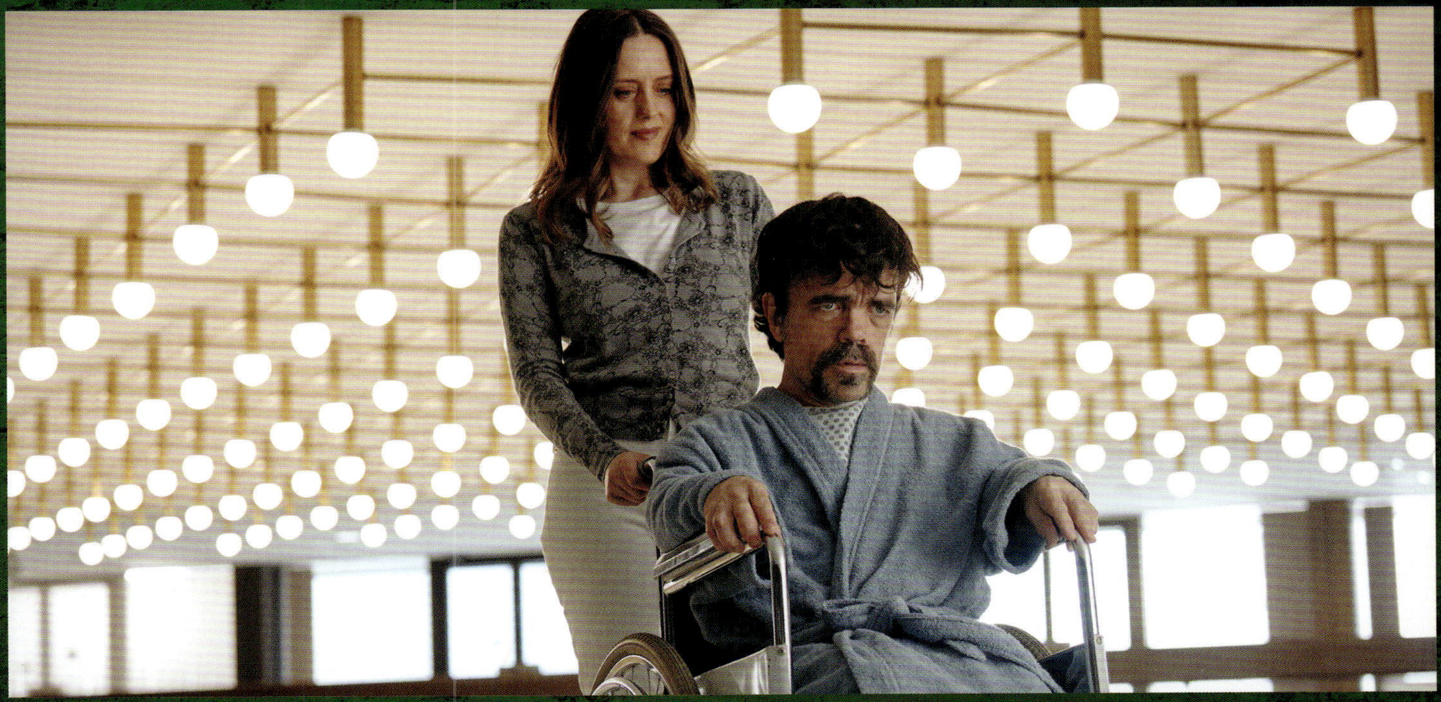

THE TOXIC AVENGER

PLAYED BY LUISA GUERREIRO

Ask anybody behind *The Toxic Avenger* who they think had the toughest job on the production, and who worked the hardest, and you can be sure they'll all give the same answer: Luisa Guerreiro, the London-based, British-Portuguese actor who donned heavy prosthetics to play Toxie.

"The costume was heavy. It was hot—nearly 40 degrees in Bulgaria. But she never complained. She was incredible," says creature effects supervisor Kate Walshe.

"She did such a great job, and then some," says Dinklage. "She is the one that had to suffer under those prosthetics in the Bulgarian summer. I applaud that lady."

"She went above and beyond. The perseverance and the energy required to be in a full-body prosthetic day in, day out is a *lot*," says Wood. "Not only to just physically move, but then also perform on top of it. Everybody bowed to her."

"We had a lot of heavy hitters on this movie that did really amazing work," says Blair. "But Luisa was the MVP. Once Winston transforms into Toxie, the whole movie is on her shoulders. And she knocked it out of the park every day."

The great, aching irony here is that Guerreiro's Herculean efforts to bring the movie's title character to Peter Dinklage-shaped life will, most likely, go unrecognized by the vast majority of the audience. Yet that is entirely her intention and her hope.

"My job was to be invisible," Guerreiro states. "My job was to *be* Peter. If anyone talking about this film says, 'Wasn't Peter great in that bit?' when I know it was actually me, I would be *thrilled*."

The team tasked with head-to-toe transforming Guerreiro into a green-skinned mutant—with a craggy hill of a face, a shovel of an underbite and a huge black-and-red left eye—was Millennium FX, based in Buckinghamshire, England. (Their previous work includes *The Wolf Man*, *Victor Frankenstein* and *Ex Machina*.)

"To have a fully prosthetic character be effectively the lead in a film and have so much action and dialogue is really rare," says Walshe, also a company director at Millennium. "We couldn't believe our luck when *The Toxic Avenger* came to us. We were really thrilled."

Toxie 2025 was born with a single sketch, rendered by concept artist Vanessa Menendez before the movie was even given the green light. "I was just getting eager and ahead of myself," admits Blair. "I started working with Vanessa so I could show things to Legendary and say, 'This is what I'm thinking of.'"

Their creative starting point, he explains, was Frankenstein's Monster, but of course they never drifted too far from the cult-iconic look of the original Toxic Avenger created in 1984 by Lloyd Kaufman and special-effects makeup artist Jenny Aspinall. "If you were to do an updated Superman or Batman, there's certain things you have to have," Blair explains. "You can

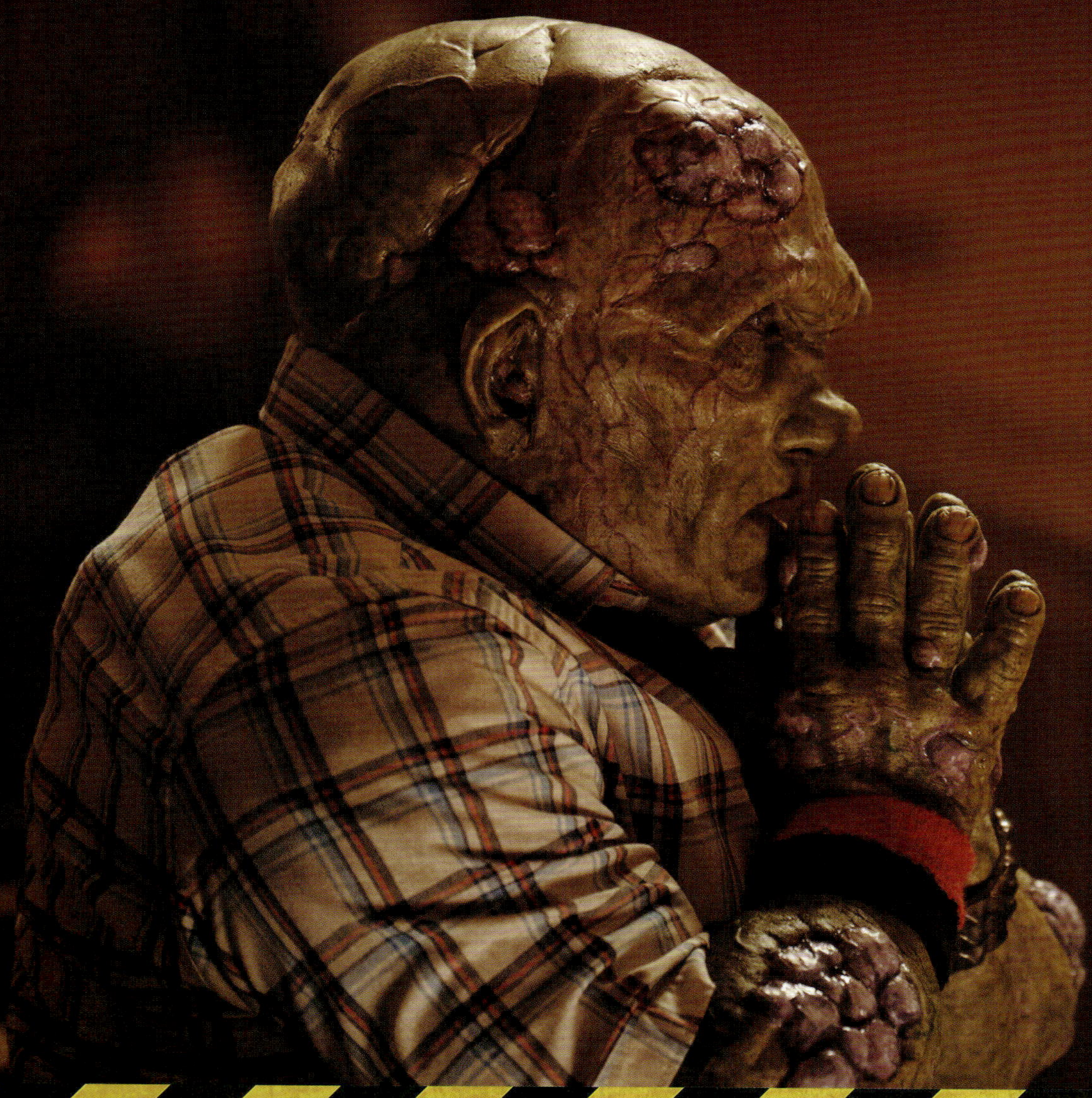

Left Winston (now transformed into the Toxic Avenger) proudly watches stepson Wade perform.

Below Toxie on stage at Troma Fest, post-fight.

Right As well as wearing all those prosthetics, Guerreiro had to wear a single contact lens so that her brown eye matched Dinklage's blue eye.

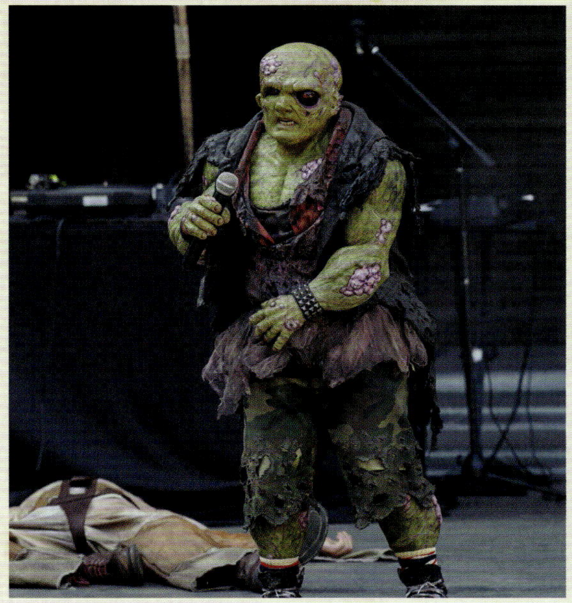

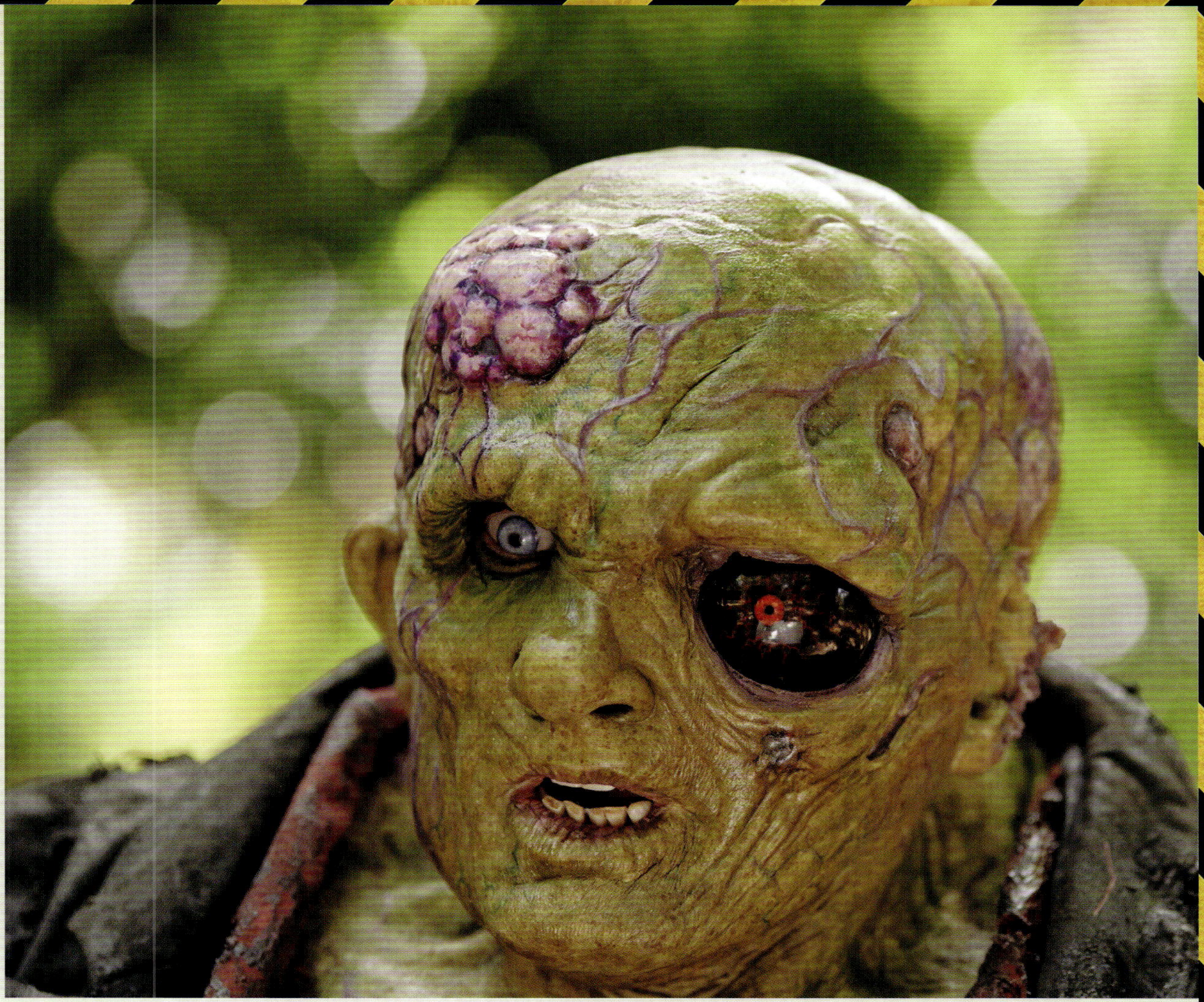

do a reimagining, you can do a remix, you could change it all up. But at the end of the day, you really do need the 'S' on the chest, or some version of Batman's pointy horns. So we knew Toxie needed some kind of physical mutation and the tutu."

Garcia describes this Toxie as retaining a "sense memory" of the original, while being "different and distinctive—a fresh way into it." Guerreiro, meanwhile, thinks, "it's like the older Toxie had a child. This design is honouring the past, and I appreciated that."

Taking that "dirty, gnarly, fun" sketch as their "style guide", Walshe's team set about using "the slickest technologies possible" to combine Blair and Menendez's design with reference photographs of Dinklage and 3D scans of Guerreiro's features, and bring this 21st century Toxie to life.

"It involved a mixture of traditional clay sculpting, digital modelling and 3D printing," says 3D sculptor Chris Goodman, "and I was able to specifically model Toxie's look to accommodate the animatronics required for his big eye." So while the decision to realize Toxie through traditional, practical effects rather than motion-capture and CGI certainly speaks to the film's grungy, retro vibe, he says, "We were using modern techniques to make sure it was going to be the best, coolest result."

Beyond the sketch, Goodman's inspirations included creature make-up legend Rob Bottin's astonishing work for Paul Verhoeven's *RoboCop* (specifically the toxic-waste-melted Emil, played by Paul McCrane) and the viridescent muscle-mass of Marvel's Hulk. "Originally we went for a far brighter green, far more luminous," says Goodman, "but Macon said, 'No, let's keep this grounded.'" With that in mind, the sculptor also paid close attention to real-life blemishes: "Boils, mutated burnt skin. Anything along those lines. Anything that's gross, that can go wrong with the human or animal body, that could be fed into the design to ground it in realism."

Constructed from a combination of foam latex and silicon, featuring airbrushed UV veining, the suit was applied in segments: torso, neck, head, arms, legs, hands and feet, with the joins easy to hide beneath Toxie's charred tuxedo/T-shirt/tutu ensemble. However, with that huge, dark animatronic eye (created by ocular specialists Fourth Seal Studios), a hefty contact lens required for the other eye, a pulsating bladder section in the skull, and a set of dentures (courtesy of Fangs FX), it was never going to be a walk in the park for the performer encased within all those prosthetics. A performer who'd not only have to spend four hours having their makeup applied every day, but who also required a very specific set of skills and attributes.

"We needed someone who was the approximate size of Peter, but who wasn't just a stunt performer," says Blair. "It is a physical performance that needs to be tuned into a very specific character that another actor will have already made a

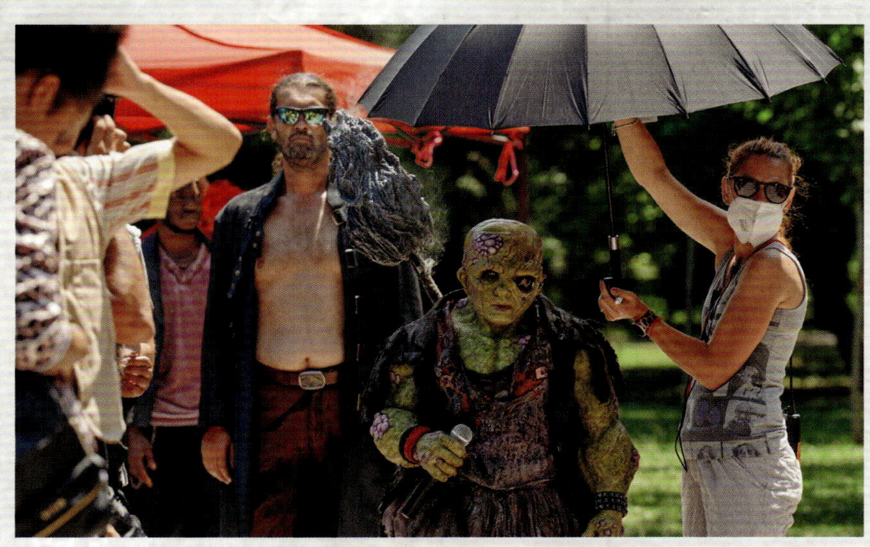

"The costume was heavy. It was hot — nearly 40 degrees in Bulgaria. But [Luisa] never complained. She was incredible."

– KATE WALSHE,
Creature Effects Supervisor, Millennium FX

lot of the choices for." The physical switch from Dinklage as Winston to the Toxie performer would need to be indiscernible if the movie was to work. Especially during its more intimate, emotional moments, such as the scenes between Toxie and his stepson Wade.

"Obviously, the physical aspect was a big part of it, because there is running and fighting and everything like that, plus there's also a comfort level with being in that type of heavy makeup," continues Blair. "But we also needed someone to have the chops for these scenes. Luisa did an audition that blew everybody away. It was not a hard decision."

At four-foot-nine, with extensive stage-combat training at the Royal Central School of Speech and Drama ("I like to play with swords"), not to mention experience of puppetry and prosthetics, Guerreiro was uniquely qualified to play this role. "It was like everything I've been keeping in my arsenal was suddenly needed," she says.

The only minor complication was the fact that she didn't share Dinklage's gender. "It can be harder physiologically because you're made different to men. But also, I'm quite a tomboy. I've never been very feminine."

Also, it wasn't too difficult for Millennium FX to work around during the suit design process. "When we got Luisa in to be life-cast for our first scans, we used a female-to-male binder that crushes the boobs down," says Walshe. "Then we just looked at the areas where the suit would need to be bulked out to give it a 'triangle' shape, so we didn't make her too curvaceous. Just little tricks to make her feel as masculine as possible. She took it all in her stride."

Ultimately, Guerreiro saw gender as irrelevant. "I'm not about mimicking, I'm about energy," she says. "My job was to observe Peter's energy and physicality, and communicate that it's him.'"

That observation process began in Sofia about three weeks before shooting commenced, relates Dinklage. "We rehearsed every day. We'd do a scene with Jacob or Taylour, and I would do it as the monster. Macon would tape it, while Luisa was in the room there with me, observing. It really helped, because Luisa had all the footage after I left—they had about two more months of filming—and she had that in her back pocket for the whole shoot."

This footage was far more valuable to Guerreiro than simply going back and watching Dinklage in his previous roles. "What I don't want is to be getting these stock mannerisms, or trying to be Peter in

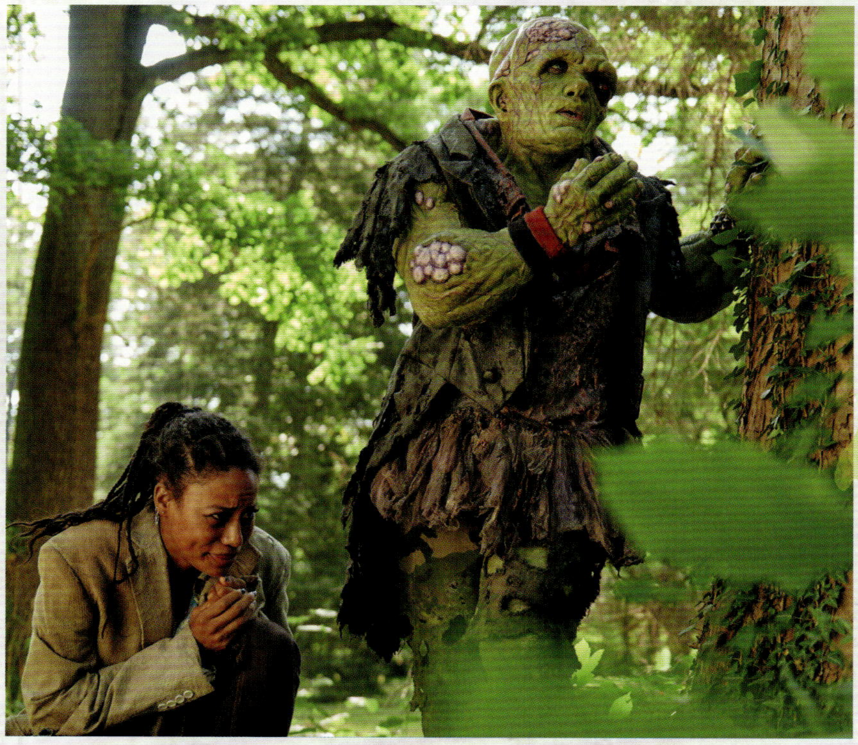

Top left A crew member kindly shades Guerreiro (in full Toxie prosthetics) from the worst of the Bulgarian summer heat with an umbrella.

Left JJ Doherty and Toxie assess the threat of the Killer Nutz from afar.

Top Right Toxie can handily detatch his big eye when he needs to engage in a little espionage.

Right Guerreiro, in Toxie garb, talks with Blair on the set of Tromafest.

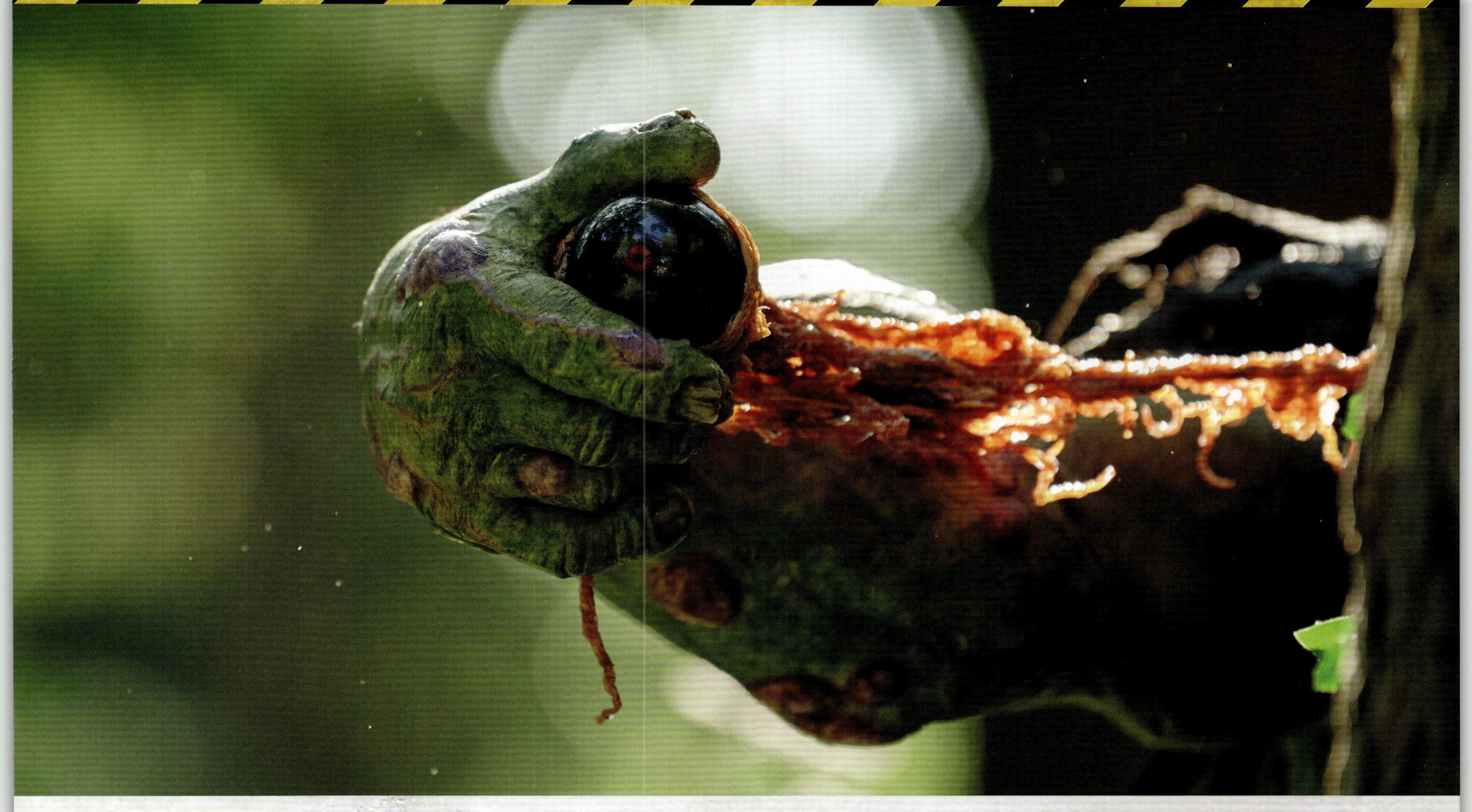

Game of Thrones, because he's playing a different character," she explains. "I said to him, 'I need to know your intentions for this scene. I need to know what your back story is. I need to know what choices you would make in this moment.' It was quite scary. You've got a lot of responsibility. You've got one of the finest actors giving you the reins and saying, 'I trust you to be me in this movie.'"

When time came during post-production for Dinklage to record his voice performance as Toxie ("I tried to tap into a softer, sweeter voice"), he was deeply impressed by what Guerreiro had achieved. "It was quite extraordinary to see because it's not me, but it kind of is. It was an out-of-body experience. And *she* was the one who had to suffer under those prosthetics in the Bulgarian summer..."

Ah yes, the Bulgarian summer. The production shot during the most sweltering months in Eastern Europe, from 21 June to 21 September 2021. Enervating conditions, even if you aren't entirely swathed in foam latex and silicone—especially on locations like the exposed, dust-blasted "Hellscape", an industrial waste-zone that Blair's team created in a quarry near Sofia, where the climactic fight sequence takes place.

"It was tough, I'm not going to lie," says Guerreiro, who was closely monitored by Millennium FX's on-set supervisor, Charlie Bluett. He would regularly check in with her on her level of discomfort, on a scale of one to 10. "The default was always six," she says. "I think I got to a nine when we did the Hellscape scenes. There was absolutely no shade, and they had these white tents, which of course did nothing. I had these

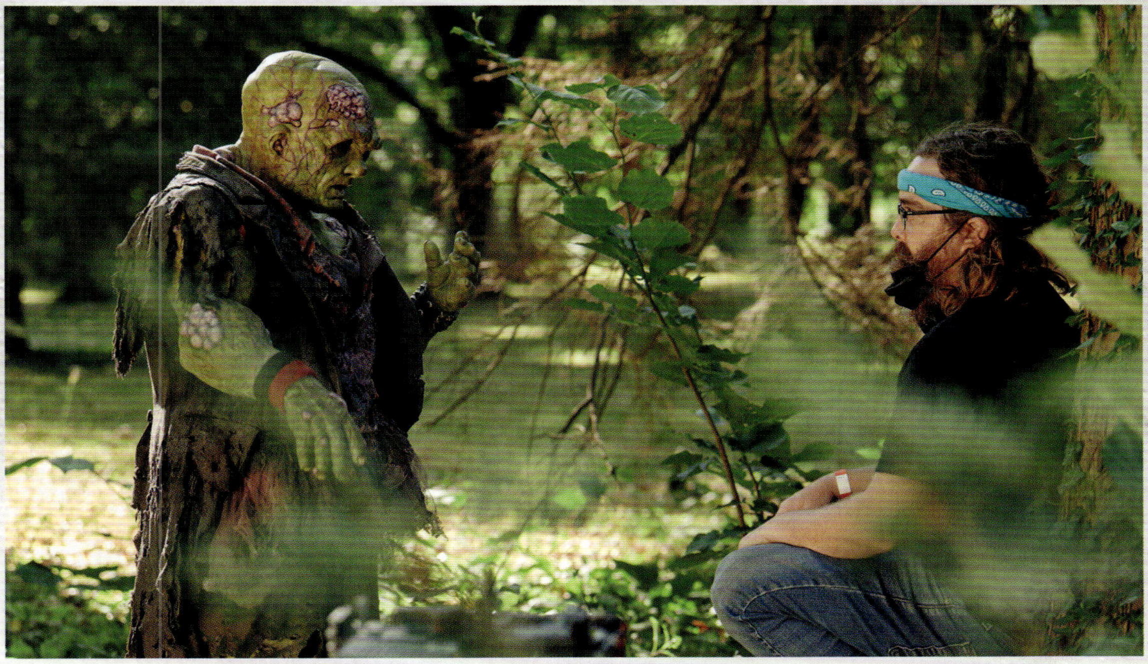

industrial fan heaters with aluminium pipes that came out and stuck down my back, and I had leaf blowers up my legs and down by my coccyx, just to keep me cool." Guerreiro was also, to her delight, given her own Slushie machine. "I just drank Slush Puppies all day," she beams. "I was living the dream of my 11-year-old self!"

While out in the open, performing her combat moves with six-foot-six Welsh actor Spencer Wilding, also covered in prosthetics as the troll-like Monster Garbinger, she had no such cool, saccharine relief. Even so, she bore up remarkably well.

"I think it can only be unbearable if it's a surprise," she reflects. "I knew it was going to be hot. I'd psyched myself up for it. I knew I wouldn't be doing it for more than 10 minutes at a time. So let's just get on with it. I'm just lucky I'm not claustrophobic!"

It wasn't merely the heat that tested Guerreiro's stoicism. Thanks to the animatronic eye/contact lens combo (Guerreiro's dark brown irises had to be obscured to match the crisp blue of Dinklage's), she couldn't see too well. Due to her Toxie dentures, she wasn't able to consume solid food (or even hot soup) without fear of ruining them or Millennium FX's fine makeup work. And, as she discovered during her first day of shooting, with that lumpy, misshapen head donned, she could barely hear a thing. The clicking and whirring of the animatronic mechanisms drowned out people's already muffled voices.

"Macon was shouting directions at me, and I was just standing there in the middle of this take with the film rolling, doing nothing. I wasn't going to move because that would have been dangerous. In the end, he fixed it by giving me a little earplug so I could hear wirelessly, which helped massively. Although you had to put the earphone in before the head went on."

It is one thing to hear from Guerreiro's co-stars and director that she never once complained during the shoot. It is something else entirely to realize that she'd go back and do it all again, without hesitation. "Would I want to play Toxie again? Yes! Absolutely! Unashamedly, unapologetically," she exclaims. Much of this enthusiasm is to do with Guerreiro's positive experience with Millennium FX and Blair and his crew, but it's also rooted in the character's essential appeal.

"There's that very traditional underdog thing," believes Blair. "A lot of people can relate to getting the short end of the stick and feeling like you don't have power. Then there's the wish-fulfilment thing, in getting an extreme version of power back for yourself. But I think the extra layer that's cool is that he becomes even more of an outsider when he gets the power, so there's even more of a low point to recover from. It's like taking that outsiderness and having it become your advantage."

Guerreiro agrees. "I love that he doesn't change back," she says. "I love that it isn't this fairy-tale ending where there's a cure and he goes back to what's meant to be the best version of him. He *is* him. He hasn't really changed. He's always this battered person who's just doing his best in a world that tries to crush him, and I think a lot of people relate to that. That's what I really loved about playing him: he's just this flawed individual who didn't have to be a superhero."

Interestingly, she does not distinguish between 'Winston' and 'Toxie'. "Toxie is always Winston to me. He's never 'Toxie'. That's just a nickname. I think we've all got a bit of Winston in us." And, of course, there is a lot of Guerreiro in Winston. Even if most of the world will never be aware of it.

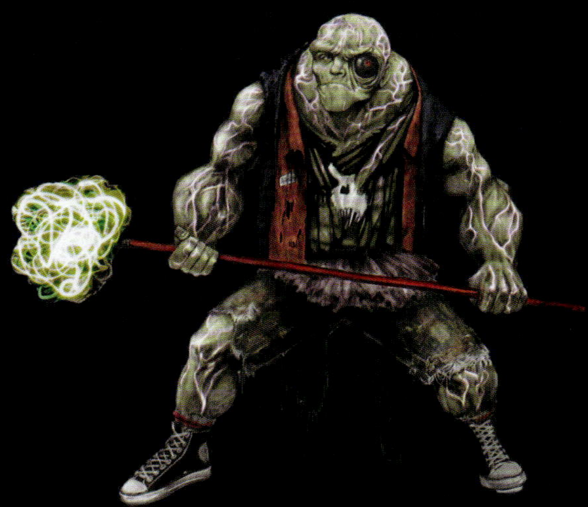

Above The first piece of concept art created for Toxie, by artist Vanessa Menendez.

Below A more detailed concept piece of Toxie's head, used as reference by Millennium FX.

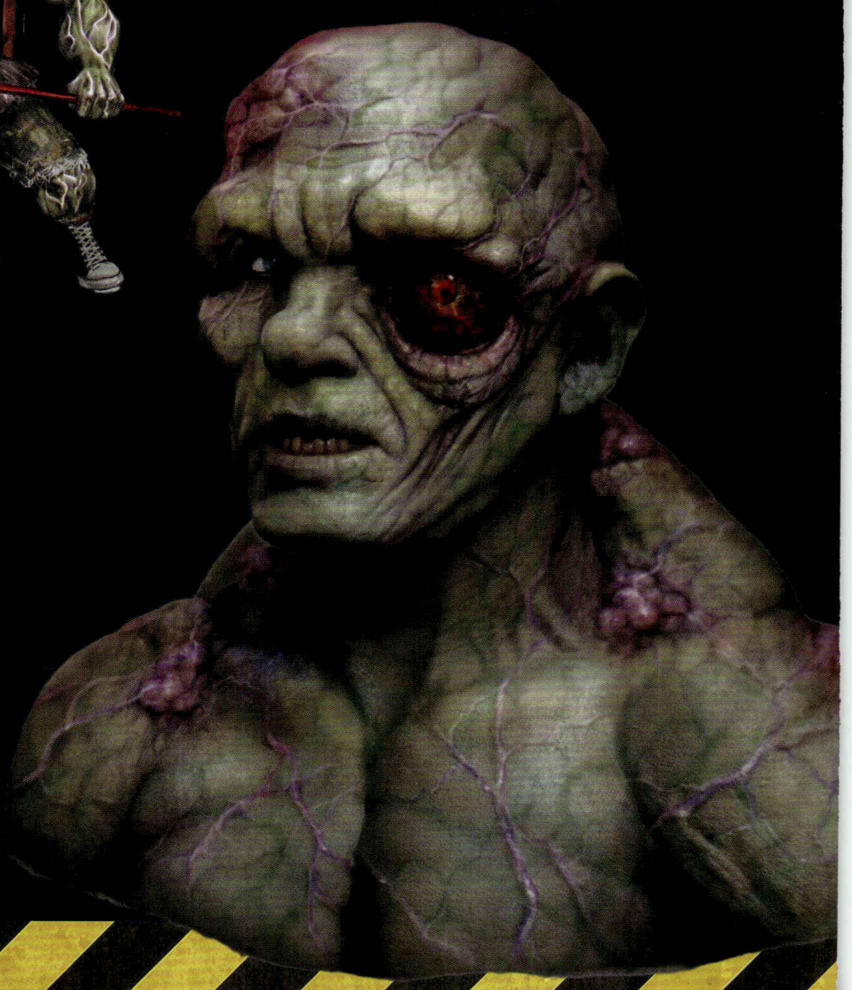

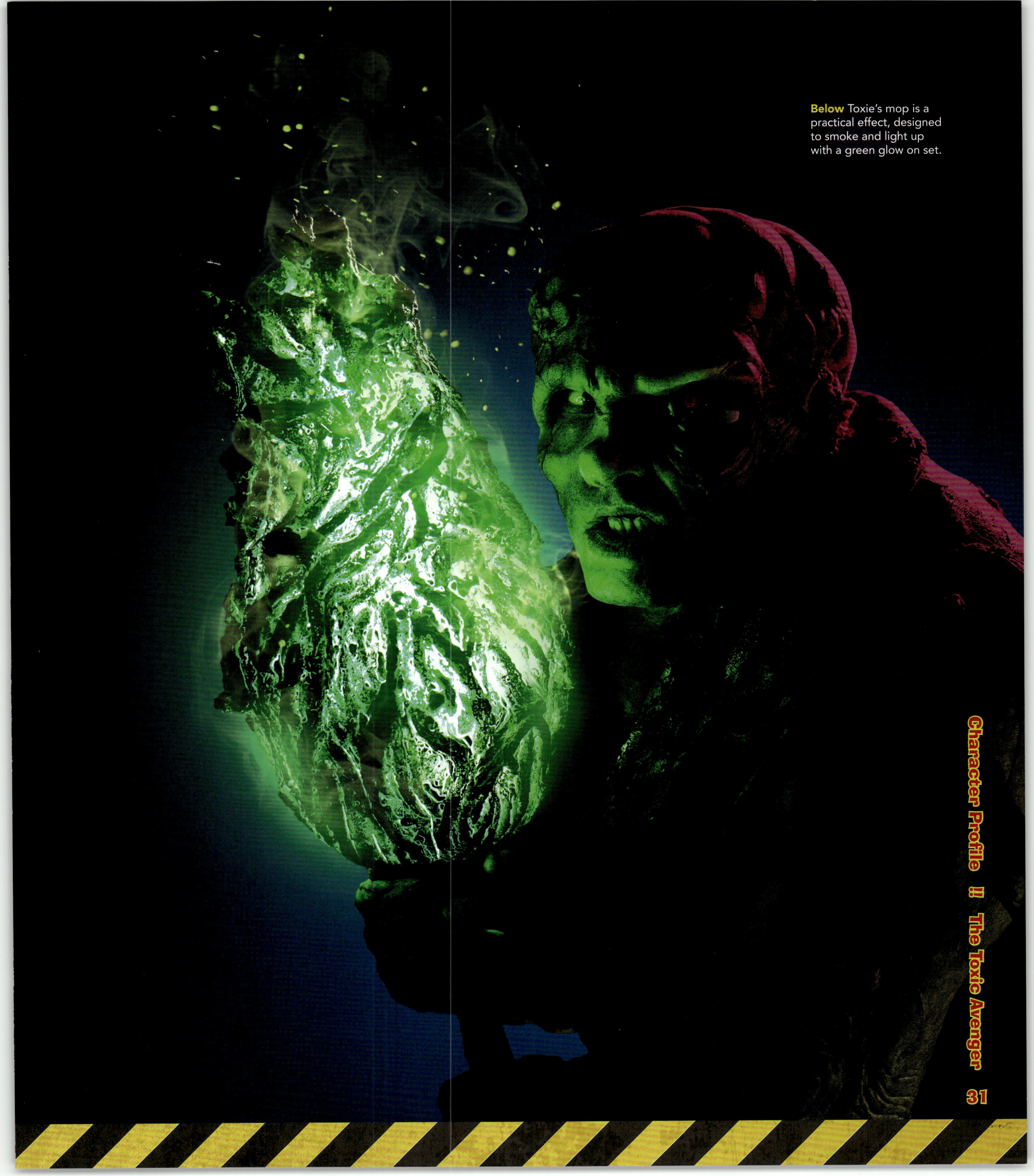

Below Toxie's mop is a practical effect, designed to smoke and light up with a green glow on set.

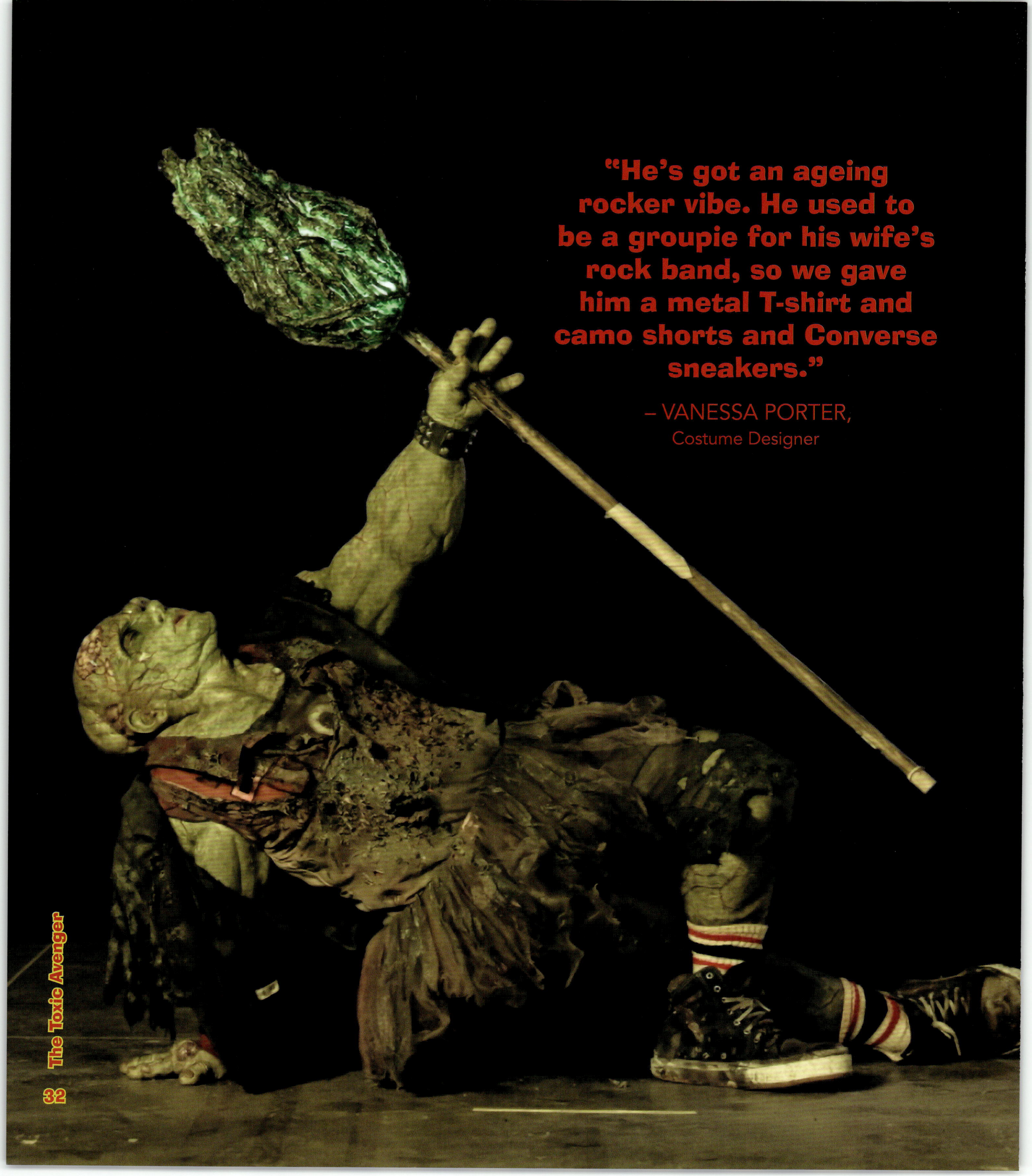

"He's got an ageing rocker vibe. He used to be a groupie for his wife's rock band, so we gave him a metal T-shirt and camo shorts and Converse sneakers."

– VANESSA PORTER,
Costume Designer

Mopping Up

Getting to grips with Toxie's weapon of choice

To Macon Blair, it is nothing less than the Toxic Avenger's Excalibur: "A mystical weapon in the form of a mop." With a greenish glow and a perpetual wisp of smoke curling from its chemically augmented tip, this unconventional polearm called for a far more advanced prop than the everyday, grey-tousled swab swung about by Mitch Cohen's Toxie in the original movie.

After much lengthy discussion with Illusion Industries about how it was going to look, they settled on something with a head "that's almost like molten lava," visual effects supervisor Chris Ritvo explains. "It's always steaming and creates this strange, heavy smoke which I haven't really seen before. It really sticks around and hangs to things. It's also got this green glow inside, created by lights that Dana put in there."

Dana Gonzales, the movie's cinematographer, confesses that "the scariest conversation of the whole production was talking about the mop and how we're going to pull it off. It glows more and smokes more as he's being threatened more, and he also fights with it so much." However, the combination of the lighting mechanism and the small smoke machine in the head added considerably to the weapon's weight—to a challenging degree, as Luisa Guerreiro soon discovered.

"I'm quite strong, but every time I wielded it, I was being pulled with the mop, like I was on a seesaw, or the end of some rope," she says. "With the mini smoke machine inside, it was difficult to take that weight away."

In the end, the FX team created a lighter, stunt version for wide action shots. Without all the cumbersome, interior mechanisms of what became known as the "carry mop", it was far easier for Luisa (and her stunt double) to use. Not that she didn't appreciate the weightier incarnation. "It did look amazing," she says. "So kudos to the SFX department!"

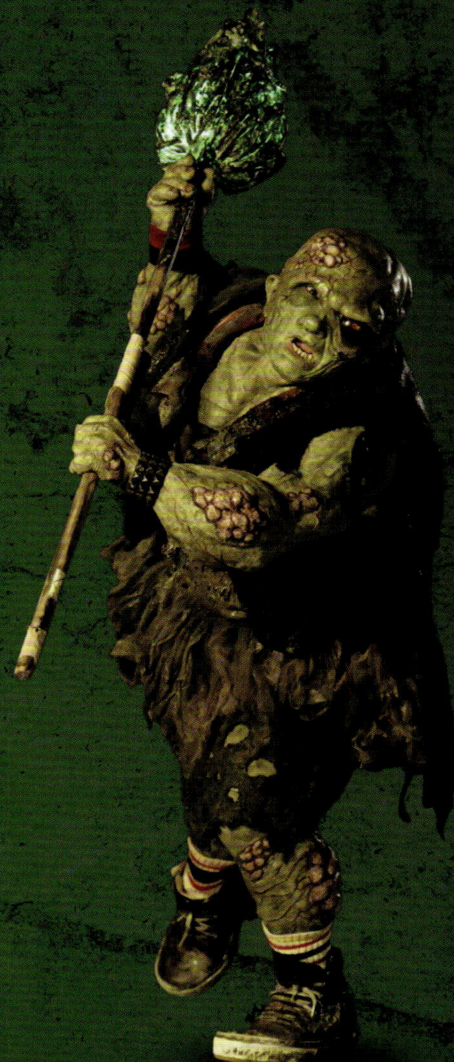

WADE

PLAYED BY JACOB TREMBLAY

Like Winston, Wade is another person who feels they don't fit into the world, and can't figure out how to change that. He's still grieving his mother, living with a stepfather he's struggling to connect with, and suffering from anxiety. However, he has a passion for dance, which is stymied at first by his adolescent insecurities, but becomes a means of joyous expression during the film's heart-warming finale.

"It's only through being thrown into this weird life-and-death situation, where he gets kidnapped and his life is threatened, that he gains the confidence to be who he is and feel good about that unapologetically," says Blair. "He's a character I had a lot of empathy for and felt very protective of. I thought if I could transfer that feeling onto the audience, then that would help propel the jeopardy of the story, where Wade is thrown into the deep end very quickly and has to figure out how to swim."

Blair says there was "a pretty short list of actors" in the required age range who had "movie-star visibility" and were capable of playing Wade. He felt he needed "a Jacob Tremblay type," thinking of the then-14-year-old Canadian actor who starred in *Wonder* and *Doctor Sleep*, and in 2016 was the youngest-ever actor nominated for a Screen Actors Guild Award in the category of Outstanding Performance by a Male Actor in a Supporting Role, for his astonishing turn alongside Brie Larson in *Room*. Then Blair got word that the *actual Jacob Tremblay* wanted to do it.

"Wade is so interesting," says Tremblay. "I've never played anyone like him before, and I was really excited to explore this character and play with it. There's a lot of fun things I get to do in this movie." For the dance sequence, for example, he worked with a choreographer, but was also able to add in some moves of his own. "It's a very artistic, emotional dance style," Tremblay explains. "Very expressive. And what's

Right Wade is described in the script as "a slight kid entering uncertain adolescence with a bone-deep melancholy".

Left below Wade looks on, unamused, as his step-father Winston attempts to make him laugh in their apartment.

Below Wade is held captive by Fritz's goons. Tremblay brought his own ideas to Wade's look, including his painted fingernails.

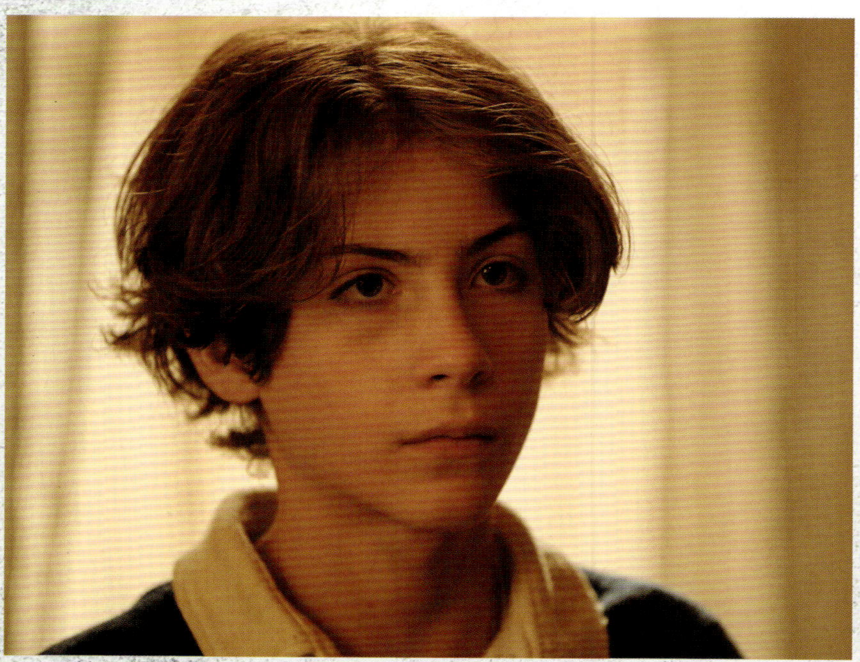

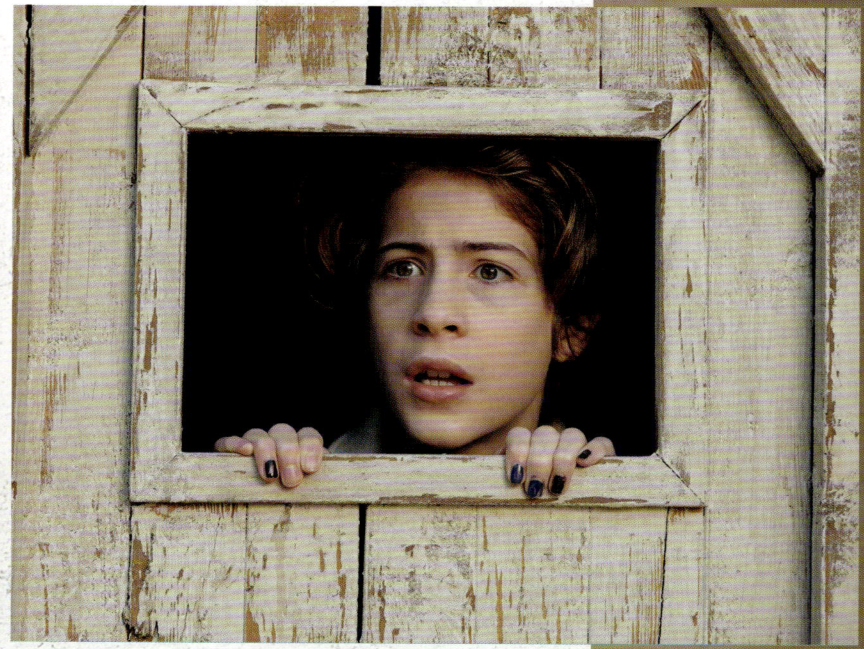

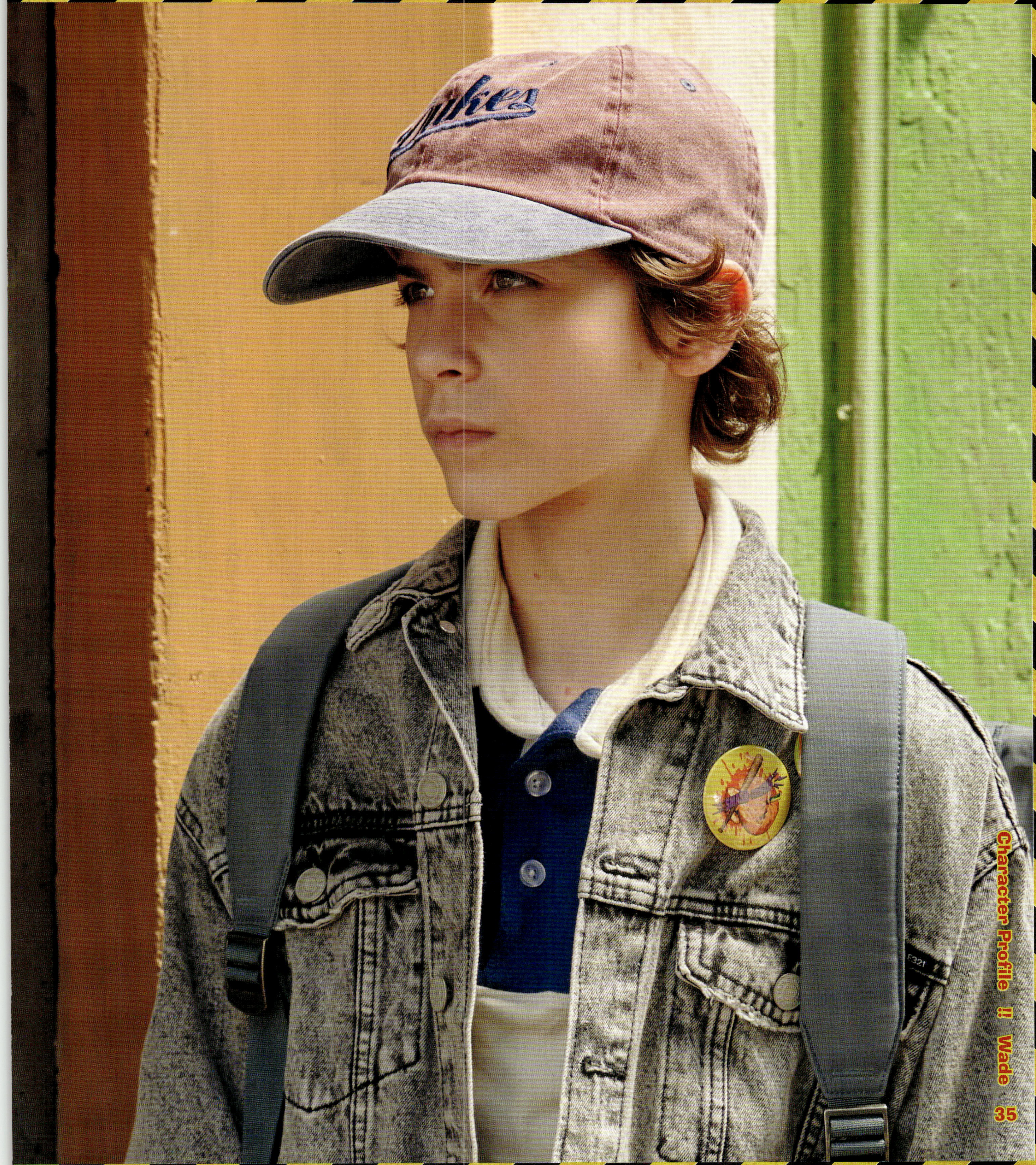

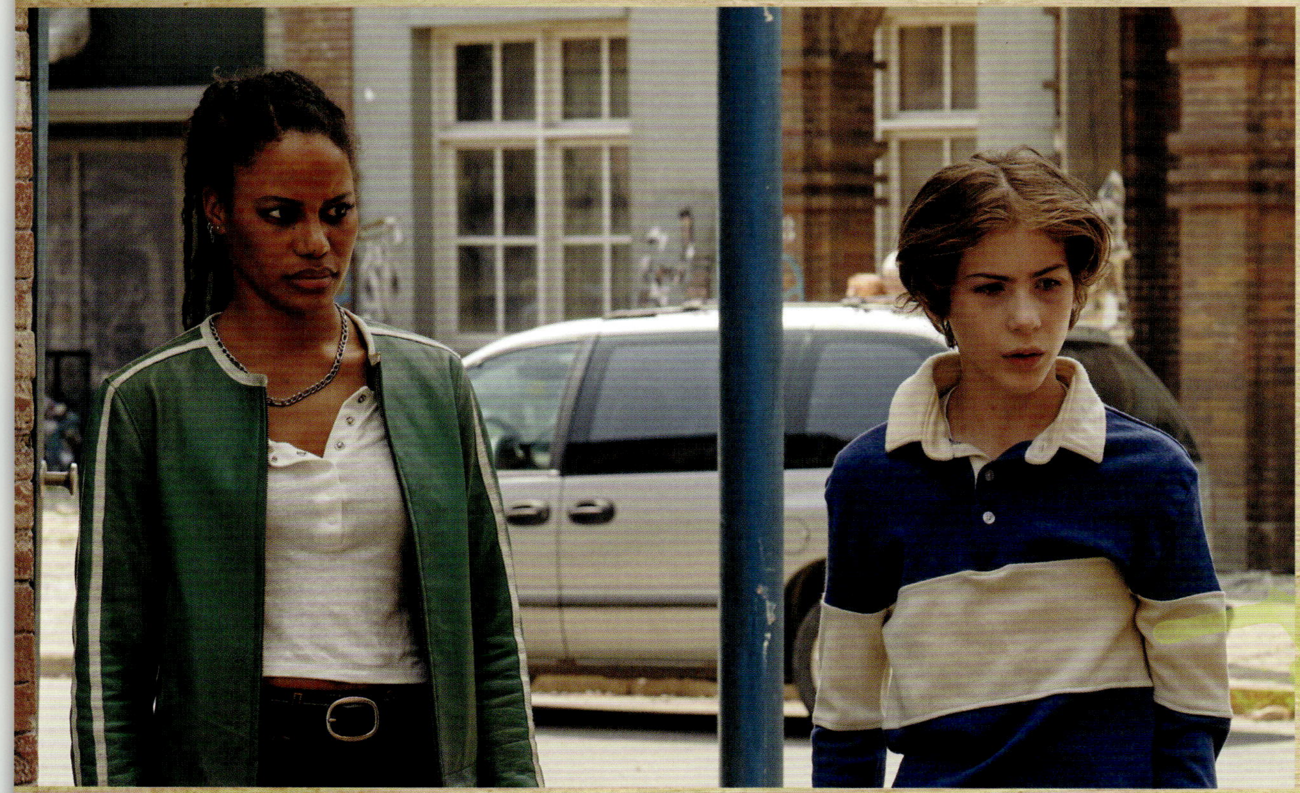

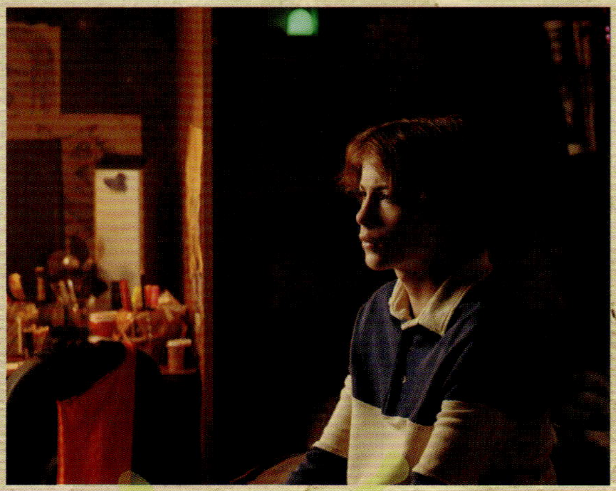

Above Wade sits alone in his bedroom. Like Winston, he is grieving his mother Shelly.

Left Wade with J.J. on the streets of Tromaville.

Left below Wade performs on stage.

Below Wade is kidnapped by Fritz's goons.

Bottom Blair directs Tremblay on set.

Opposite page In a sense, Wade undergoes his own transformation when he takes to the stage for the film's finale.

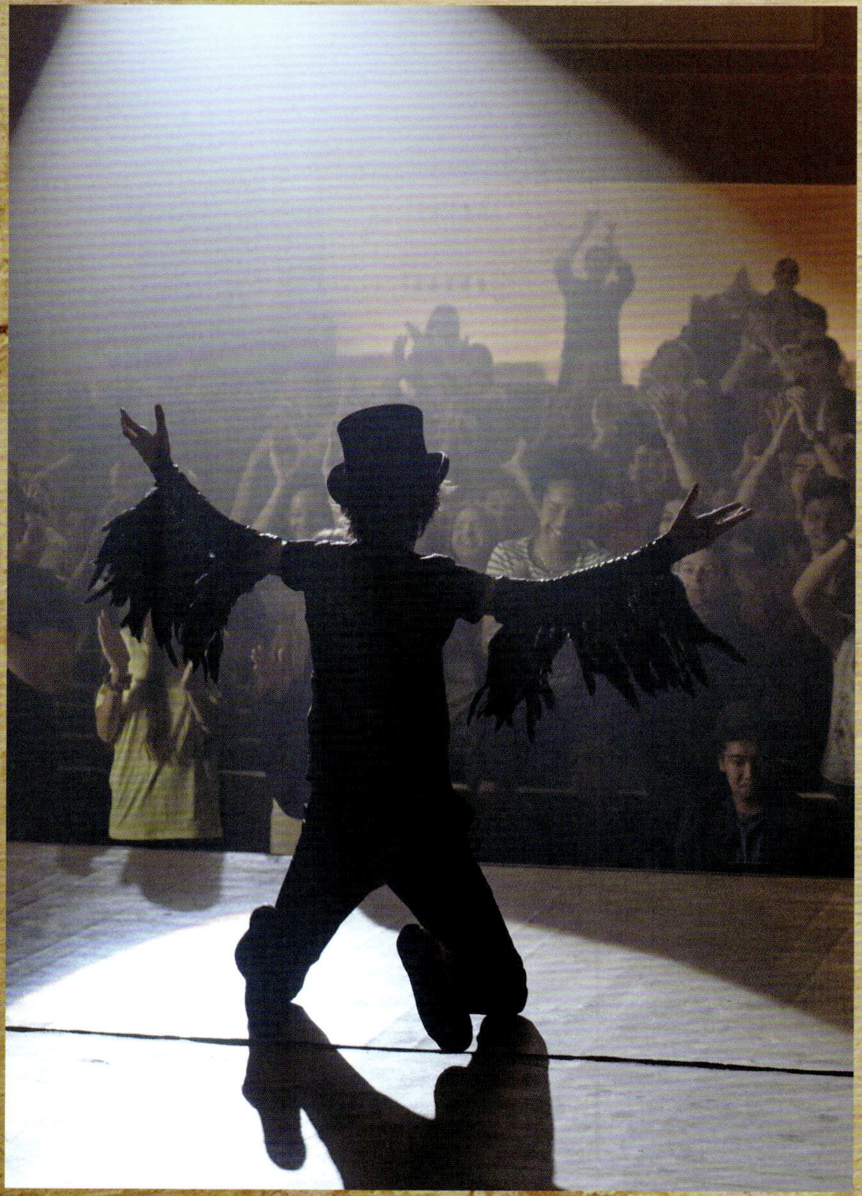

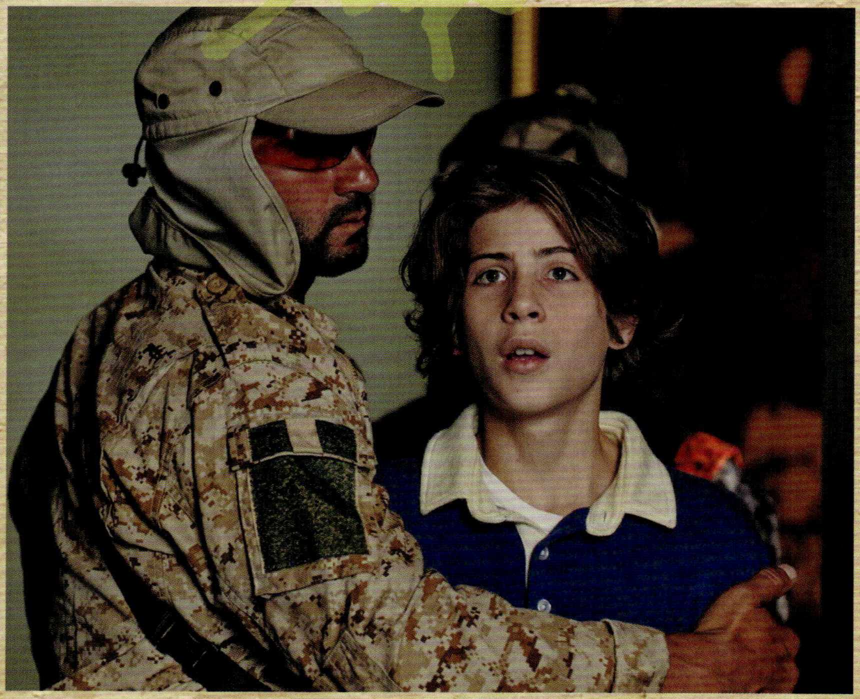

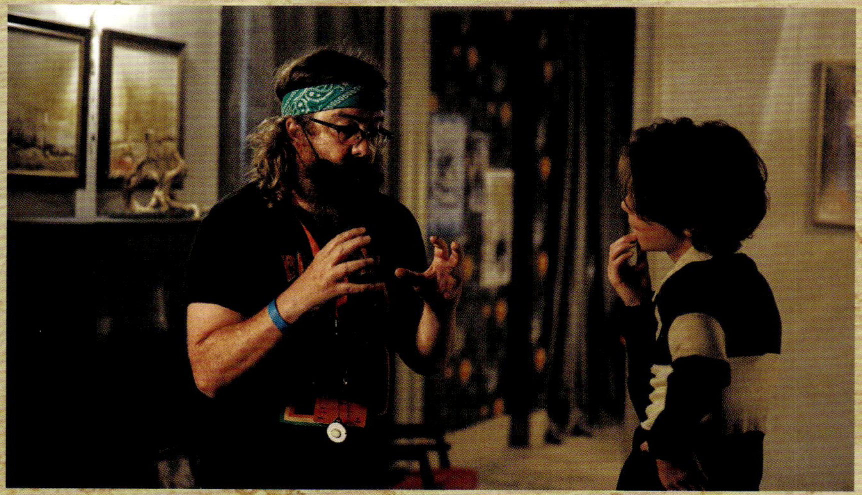

funny is Wade is very specific about what his dance is. He calls it 'a property movement piece.'"

Performing this prop-comedy-inspired act—which involves smashing pumpkins with a baseball bat—was Tremblay's most challenging sequence, but also his most satisfying. "I was so excited, but also nervous, dancing in front of an audience of probably a hundred background actors," he recalls. "We shot it multiple times, and also I had to freestyle a bit. But it's such an important moment, I really wanted to do a good job and make sure that I wasn't holding back at all, that I could just let go."

He also has very fond memories of working with Dinklage during the early scenes. "Peter is a great actor. I'm a big fan of his. But one of the big problems was trying to keep a straight face during my scenes with him, because he's so hilarious. I had a blast working with him and Macon. We were able to have a fun time on set, doing improv and changing up the scenes however we like."

Blair's trust in Tremblay went beyond allowing him to improvize. He even encouraged his input into Wade's look and style. "He gave me so much freedom with my character," reports Tremblay. "I was the one who came up with Wade's nail polish and his hairstyle." Unlike anything he'd made before, *The Toxic Avenger*, in a sense, became Tremblay's coming-of-age experience, as much as it was Wade's.

"This movie is unique," he says. "You can't really compare it to anything else. I didn't really have a reference for it. But that was what was so fun about this. I could make it my own thing."

"I've never played anyone like [Wade] before, and I was really excited to explore this character and play with it. There's a lot of fun things I get to do in this movie."

– JACOB TREMBLAY,
Actor

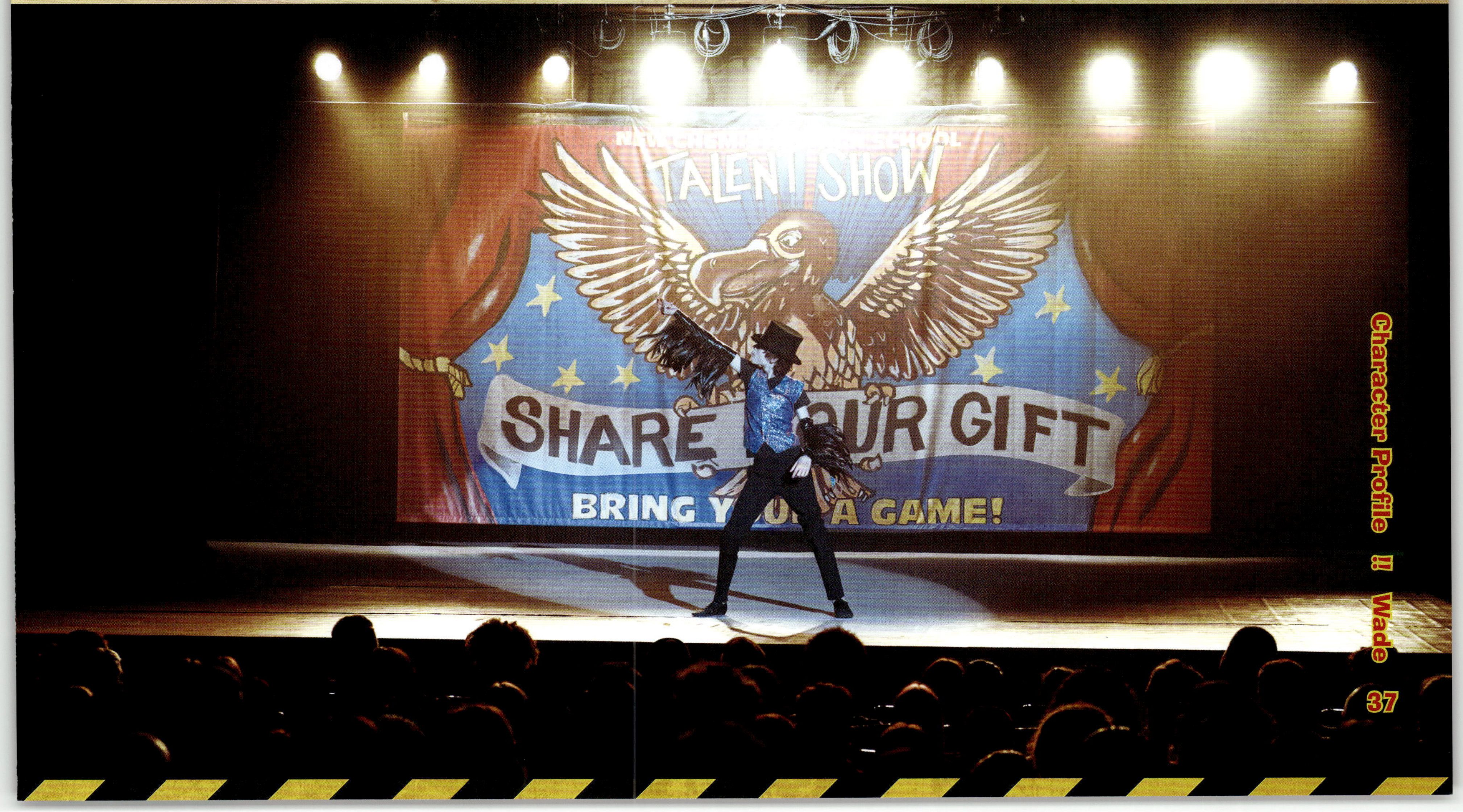

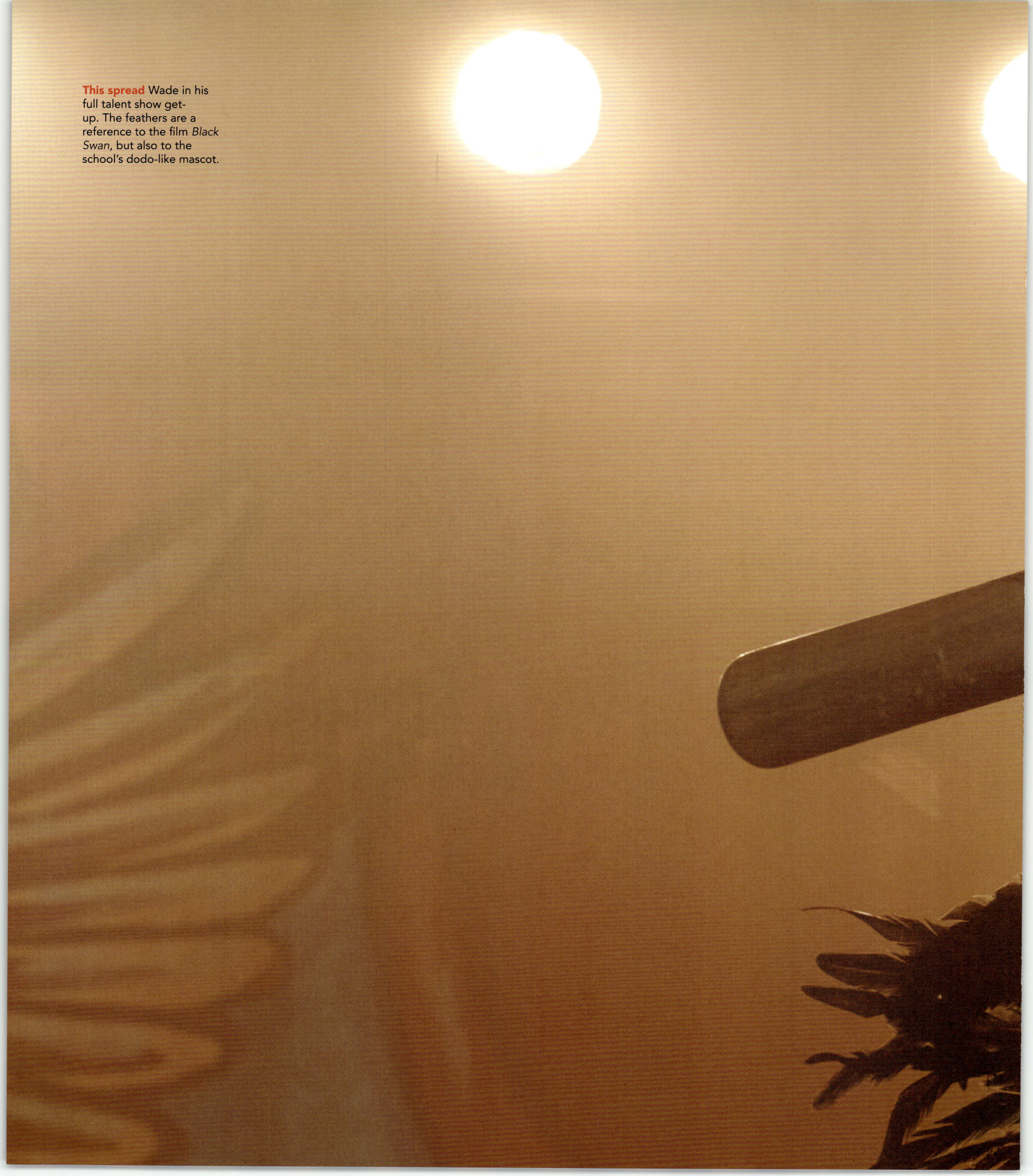

This spread Wade in his full talent show get-up. The feathers are a reference to the film *Black Swan*, but also to the school's dodo-like mascot.

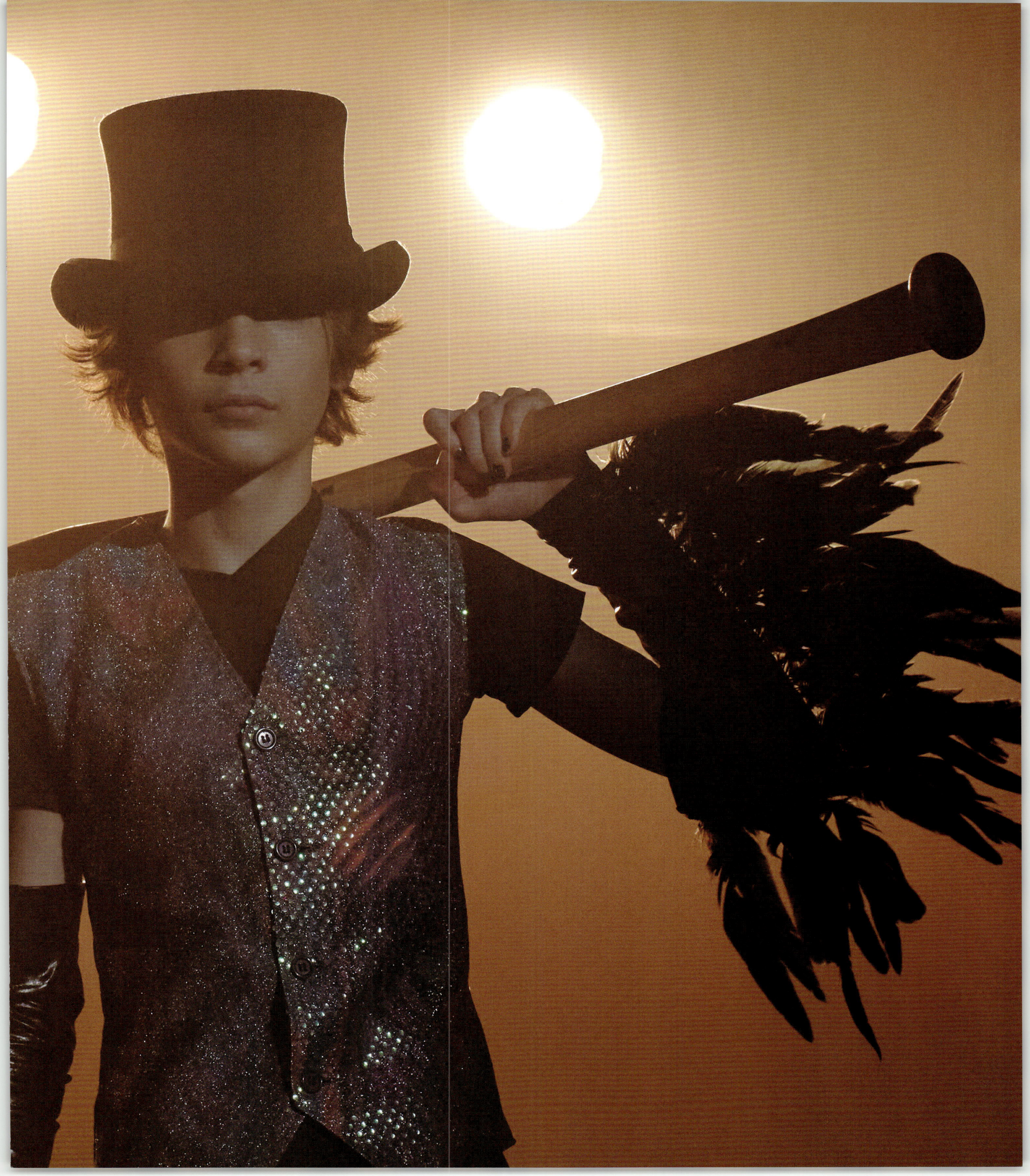

WINSTON'S APARTMENT

Though the Gooze home is based on a Brooklyn apartment that Macon Blair once lived in (albeit roughly quadrupled in size to allow room for shooting), it primarily had to convey the aching absence of Shelly, much-missed wife to Winston and mother to Wade. "Her presence is still felt there," says Blair, "even though she's gone. You see it in little bits of decoration or organisation or something that makes more sense for her than it would for Winston."

British production designer Alexander Cameron (*The Hallow*, *The Foreigner*) points out that if you look carefully in the apartment, you'll spot "some nicely organised china," and her toiletries are still arranged around the dressing mirror in the bedroom. "It shows Winston hasn't changed a lot of the décor from when she was alive," he says.

The intricate set, which was built at German Studios in Sofia, Bulgaria, is full of such fascinating touches, which offer subtle insights into the characters of both Wade and Winston, as well as the wider world of Blair's Tromaville. For example, Winston has a retro two-track tape recorder in one corner, and an old-fashioned box TV in another, suggesting this might not be the same 'present day' that we, the audience, live in. "His laptop is old and clunky, too," Blair notes. "We wanted to underline the idea that Winston is a little stuck in the past, but also the movie in general is a little bit outside of time. Not necessarily like a period piece, but it is in its own little time bubble that is separated from reality."

To bring a splash of color and character to the apartment, Cameron was able to enlist the help of a true fan of the original film. "The tapestry artist Ben Venom was very keen to get involved," he says. "He allowed us to use his artwork for free, so we have a couple of his quilt-work pieces on the walls—something different and quirky that you don't normally see in an environment like this. I was pleased to introduce something like that because it

"Winston hasn't changed a lot of the décor from when [Shelly] was alive."

– ALEXANDER CAMERON, Production Designer

Below left Winston kicks back at home.

Below Wade's room hints at his theatrical talents.

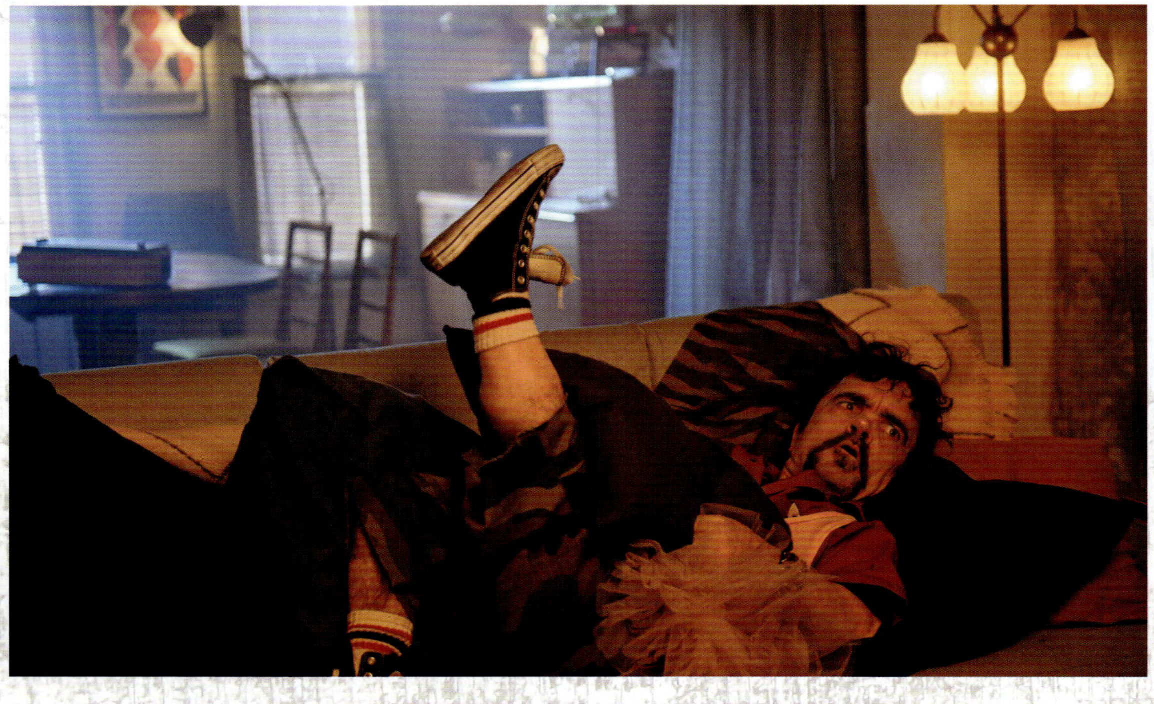

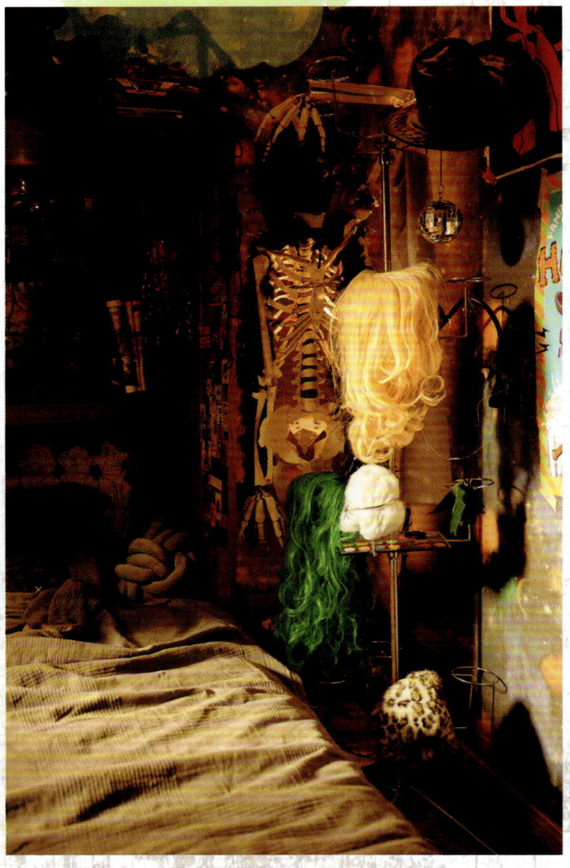

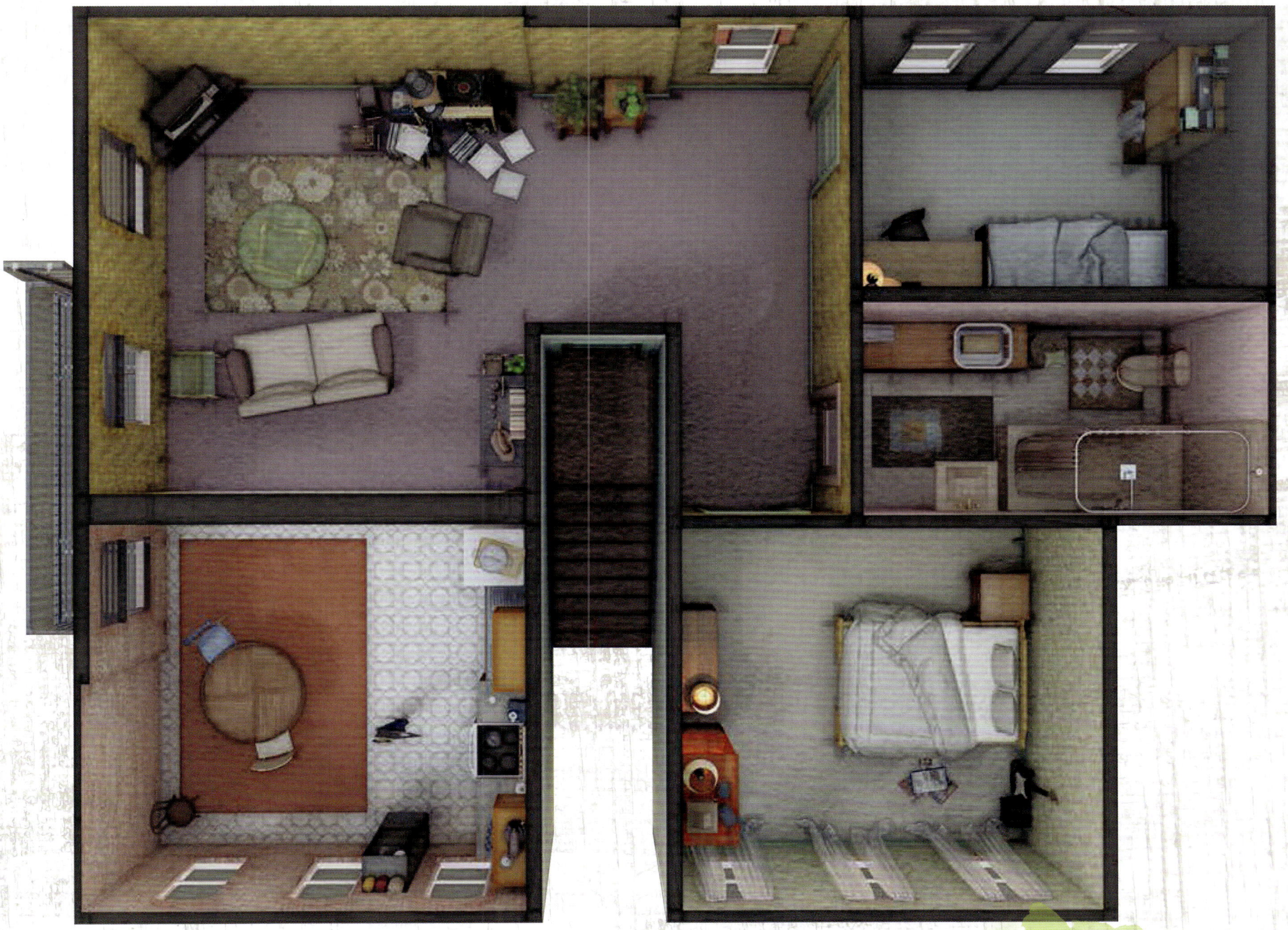

mirrors Winston's off-the-wall-ness."

Fans in the audience might also be able to spot some Troma-flavoured Easter eggs among the decor. On the wall of Wade's room, for example, is a poster for a fictional prop-comedian named Hathead (inspired by real-life comedian Gallagher), shown with a baseball bat and some smashed pumpkins. Designed by the production's graphic artist John Pundt (another "massive fan" of Toxie, according to Cameron), its framing and color scheme distinctly resemble the title design for Troma cartoon *Toxic Crusaders*.

"Yeah, there's a little connection in the font and the lettering," says Blair, though he points out the poster also foreshadows the ultimate revelation of what Wade's dance piece *really* involves. "When Wade is talking about his 'property movement piece,' it sounds kind of pretentious, but what he's really talking about is basically a low-rent Gallagher routine, which involves smashing fruit and stuff. I don't think anybody would clock that from the poster initially, but if someone were to watch the movie a second time, maybe they would."

Above Production designer Alex Cameron's floorplan for the Gooze domicile.

Below Winston's home is full of retro-tech touches, such as the two-track tape recorder in the lounge.

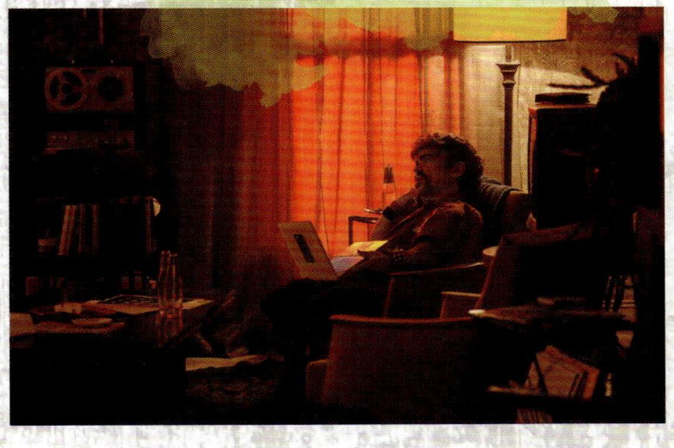

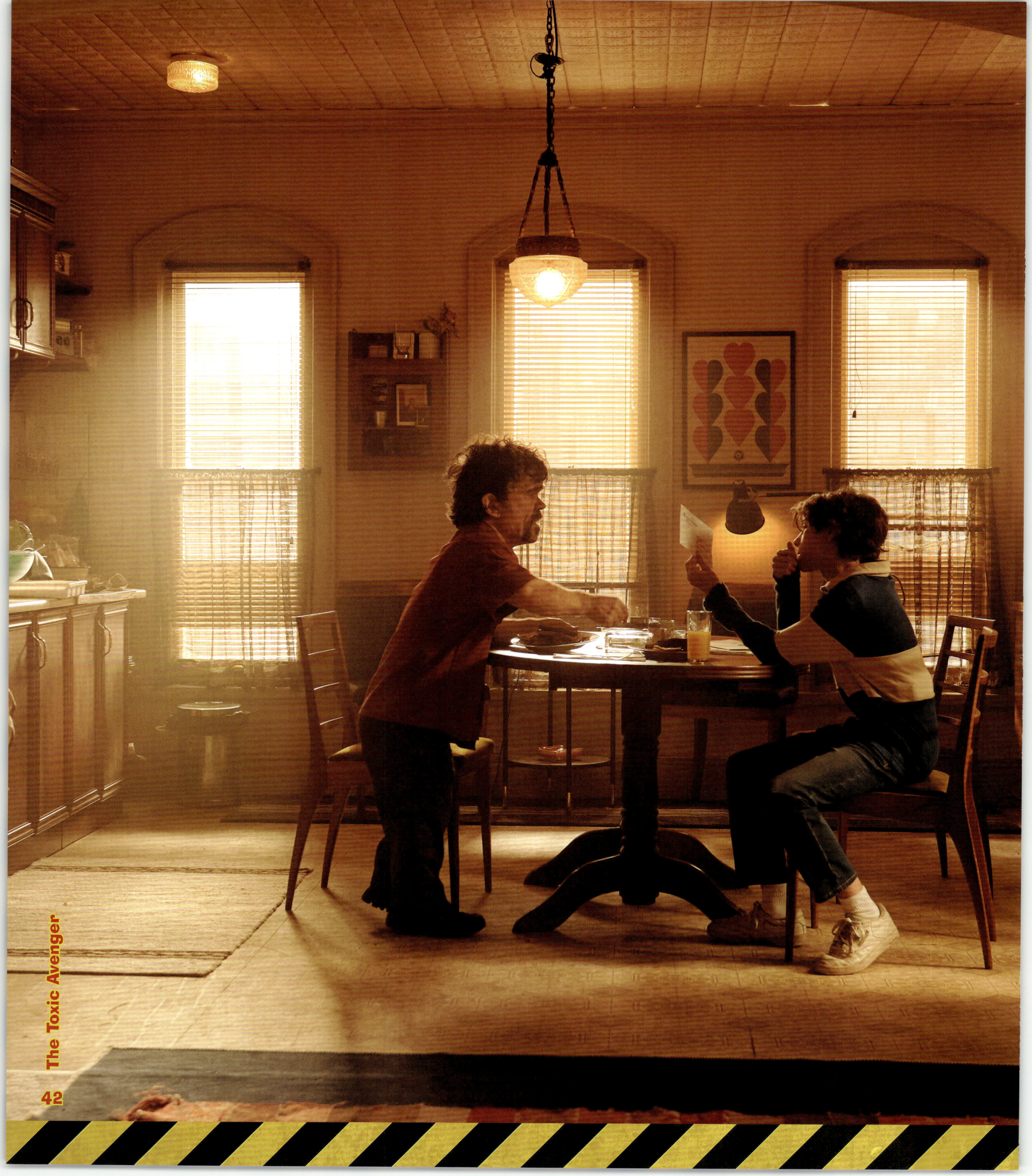

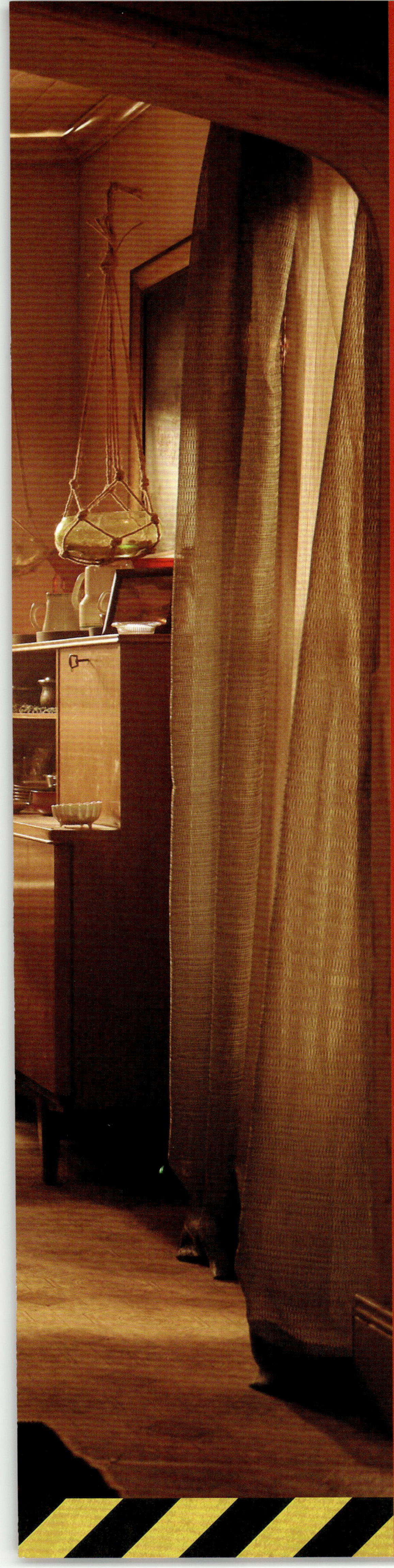

Daisy's Bodega

What's in store below Winston's apartment?

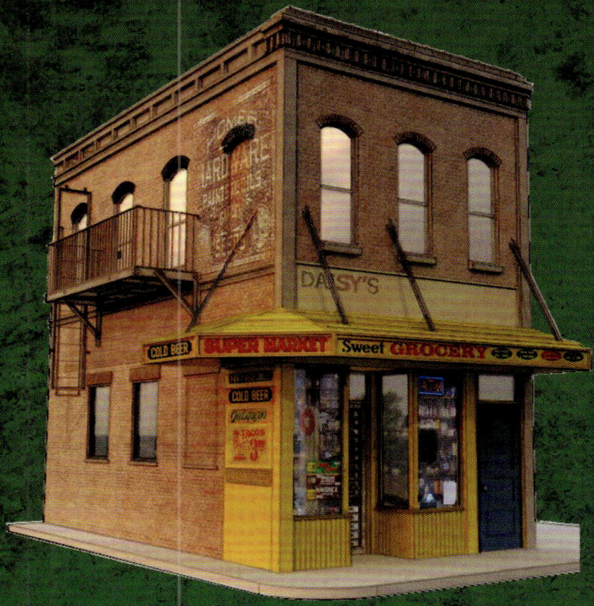

The shop located just beneath Winston and Wade's home provides another example of a Macon Blair personal touch. "My apartment was above a bodega very similar to this," he reveals. "It's 100 percent a Flatbush, Brooklyn bodega-apartment set-up. I gave the art department photographs of that building and said, 'Just do this.'"

Another touchstone was 1984's *Repo Man*, which features obviously non-branded products on its store shelves, such as "Yellow Cling Peach Slices" and "Corn Flakes", all in plain white containers with blue lettering. You find something similar in the bodega, except the rationale here is that they're all B.T.H. products; an indication of how far the company has infected everyday town life.

Above Concept art of the building's exterior, showing both Daisy's bodega on the ground floor and her apartment that sits above it.

Right The set for 'real', on the German Studios backlot in Sofia, Bulgaria.

Opposite page Winston and Wade share a tense moment over breakfast.

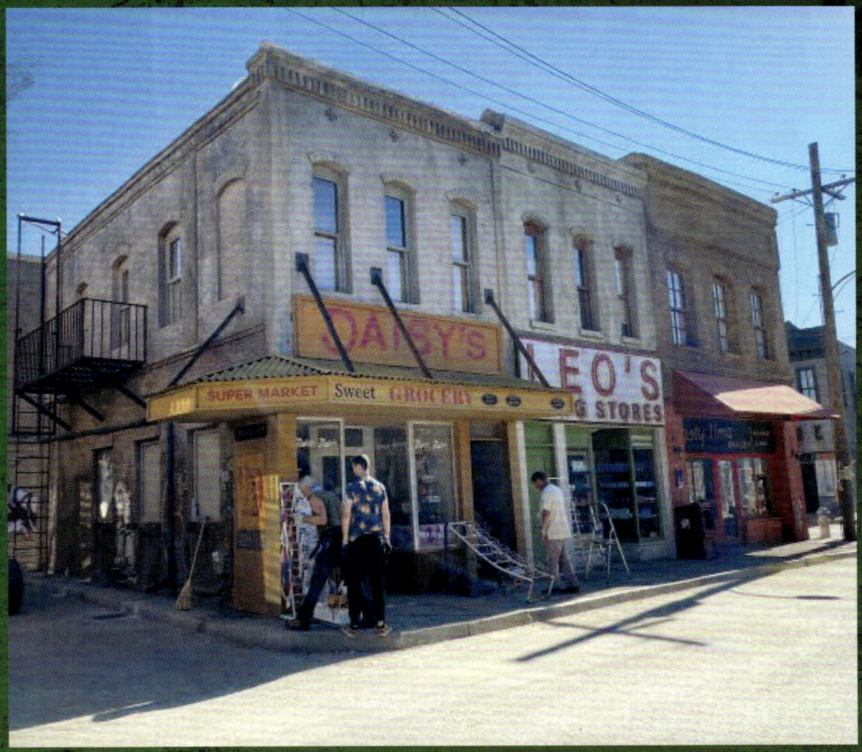

J.J. DOHERTY

PLAYED BY TAYLOUR PAIGE

Where Toxie is the hero who gradually rises during this story, finding his way to acceptance and adulation, J.J. Doherty starts out as a fully-fledged kick-ass vigilante with a take-no-crap attitude. Having been mentored by ill-fated investigative journalist Mel Ferd (Shaun Dooley)—who, thanks to a tactical misstep by J.J., is brutally dispatched during the film's opening sequence—she's already on the road to bringing down Bob Garbinger's evil, environment-destroying empire when we meet her.

"J.J. is trying to make amends for what happened to her mentor, and the way she ends up doing that is by transferring some of her bravery and her willingness to fight and stand up to injustice onto Toxie," explains Blair. "She is the one who says: 'Here's how we can win this fight.'"

Originally, Blair envisioned J.J. as "much more strait-laced and humourless", but once he'd cast Taylour Paige in the role, he realised she didn't need to be so relentlessly badass. "Her vibe on screen just felt real and lived-in," he says of Paige's impressive work in *Ma Rainey's Black Bottom* and intense indie drama *Zola*. "It was not this refined, cooler-than-thou starlet quality."

During rehearsals with Paige, Blair began to reshape the character, solving problems with it that he hadn't even been

Below J.J. takes Wade back to his apartment.

Bottom J.J. is a crusading hero driven by a lot of personal pain – something which attracted Paige to the role.

Opposite page Unlike many characters in Macon Blair's *Toxic Avenger*, J.J. has no equivalent in the original film.

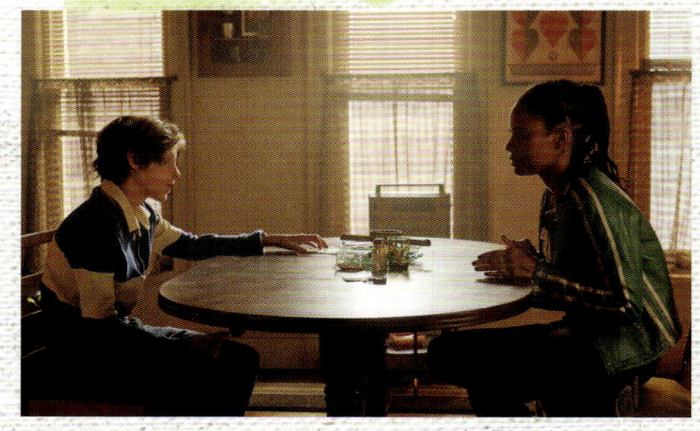

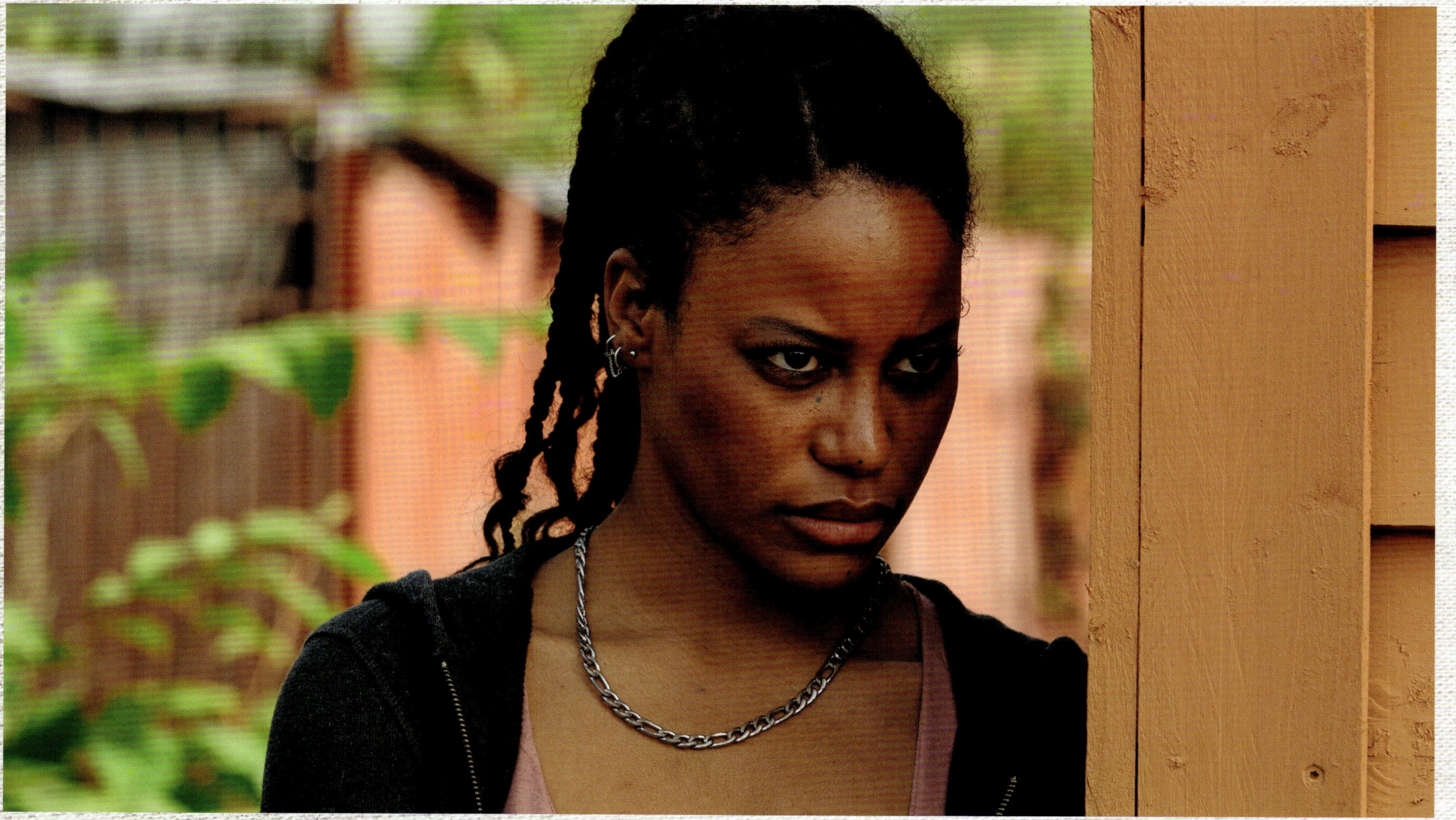

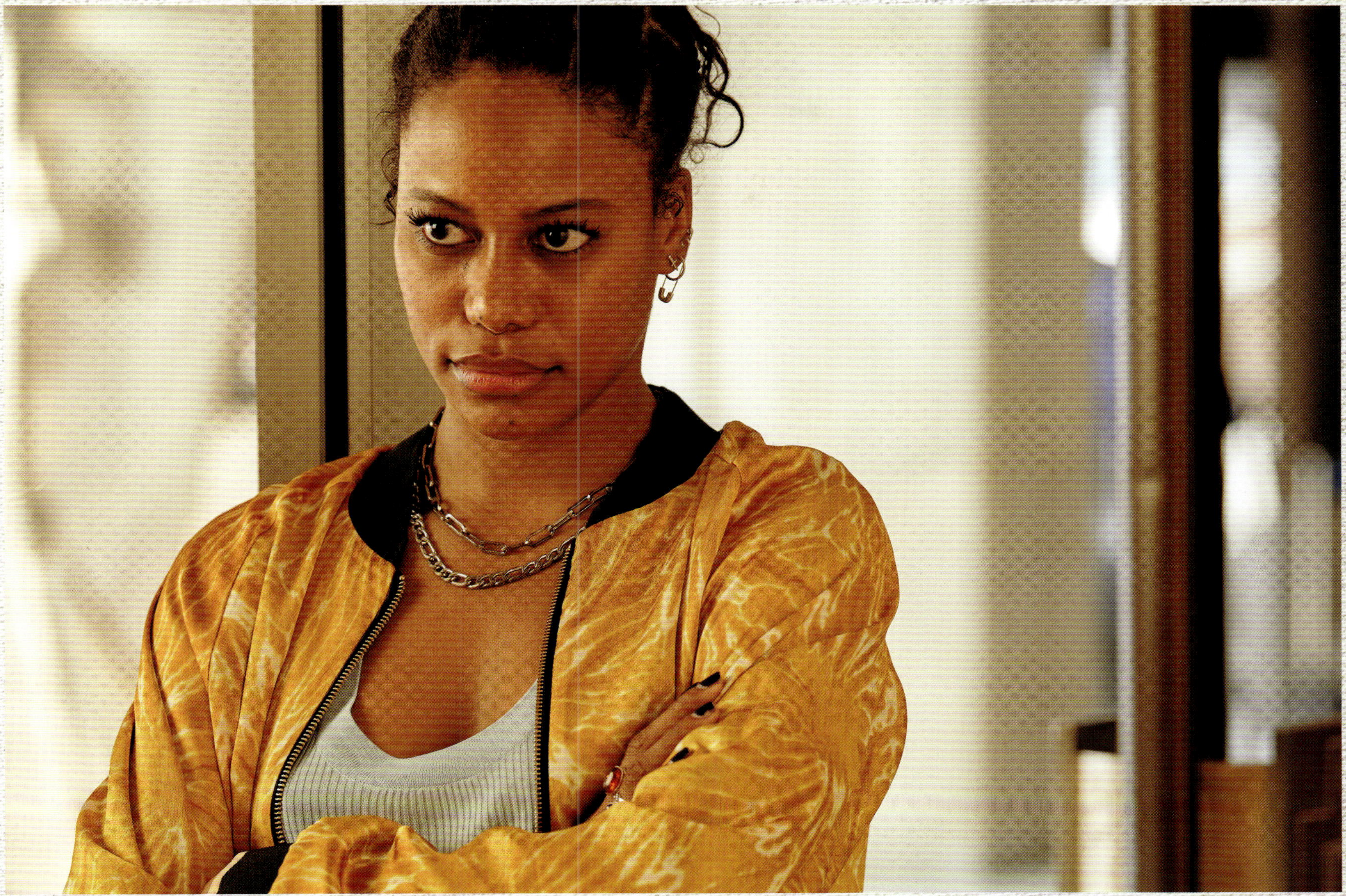

"Her heart is in the right place. She wants to do what she can to make it feel better, even though it feels pretty hopeless."

– TAYLOUR PAIGE, Actor

aware of before. "J.J. seemed inaccessible because she's so cool, and making her a little less cool helped. Taylour was the one that brought that to the forefront. I mean this in the best possible way, but an imperfect version of the role made a lot of sense with her. She didn't need to be super-slick and super in control all the time. She could lose her temper a little bit. She could be unaware of how she's affecting other people. She has a scene with Wade where they meet in the kitchen for the first time, and she dumps a lot of very personal, heavy stuff on him, and is totally unaware of how inappropriate that is. For me, that was a 'click' moment of her being so involved in her crusade that she's become, to a certain extent, socially inept. I found that very charming."

Paige herself was also attracted to this emerging aspect of the character. "J.J. has a lot of heart, a lot of pain, a lot of frustration and resentment at the world," she says. "She lost her mother. She lost her sister. She's a bit righteous, and sometimes her righteousness defies logic and gets her into trouble. It's almost like she's in a state of arrested development. When you know the world is going to shit everywhere around you—like this city that we're living in where everyone's sick, everyone's dying—I think that would do a number on anyone's psyche. But her heart is in the right place. She wants to do what she can to make it feel better, even though it feels pretty hopeless."

Paige admits she hadn't previously seen the original *Toxic Avenger*, but was aware

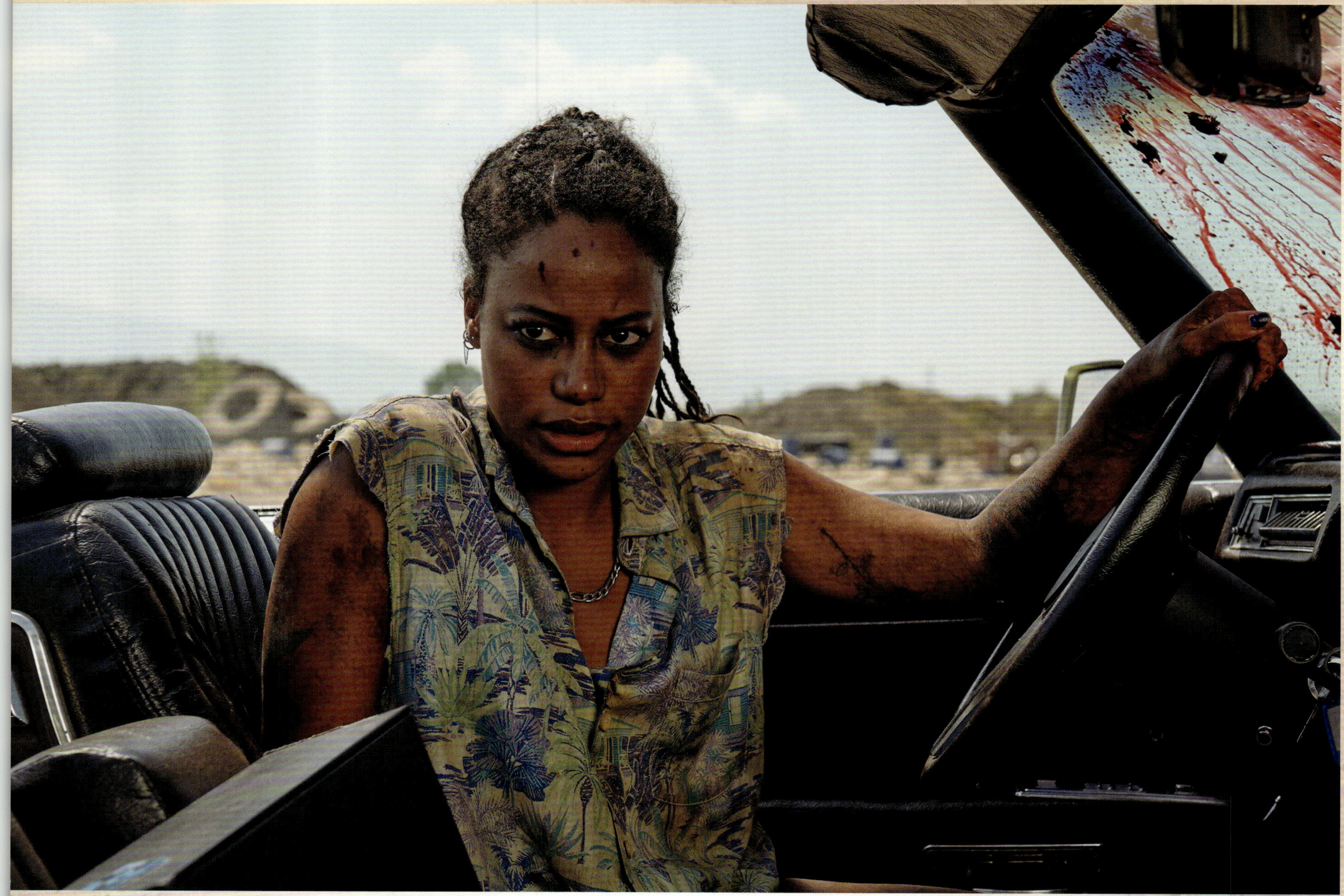

of its "really big cult following", comparing it with *The Rocky Horror Picture Show* in terms of the passion of its fandom. "Then I watched it when I found out I was doing it and I was like, 'Whoah!'," she laughs, "'This is gnarly!' It's so gnarly. Really bold for the time and different, which I appreciate."

Beyond familiarizing herself with the 1984 version (which has no J.J. equivalent character), preparing for the role was primarily a matter of combing through Blair's script and teasing out as much psychological authenticity as she possibly could. "When she loses her mentor, it drives her. She's ready for a suicide mission," says Paige. "So I wanted to feel emotionally truthful and free, even though there's a lot of hyperbole in this world—it's like our world, but on steroids. The prep was all about acknowledging the circumstances of this world as truthfully as possible."

For Paige, who grew up in Inglewood, California and trained as a dancer before she moved into acting, the role presented a valuable challenge. "I'm always up to do something different," she says. "I just want to keep myself guessing, and I want to keep people who are interested guessing. And this is a different style of storytelling, and it's big, and it's a studio film, so I felt like I was being stretched as an actor."

The character was also very different in appearance to anyone Paige has played before. Porter describes J.J.'s look as "a little bit punk, but not over the top. It's sort of effortless; we didn't want to make it feel like she put a lot of time or effort into how she dressed. She's got this green leather jacket that she wears for most of the movie; green is our protagonist colour in this movie, because Toxie is green. But also, I think it just looks good!"

Paige's favourite visual aspect of J.J. was her tattoos, some of which the actor herself designed, drawing in one case from

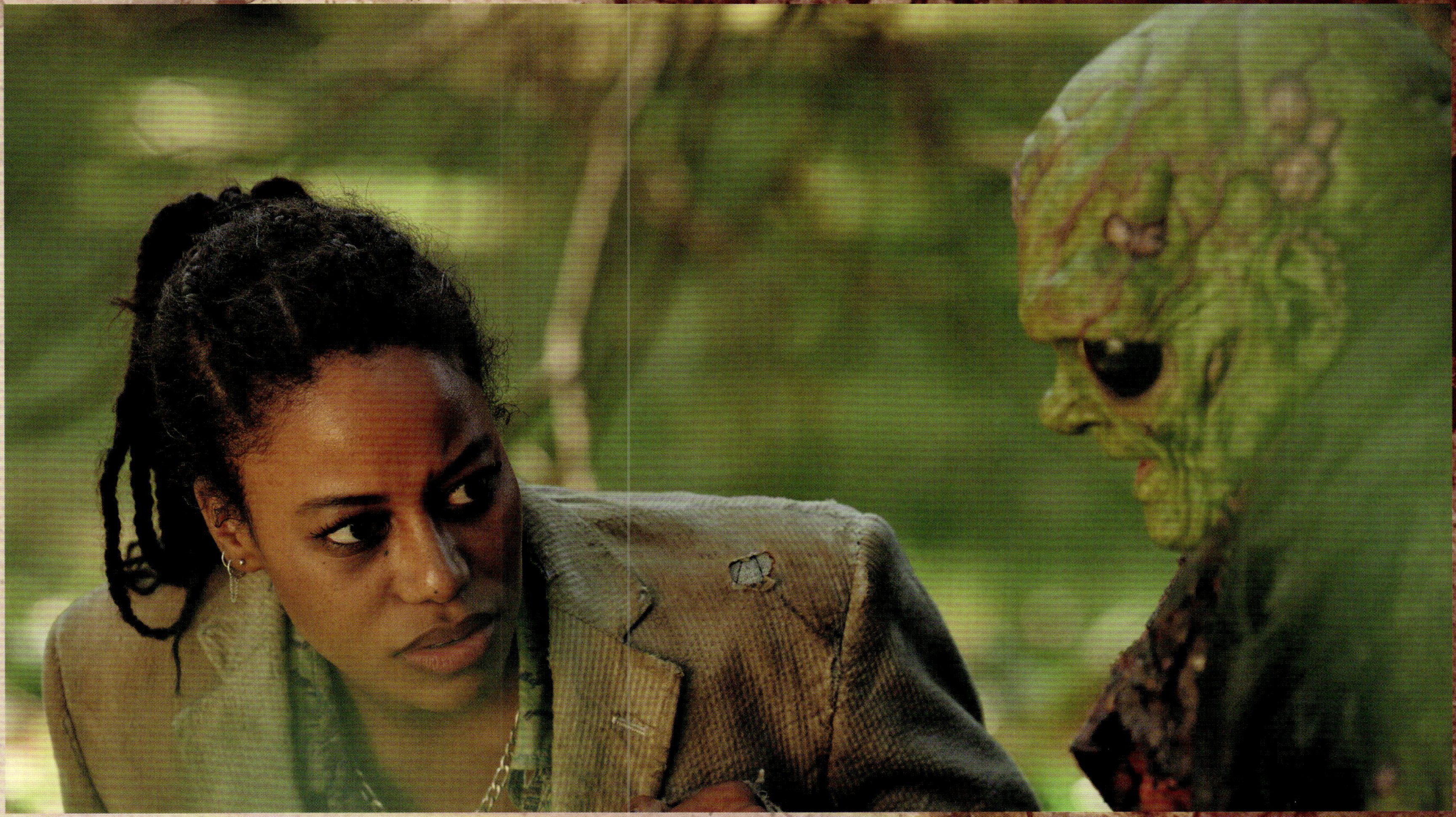

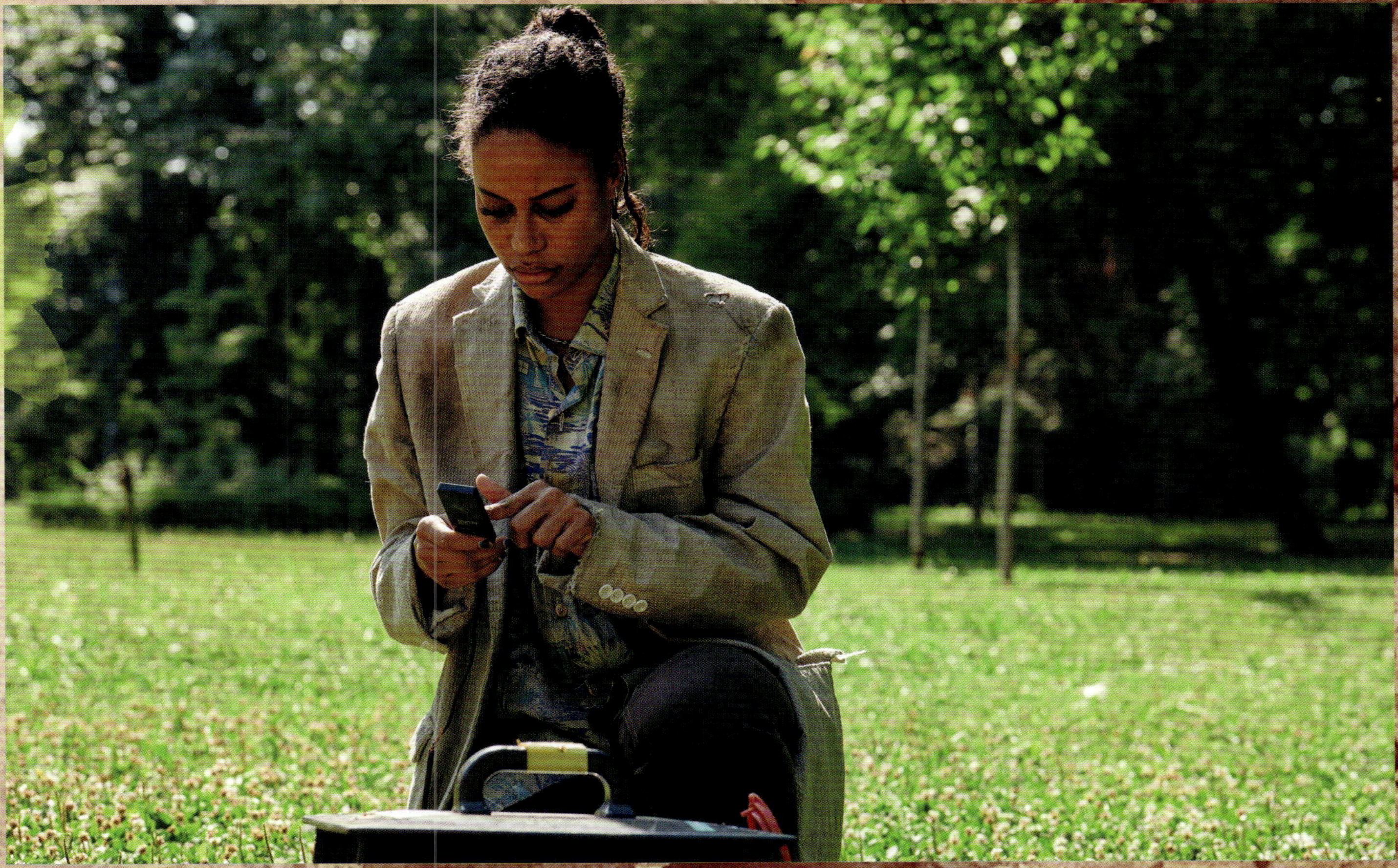

Above J.J. and her new crimefighting partner: the Toxic Avenger.

Left Some of J.J.'s tattoos were designed by Paige herself, bringing a personal visual touch to the character.

Right In the script, Blair describes J.J. as having a "punk librarian vibe" – hence the oversized grey blazer and printed shirt.

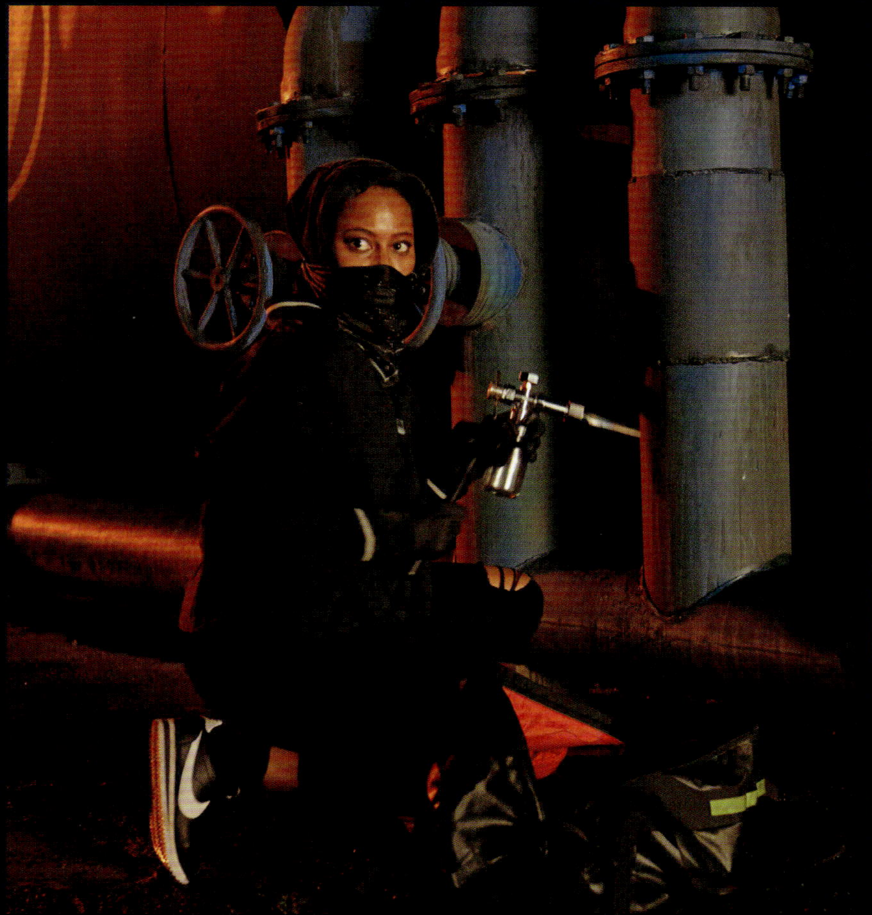

"Her style is: 'I got shit to do. Time is of the essence. Don't fuck with me.'"

– TAYLOUR PAIGE,
Actor

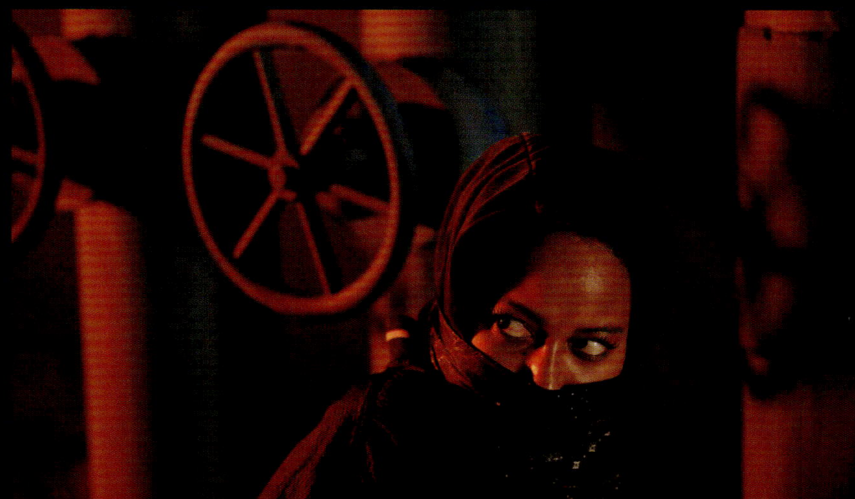

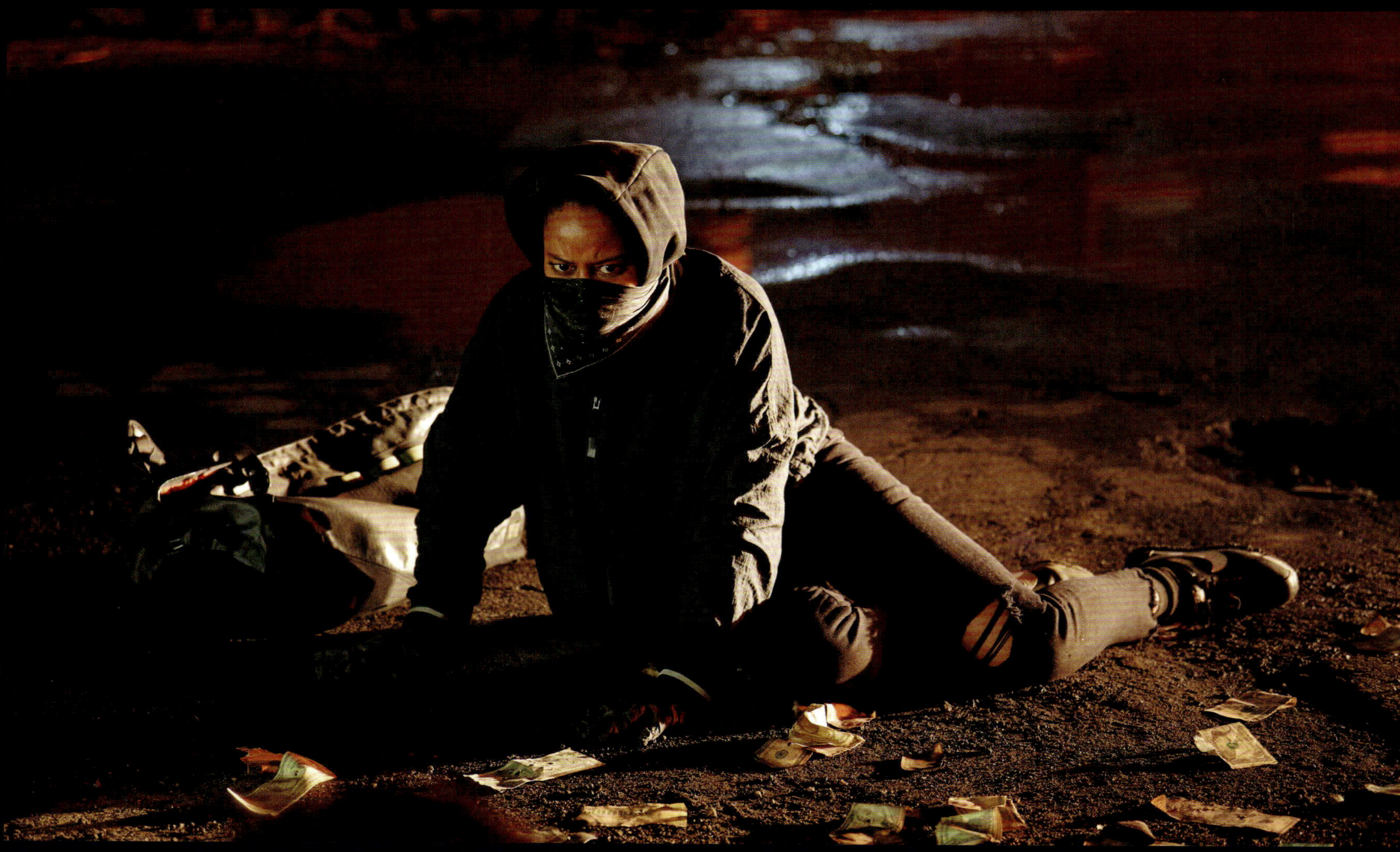

a very personal source. "She's got these really cool, psychedelic tats, very spiritual, otherworldly, occult. One of them is a stick figure of her sister, and it says 'Steph.' Actually, personally, I had a friend and sister pass away in 2014, and her name was Stephanie, so I put her on my arm. J.J. also has a tattoo on her hand that says, 'You Wish', because she's like, 'Don't even *try* me'. Her style is: 'I got shit to do. Time is of the essence. Don't fuck with me.'"

Getting shit done in Tromaville means putting your body on the line—dealing hurt and getting hurt. "There was a lot of running and jumping around on hot days, and in one sequence I got to slide down a mountain with sand, with all this trash they'd put everywhere. It was so fun," says Paige. J.J.'s biggest fight sequence takes place during the final act, when she goes toe to toe with Garbinger's demonic executive assistant Kissy Sturnevan (who's imbibed a small amount of the same serum that transforms both Toxie and her boss), played by British actor Julia Davis. Though a veteran improv comedian, Davis had never done action before, and before shooting the scene, confessed to feeling nervous. She requested one more practice session, going over all the moves with Paige.

"I panicked and basically punched her in the side of the head," recalls Davis. "I've literally never hit anyone in my life. And she's really strong, really cool, but she had tears in her eyes and I felt so, so guilty."

For Paige, it was no biggie. All in a day's work. "It was okay. I didn't mind it," she says. "We were in it, we were in character, and she was playing a terrible person! But Julia is really the best person, and we hung out all the time."

Opposite page J.J. in full environmental activist mode at the BTH factory.

Below J.J. and Toxie, partners in crime, look on at the Killer Nutz.

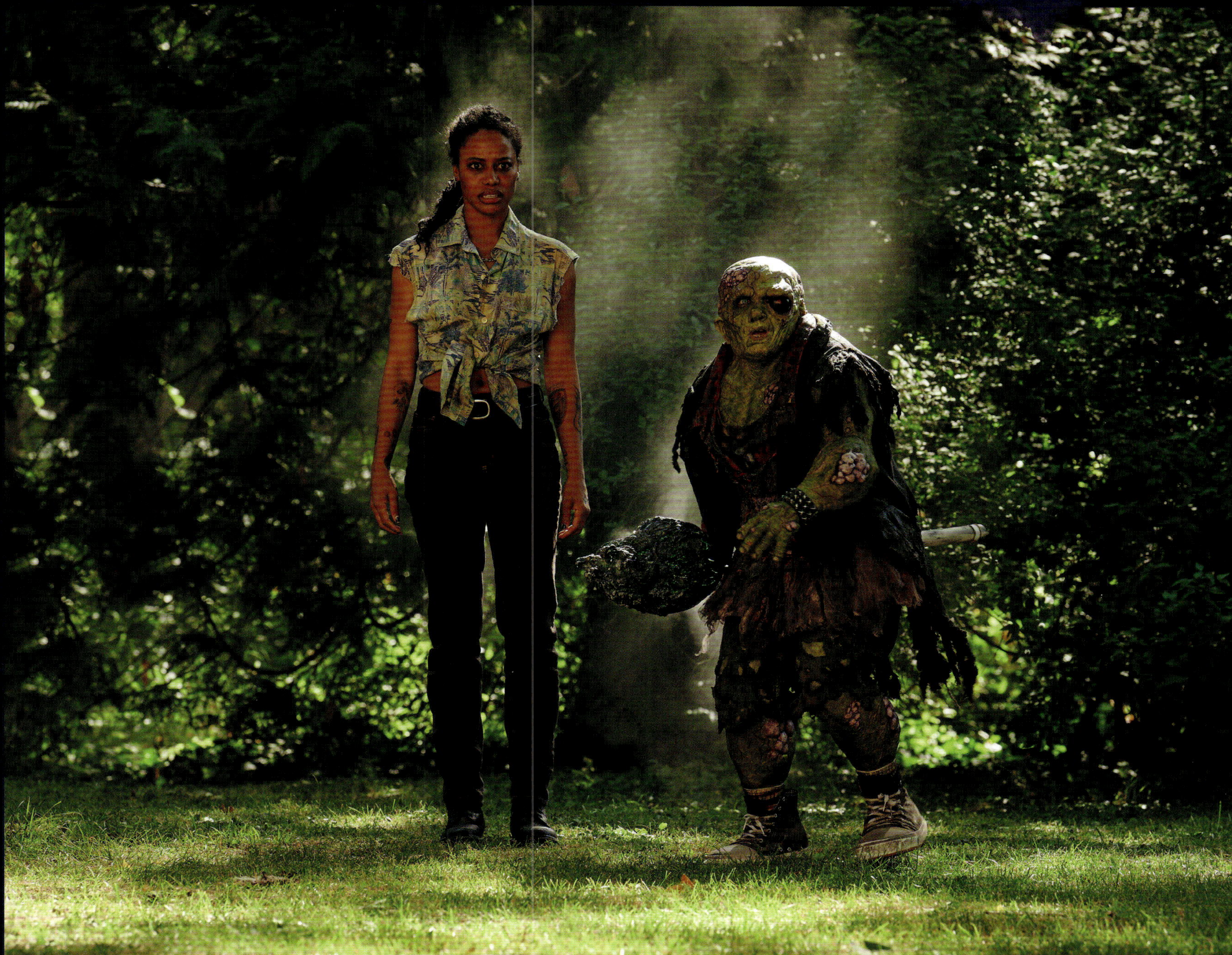

J.J.'S FLOP HOUSE

For J.J.'s humble base of operations, Cameron found a building that already existed at the studio, one that worked well for both the location's interior and exterior.

"On a different part of the backlot there was this weird little street, and we thought 'We'll use this,'" says Cameron. With its wood cladding and picket fence, the house proved an ideal match for the shabby Americana of the Tromaville Strip his team were creating just around the corner.

Given that the location is technically the home of J.J.'s roomie Dennis, and given that Dennis is played by none other than *The Toxic Avenger*'s writer-director Macon Blair, the main inspiration for the flop house came from Blair's own life. "I guess you can say it was based on places I had lived when I was younger," he says. "It's just a cheap, poorly-taken-care-of place. A scuzzy little Hobbit hole."

However, by the time the audience moves inside, this scuzzy Hobbit hole has already been ransacked and trashed by Garbinger's monster-rock goons The Killer Nutz—who have also bloodied Dennis' nose—so it doesn't give us the best sense of his taste (or otherwise) in interior decoration. Although Cameron did have one significant aesthetic touchstone: Tony Scott's Tarantino-scripted crime classic *True Romance*. Specifically, the house where we find Brad Pitt, as the perpetually stoned Floyd, lying on the sofa.

"I had really long hair, with a big beard—that's just how I looked," says Blair of the decision to make Dennis a Floyd-type character. He always knew he'd want to

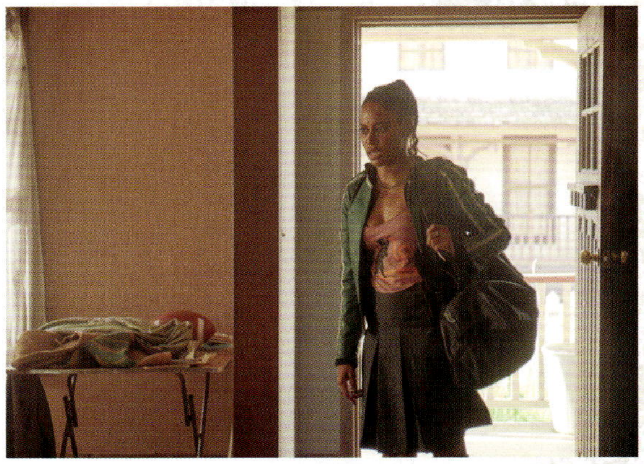

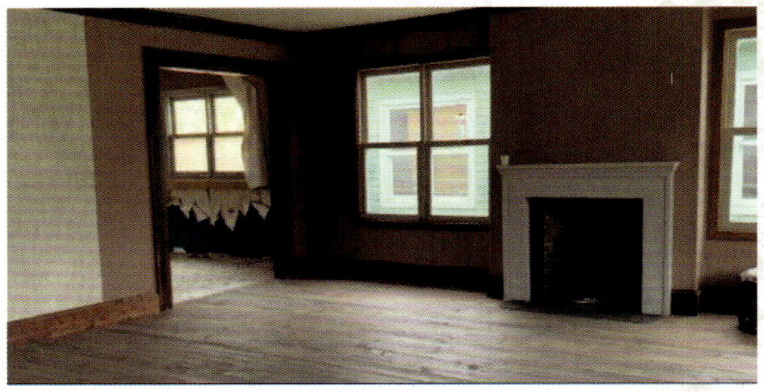

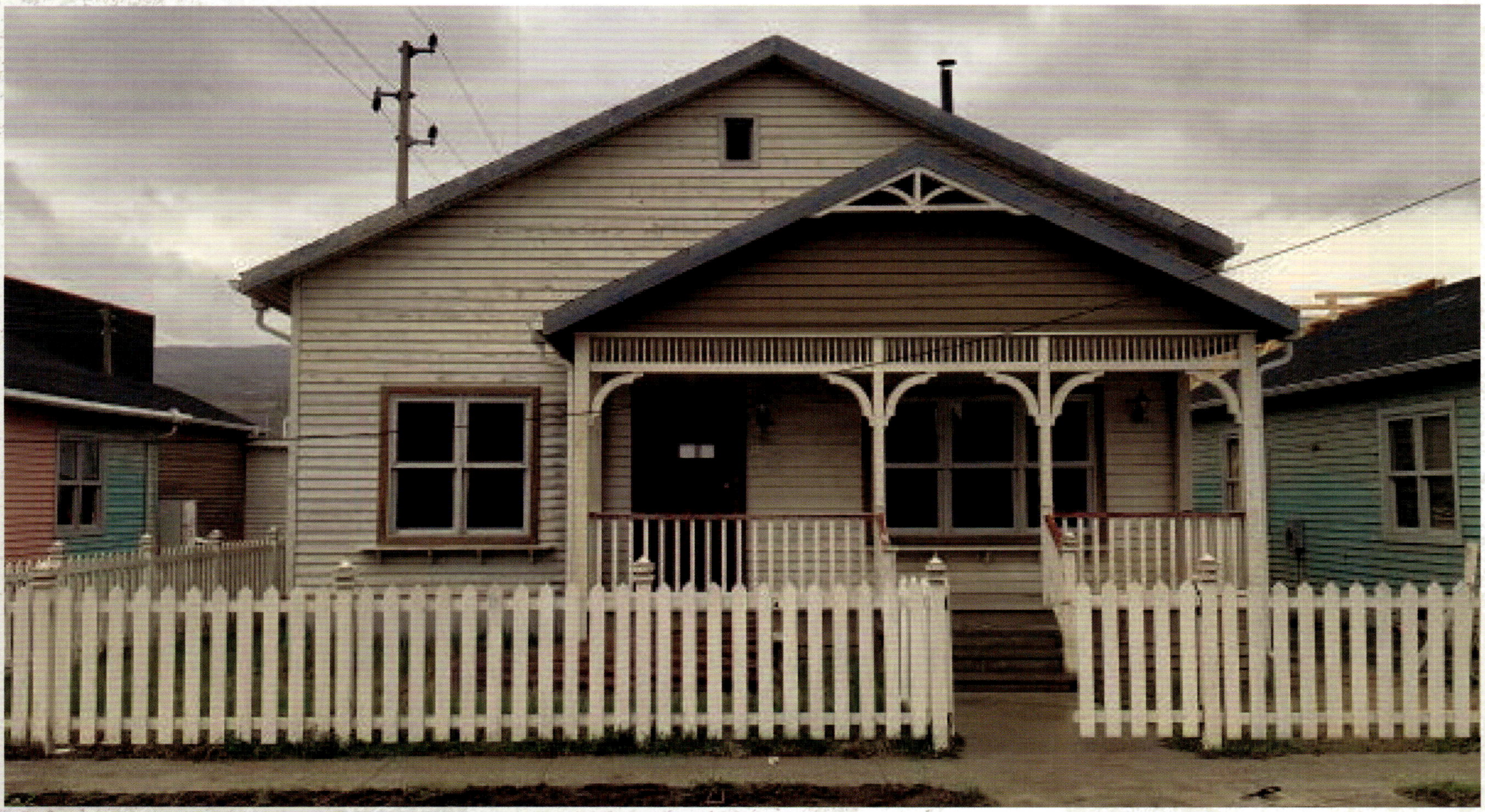

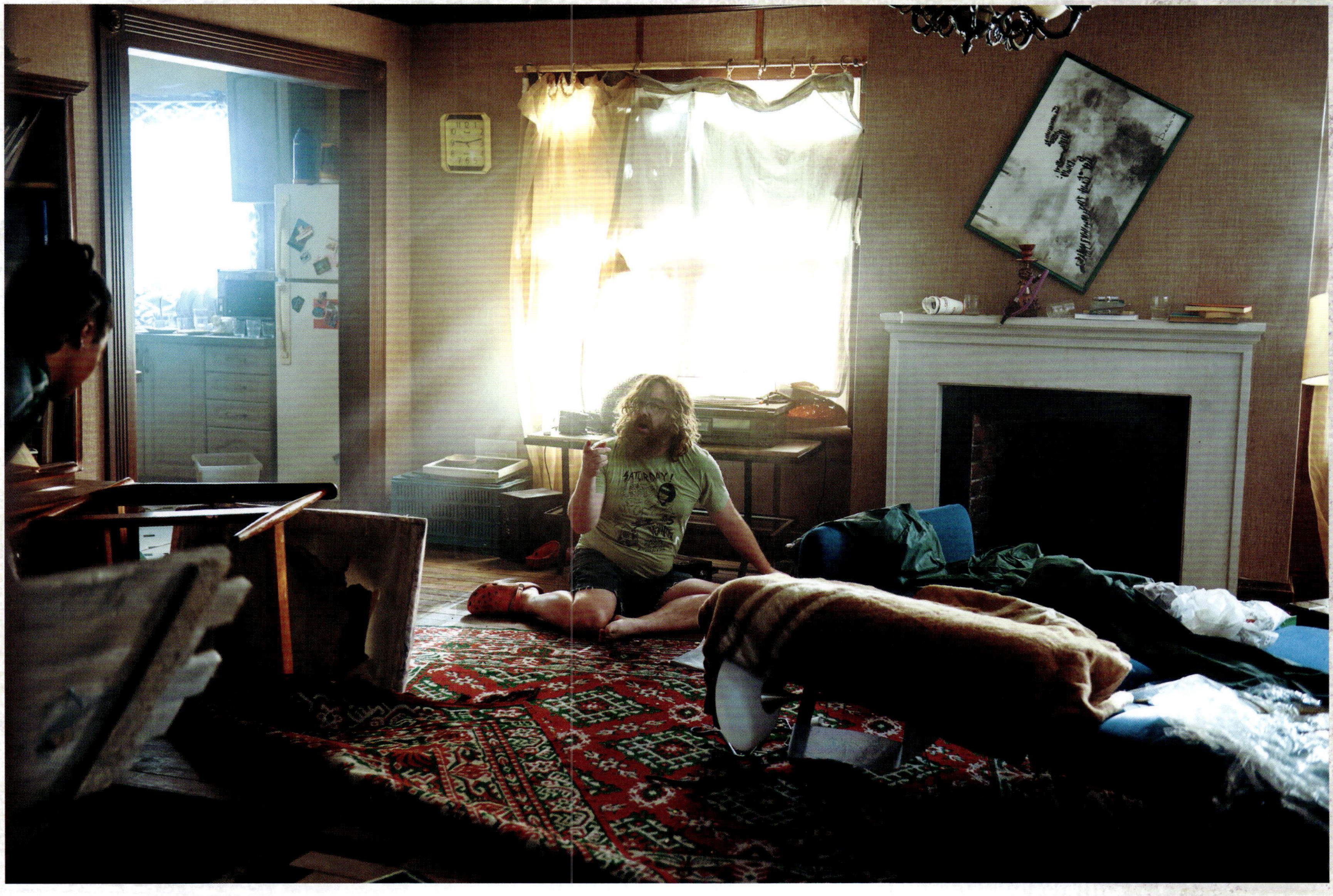

make a cameo in the film, with the express intention of including a playful on-screen moment with the original Toxie's creator, Lloyd Kaufman at the end of the film. But he didn't want it to be some "weird random director cameo that doesn't serve any purpose," so he decided to build Dennis into J.J.'s world, and establish him as "a noisy loudmouth," and the eventual meta payoff would feel more organic.

"He's been beaten up by The Killer Nutz the first time we meet him, so when we see him the second time at the Killer Nutz concert, he's the one person in the background, shouting, 'You suck!' Which makes you wonder, 'Why did you go to the concert?'" Blair laughs. "But it was just a running gag about what Dennis' purpose in the movie is—which is apparently to just comment on things noisily and rudely, so he can get taken to task for it by Lloyd in the last scene."

Left top J.J. arrives home to find it's been ransacked by The Killer Nutz.

Left mid The original set interior, as discovered by Blair and Cameron.

Above Blair in his guest role as Dennis, J.J.'s loudmouthed roomie.

Left bottom The set exterior on the German Studios backlot.

"It was based on places I had lived when I was younger."

– MACON BLAIR,

Director

MEL FERD

PLAYED BY SHAUN DOOLEY

The first person we meet in *The Toxic Avenger* is grizzled bulldog journalist Mel Ferd, played by British actor Shaun Dooley. Ferd sets the plot in motion, having uncovered proof that B.T.H. is poisoning the environment, with the help of a mysterious informant codenamed Sneaky Cheetah. "Mel is a capable, world-weary-type guy who really believes in what he's doing and has some real affection for his apprentice J.J.," says Blair.

With Cameron, he designed the opening scene to make it feel like "a private-eye movie, with striped Venetian blinds and the city in the background." The interior of Ferd's office was built on the studio set but, rather surprisingly, Cameron found the perfect place for the exterior in an abandoned Bulgarian train station.

"It was such a cool location, with this big atrium and these fantastic windows," says Cameron. "It's a little eastern European in its look, but when we shot it at night, with moonlight through the windows, it looked very moody."

Blair was particularly impressed by the way it reminded him of Los Angeles' Bradbury Building, which featured at the end of Ridley Scott's future-noir masterpiece *Blade Runner*. "We lit it with that in mind," he says, noting that the station's two-story structure allowed him to add an extra dimension to scenes which he'd written to take place on a single floor.

It is here that, only a few minutes later, Ferd meets his untimely and messy end at the hands of the Killer Nutz, who have tracked J.J. to his office and proceed to blast the reporter out of a window. Blair reveals that his protracted, brutal death scene is an unveiled tribute to the sequence in *RoboCop* where Peter Weller's Murphy is murdered by a criminal gang. But it's also intended to toy a little with the audience's expectations. "He's uncovered some sort of scheme and he gets blown apart by a team of bad guys. It stands to reason that he's going to become 'RoboCop', or he's going to become Toxie—the next version of the hero. But he's not. He's just been blown out of the window. And we cut to a

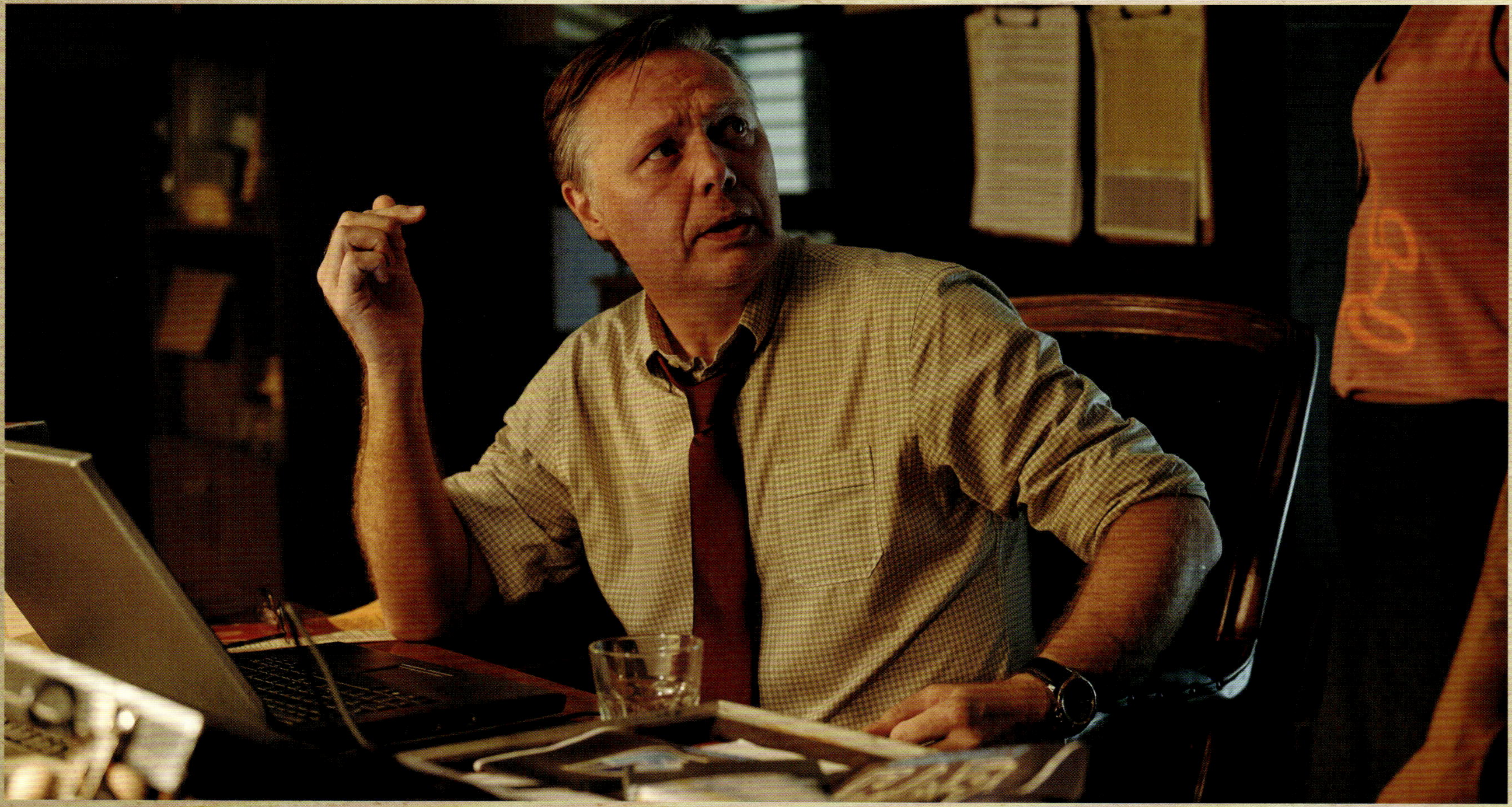

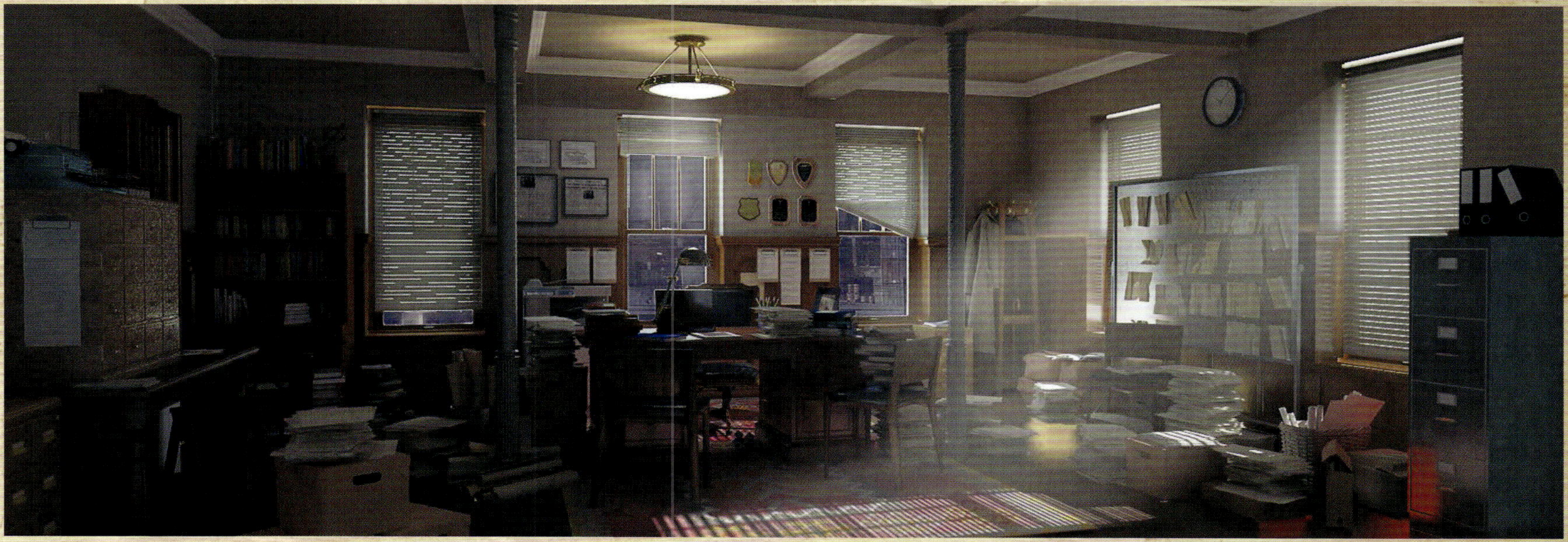

much less impressive person, just snoring in bed."

Fans of the original *Toxic Avenger* will have already noticed that Ferd is named after the kid played by Mark Torgl, who in that movie transformed into its Monster Hero: Melvin Ferd Junko III.

"Yeah, that is a little bit of a nod to the fans," says Blair. "I thought of it as an alternate timeline, where Melvin avoided that accident and just grew up and figured out things his own way, putting his energy into being a justice-seeking, muckraking investigative reporter. It doesn't make a ton of sense, but I related it to what they did with the first *Mission: Impossible* movie, where you get a little bit of a hand-off from Jim Phelps (Jon Voight) to Ethan Hunt (Tom Cruise); so it's sort of a hand-off from Mel Ferd to Winston. From the guy that was probably prepared to be a hero, to a guy that is totally *not* prepared to be a hero."

Opposite page Mel Ferd speaks to J.J. Doherty in his office.

Left below Ferd is very much a mentor for Paige's character J.J.

Left bottom Blair and Gonzales gave the opening scenes in Mel's office a film-noir look.

Above Concept art of Mel's office, which is full of paperwork.

Right below Mel joins the dots between B.T.H. and Tromaville's environmental devastastion.

Right bottom A close-up of Mel's corkboard wall of investigation.

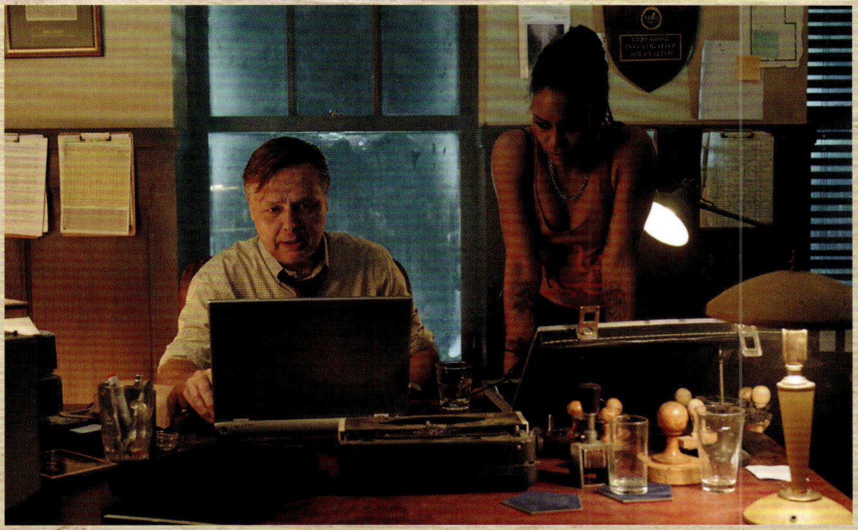

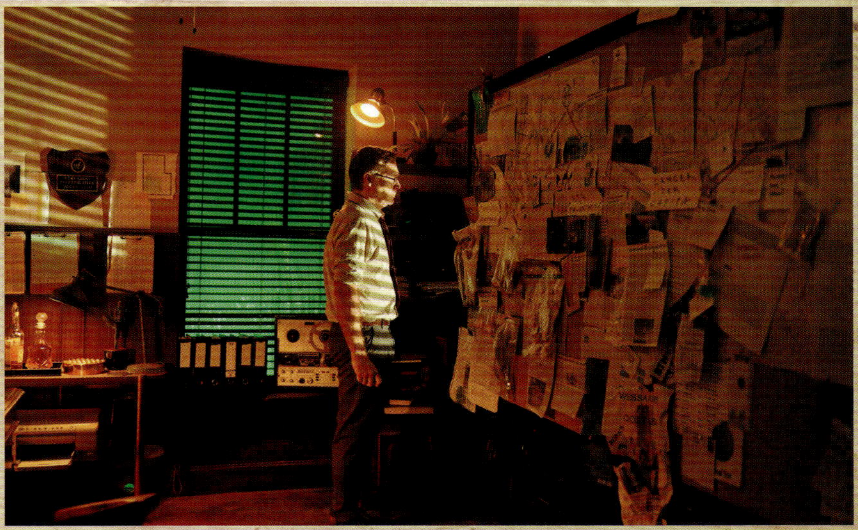

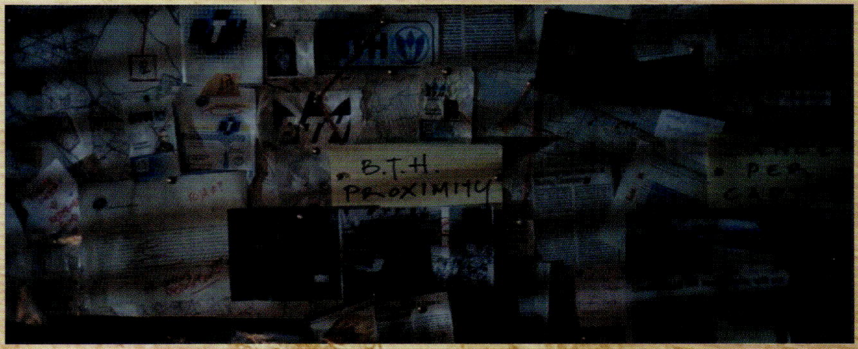

BOB GARBINGER

PLAYED BY KEVIN BACON

For a movie whose hero is a lumpy, green-skinned monstrosity, it makes perverse sense that its villain should be the exact opposite: a smooth, shining apparent paragon of humanity. Buff. Charismatic. Handsome. But where the original *Toxic Avenger* pitted its Toxie against a malevolent gang of well-honed, good-looking gym rats, Macon Blair's remake takes things to the next level. Toxie '25 nemesis Bob Garbinger doesn't just work out; he has regular transfusions of gorilla blood (please don't try that at home). And he isn't just someone who hangs out in a health club; he *owns* the health club. All of them, in fact… Along with pretty much every healthcare product used by the long-suffering people of Tromaville.

"I took the health-club premise of the first film and pushed it to the furthest possible extreme," Blair explains. "Garbinger is selling something he tells people will make them feel better about themselves, or instantly feel skinnier, or suddenly more energetic. There was a lot of room for dishonesty there. He's selling snake-oil products. And having Winston fight against a big corporation that's built around the idea of people becoming their perfect selves seemed like a good basis for friction between them."

Originally, Blair saw his blond, baby-oiled antagonist as little more than a slick grifter who's conned his way to the top of the tree. "He's made a lot of money by wringing the system and cutting every corner he can,

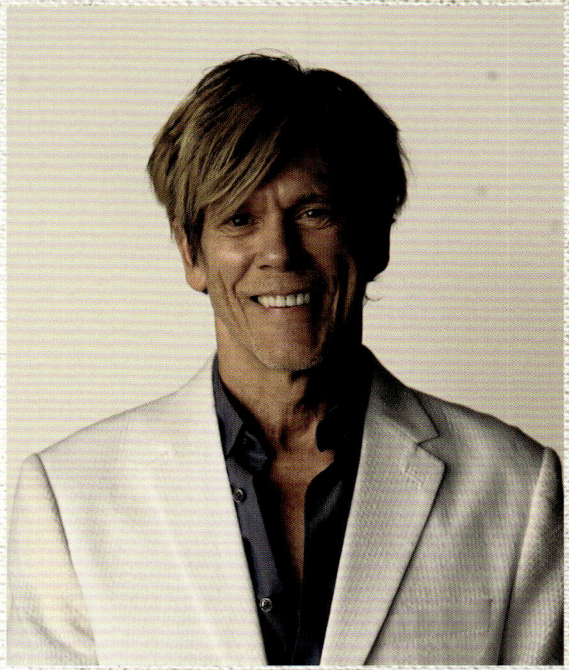

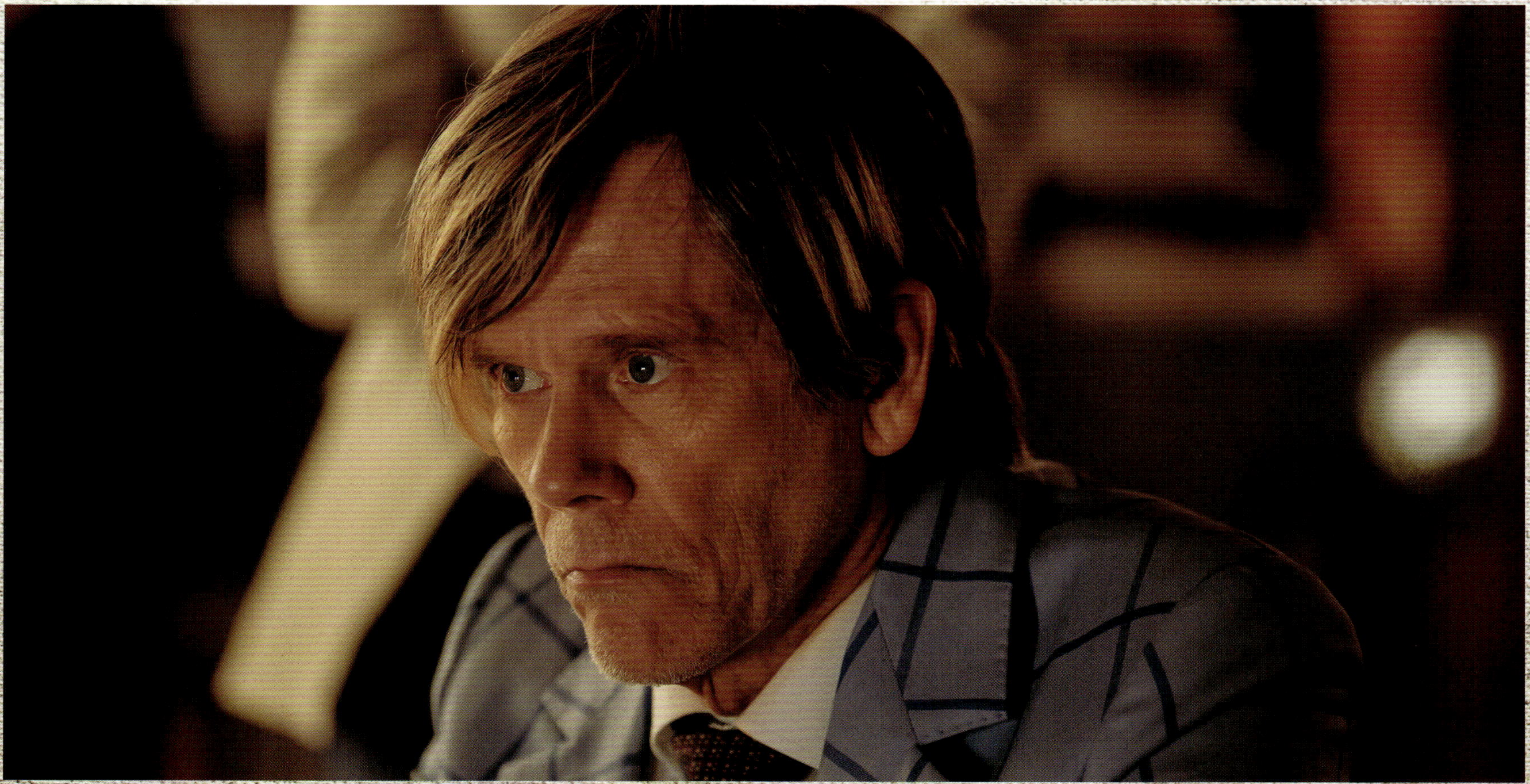

Left B.T.H. company photo of Bob Garbinger, health-product pusher and ruiner of the planet.

Left below Bacon brought some valuable vulnerability to this preening villain.

Right & below Garbinger in his signature blue-and-gold robe, plus the shark-tooth pendant that suggests his predatory ways.

so we wanted him to be this larger-than-life, megalomaniacal type of character." However, as he revised his script, Blair realised it would be far more interesting to recalibrate that character as a little past his peak, a little out of his depth, and far less in control than he at first appears—especially once we discover he's being menaced and manipulated by underworld kingpin Thad Barkabus.

"Bob's best days are behind him and the walls are closing in. He knows he's not as smart as he's presented himself to the world, and that his grift is unsustainable. Which, in a way, brings him closer to what Winston is going through. They're both desperate and they're both at loose ends. That seemed a fun direction to take it."

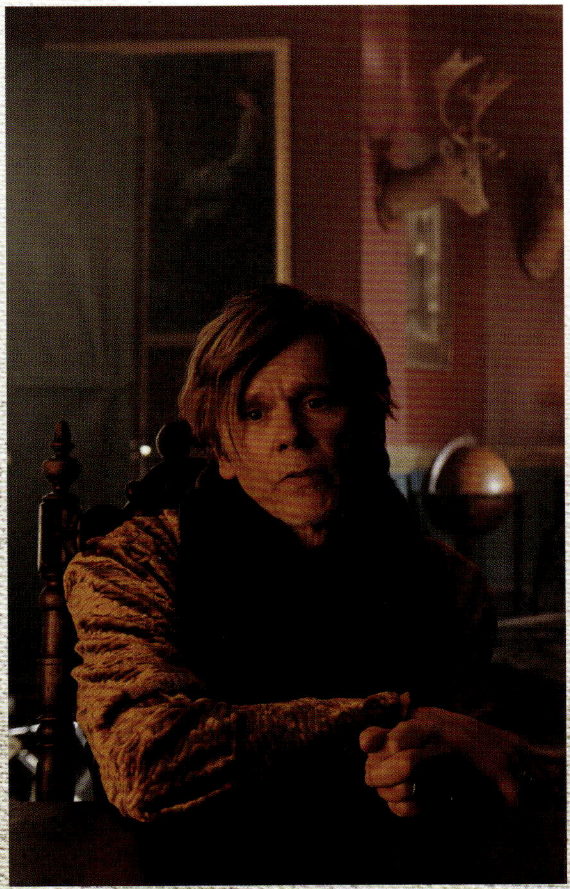

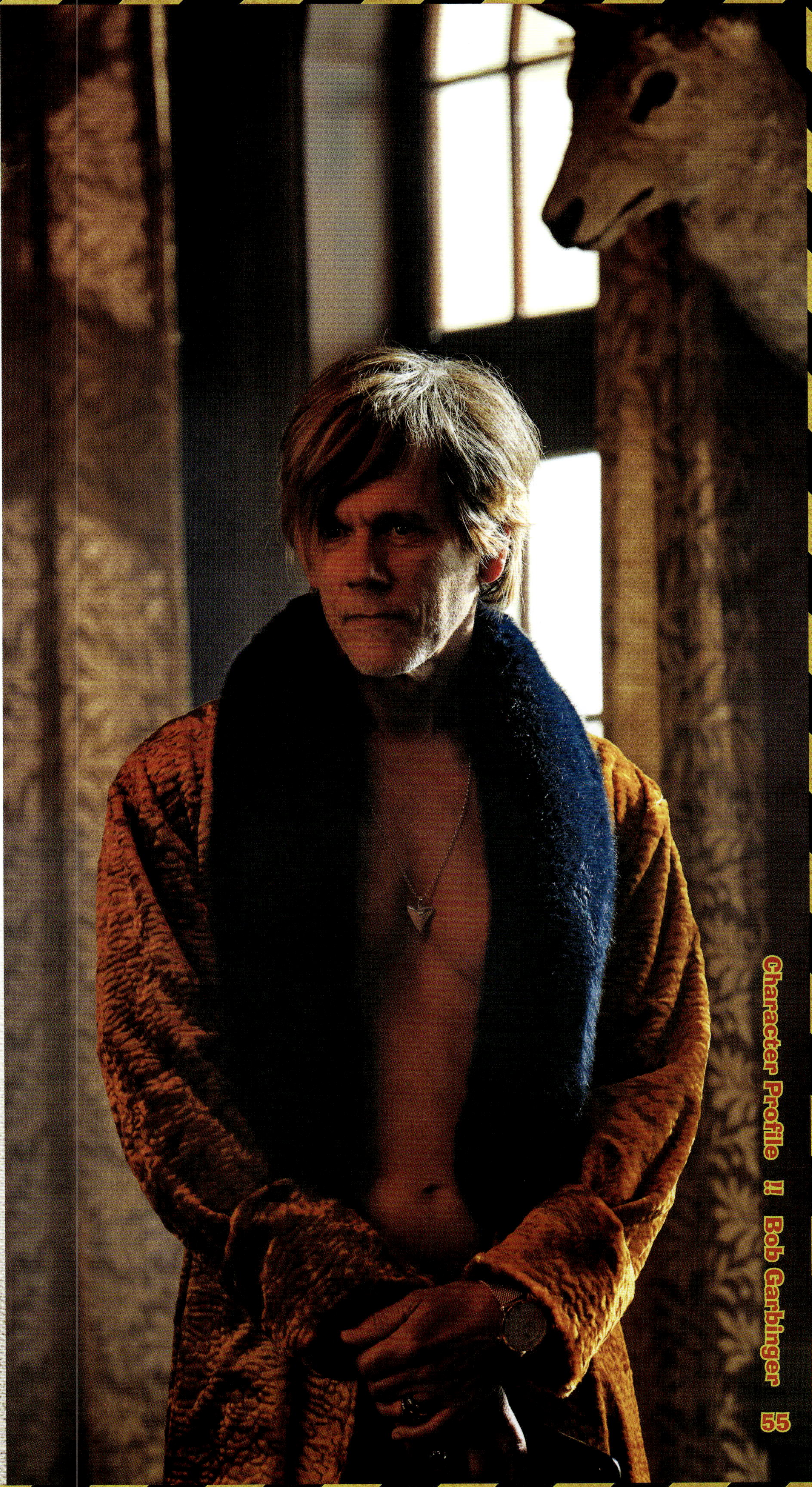

> **"We had one conversation at the top, to discuss what we're going for, and he said, 'I got it.' Then he shows up and knocks it out of the park with the first take."**
>
> – MACON BLAIR,
> Director

Though it did present a challenge when it came to casting Garbinger. Blair needed someone who could channel that 'golden god' charisma and metaphorically twirl their moustache, but also undercut all the bluster by injecting the requisite degree of vulnerability. That someone was Kevin Bacon: a veteran star four decades into a career that's already turned out movies as diverse as classic slasher film *Friday The 13th*, teen dance drama *Footloose*, cult comedy monster adventure *Tremors*, true-life disaster movie *Apollo 13* and sober mystery thriller *Mystic River*.

"We thought it would be cool to take someone who has a big presence in the audience's imagination and then get them to do something different and new," says Blair. "Certainly, Kevin's played good guys and bad guys and all sorts of different types of roles. He's been around forever. He's got the genre credibility coming in from *Tremors*, but he also has this Oscar®-calibre type of credibility. Garbinger has a lot of big, florid monologues, so there's definitely some chops that are required for those. Kevin felt like he could check a lot of different boxes."

Thankfully, when Legendary approached him, Bacon said yes. "I don't know how familiar Kevin was with Troma," admits producer Alex Garcia, "but he loved the script, and the world and the characters, and he was excited to work with Macon."

The feeling was mutual. "There's a reason why he's been around forever," says *The Toxic Avenger's* director. "Because he's such a pro. With this character specifically, you could easily go too big, or miss the mark. It requires you to jump through a number of hoops simultaneously. So I was prepared to have a lot of conversations with Kevin about, for example, 'How funny is *too* funny?' There wasn't really any of that. We had one conversation at the top, to discuss what we're going for, and he said, 'I got it.' Then he shows up and knocks it out of the park with the first take. He instantly dials-in to what the needs are for the scene. He intuitively gets it."

Bacon's on-screen brother concurs. "The last two weeks of the shoot was all with Kevin—the primary relationship stuff with Bob Garbinger," says Elijah Wood, aka hunchbacked henchman Fritz Garbinger, who's locked in a perpetual emotional battle for Bob's approbation with his executive assistant Kissy Sturnevan (Julia Davis). "It was a joy. It was a blast. Kevin's such a lovely human, super-game for anything. I'm a real admirer of his and I have been for a long time. He's an incredible actor and he's also not afraid. He's not afraid of genre, he's not afraid of looking ridiculous. His character is ridiculous at times, and he leapt into it with such vim and vigour. It was really fun to see."

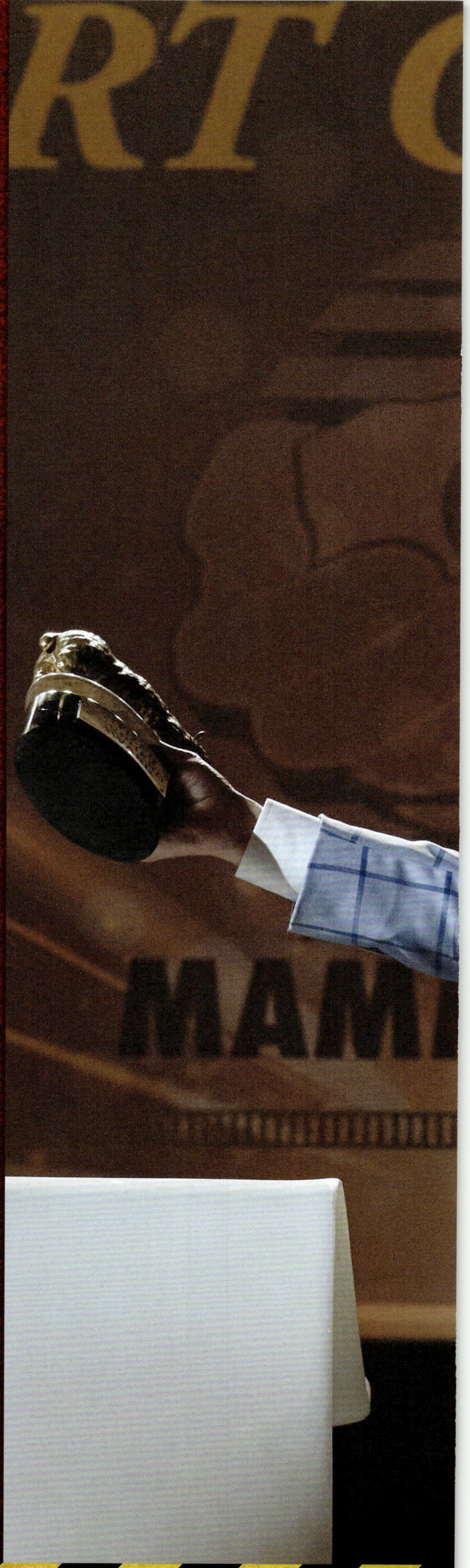

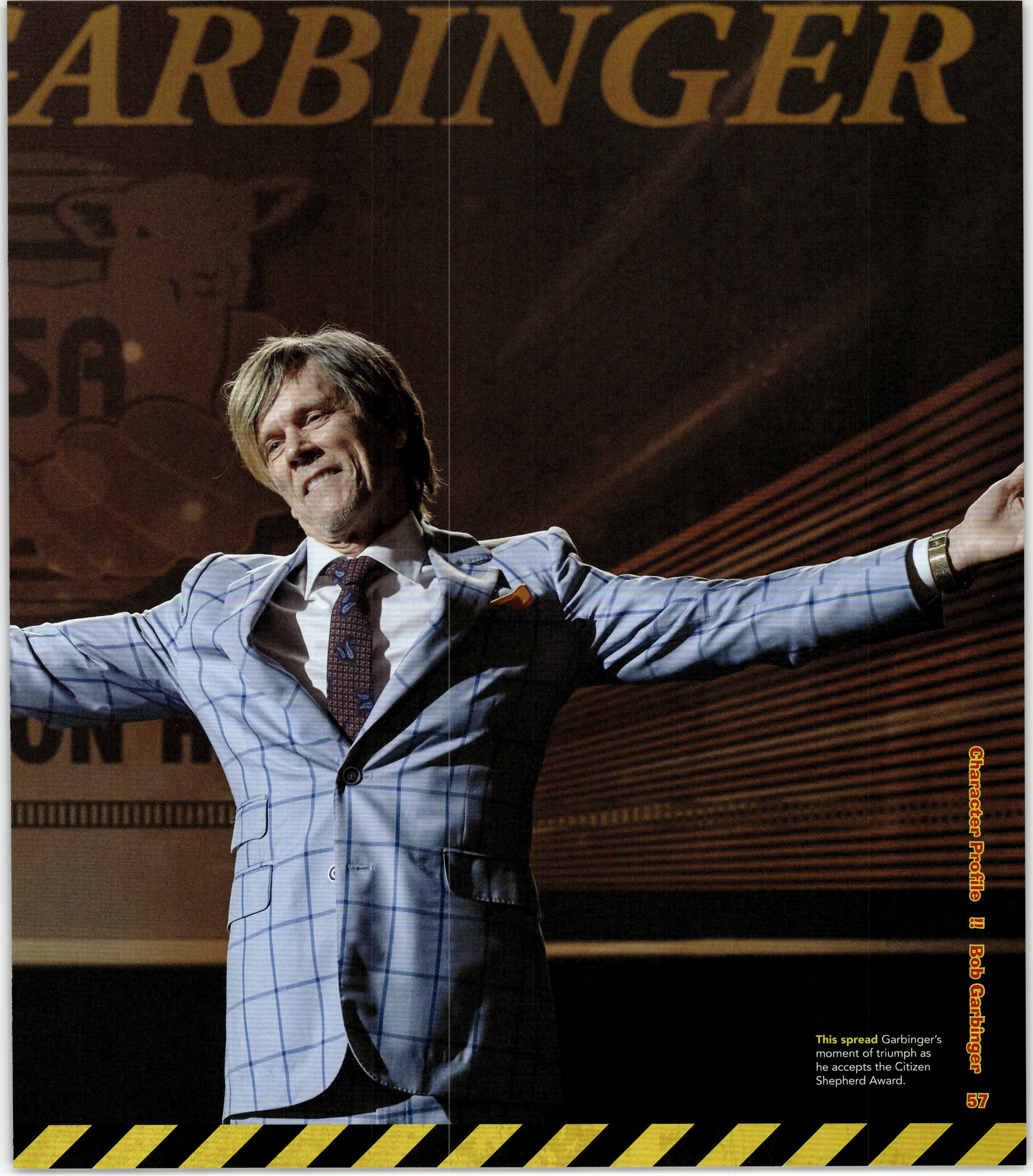

This spread Garbinger's moment of triumph as he accepts the Citizen Shepherd Award.

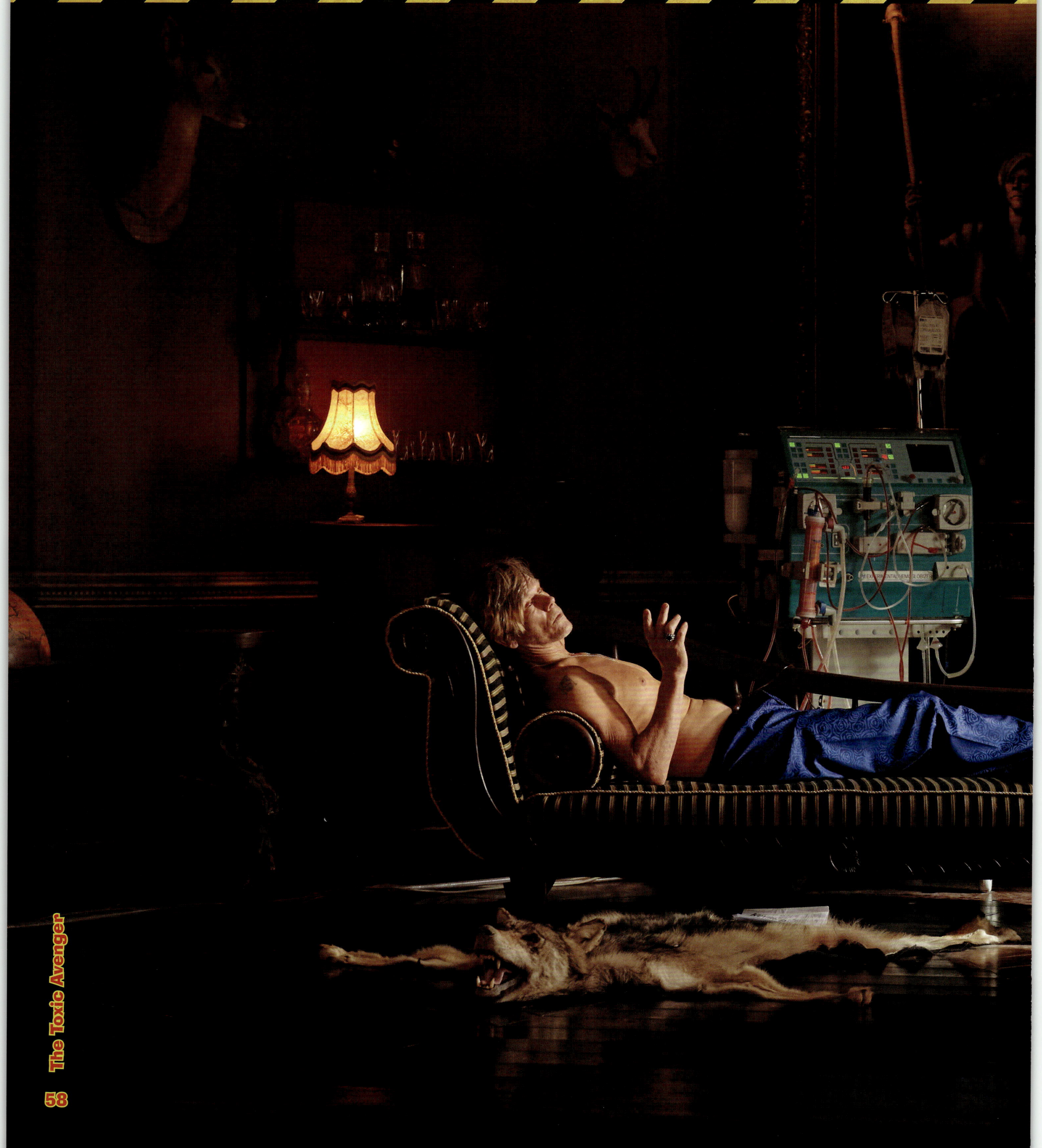

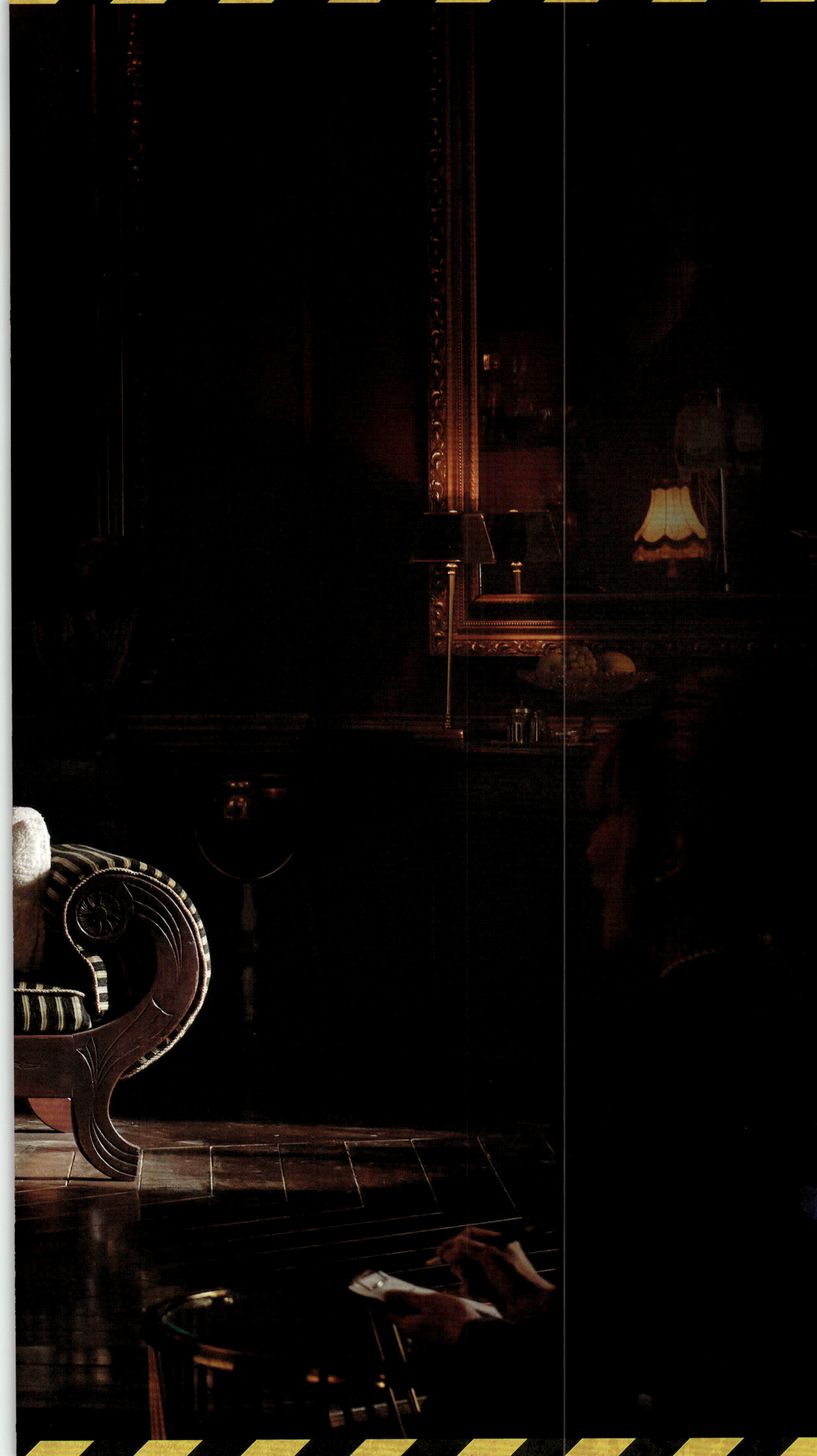

That ridiculousness exhibits itself largely through Garbinger's colossal vanity—he is described in the script as "a blond comet of blasé narcissism"—which is reflected in his outré sartorial choices, foremost among them a gold-coloured, fur-trimmed robe (worn with bunny slippers). Although the robe was originally intended to be purple, reveals Porter. "I felt like the blood that was going to cover it later wouldn't show up on purple," she says. "So we shifted the colour to a yellowish gold, which also felt like it would pop against all the dark interiors that are in the movie, and then also pop in all his big fight scenes."

Garbinger's signature outfit also contains a few clues as to his ultimate fate: after drinking a Toxie-extracted serum, he transforms into the huge, hairy Monster Garbinger (played by Spencer Wilding). "I wanted to foreshadow that with the robe," says Porter, "so I gave it a blue fur collar, while the yellow is like a Mongolian pelt, with an unusual fur pattern in it—it's all fake fur, by the way. And then he has a necklace that's a shark tooth, and these rings that have claws on them."

The other implication here, of course, is that Garbinger's always seen himself as an apex predator, at least in the business sense. One who cares little for the trail of destruction—ruined lives, ruined environments—he leaves in his ravenous wake. The irony being, when he finally becomes a true predator (or perhaps his true 'perfect self') he's set the course for his own spectacularly bloody destruction.

This spread The secret of Garbinger's gleaming success, apparently, is transfused gorilla blood.

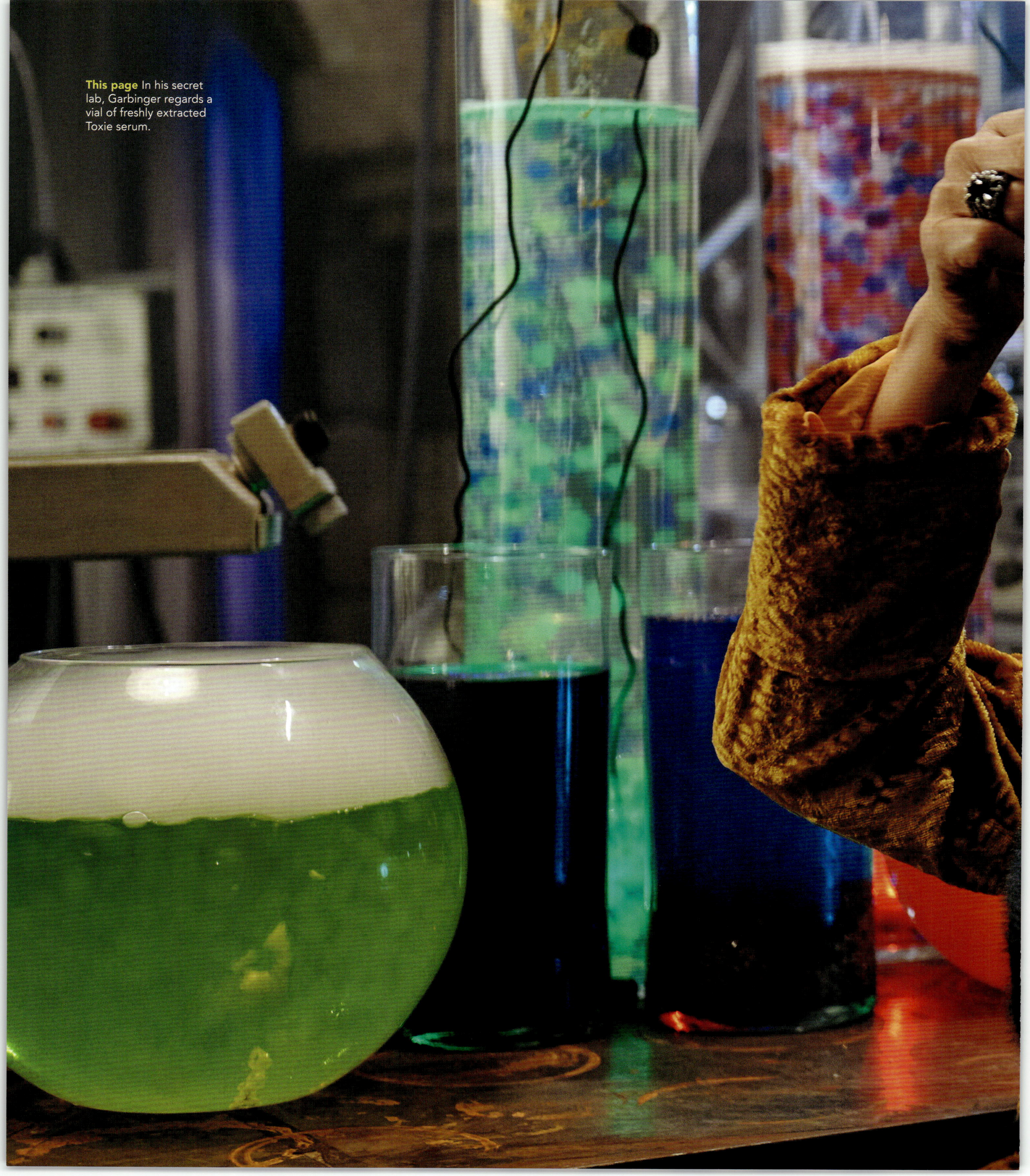

This page In his secret lab, Garbinger regards a vial of freshly extracted Toxie serum.

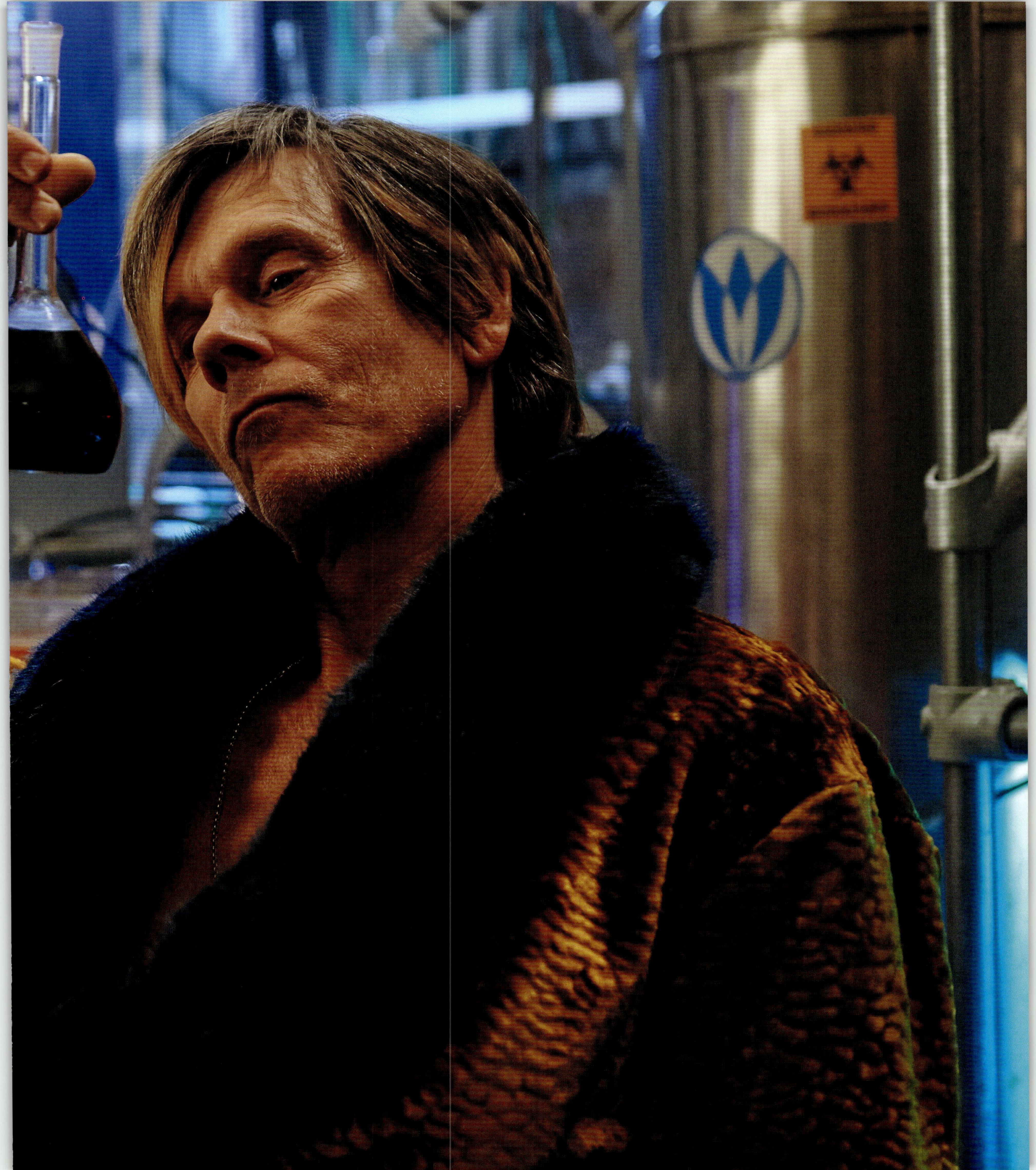

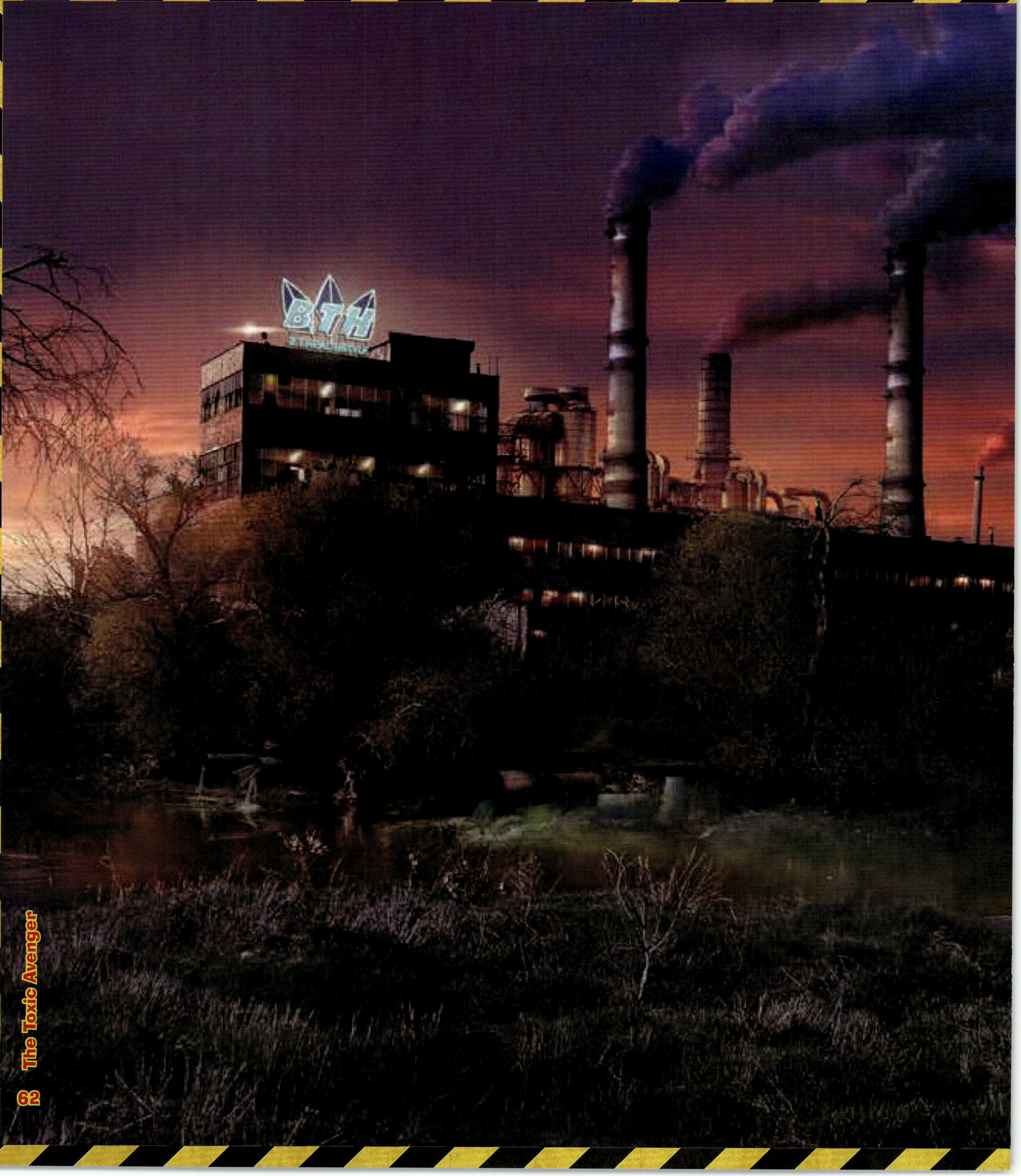
BTH

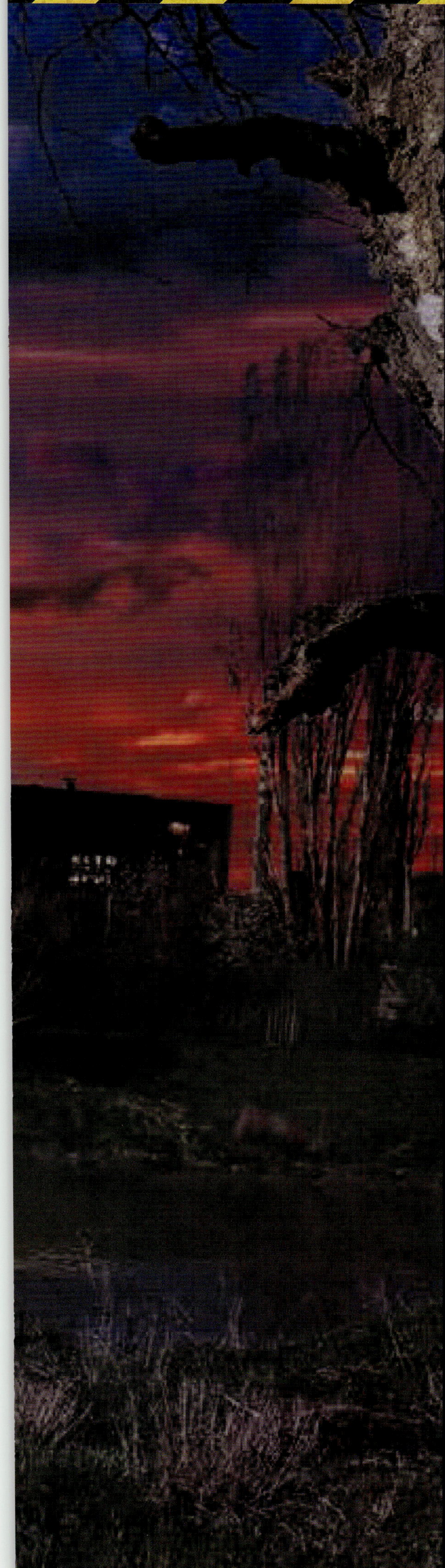

THE B.T.H. FACTORY

Looming over St. Roma's Village, like a filth-spewing beast, is Bob Garbinger's factory. It is the source of all that is evil and corrupting in the town, retching toxic sludge into its waterways and belching fumes into the sky. It is here that Winston works, pushing his mop around the factory floor, and it is here that he will meet his destiny, apparently shot to death during an unsuccessful robbery by Garbinger's weirdo hit squad, and dumped in the sludge, where he mutates into the Toxic Avenger.

For the exterior shots of the factory, Blair and Cameron sought out a real location which they would augment and tweak with the help of Canadian visual-effects supervisor Chris Ritvo. After scouting the outskirts of Sofia, Bulgaria, they found the ideal spot in the form of a still-active rubber factory, located about half-an-hour's drive north from the city.

"We looked at a lot of different factory locations," says Blair. "Some of them worked for the interior, and some of them worked for the exterior, but this was the only one that offered a little bit of everything, and it had this nice view from across the river, too. It was the obvious choice."

The existing factory was so close to what they had envisioned, in fact, that it required very little work, in terms of art-department dressing. "It was 95 percent ready to go," says Blair, from the rusting barrels that were stacked around its environs to the huge pipes that coiled around the site. Primarily, says Cameron, it was a matter of changing the signage, covering up what was already there with the B.T.H. Logos. "I mean, it looked pretty horrible, which is what we wanted!"

"I mean, it looked pretty horrible, which is what we wanted!"

– ALEXANDER CAMERON, Production Designer

However, for the wider shots of the site—most importantly the establishing shot which opens the film—the VFX team applied some digital set extension. "We kept the foreground building much the same," says Ritvo, "but we added pipes in the foreground to gush green liquid into

Left Bob Garbinger's factory in all its filth-spewing glory.

Right The original location: a rubber factory, just outside Sofia, Bulgaria.

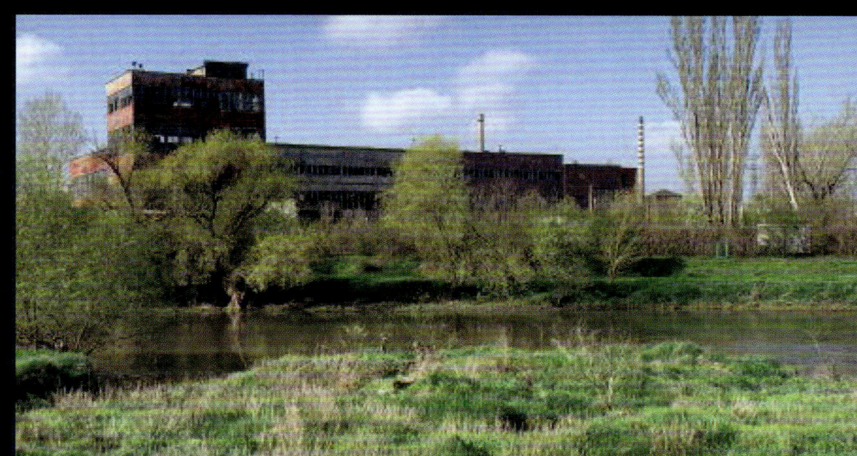

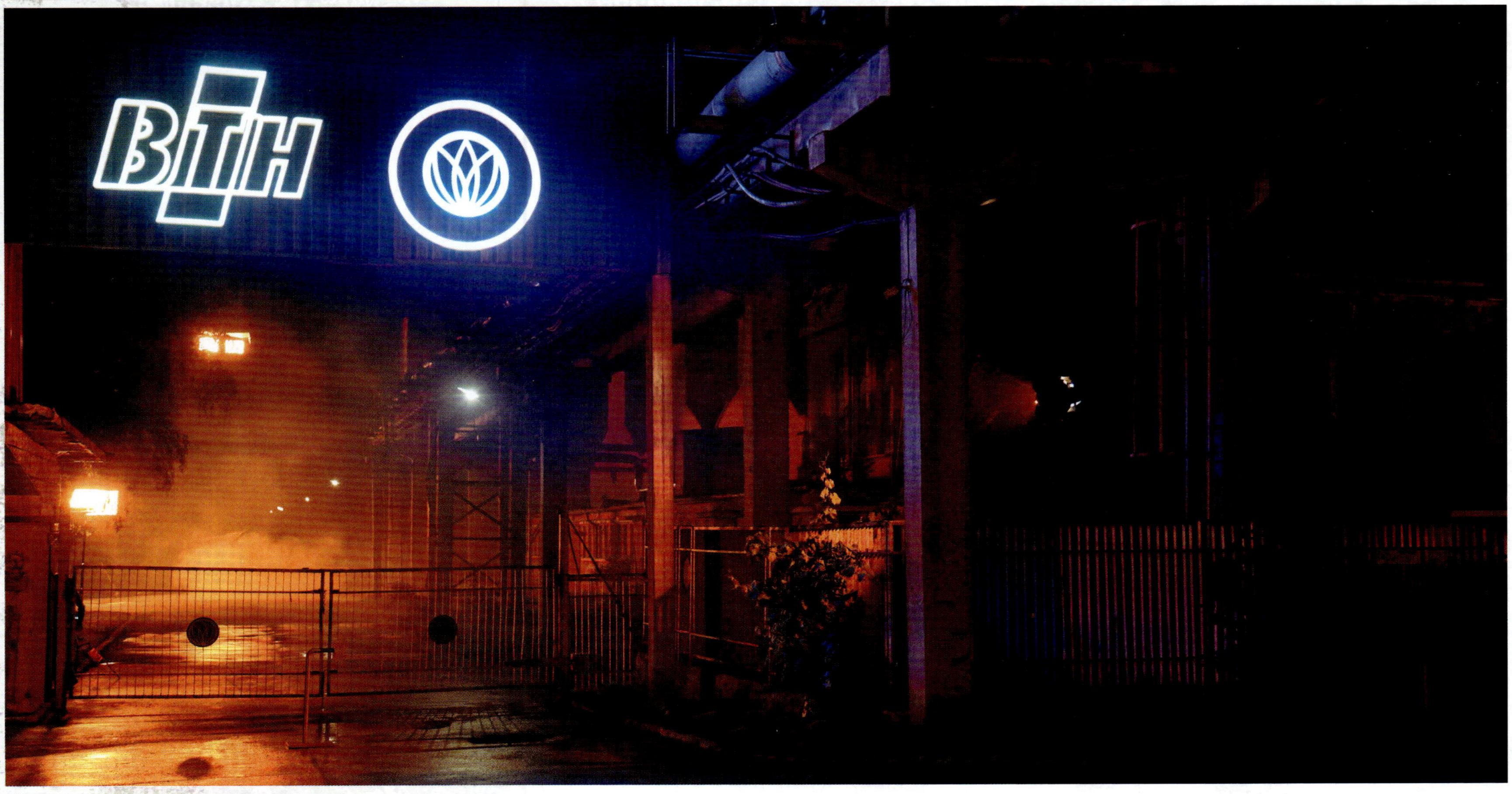

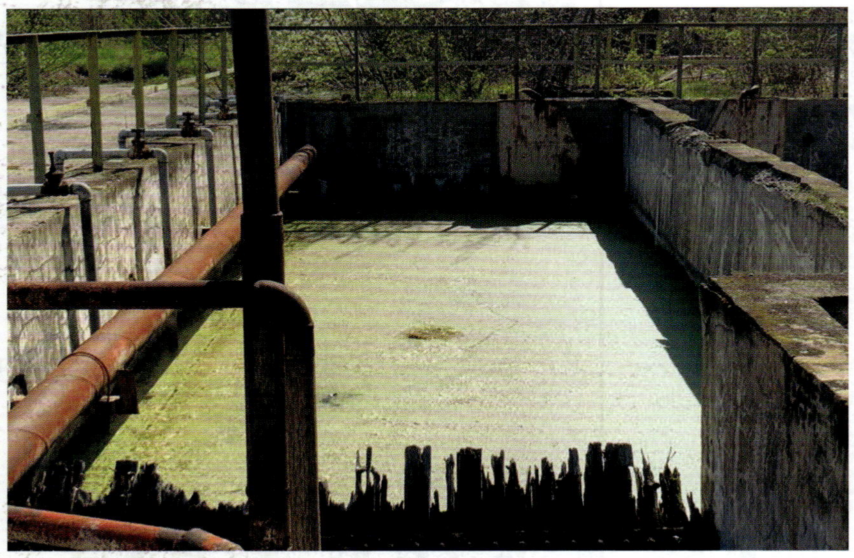

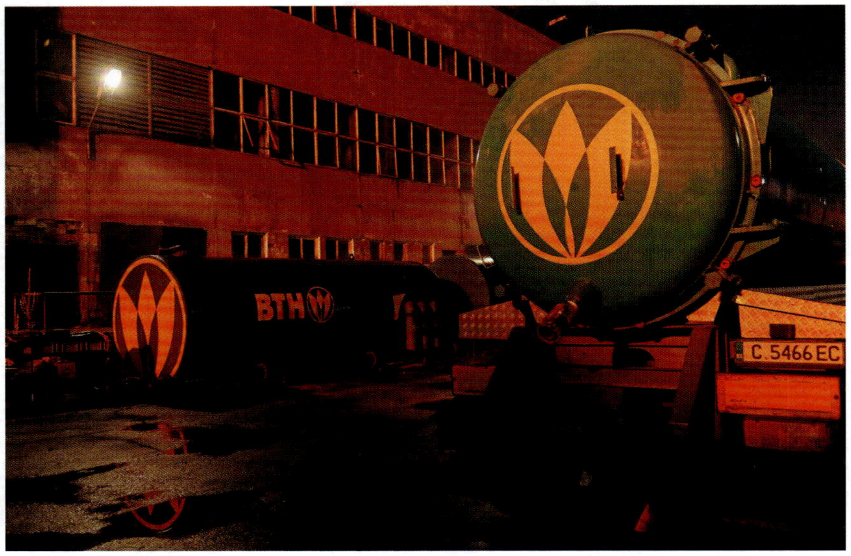

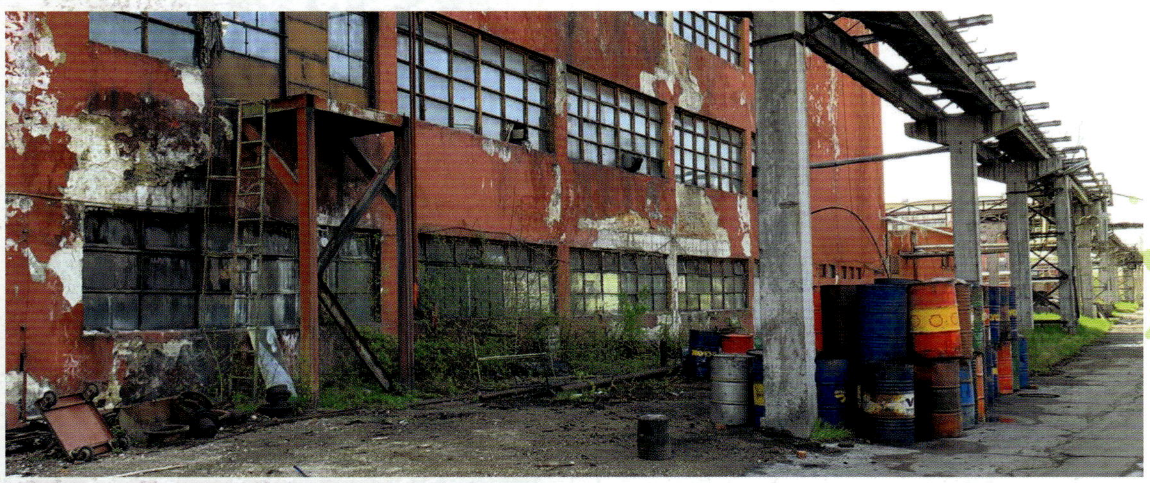

Top The dark, mysterious and smoky B.T.H. factory by night.

Above left The algae-smothered pool which inspired Blair to re-conceive Winston's death-and-rebirth scene.

Above right Some B.T.H.-flavoured set dressing on the factory site.

Left The exterior of the rubber factory, as Blair and Cameron found it during their initial location scouting trip.

the river, we added the chimneys, spewing dark, black smoke into the atmosphere, and we added the big neon sign. But it's blinking on-and-off, because we thought it would be funny that the sign doesn't quite work. They're trying to keep everything super low-budget, with costs kept to a bare minimum."

Another touch added by the VFX team was the almost incongruous presence of a windmill, which Ritvo says was probably the result of B.T.H. at some point making a half-hearted, media-pleasing attempt to look environmentally conscious. "But it went derelict very quickly. There are vines hanging off it. That was just one of the many ideas and inside jokes we'd throw at each other, saying, 'Oh, this could be funny.'"

Aside from an interior establishing shot showing Winston mopping up some mess in a corridor, and a glimpse of a conveyor belt on which people are packing boxes, little is seen of the factory floor in the movie. This was partly due to budgetary constraints, Cameron admits. "There was talk of doing it all with green screen and showing this huge space inside, but it was too expensive, so we ended up simplifying it and abstracting it and putting smoke in and lighting effects. And it worked."

Yet according to Blair, there was a strong narrative purpose to obscuring the specifics of the factory's mechanical guts. "The idea was to be suggestive and hide the ball a little bit about what the factory is producing and how it's producing it," he explains. "We just wanted it to look sinister and unknowable and dangerous. We built a version of the floor, but you only see it through windows, and it's lit in such a way that you kind of get a sense of it, but we're not really participating in it."

There's one thing we know for sure the factory is producing: disgusting and harmful toxic waste. As mentioned above, this is the site of Winston's demise and the place of Toxie's violent birth, a crucial moment in *The Toxic Avenger*'s storyline. Originally, Blair had written the Killer Nutz

"We just wanted it to look sinister and unknowable and dangerous."

– MACON BLAIR,
Director

Below Various corporate logo designs for B.T.H.

Right Winston's pass card, complete with B.TH. QR code.

BTHealthstyle

disposing of Winston by stuffing him into "a pipe structure" which he was expecting to construct on set. However, while scouting around the Sofia rubber factory during pre-production, he found a "weird pool", with crumbling masonry, rusting pipes, and thick green algae blanketing the water's surface.

"I loved the quality of the water," he says. "You would throw something in, and all the green stuff would retreat, and the water would become black. Then slowly the green stuff would congeal again and close over the top. So it was a better version of what we had written, but existing in reality!" As a result, Blair re-conceived the scene to match the location.

Ironically, when time came to shoot it during the summer, Cameron says, all that lovely "green stuff" had disappeared. "So then we put our own kind of polystyrene green crap on the top," he laughs. "But it still looked great."

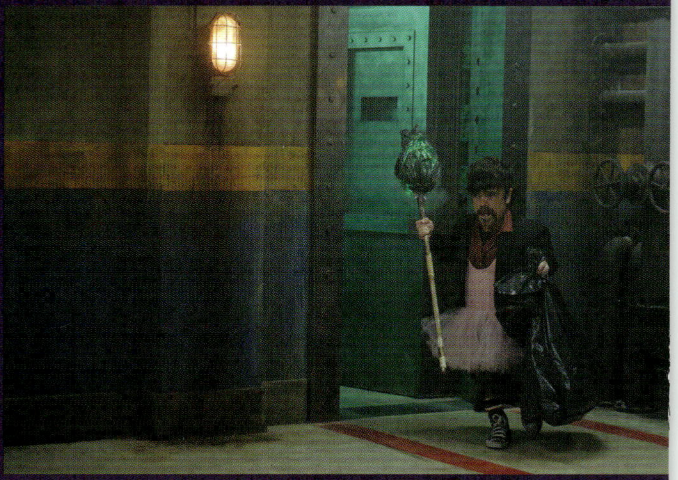

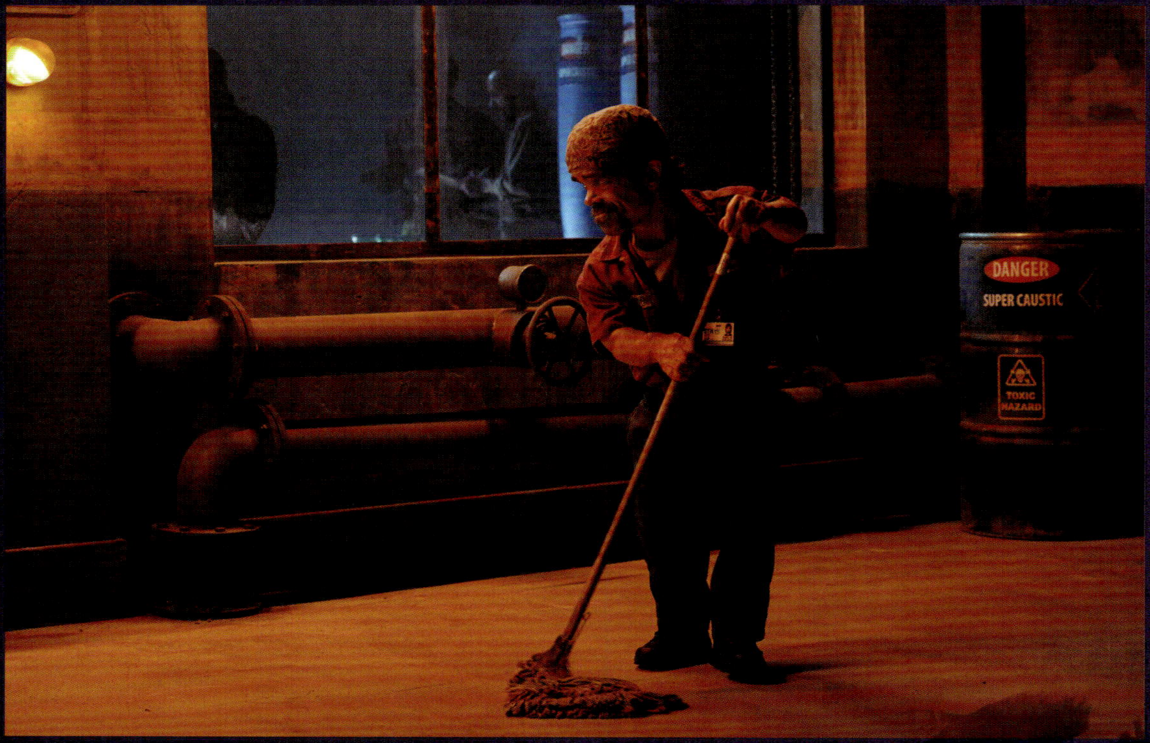

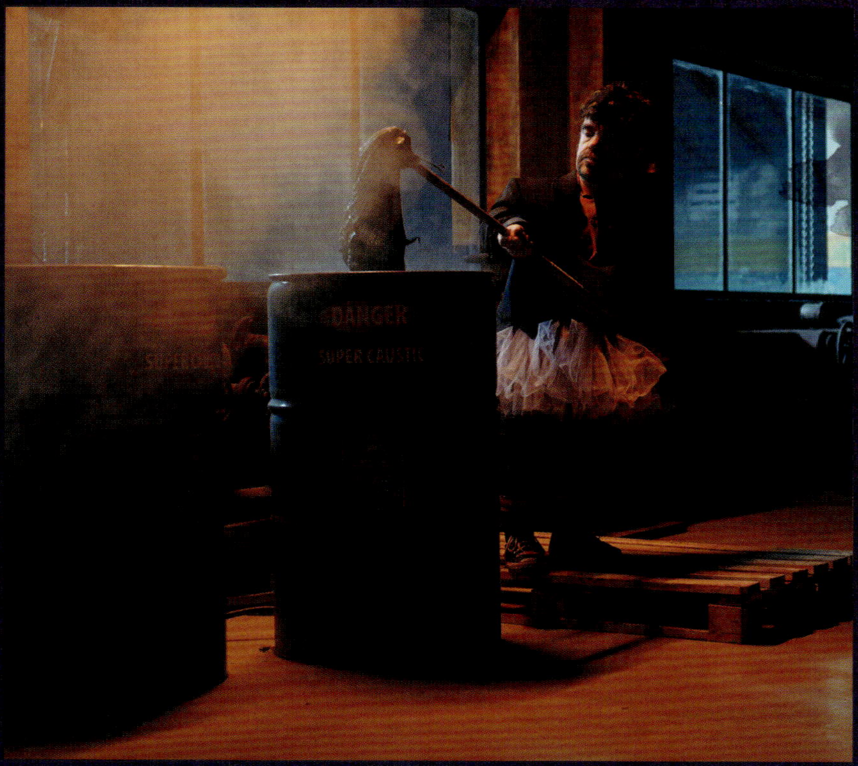

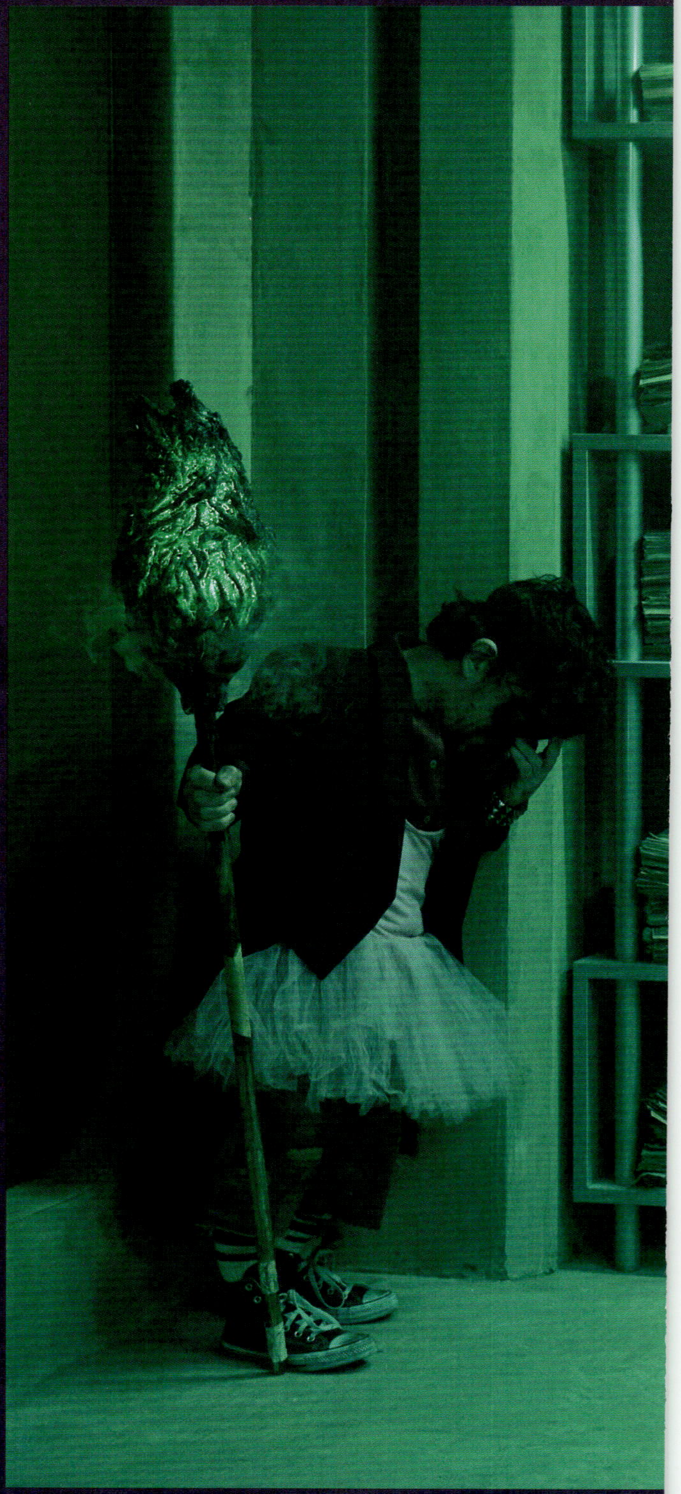

Top left Winston breaks into the factory to take the money he feels he's owed for his healthcare.

Top right Concept art of the B.T.H. vault.

Above Winston at work. (Note the foreboding barrel behind him).

Left Winston uses B.T.H. toxic waste to upgrade his mop, and make this a uniquely armed robbery.

Right Winston in the B.T.H. vault, getting his trash bag filled with cash.

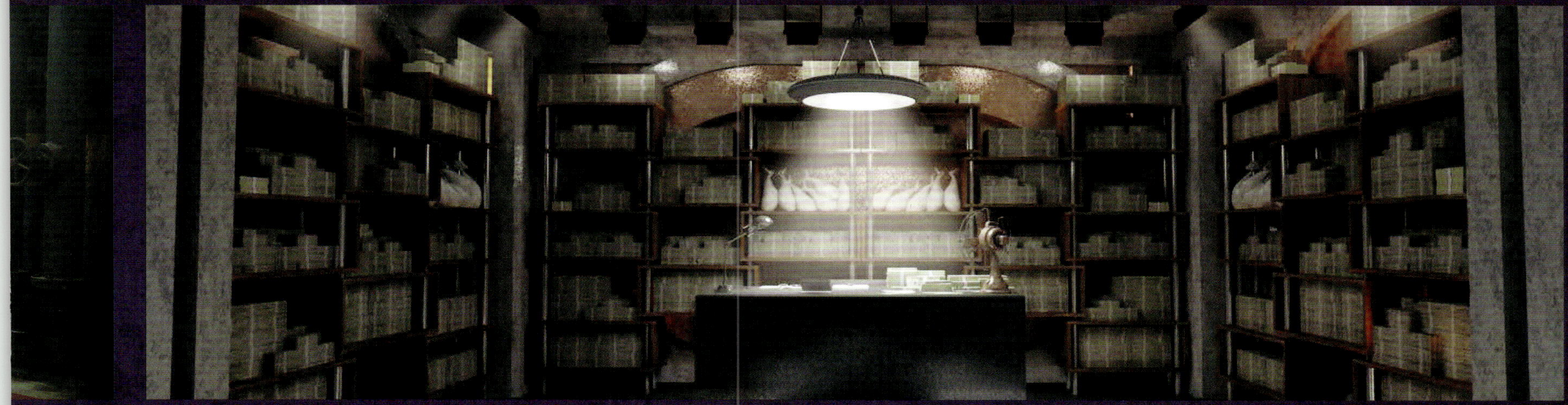

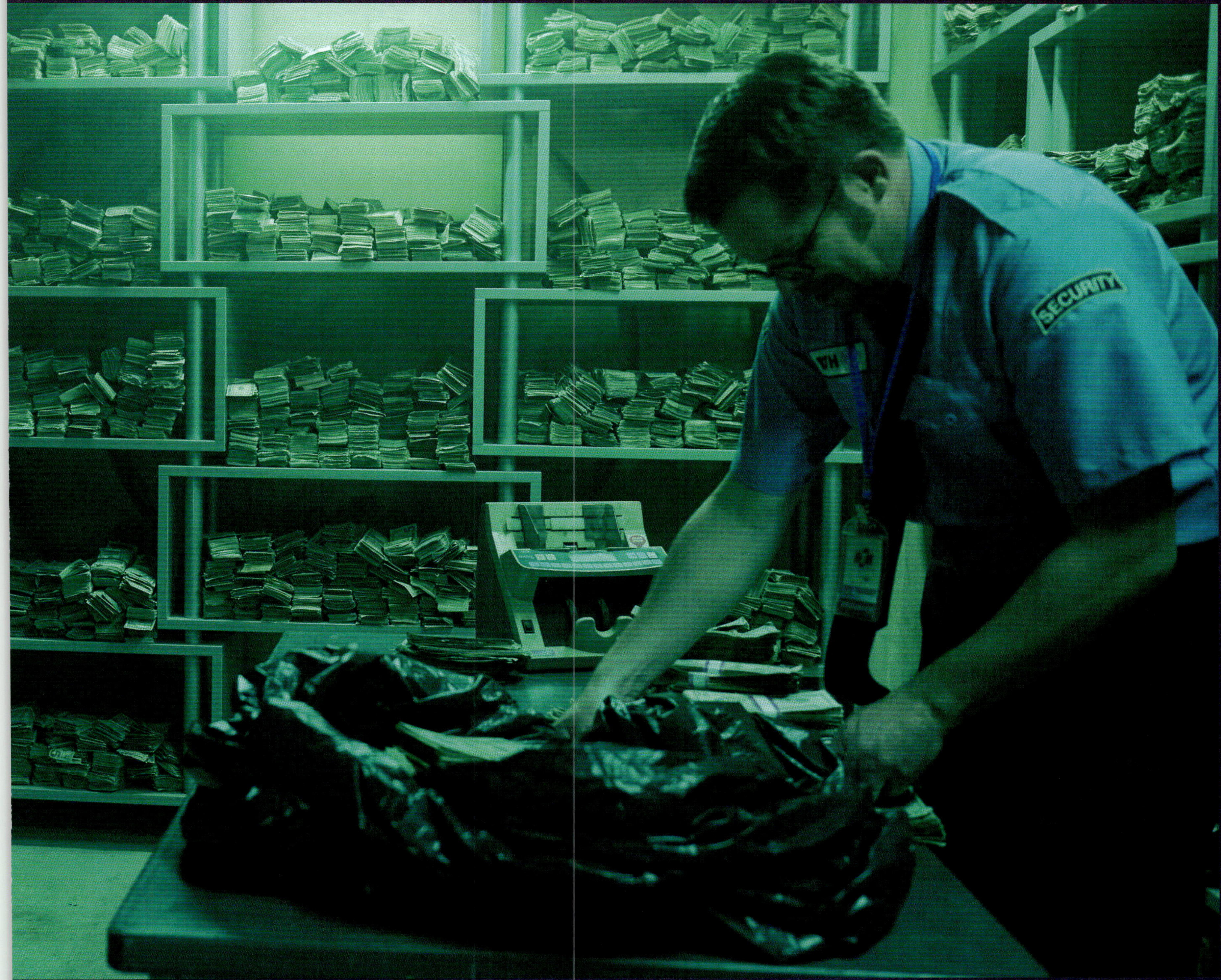
SECURITY

INDUSTRIAL AREA AND THE TALL HILL

To create the semi-derelict, heavily worn industrial backdrop for much of the film's action, Blair and *The Toxic Avenger*'s art team made the most of Bulgaria's brutalist, artificial environments. For example, they found the industrial area, where J.J., Wade and Toxie battle with Garbinger's mercenary goons in Sofia, around an active boiler-manufacturing facility with a disused railway line running through it. "It was a pretty interesting place," says Cameron. "We used this area for quite a few scenes. All we had to do with it was add some more crap, to be honest!"

Meanwhile, for the Tall Hill location near Guthrie's camp, where Toxie and J.J. have a moment of respite and a heart-to-heart about the state of the world, the production found an oddly beautiful flooded quarry next to a shuttered steel factory. Described in the script as "a massive strip-mined and calcified crater, like an atomic blast zone," the location had to be "kind of gross and sad, but also legitimately a nice view," says Blair.

Like the B.T.H. Factory, this was somewhere which required digital augmentation to bring it fully into the Tromaville idiom. "It looks incredible," says Ritvo. "It is absolutely massive. Originally, the idea was that we were going to take away the lake and make it a big sandpit where barrels have been dumped, but then we thought it would be better to turn the water green and make it more of a toxic-waste dump rather than a pit."

Blair loved the idea, which opened the way for Ritvo to add one other new concept—or rather, resurrect an old one. Early on in development, he says, Toxie was going to battle a huge, albino alligator, but this sequence was axed "due to expense." Keen to keep the big, pale reptile in some form, he found it a home, of sorts, in Tall Hill.

"I kept trying to find a place where we could add in an albino alligator and do it

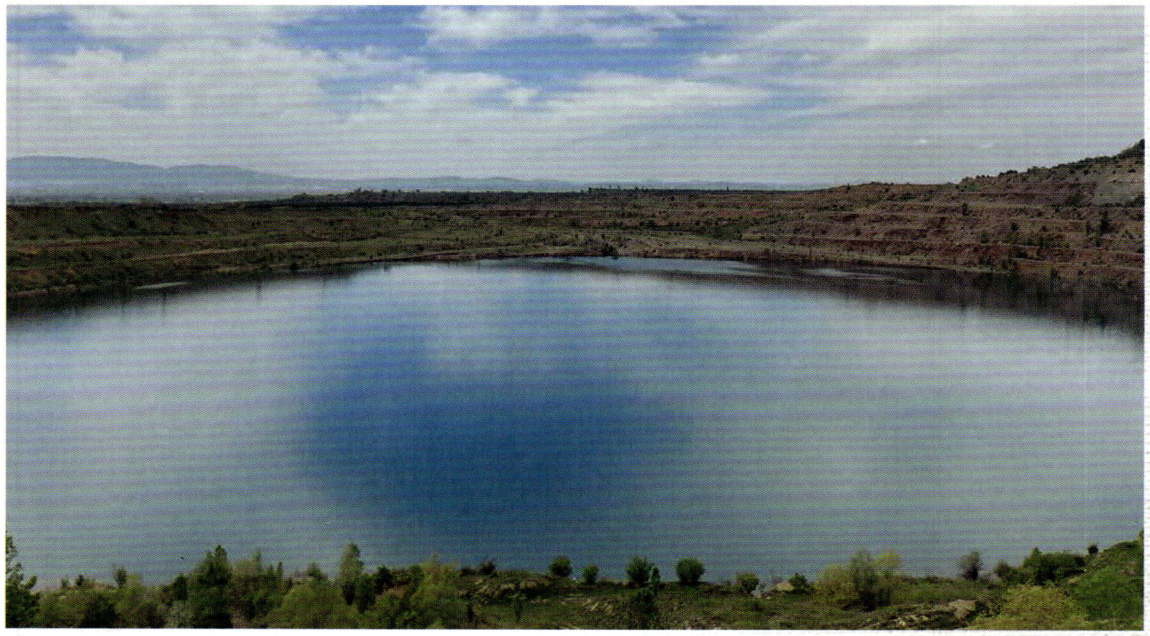

Below Exterior of the Bulgarian boiler factory. Location scouting shot.

Right The flooded quarry where Toxie and J.J. have a heart-to-heart.

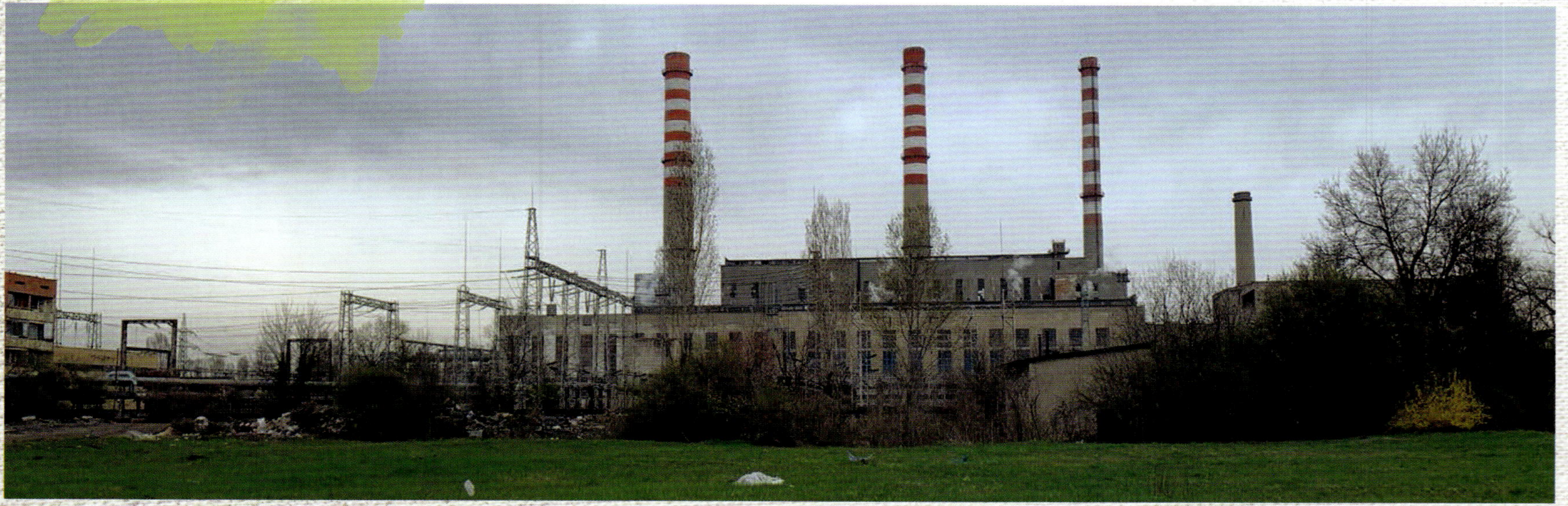

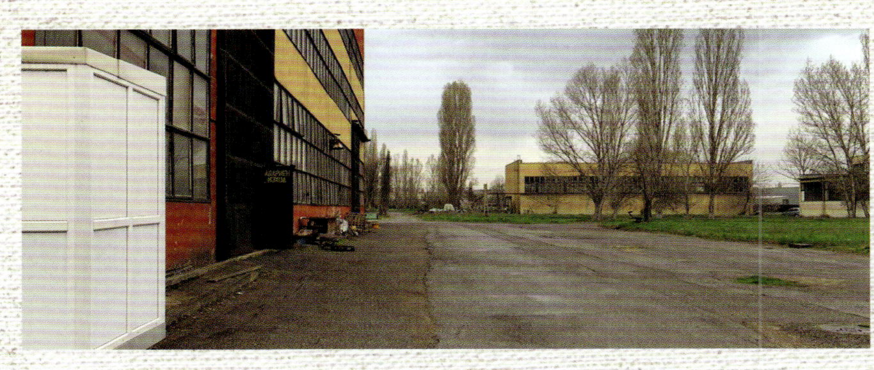

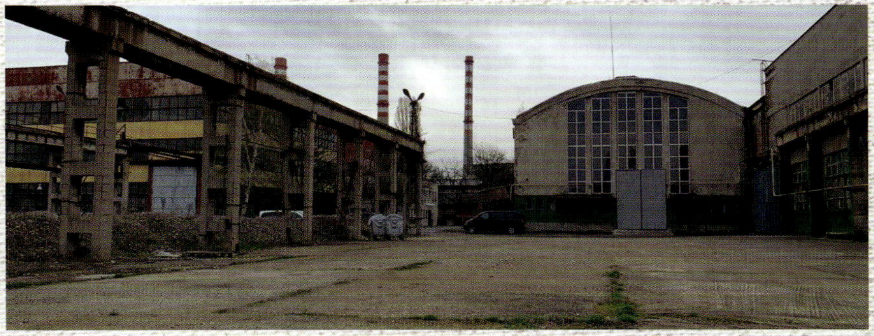

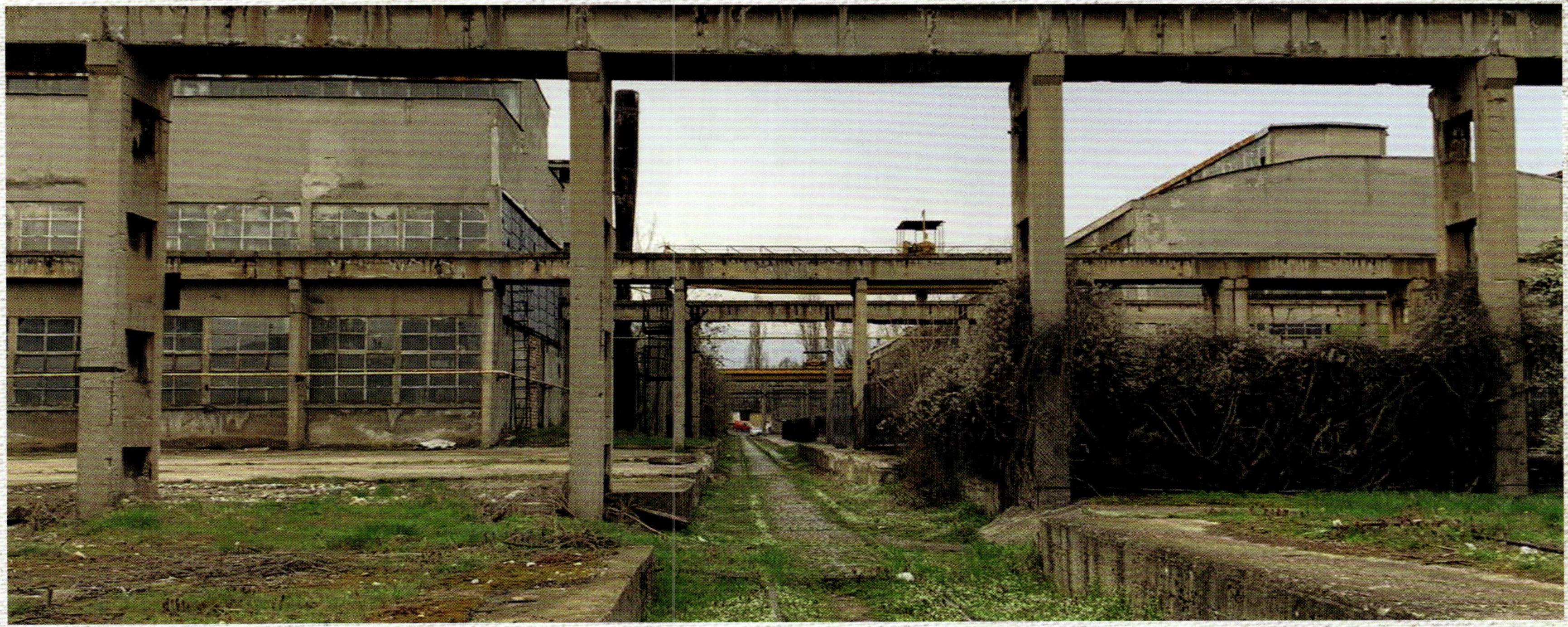

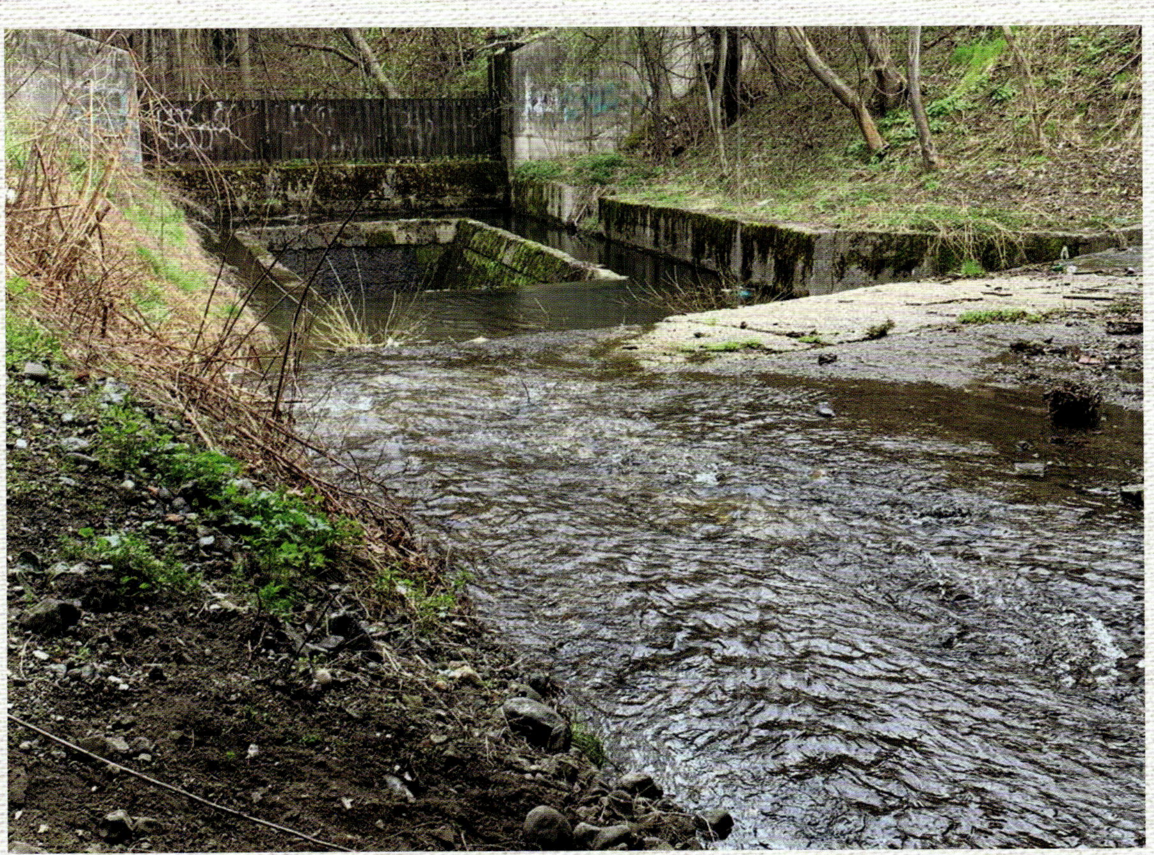

within my budget," he says. "So, in the slime pool, we do have the bones of the alligator, in the distance, on the left." While its presence is something of a production in-joke, it does add some depth to the world-building, Ritvo believes, suggesting that B.T.H.'s pollution has created other monsters in the area. "Maybe in a sequel, if our dreams come true, we'll see some of these strange animals."

This page A Bulgarian boiler-manufacturing facility became the real-world basis of Tromaville's industrial wasteland. These photos were taken during the initial location scout.

THE MUTANT BIRD

If *The Toxic Avenger* has a mascot, it is surely the "deformed mutant bird" we first meet outside the B.T.H. Factory, perched on a stump and squawking "in despair," as the script describes it.

It was also one of the first things that Blair conceptualized, at the very beginning of the development process. "Before we got a green light, there was a long period of time where I did a lot of my own concept art, just little sketches and watercolours. I did a bunch of sketches of the bird." Even this early on, Blair knew this miserable, mangy creature would need to be realized on screen by puppetry, rather than digital effects.

"The thinking was, we've got the main character, Toxie, as a mutant, so we wanted to fill out the world a little bit and show how the factory is causing all this wreckage and mutations," he says. "We also knew Toxie was going to be a person in a suit, so it seemed important that this should be a puppet. It's a little bit of a joke at the beginning, but it also sets the expectations for what kind of movie this is gonna be, with its prosthetic makeup and a lo-fi approach."

Ritvo thinks the bird is "awesome," and says it's his favourite thing in the film. "I was secretly hoping I would get to create it in CG, just because I like the idea so much," he says, "but I am a big proponent of puppets, so practical was definitely the way to go. Macon and I talked a lot about why puppets work. You don't necessarily think they're alive or they're real, but you fall in love with them, and they come to life on their own. It's like the audience is in on the joke."

Working from Blair's own sketches, Bulgarian special-effects makeup team Illusion Industries (with whom Ritvo collaborated on his previous project, *The Texas Chainsaw Massacre*) created a bird that the VFX supervisor describes as "very weird and unique. It's had a pretty hard life. It's obviously been hanging out in a lot of toxic-waste dumps and is pretty strung out. Whatever it's been breathing in, you can see in its eyes it's really messed it up." He did have some involvement with the creature's creation, however, with the VFX team painting out the puppet's rods and adding digital eyelids and a tongue, "just to keep it alive a little bit."

As the film developed, the bird began to grow in importance. For the scene where Winston first realizes he's been transformed into a monster, Blair originally envisioned him emerging from a river, to see himself reflected in the moonlit water. However, the realities of achieving this one, brief moment in an actual river, at night, with an actor in a full-body prosthetic, quickly hit home. "We reworked that scene," he says. "Now Toxie has already emerged onto dry land and the recognition that he's become a monster is given to us through his interaction with the bird, which is grossed out by him. What was originally intended to be a little fun extra detail became the focus of the scene."

The bird also received a further "promotion", as Blair puts it, to become a true icon. Actually a "nervous red warbler," that is indigenous to Tromaville, it appears on the town seal (mounted on the mayor's lectern in Mammon Hall) and its police uniforms. "It is the symbol of the town," says Cameron, who created all these visual elements himself, positioning the dodo-like creature in the same kinds of places and poses you'd usually expect to find a proud bald eagle.

But the poor warbler is also, Blair says, a symbol of what St. Roma's Village has become. "It represents the way the town has kind of decayed and lost something since the Garbinger presence arrived," he says. "That is embodied in this weird mutant bird."

Right & far right
The puppeteers of Illusion Industries bring the "nervous red warbler" to life on set.

Opposite page
Tromaville's mangy dodo-esque mascot during production, before the puppetry rods are digitally removed.

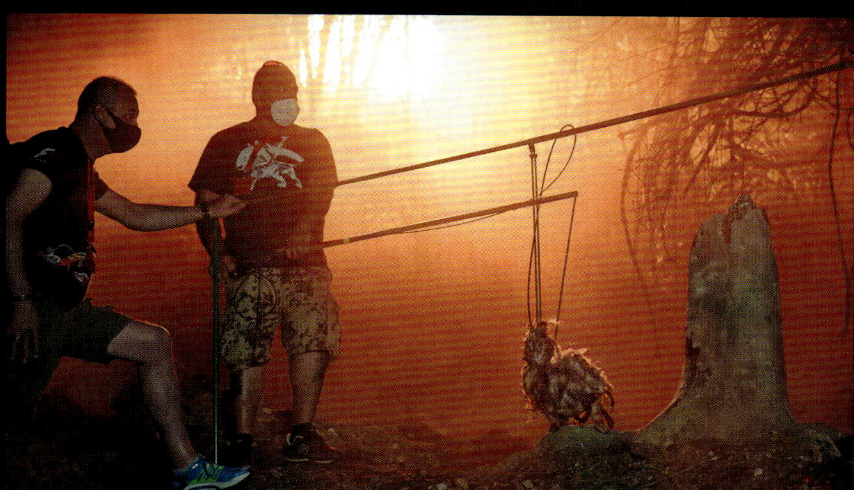

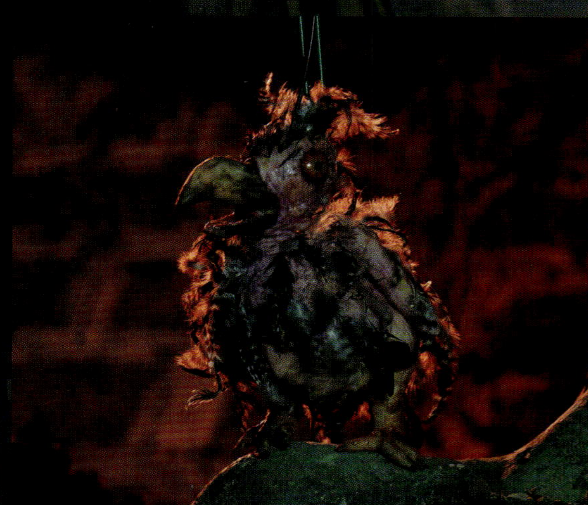

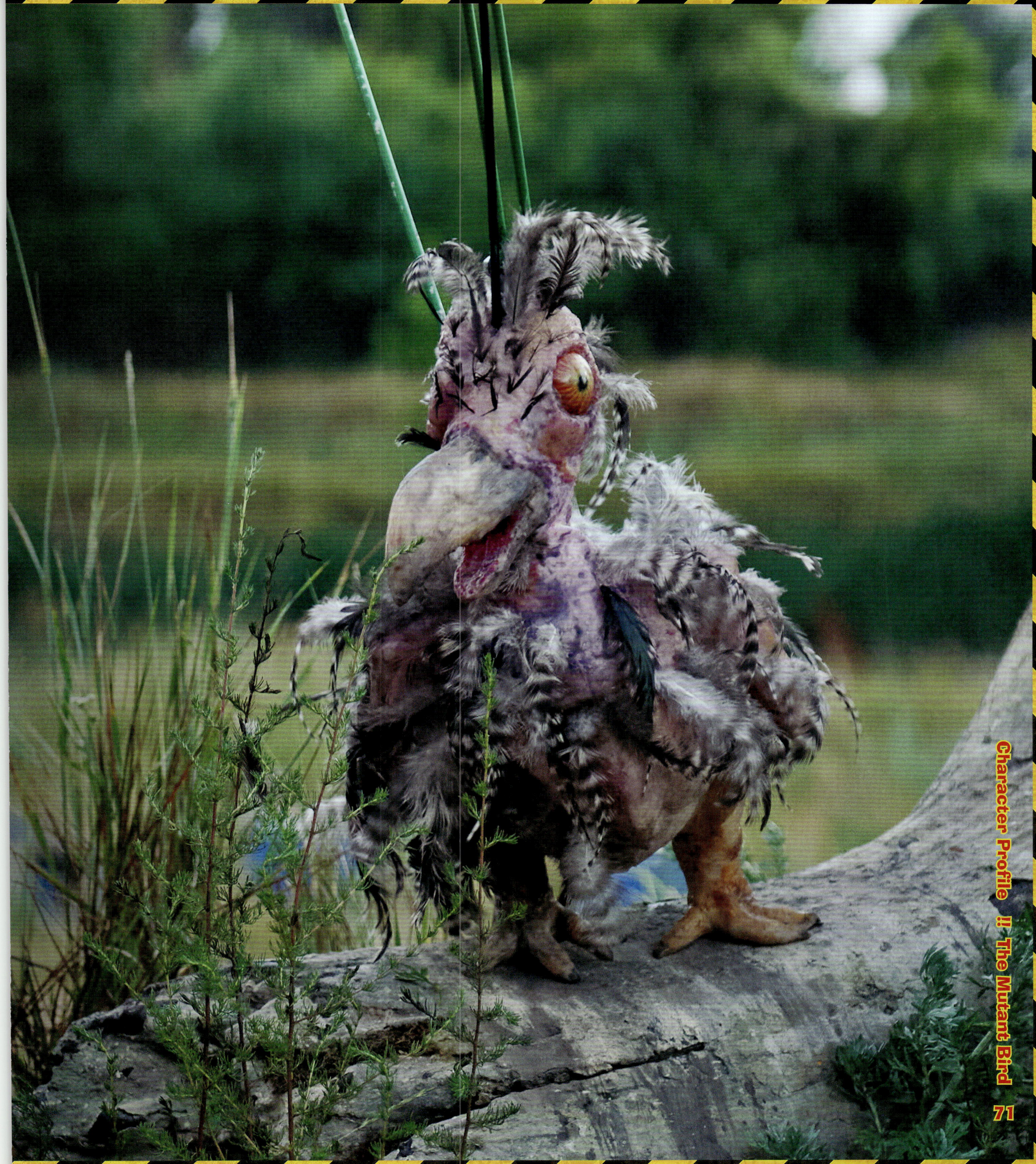

ST. ROMA'S HIGH SCHOOL

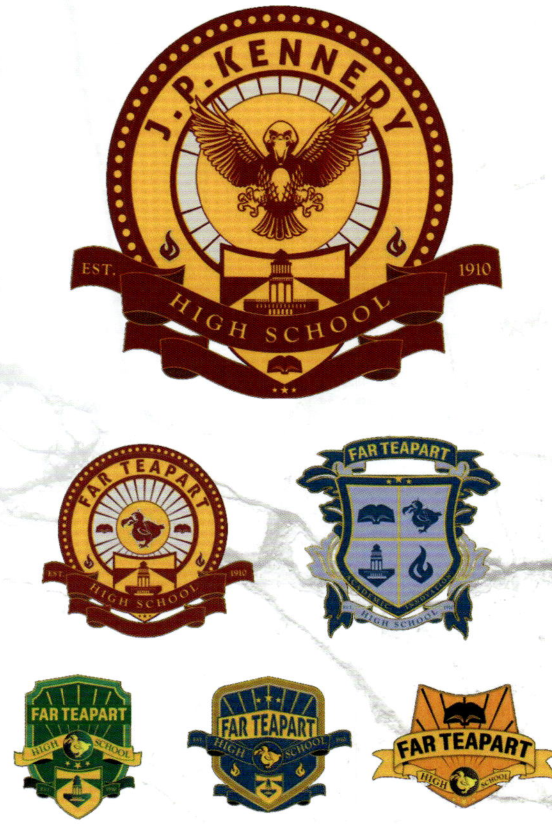

As with many of Tromaville's landmarks, Wade's high school presented the challenge of finding a building in Bulgaria that could convincingly double for Macon Blair's slightly askew America. In this case, the task was made a little easier by the fact that, in terms of interiors, they only really needed to show the school auditorium, where Wade takes the stage at the film's conclusion to achieve his final triumph of creative expression. Blair and Cameron found their St. Roma's High School in a town close to Sofia, which, despite being "a very communist-looking place," as Cameron puts it, had all the required elements for the sequence.

"It had this nice balcony, where Toxie could observe the show from a little pocket of darkness," says Blair. "And given that's the last shot of the movie, it was very important. As soon as we saw that, we knew it was the right place."

Serendipitously, the auditorium also had some other features which, it struck Blair, echoed another important and emotional scene in the movie. "The architecture felt like it had a certain connection to the architecture in Winston's dream (which was unfortunately cut), where he's talking with Shelly," he explains, pointing out the globe-like lamps which hang from the ceiling. "It just fit the vibe of what we needed."

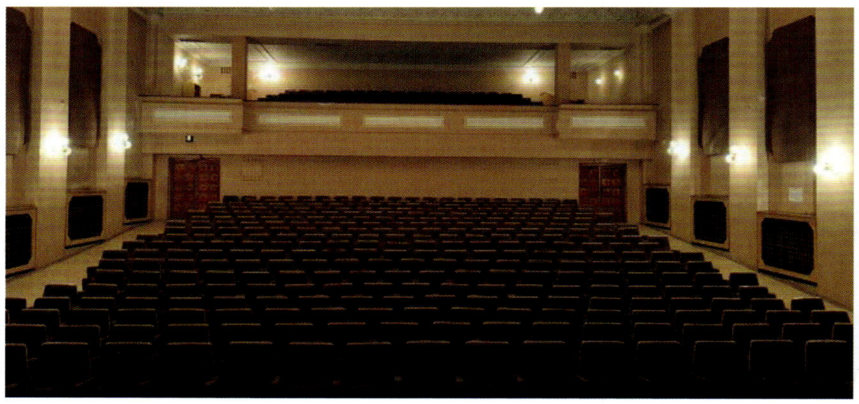

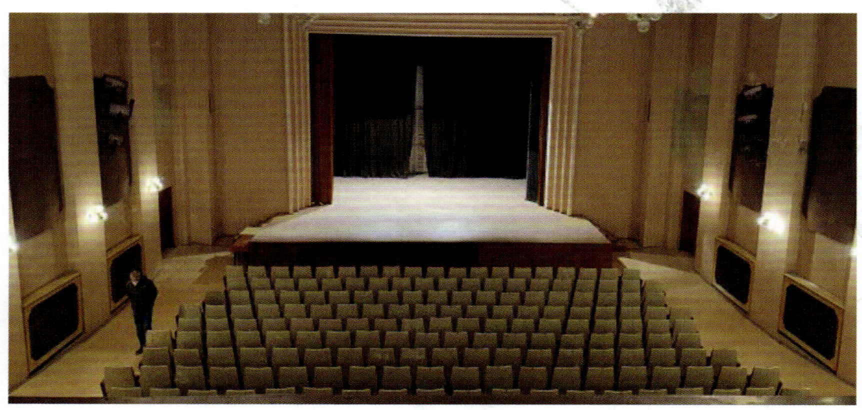

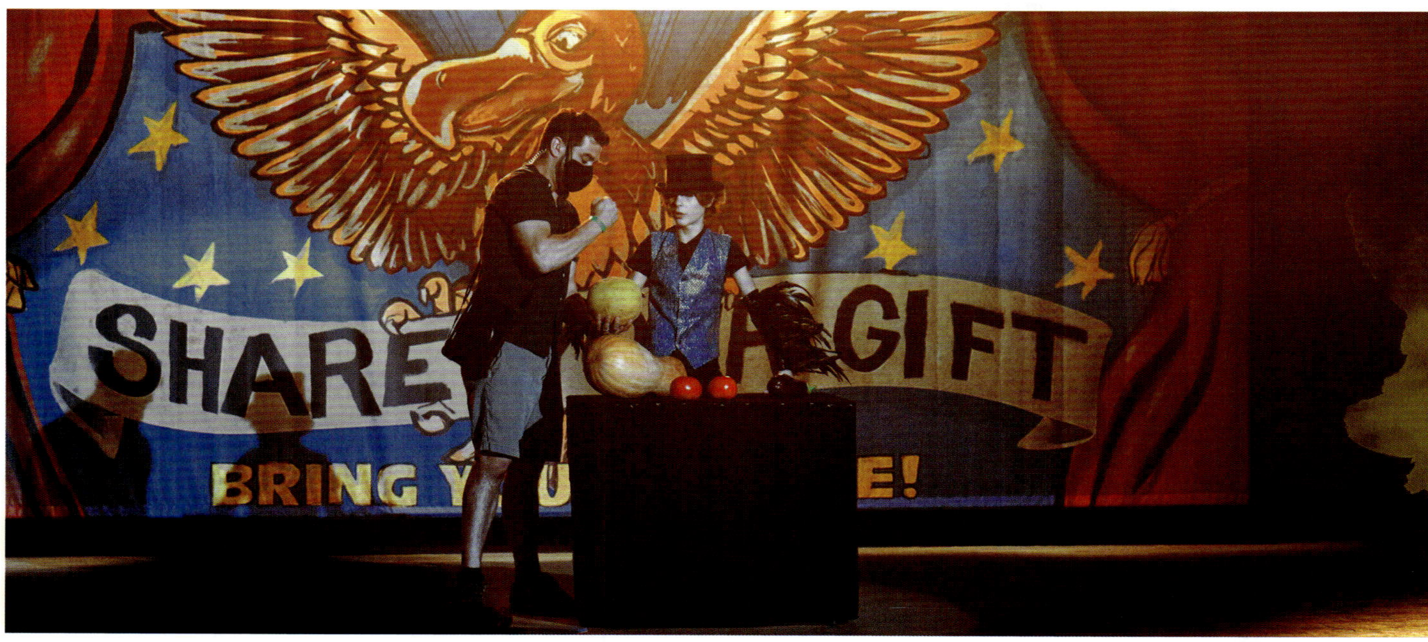

Top A variety of crest designs for Wade's high school – all of which feature the iconic town dodo-like bird.

Above The auditorium (that is set for Wade's performance) viewed from the stage (left) and from the balcony (right).

Left A crew member helps Tremblay prepare to start smashing fruit and veg, for Wade's big moment on stage.

ST. ROMA'S HOSPITAL

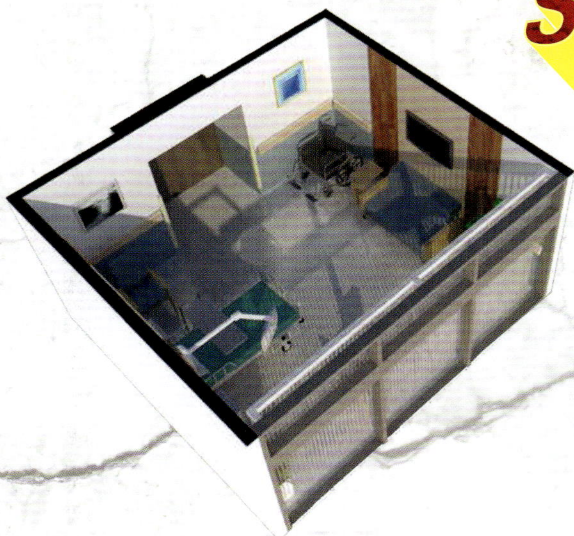

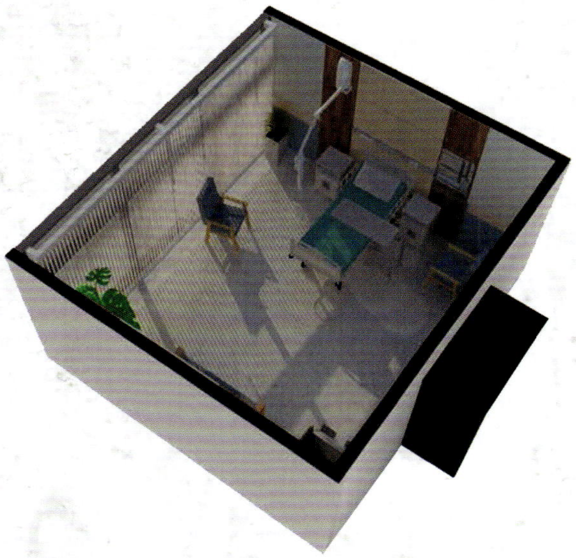

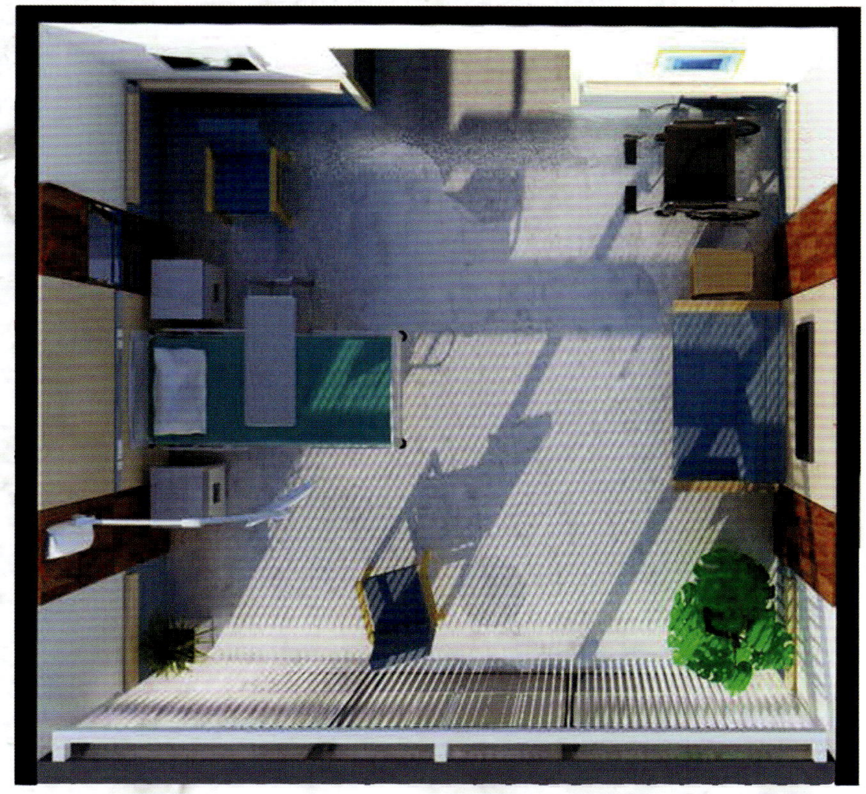

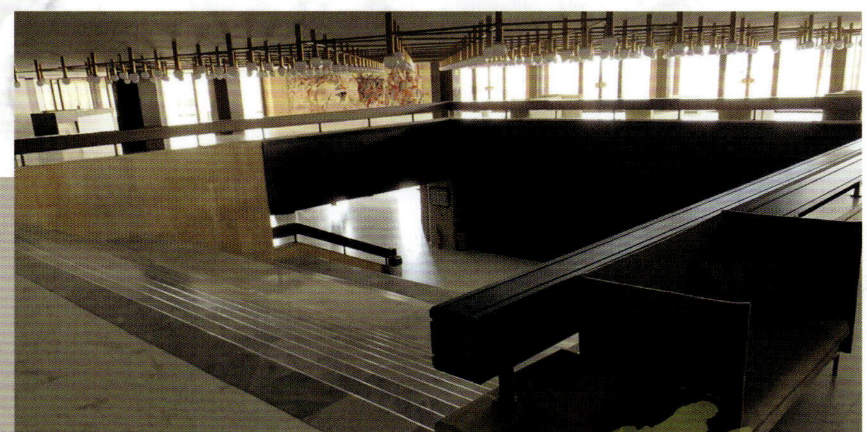

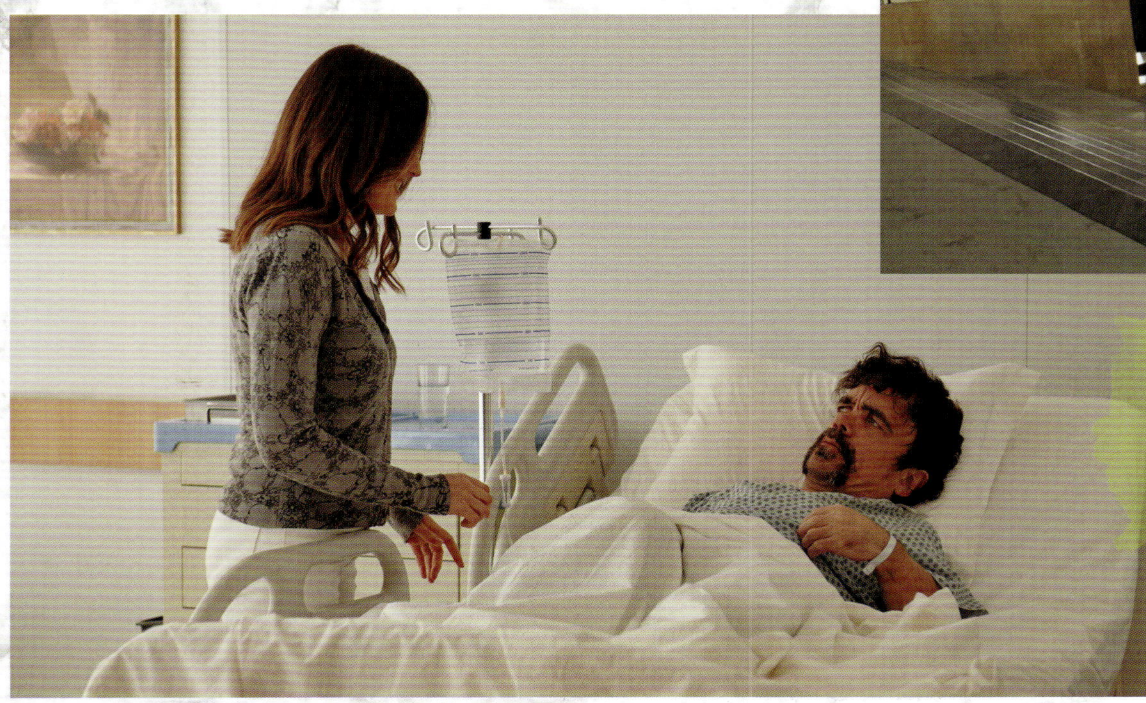

Top Concept art floorplans for Winston/Toxie's hospital room.

Left Winston encounters a vision of Shelly.

Above The location for the hospital shared features with the auditorium, specifically its globe-like lamps.

THE TROMAVILLE STRIP

St. Roma's Village—better known by its unofficial name of Tromaville—is far and away *The Toxic Avenger*'s most important location. Particularly The Strip that runs down the town's centre, like the spine of the community. It is here that Winston/Toxie lives, and it is the place he must defend and protect, aiming to rid it of the pernicious influence of Bob Garbinger's B.T.H., much like Batman had to cleanse Gotham City of its corruption. Although, this is no Gotham.

"It's a place that's past its prime," says Garcia. "It's fallen on some hard times. It's sort of an amalgamation of struggling small towns everywhere, but with a very distinctive twist to it."

While there is a "decaying vibe" to Tromaville, Blair felt it was important not to make the town feel too depressing. "I think you can very easily veer into misery porn," he says. "We wanted to convey the idea that, yeah, it's a little rough around the edges, but as a viewer—maybe not as a citizen—you would want to return to Tromaville. The reference we used a lot was *Repo Man*, which takes place in a fictional city. It's got all these sleazy, weird sort of details, but it always feels very fun to return to."

While Lloyd Kaufman and Michael Herz had created their 1984 Tromaville on the streets of Jersey City and Boonton, New Jersey, Legendary gave Blair an entire backlot to play with, at German Studios in Sofia, Bulgaria, where they had just previously shot the horror sequel/reboot *The Texas Chainsaw Massacre*. "Given the good crew experience we had there, and the ability it gave us to build our own Tromaville, it was a good turnkey solution," Garcia explains.

Most usefully, the backlot already contained a standing street set rendered in wood and polystyrene brick, which had originally been built for 2018 action thriller *The Hurricane Heist*, and was repurposed by Legendary for *The Texas Chainsaw Massacre*. "It's essentially one street, but at each end the road kind of dog-legs off," explains Cameron. "In its basic form, it was

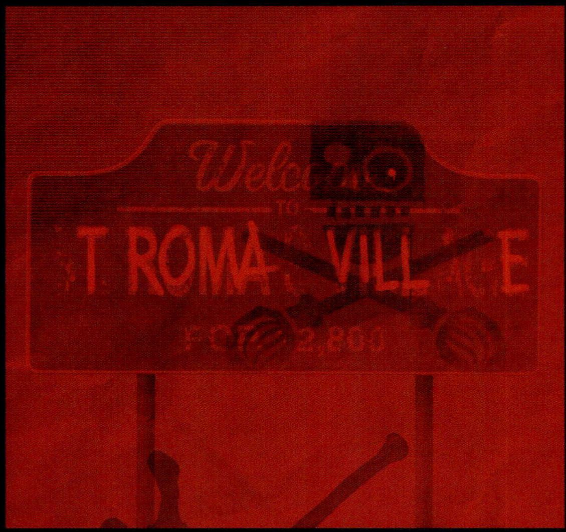

Above Concept art for the town sign.

Below Concept art of the Tromaville strip.

Below left A panel from the comic-book series *Watchmen*, which was an inspiration for Blair and Cameron's Tromaville.

Opposite page Some fictional reference used by Cameron to design the Tromaville Strip.

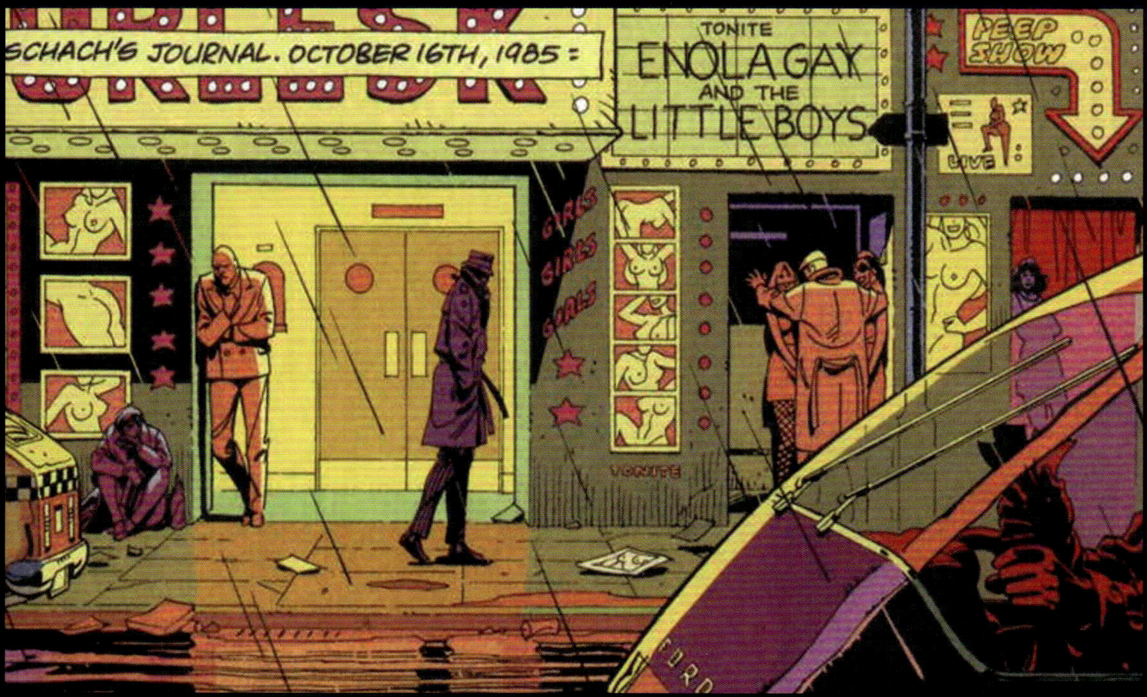

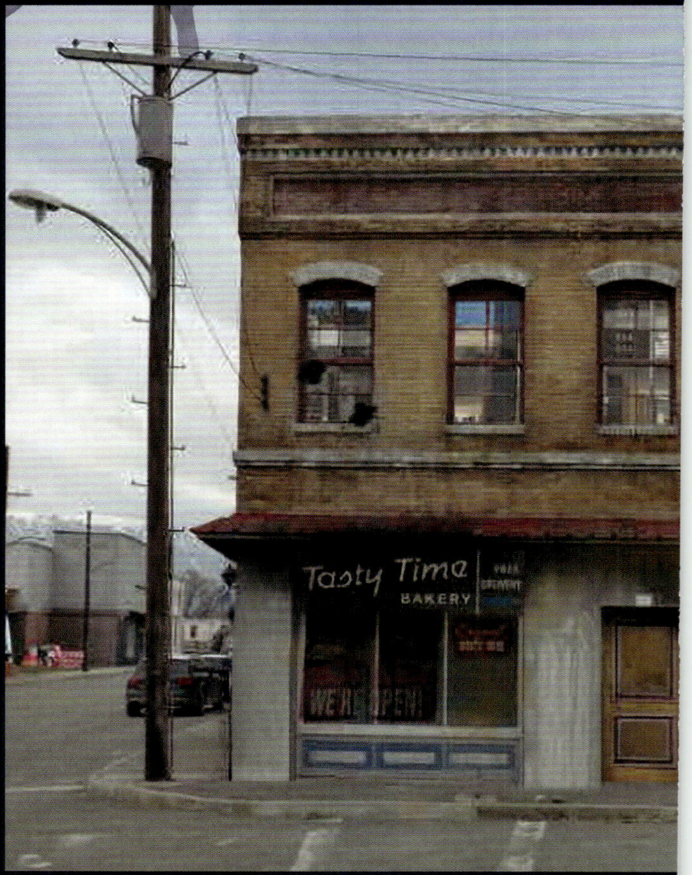

already there, but in *Texas Chainsaw* it was a deserted town, so we had to pump life into it. It looks completely different now; in fact, we completely changed some of the facades."

Given Blair's previous movie, *I Don't Feel at Home in This World Anymore*, was shot primarily on location and with a much smaller budget, working to such a scale was an exciting new experience. "It was completely insane," he admits. "Very difficult to get my head around. Luckily there were so many small-picture things to deal with, there wasn't an opportunity to really get my mind blown about the big picture. Early on, there were discussions about this maybe being more of a location-driven movie, but we felt that even if we found an existing location where we could shoot up and down a whole street, there would still be this layer of art department work that would have to happen. We figured we might as well go the backlot route. That's how the choice of filming in

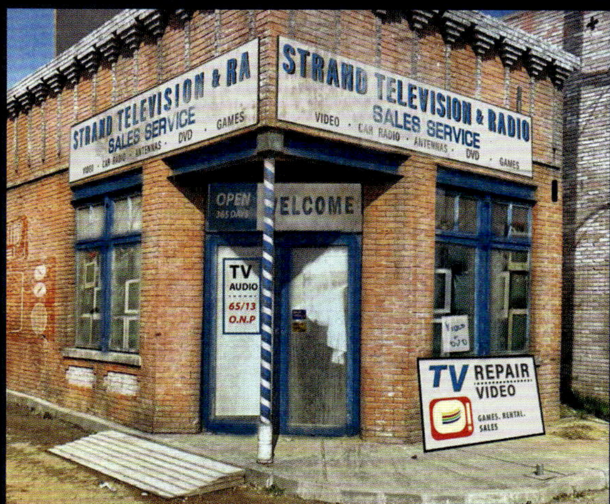

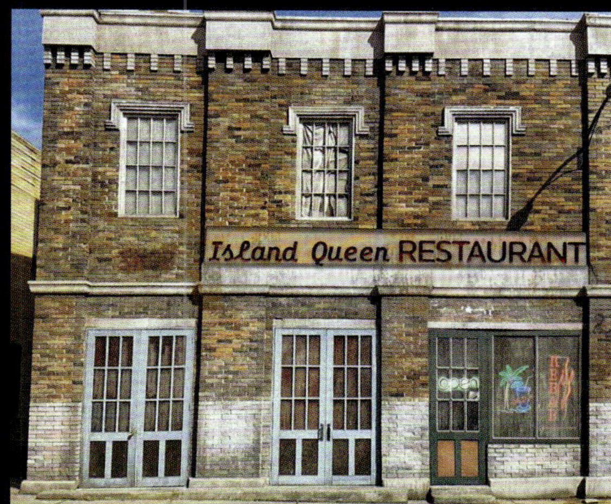

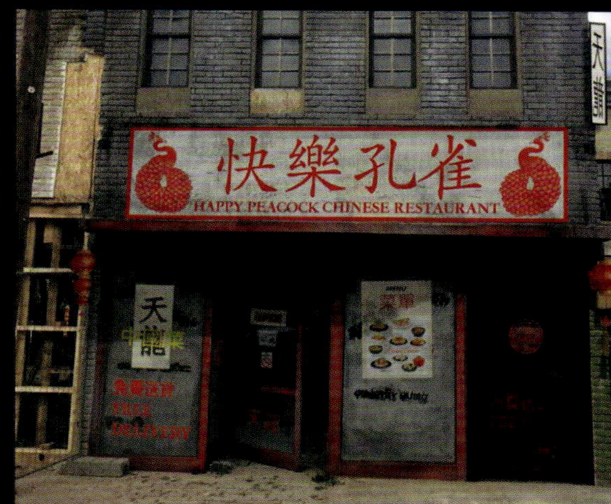

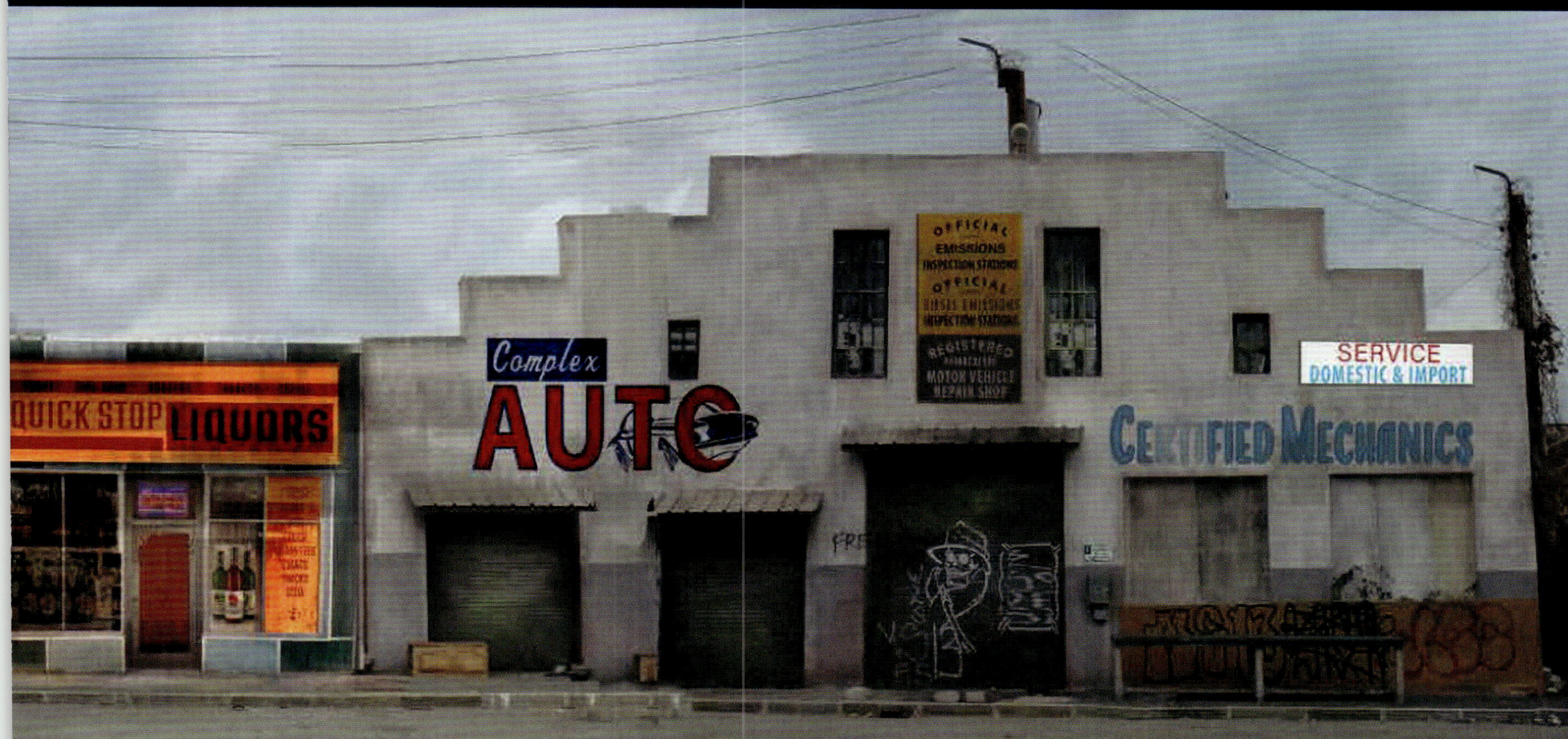

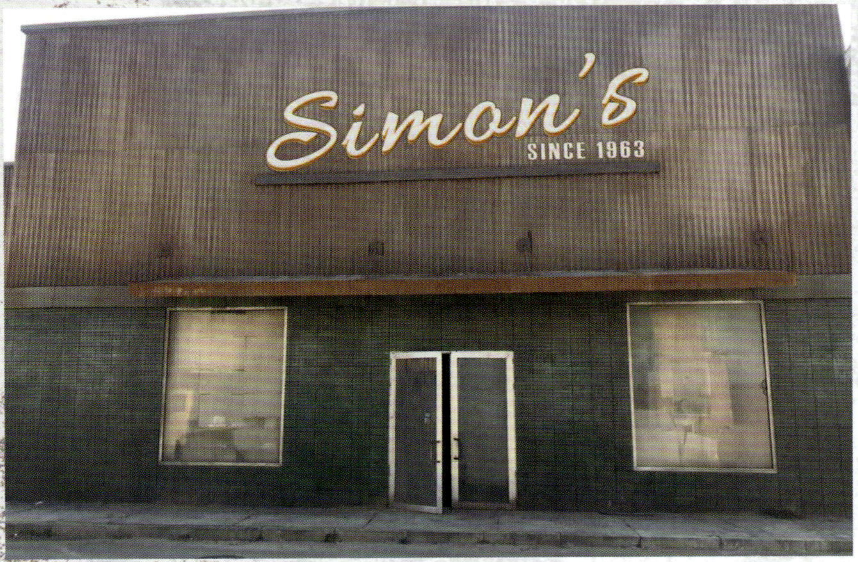

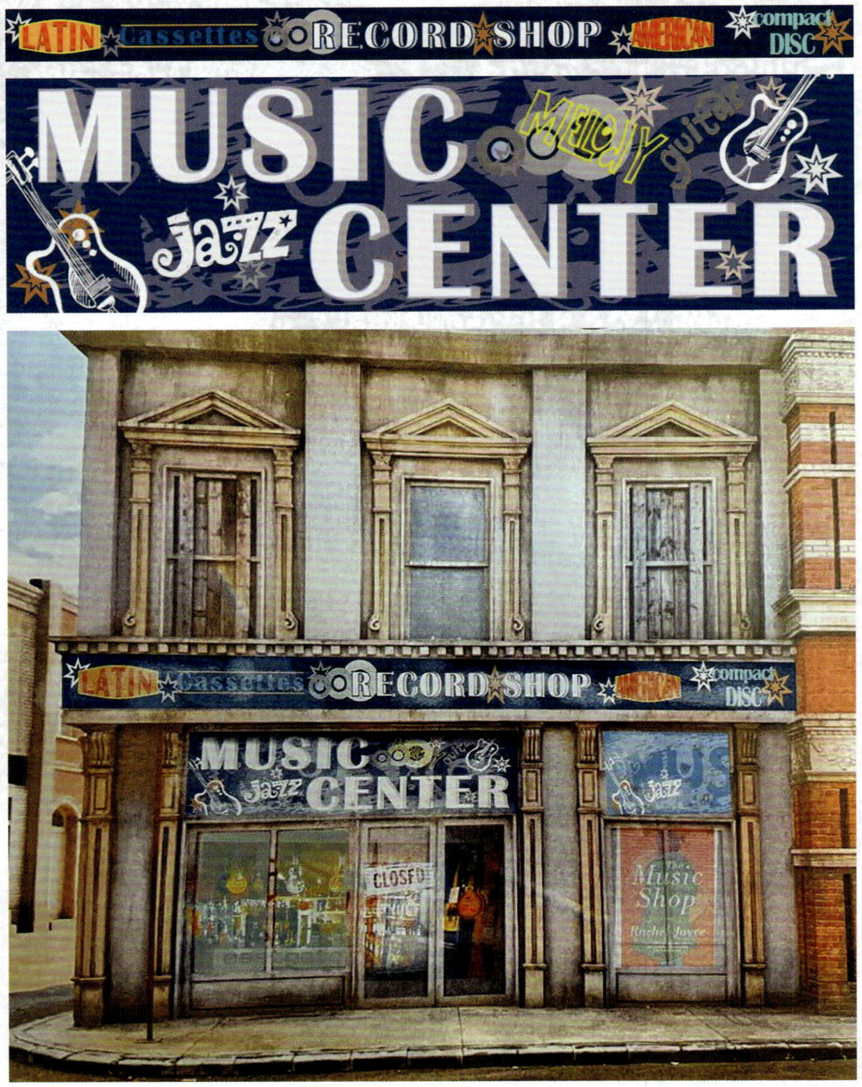

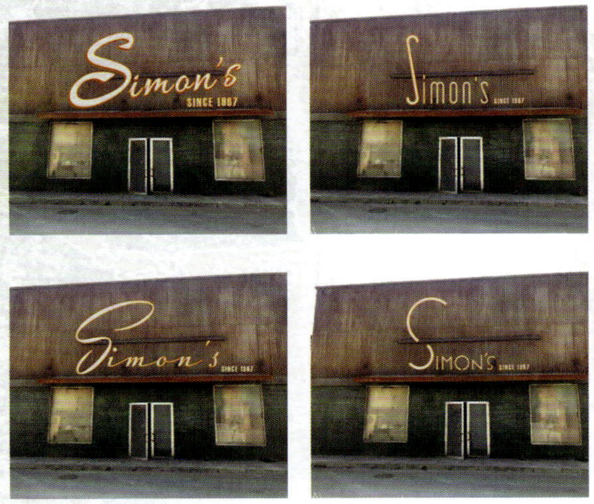

Above & right The production team experimented with different typefaces for a particular shop called Simon's, located on the Tromaville Strip.

Right Concept art for a Tromaville music store.

Bulgaria clarified the way to get it done."

Dinklage was impressed by the results. "It reminded me of what it must have been like back in the old Hollywood days where you'd turn a corner and suddenly you're in the Old West, with all the storefronts and all that," he says.

Of course, Tromaville is not the Old West, though its Strip does have an intentionally retro feel. Cameron was keen to give it a 1970s texture — similar to New York during that era, but also the Philadelphia setting of the first *Rocky* movie. "I love the hand-painted signs and that more home-made look and individuality the shops had then, rather than nowadays when everything looks the same," he says. There is also plenty of neon, in particular the flashing red sign for Belgoody Bail Bonds, adjacent to Winston's apartment. This is partly a reference for fans (Peter Belgoody is the town mayor in the original *Toxic Avenger*), but also a kind of visual lodestone for Toxie and the audience.

"There's a point later in the movie where he sees the sign and realizes if he heads towards Belgoody Bail Bonds, he could just go home," Blair explains. "But he chooses instead to stand up to the bad guys that are holding hostages in the restaurant. That's a little bit of an Easter egg, but it's also meant to orient you to where Toxie is in the neighbourhood."

Precisely where in America Tromaville itself is oriented was a matter of much discussion during the early stages of production. "When we first started, it was decided this was kind of a nondescript place in the States," says Cameron; in addition to '70s New York and Philadelphia, Portland, Oregon was mentioned as a key reference. Then, about three weeks into production, it was decided that St. Roma's Village would, in a nod to the original Tromaville, be based in New Jersey. Or at least a scuzzy, sleazy, alternate take on the Garden State. "We had to change all the number plates on the cars," the production designer laughs.

The final visual element that needed to be woven into Tromaville was the impact of B.T.H. on the community. Although, how that evidenced itself required a little finessing. "Winston and Wade are almost isolated in this environment where they're surrounded by people who are under the influence of B.T.H.," explains Cameron. Originally, there were to be citizens on the street wearing bizarre B.T.H. contraption-products, such as a "Belly Rip" corset (supposedly designed to slim the fuller figure) and the "Mental Stim", which looks like a steampunk sex toy on a head rig. Cameron went as far as designing these strange devices, but, "the studio said, 'Actually this might be too much.'" So, while less fantastical B.T.H. products still litter the film's background and foreground, from headache medicine ("Fast, Safe B.T.H. Pain Relief For Everyone") to orange juice, Cameron opted for a rather more subtle approach.

"It is definitely the case that the town is under this kind of evil spell," he says. "So the colour blue that we used in the factory is actually in the street as well. There are buildings that are painted blue, giving the sense that B.T.H. is physically seeping into this world."

"It reminded me of what it must have been like back in the old Hollywood days where you'd turn a corner and suddenly you're in the Old West, with all the storefronts."

– PETER DINKLAGE, Actor

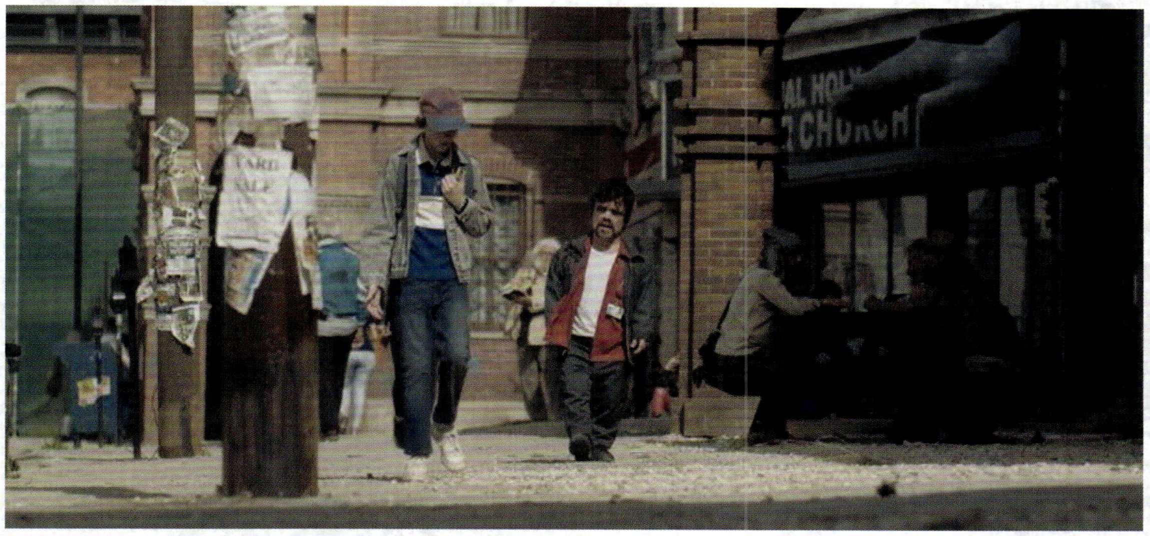

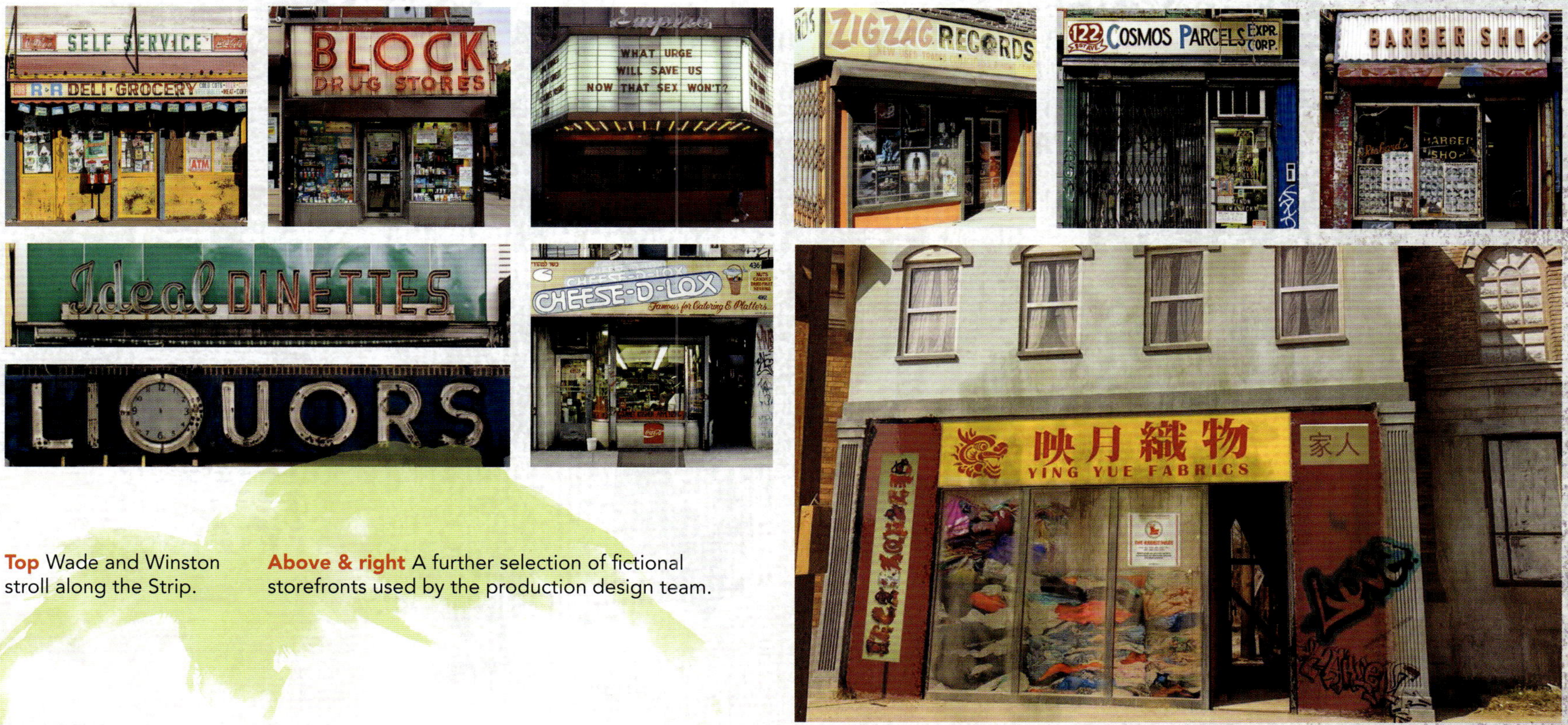

Top Wade and Winston stroll along the Strip.

Above & right A further selection of fictional storefronts used by the production design team.

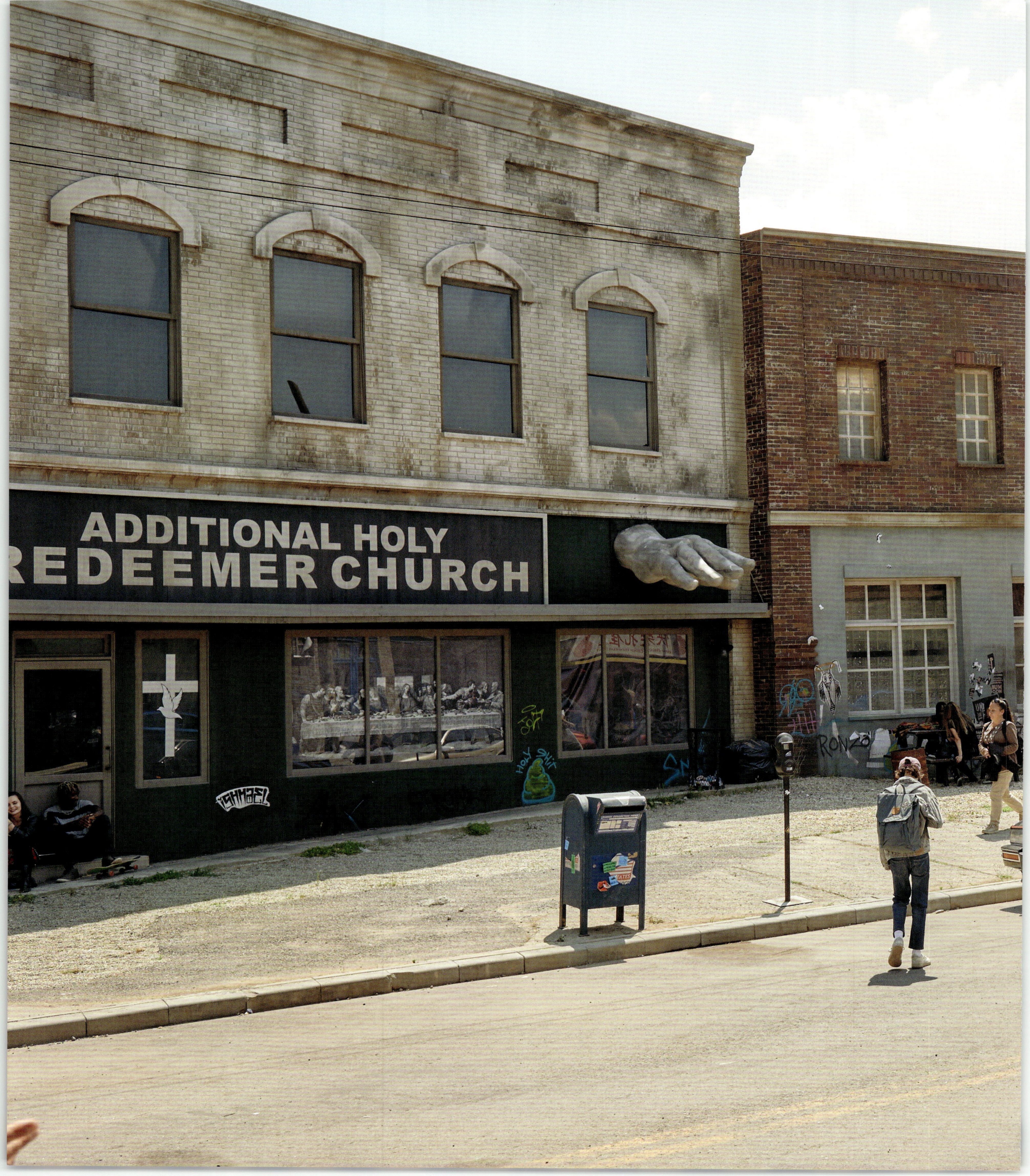
ADDITIONAL HOLY
REDEEMER CHURCH

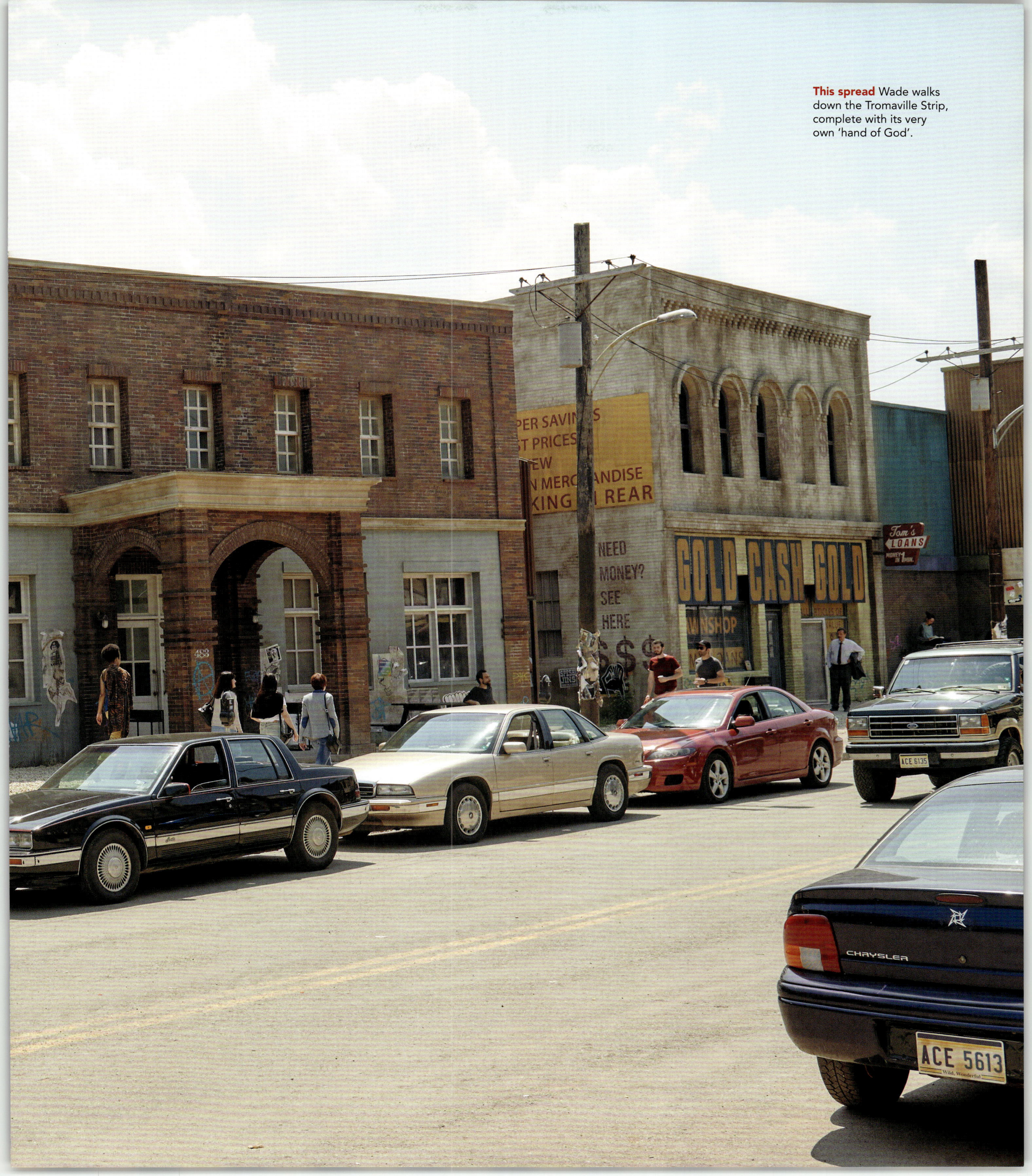

This spread Wade walks down the Tromaville Strip, complete with its very own 'hand of God'.

THE KILLER NUTZ

When Macon Blair returned to the original *Toxic Avenger* during the scriptwriting process, one thing he noted was how colorful and extreme its bad guys were. They often wore elaborate face paint and almost clownish costumes, while in the sequels they became more bizarre and animalistic; one foe in *The Toxic Avenger Part II* inexplicably had the face of a dog. (The reasons why were never revealed.) Blair wondered how he could introduce his own take on such malevolent outlandishness, while keeping it, to some degree, grounded. "Not that we were being realistic this time around," he insists, "but we wanted things at least to have a reason, as opposed to some bad guy showing up who happens to have safety pins in their nose, or whatever extreme detail it's going to be."

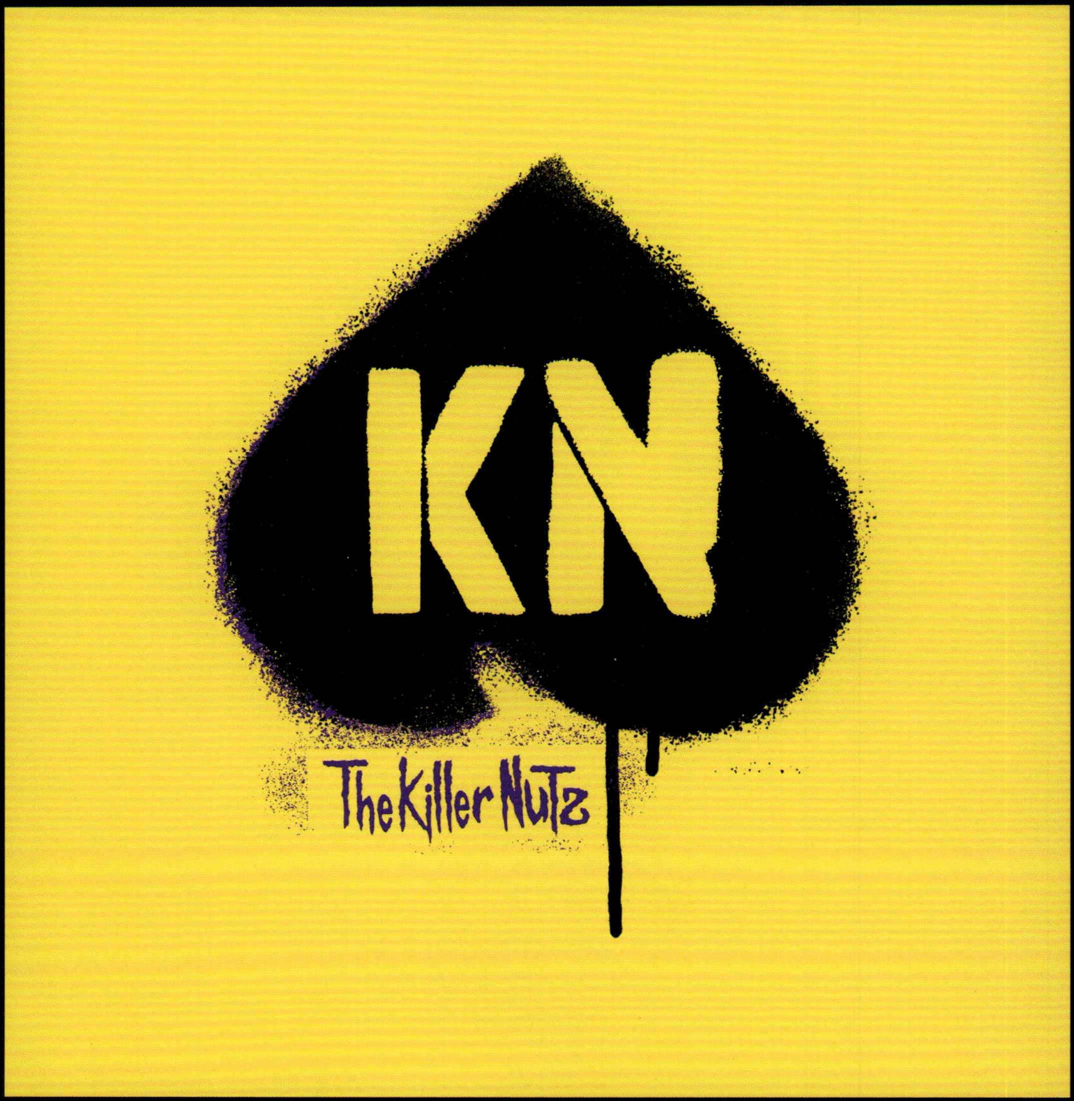

He was also keen to include a core group of villains who would echo the gang in *RoboCop*, a huge influence on Blair while making this film. "One of them's a heavy metal guy, and one of them's a disco guy, and then you have Clarence (Kurtwood Smith), who is kind of the evil, geeky brain guy. They all have this little function to fill." At the same time, Blair knew he wanted music to feature prominently in the movie, and that at some point Toxie would have a musical number. As those two strands entwined in his mind, he started to envision this gang of villains as a rock band.

"I thought about bands that have this very extreme, threatening persona that's part of their stagecraft. From Alice Cooper and Kiss, up to Slipknot and Ghost, it's a long tradition. What made me chuckle at the time was the idea of a band that has this sinister and evil performative aspect, but who turn out to be *literally* sinister and evil. When they sing about being crazy and psychotic, it's not stagecraft. They are actual professional killers who are also aspiring musicians. This idea of a rock and roll band that moonlights as contract assassins just made me laugh."

After much scribbling in a notebook, drawing doodles of costume ideas and writing down "cheesy lyrics," Blair ultimately formed The Killer Nutz: the "Insane Clown Posse/Slipknot/Limp Bizkit wannabe-supergroup," who stalk and smash their way through the film, wreaking murder and mayhem…

This spread Production-created artwork for Tromaville's biggest – and baddest – band.

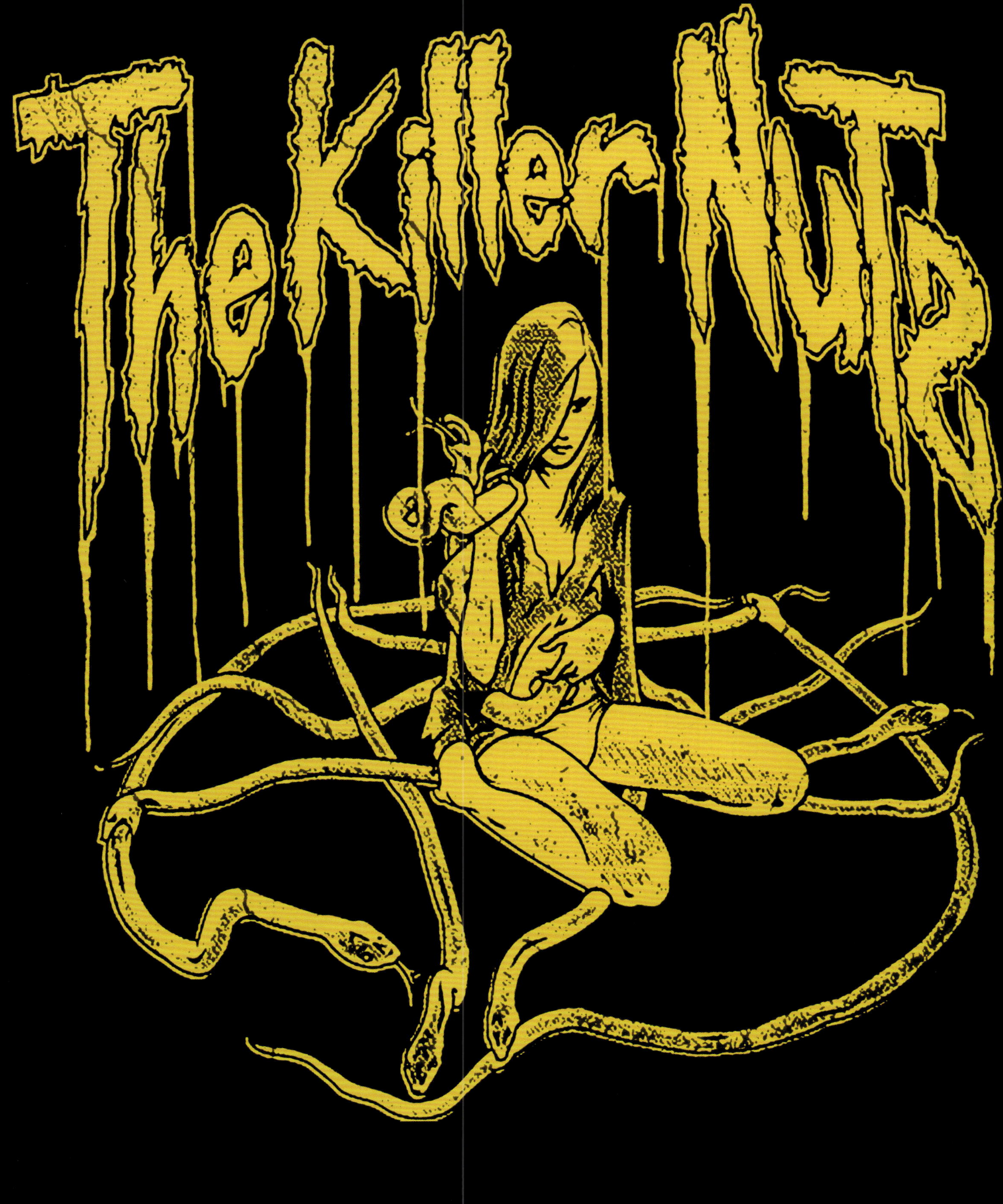
The Killer Nutz

This spread The Killer Nutz – a motley crew.

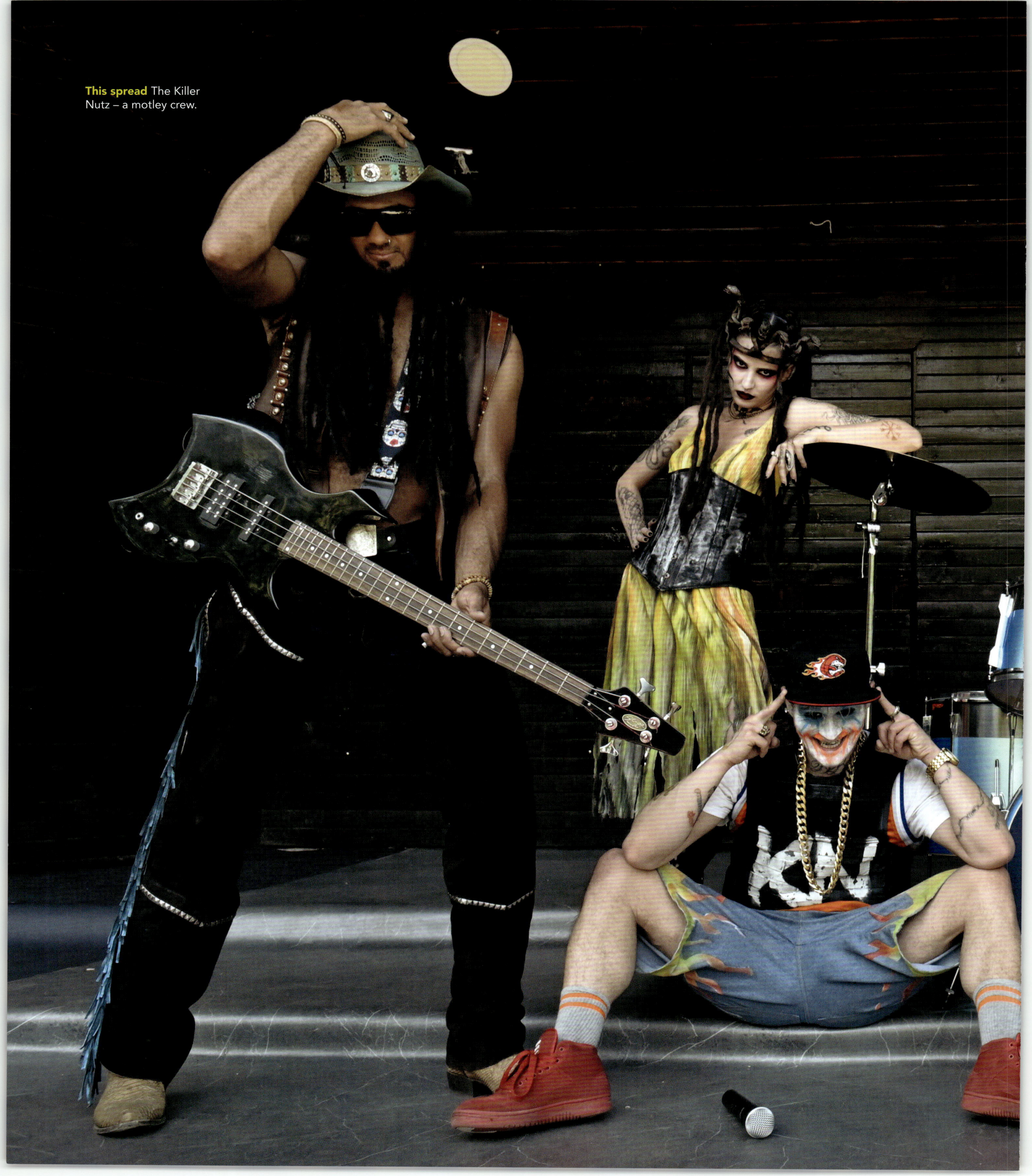

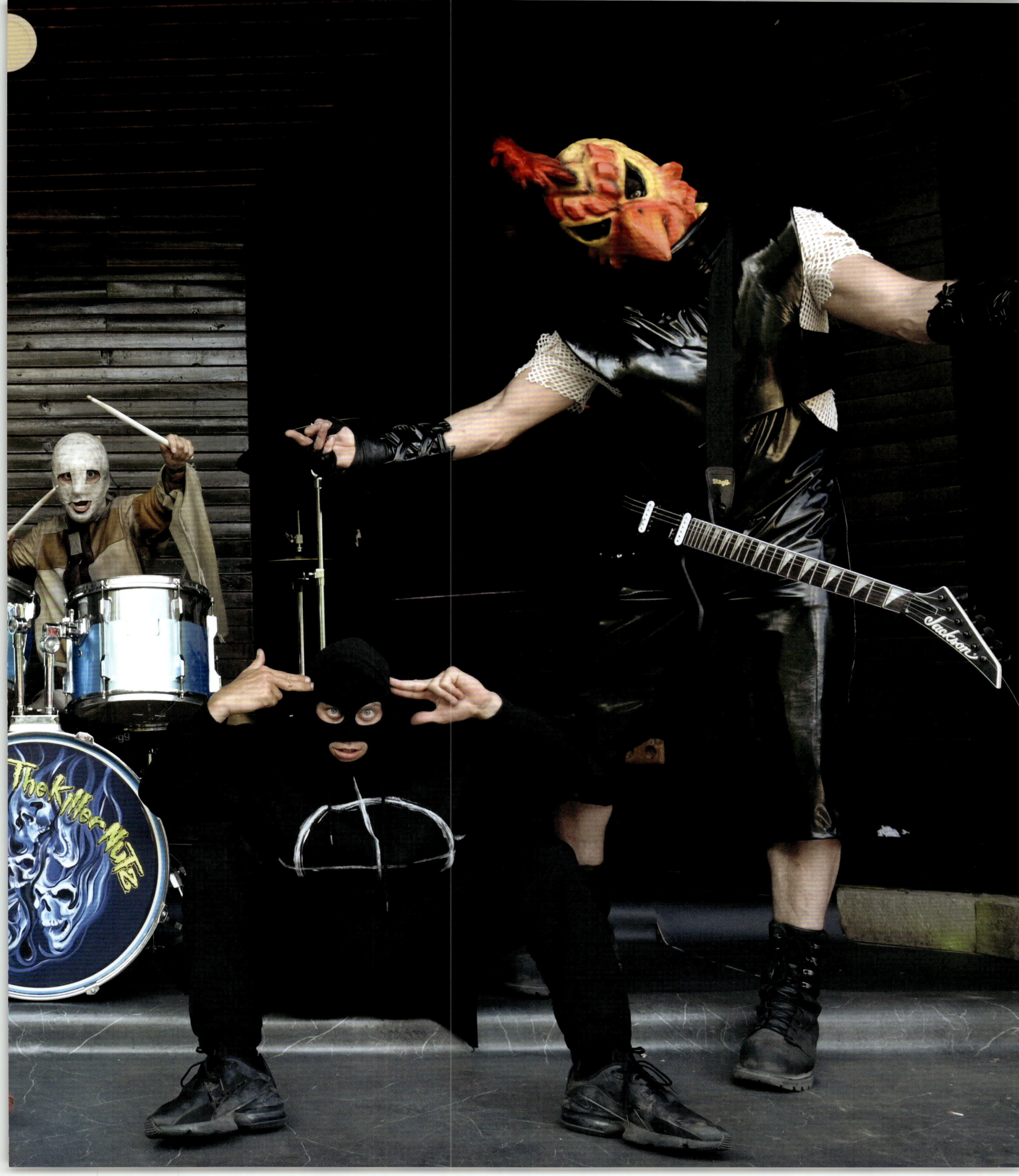
The Killer NUTz
Jackson

BUDD BERSERK

(VOCALS) PLAYED BY JULIAN KOSTOV

Envisioned in the script as "The Joker as white-guy frat rapper," Budd Berserk is the Killer Nutz' frontman and leader. Drawing inspiration from the likes of Detroit hip-hop duo Insane Clown Posse and popular rap-rock outfit Limp Bizkit, Porter appropriately decked him out in a basketball jersey, a pair of fire-decorated shorts, and a graffiti-scrawled bulletproof vest. "He's meant to be a pretty literal reference to those types of bands," she says.

Like all but one of the Nutz members, Budd was drawn from a pool of local, Bulgarian talent. "Julian Kostov is a phenomenal actor," says Garcia. "He's fantastic. He really brought that character to life." A former professional swimmer, Kostov has made small-screen appearances in the likes of Sky One's *A Discovery of Witches* and Netflix's *Shadow and Bone*, and he's also starred in British war drama *Another Mother's Son*, the Gerard Butler-starring *London Has Fallen*, and *Texas Chain Saw Massacre* prequel *Leatherface*.

The role of Budd is one Kostov closely related to—thankfully on the musical side of the character's personality, rather than his murderous side (though Kostov was originally inspired to start acting by Heath Ledger's astonishing turn as the Joker in *The Dark Knight*). During auditions, he revealed his aspirations to be a rapper, so he held nothing back on set, Blair reports.

"He threw everything of himself into that part. When we were between setups, he'd come up to me and say, 'I wrote these other songs!' and I'm like, 'Okay man, let's talk about it at wrap. I'm trying to shoot this shot over here,'" the director laughs. "But he was constantly saying, 'What if we do this? Would I do that?' He was really invested in the character, which was a lot of fun to harness."

Below Bulgarian actor Julian Kostov as the Killer Nutz frontman, proficient with both gun and mic.

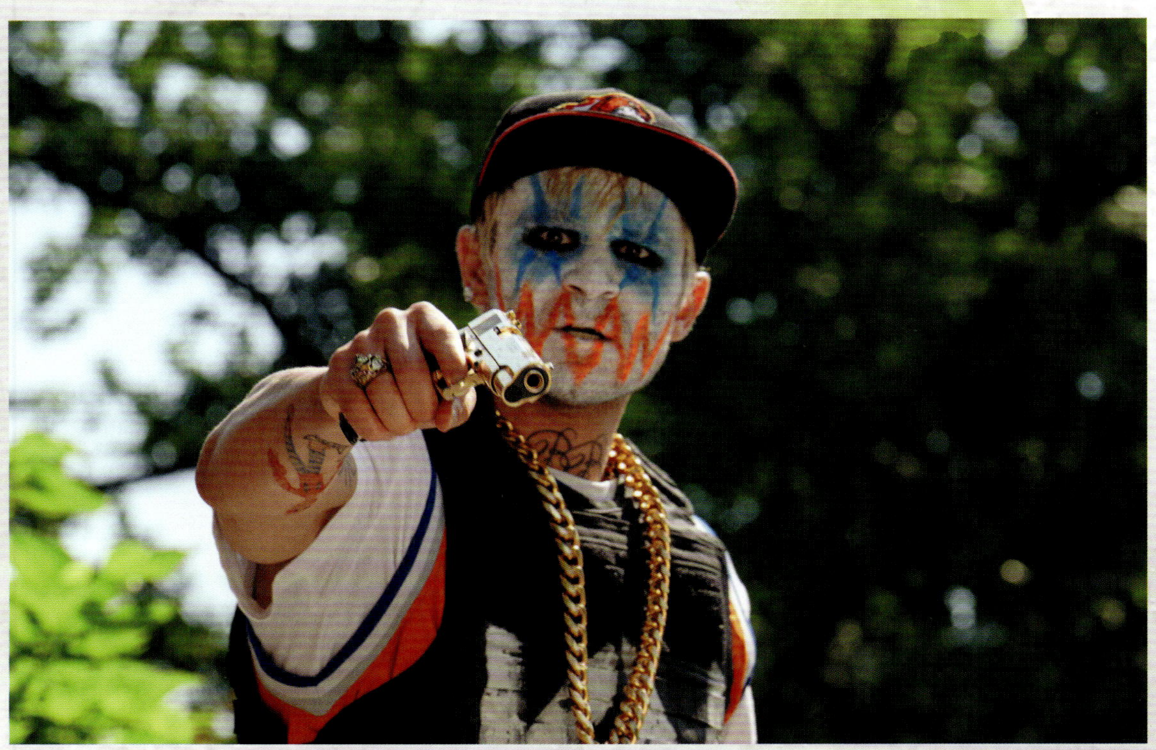

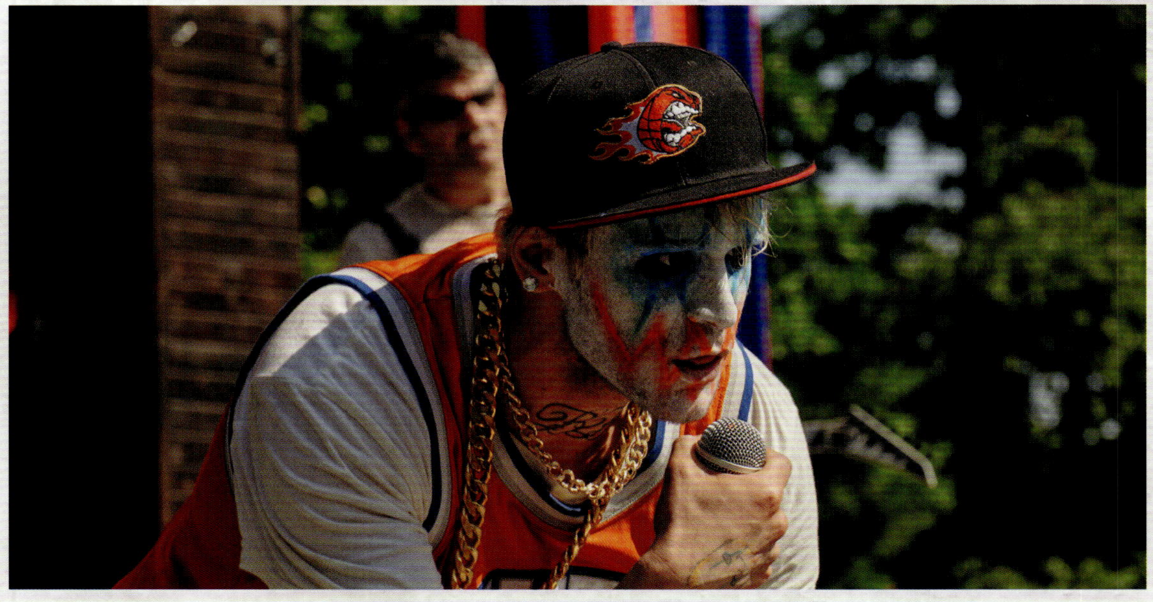

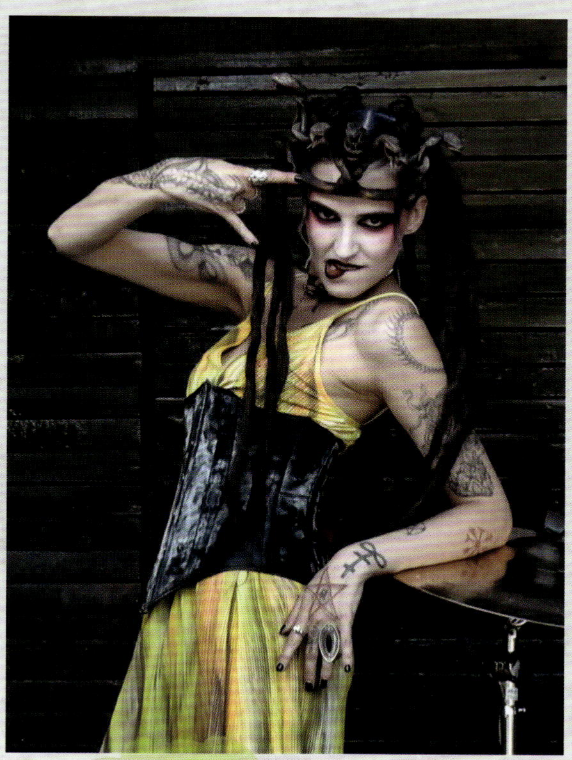

DJ COOL CTHULU

(TURNTABLES & KEYS)
PLAYED BY NEEDA SPASOVA

The Killer Nutz' DJ and keyboardist is named after the tentacled, demonic entity Cthulhu, created by horror visionary H.P. Lovecraft, so it's unsurprising to learn from Blair that she brings "black magic and hexes and curses to the band." In the script, he pithily describes her as "a demonic river witch," and this outline gave Porter all the inspiration she needed to conjure this marshy miscreant (played by newcomer Needa Spasova) into reality. "It spiralled from there," she says. "She looks like a swamp creature!"

Similar to Budd Berserk, DJ Cool Cthulu's look references hip hop's eccentric fringe, in particular South African act Die Antwoord, but it also taps into Greek mythology. "She has a crown that she wears when she performs, which is made from rubber snakes," Porter says. "So there is a little bit of a Medusa vibe. It was fun, playing with her witchy rocker style."

Above Spasova as the Nutz' "witchy rocker".

Below Nwamerue as "the hot one".

VENUS DEVALERO

(BASS)
PLAYED BY DUKE NWAMERUE

Given the band is so packed with Troma-appropriate bizarros, Blair felt that he needed "a hot guy" to provide a little visual balance. "So that was Venus. Venus was the hot one."

He found his Venus in Bulgarian actor Duke Nwamerue, who delivered "a very charming, charismatic audition." Nwamerue is primarily a stunt performer, whose credits include *Hitman's Wife's Bodyguard* and Netflix show *The Witcher*, so he is more than just a pretty face. Though, much to Venus' chagrin in the movie, he doesn't get to do any parkour.

"We made him a little bit of a cowboy, with a slight Kid Rock vibe," explains Porter, who once again took a single-line description in Blair's script—"Rasta-cowboy Lothario, long braided goatee, nip rings" — and ran with it. "He's got some chaps, a big hat, and we made him this leather vest which has a skeleton embossed on the back. He also has sunglasses that he wears most of the time. Douchey sunglasses."

As for that elaborate goatee, it ultimately proves to be Venus' downfall, when Toxie throttles him with it during the Troma Fest sequence. Turns out looks *can* kill.

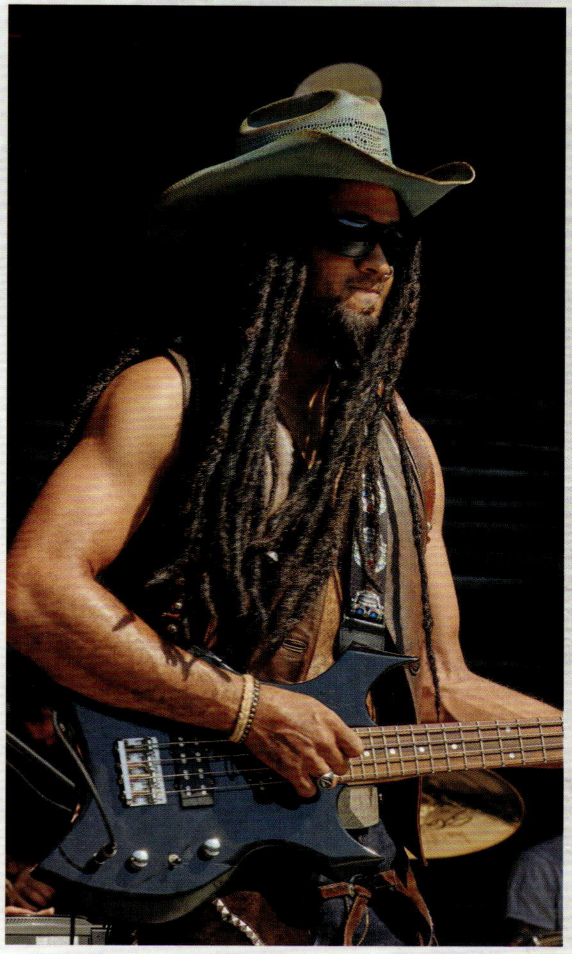

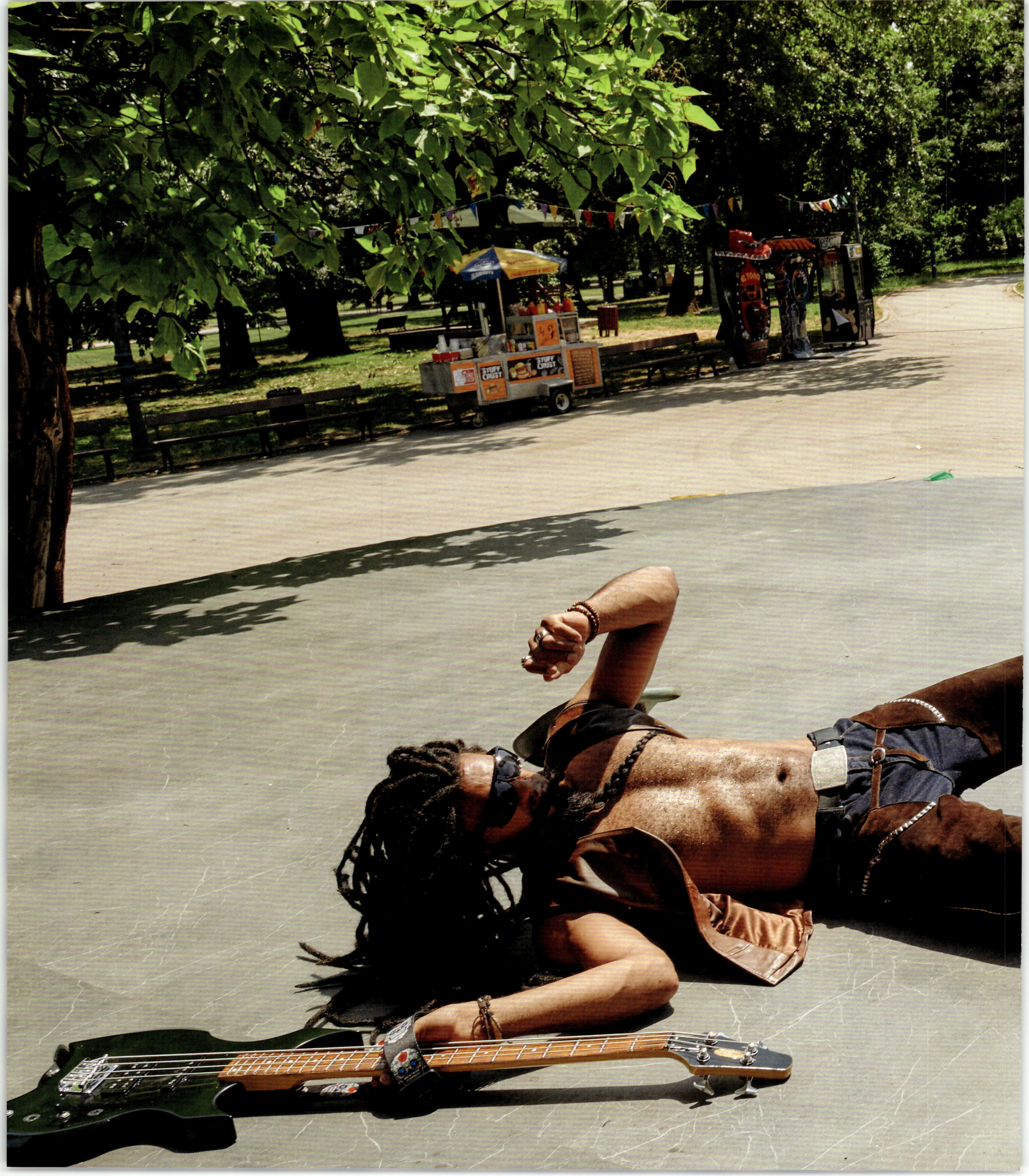
STUFF CRUST
STUFF CRUST

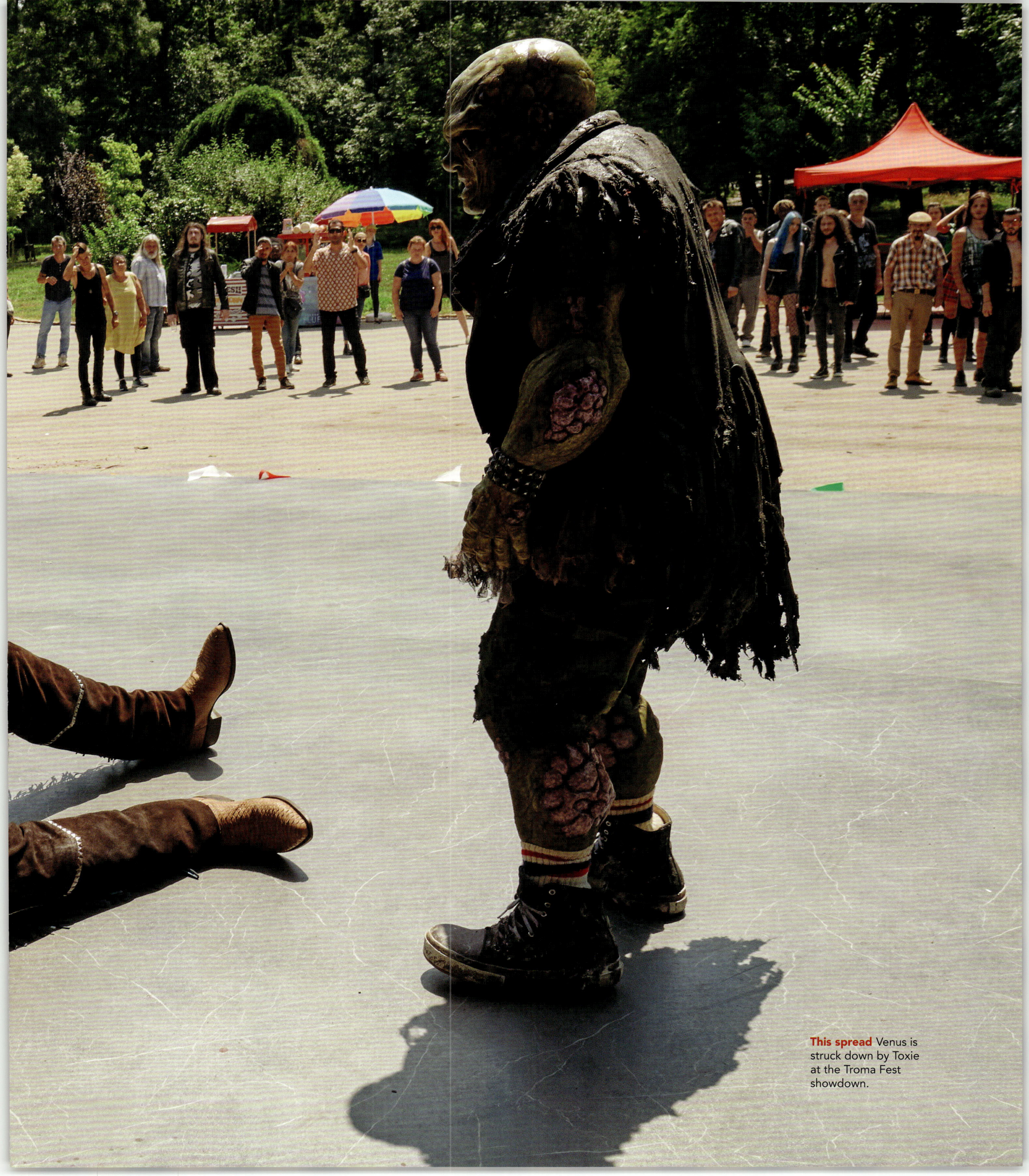

This spread Venus is struck down by Toxie at the Troma Fest showdown.

HIM UNDER THE HOOD

(MYSTERIOUS GUITAR SAVANT)
PLAYED BY SPENCER WILDING

The Killer Nutz's most enigmatic, strange and imposing member is the guitarist known only as Him Under The Hood, played by Welsh actor and former pro-kickboxer Spencer Wilding (who also plays Monster Garbinger and was one of the actors to play Darth Vader in *Rogue One: A Star Wars Story*). "Him Under The Hood is the muscle," explains Blair, who in creating this looming masked figure was thinking of "wilfully anonymous musicians" in real-life, citing rock guitarist Buckethead and the luchador-mask-wearing HeWhoCannotBeNamed from punk outfit the Dwarves. However, neither of them went quite so far as Him Under The Hood, who sports an elaborate, evil-looking rooster headpiece.

"We had the mask made in Bulgaria and designed it to be simultaneously scary and funny," reveals Porter. "We looked at some different store-bought chicken heads as reference—lots of chicken masks exist in the world—but we wanted to make it specific to this band. So then I thought of giving it a mohawk and making the facial expression much more menacing."

But… why a chicken?

Blair was partly inspired by the 2006 Troma movie *Poultrygeist*. "But mainly it was just wanting him to have an animal mask on. At one point it was going to be a monkey or gorilla mask, but there was something about a chicken which seemed like, in those early scenes, it could be legitimately frightening or disarming. Like, 'Wait. What type of movie is this?' It just seemed visually fun and interesting."

Towards the end of the movie, things get even weirder with this character. During

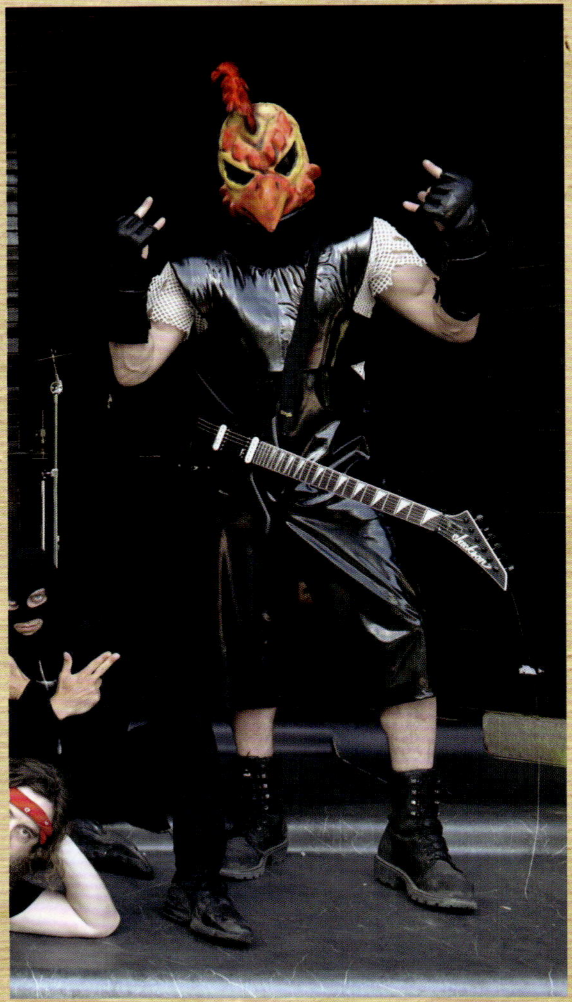

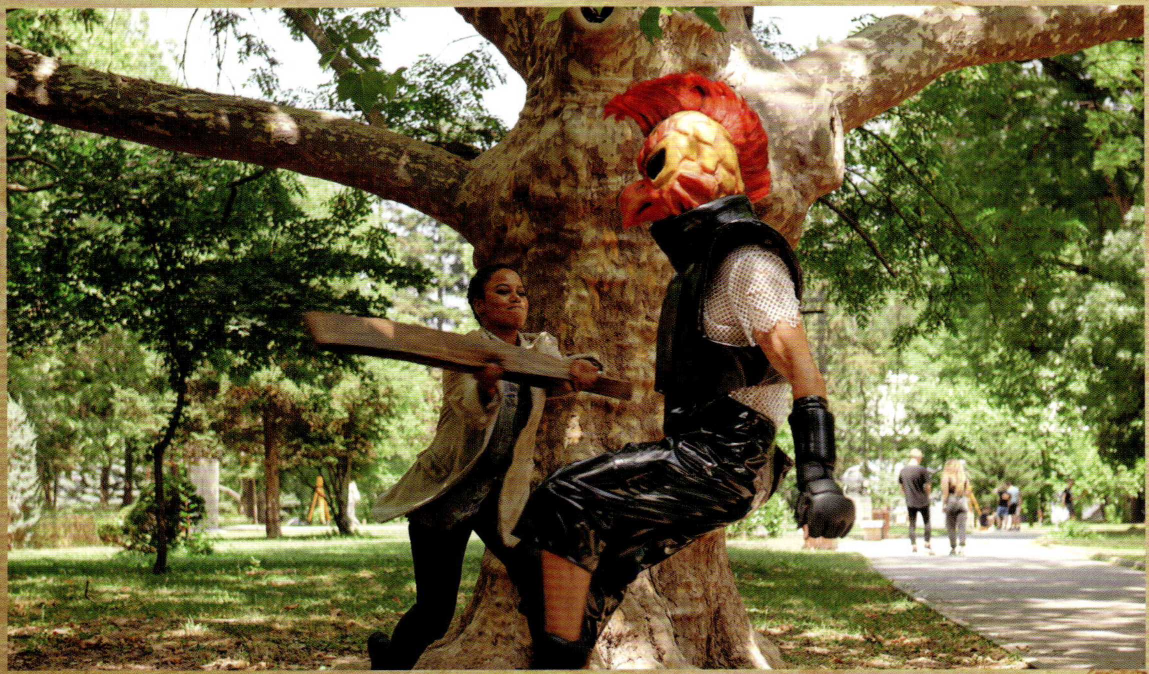

"We had the mask made in Bulgaria and designed it to be simultaneously scary and funny."

– VANESSA PORTER,
Costume Designer

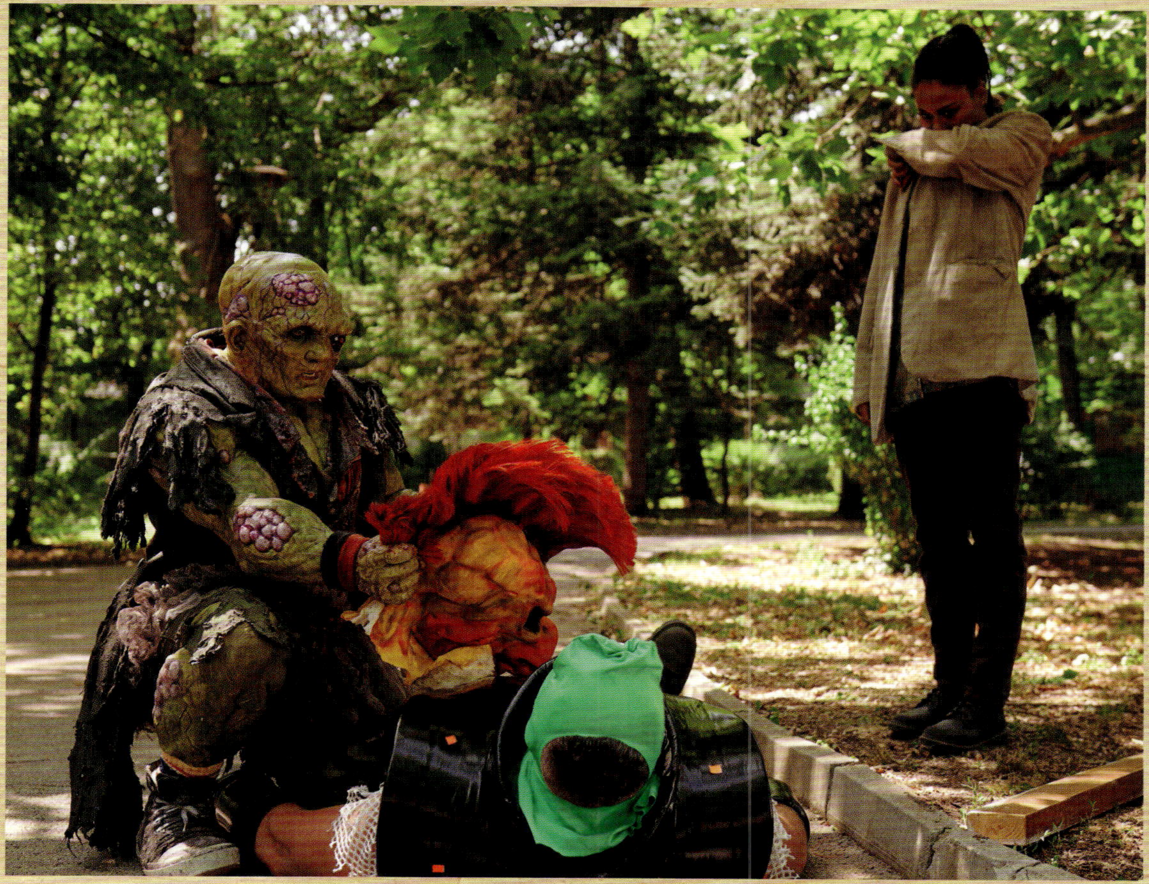

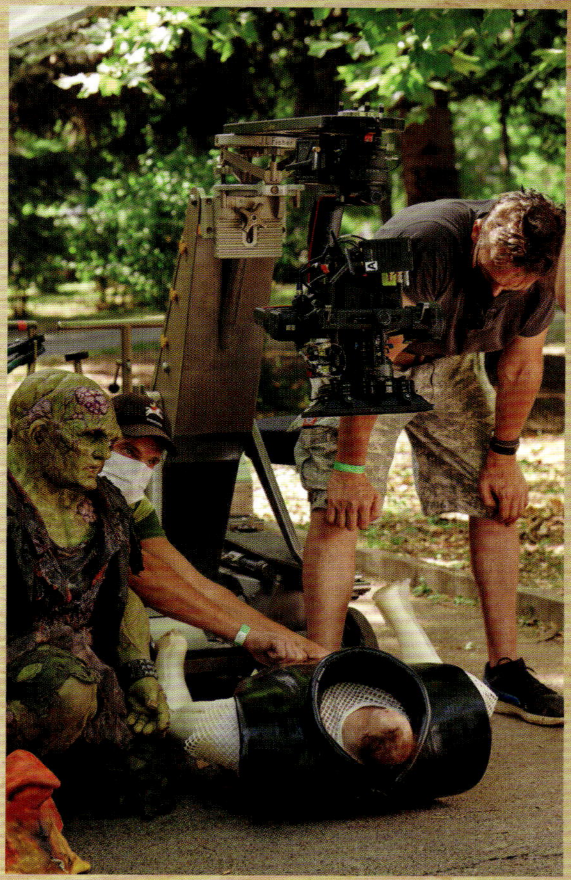

the Troma Fest battle sequence, his mask is knocked away revealing that, underneath, he has the head of a baby. "Not 'baby-like'," Blair notes in the script. "He literally has the head of a 12-month-old child."

Which begs another, bigger question: why a *baby's head*?

"Hard to answer," admits Blair. "No particular reason other than a punchline. As I was writing, it started to feel like if you don't answer the question of what's under the mask, at some point people will think, 'Oh, I guess it's just a mysterious guy'. But we've set up this idea that these chemicals Garbinger is putting out into the world are causing these awful side effects. So I figured, 'What would I enjoy the most when they finally rip the mask off?'" His main inspiration was the character of Blaster in 1985 *Mad Max* sequel *Beyond Thunderdome*. "His helmet comes off and he's got this childlike face under there, when you were expecting him to be more of a brute. It's that sort of thing, but I wanted it to be more of a gag, so I thought, 'Let's have a puppet baby head.'"

Ritvo says the baby-head reveal is one of his favourite parts of the movie (after the mutant bird) and confirms the head itself was supplied by Millennium FX, who created the Toxie and Monster-Garbinger suits. "It was from a different film, but they augmented it for us and shipped it over from England. No one knew what this thing was going to look like until it showed up on set the day before we shot it. The moment I saw it, I thought it was perfect. It reminds me of the little mutant guy in *Total Recall*."

Provided on a shoulder bust, the puppet head was used primarily for close-ups. For wide shots, Wilding wore a green mask, allowing Ritvo's team to digitally erase his real head and replace it with the baby's, whose movements were matched as closely as possible to the actor's. However, one moment, where the exposed Him Under The Hood has to sit up in a single shot, required some extra effort. "There are a lot of funny outtakes with me and the first assistant director (Derek Peterson) on the ground trying to puppeteer this crazy baby's head," Ritvo laughs. "So yeah, it's all practical. It looks amazing. And very disturbing."

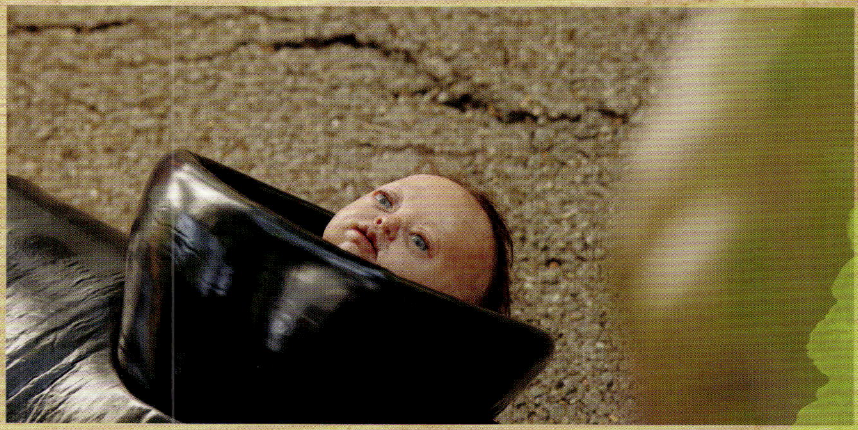

Above In some scenes, Wilding had to have his head covered by a green mask, so that it could be digitally replaced with a CG baby head.

Left Him Under The Hood's disturbing baby head was provided by Millennium FX.

Opposite page J.J. takes on Him Under The Hood.

ZODIAC 3000

(THE HYPE MAN)
PLAYED BY MAKO-DIMITAR BOZHILOV

Not every member of a band has to play something. Take dancer Ben Carr from Boston ska-punk act the Mighty Mighty Bosstones, for example. Or Bez from Madchester band The Happy Mondays (though he did shake some maracas). The Killer Nutz have their own, non-instrumentalist equivalent in Zodiac 3000: "a creep in a black ski mask."

In terms of his unsettling look, the clue to his origin is in his name. "We referenced some drawings of the Zodiac Killer," says Porter, referring to the never-identified serial killer who terrorized Northern California during the late 1960s. "He had a drawing on his chest: a white circle with lines through it. So we made a t-shirt with that drawing on it."

Originally, Blair just saw Zodiac as someone who "sometimes shakes a tambourine," but when breakdancing champ Mako-Dimitar Bozhilov revealed his b-boy skills during his winning audition for the part, Zodiac 3000 became a far more agile performer: a ruthless hitman who can do headspins and helicopters.

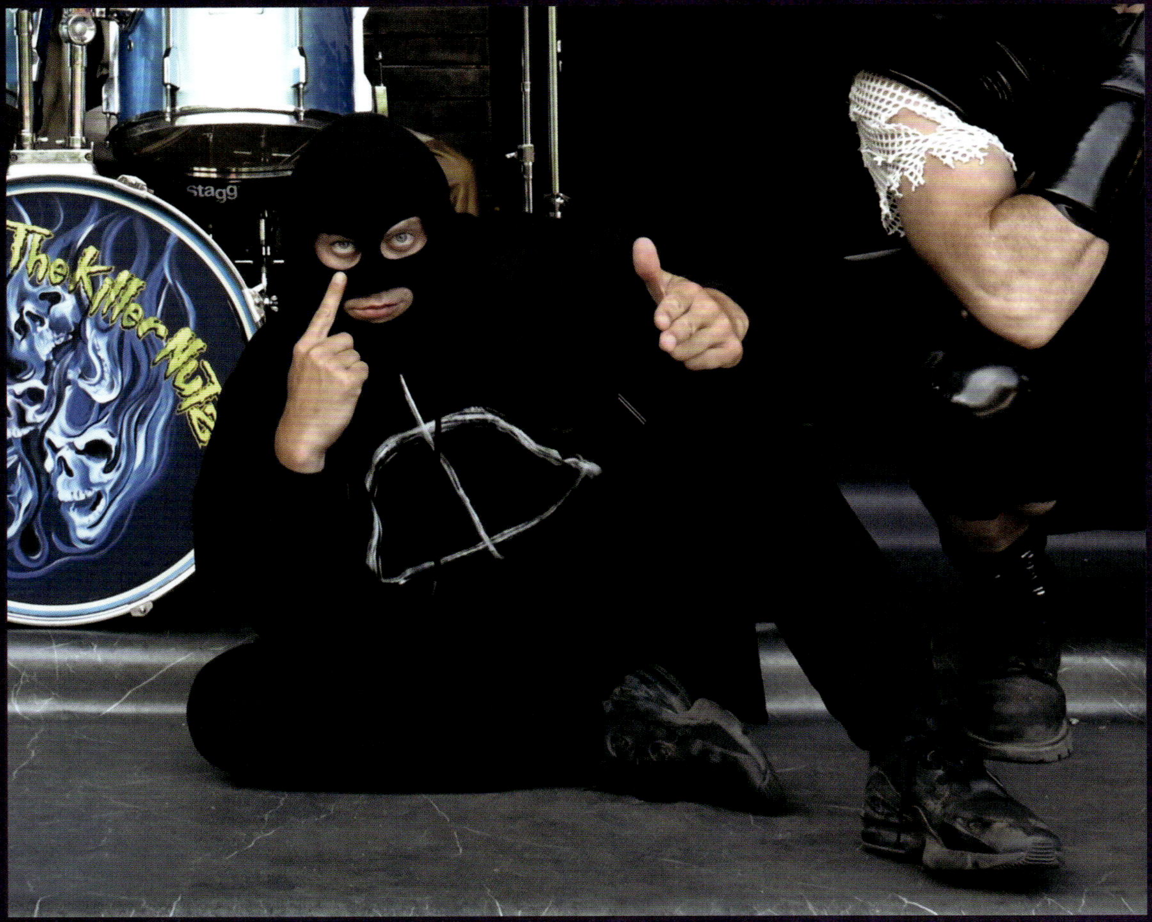

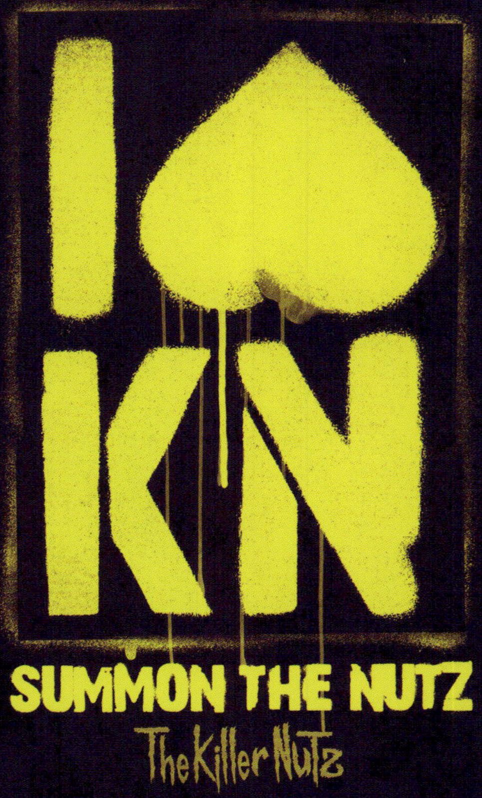

"We referenced some drawings of the Zodiac Killer"

– VANESSA PORTER,
Costume Designer

Left The Killer Nutz's unsettling hype man, Zodiac 3000.

NIGHTMARE JOSH

(DRUMS)
PLAYED BY NENCHO STEFANOV-NINIO

In the *Toxic Avenger* script, The Nutz' deranged drummer is given this simple, punchy four-word description: "Bandages, straitjacket, a maniac." Blair says the straitjacket (which brings to mind one of the weasels in *Who Framed Roger Rabbit*—you know, the one with the straitjacket) was primarily a visual joke. "What's the least efficient thing for a drummer to wear?" he asks. "It makes the least amount of sense. But it's like the band is trying very hard to say, 'Just in case you forgot, we are crazy. We are psychotic. Look! I wear a straitjacket!'"

Working with Illusion Industries in Bulgaria, Porter devised a straitjacket outfit, replete with leather and buckle detailing, and also the drummer's bandage mask, which she saw as being "kind of a classic mummy mask." This was created as a single latex piece covered in bandages, to allow local actor Nencho Stefanov-Ninio to don and doff it with relative ease, "so you wouldn't have to re-wrap it every time," Porter explains.

It was important to cast somebody, Blair says, who could really bang the drums, "since I knew they were going to play a live concert. You can fake guitar-playing a little bit if the camera's not on you too much, but drums fall apart very quickly if they're out of time, or if they're not hitting them right. Nencho was a great drummer."

That live concert, Troma Fest, is also the scene of Josh's spectacular demise, during one of the film's "signature shots", as cinematographer Dana Gonzales describes it. "You see Toxie throw the mop and it goes through Josh's head and then lands on the DJ's turntable and electrocutes her," he says. "It's such a great shot."

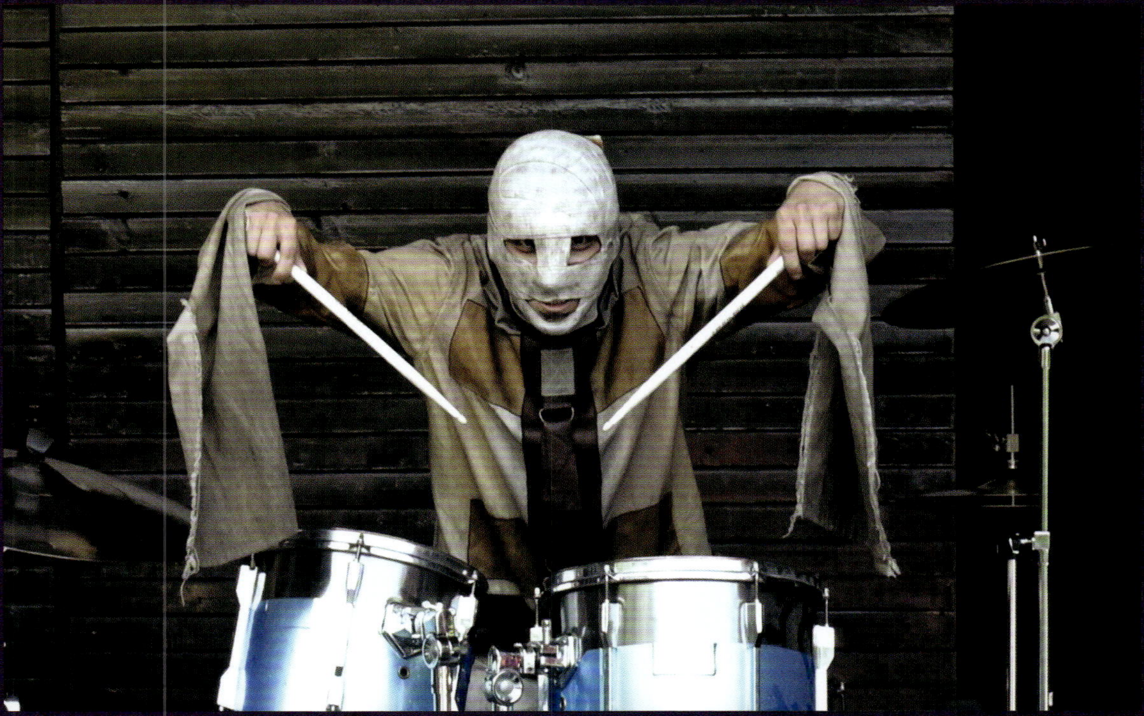

As described in the script, Josh's head was originally going to be cleaved off his shoulders, with blood erupting from the open neck. But Ritvo convinced Blair they could push it even further using CGI. "I said, 'Wouldn't it be more fun if his head exploded completely?' And he was like, 'Yeah, that's awesome.'" Blair was always up for anything that would increase what he calls "the gore score."

So now, as Ritvo puts it, "the head explodes and blood hits the camera, with Josh's eye popping out and sliding down the camera, too. Macon *loved* that. He wanted to take it to the next level."

> **"Blood hits the camera, with Josh's eye popping out and sliding down the camera."**
> – CHRIS RITVO, VFX Supervisor

Above Nightmare Josh, shortly before he loses his head (literally).

THE NUTZMOBILE

"I designed the skeleton with its hands around the bar at the front, but Macon said, 'Nah, it's better to have the middle fingers up.'"

– ALEXANDER CAMERON,
Production designer

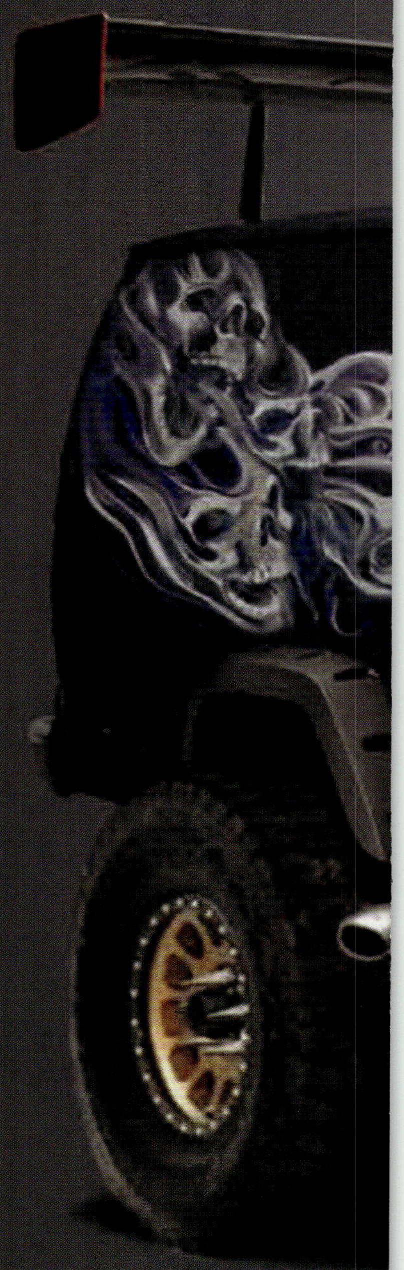

The band's tricked-out equivalent of The Batmobile (crossed with the A-Team van) went through several different iterations during the design process. "At one point it was going to be a Humvee," reveals Blair. "At another it was going to be an oversized luxury car. All we knew is that it needed to be very gaudy and over the top." As with most things concerning The Killer Nutz, Blair and his team aimed at striking a balance between menacing and absurd. "They're supposed to be this stealthy assassination operation, but they call the most amount of attention to themselves everywhere they go," Blair laughs. "It doesn't make a ton of sense, but that's part of what's funny about it."

When Blair and Cameron discussed options with their picture vehicles coordinator, he suggested an old Ford Transit which had been used in some previous films. "It was just a white van, very boring," says Cameron. But he saw it as an opportunity—a blank slate. "Rather than continue trying to find the perfect vehicle, let's do something we can have complete control over," he suggested. So, they took the van, resprayed it, added the airbrushed art, affixed a huge spoiler, changed up the wheels and mounted a chrome Angel of Death flipping the bird at the front of the vehicle. "That was Macon's idea," Cameron confirms. "I designed the skeleton with its hands around the bar at the front, but Macon said, 'Nah, it's better to have the middle fingers up.' It was something you could have a lot of fun with."

Perhaps the most over-the-top addition was the *Ben-Hur*-style spikes protruding from the wheels. "Oh my God, the wheels," laughs Cameron. Not exactly health-and-safety appropriate. "Yeah, they had to be blunted a little bit…"

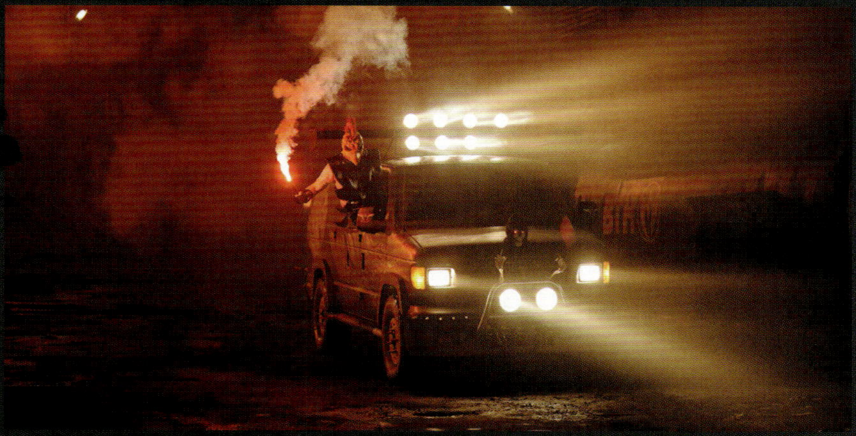

Right Him Under The Hood evidently loves to ride shotgun.

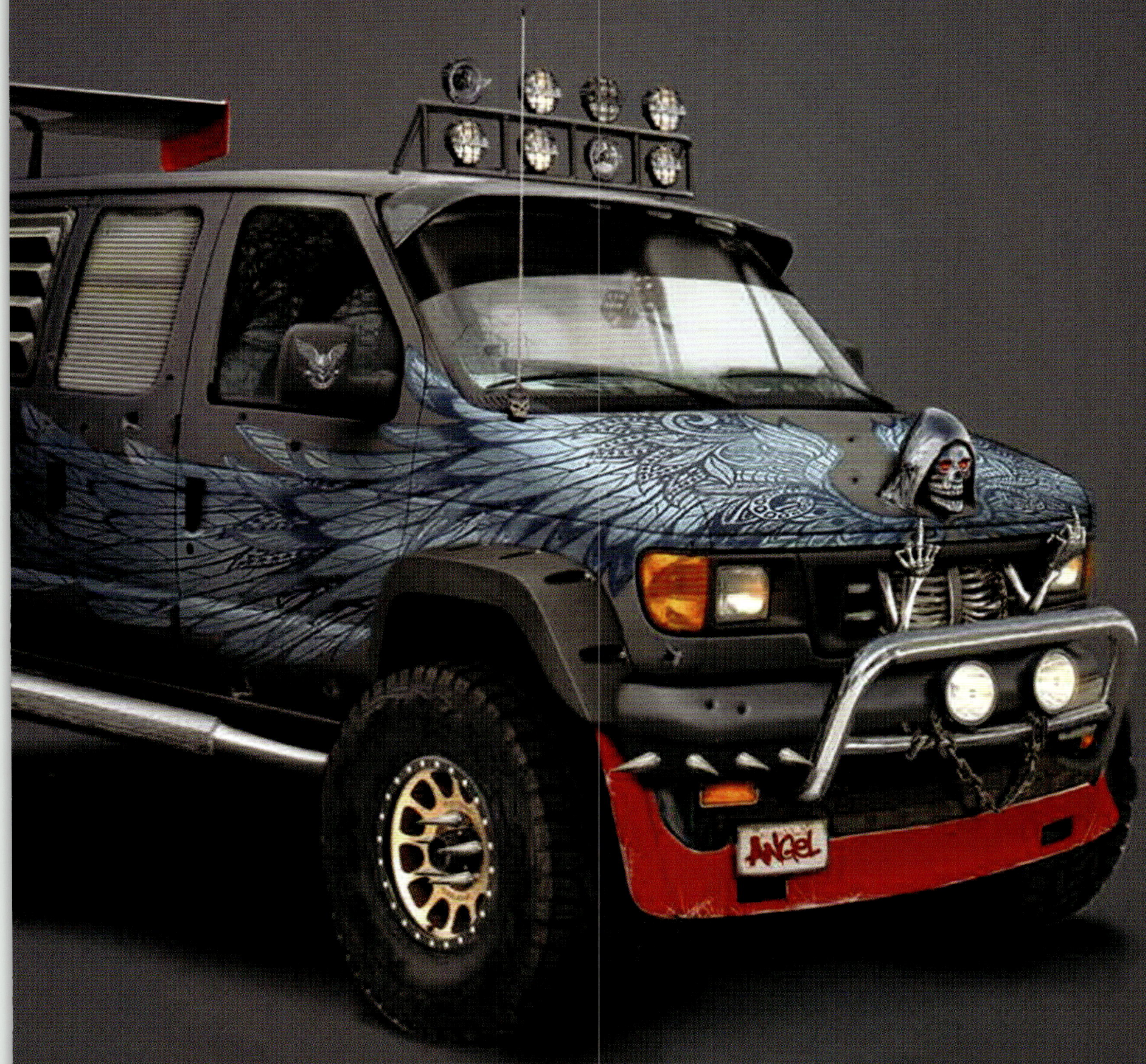

This page Concept artwork of the Killer Nutz' ostentatious ride.

DA UNDERWORLD

Given The Killer Nutz' not-so-compartmentalized double life as a rock band and a hit squad, it's no surprise to learn that their HQ needed to work both as a rehearsal space and as an evil lair. "You only really see it in one or two shots, but it provides a way to introduce The Nutz as the bad guys of the movie, and give them a bad-guy lair," says Macon Blair.

After visiting several local bars in Sofia, one in particular stood out as the best setting for the band's subterranean skulduggery. "It was literally underground and had these low arching ceilings. It felt very cave-like and potentially scary," says Blair.

For Cameron's team, it was a very easy location to dress. "We hardly did anything to it," he says. "The texture was there, and it was more a case of removing stuff, like the barrels, than adding, just to make it look less like a public place."

It also came with an added benefit, Blair reveals. "We ended up using the alleyway and parking lot around it for many subsequent scenes. When Toxie is getting chased by the mob, that's right outside of Da Underworld. The Killer Nutz taking off in their van, some close-ups of Fritz (Elijah Wood) yelling at them, all of the Nutz music-video stuff… We were able to combine a lot of other scenes into this one location, without having it seem like we were shooting in the same place."

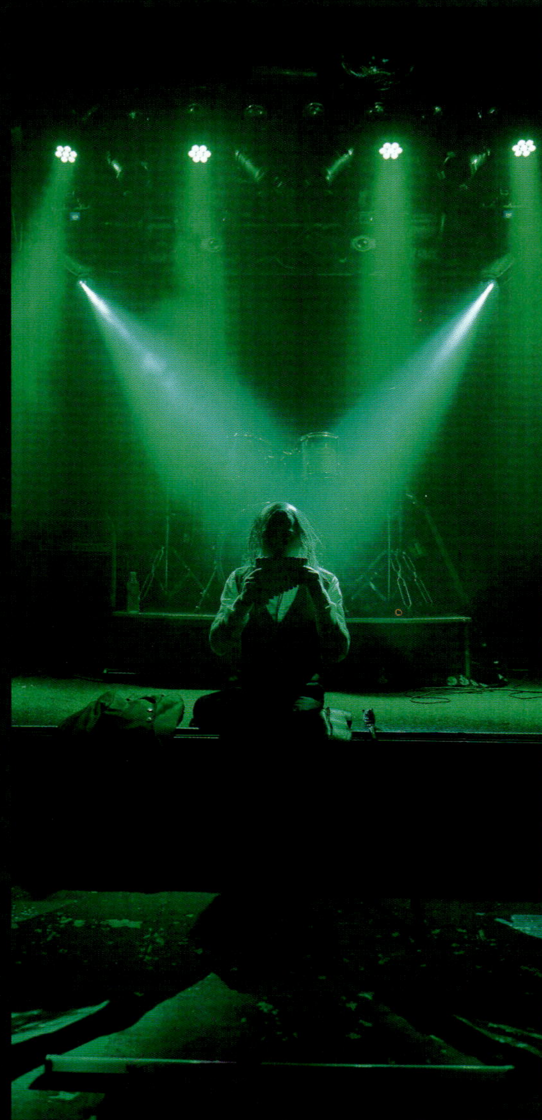

Above Band manager Fritz Garbinger on the panpipes.

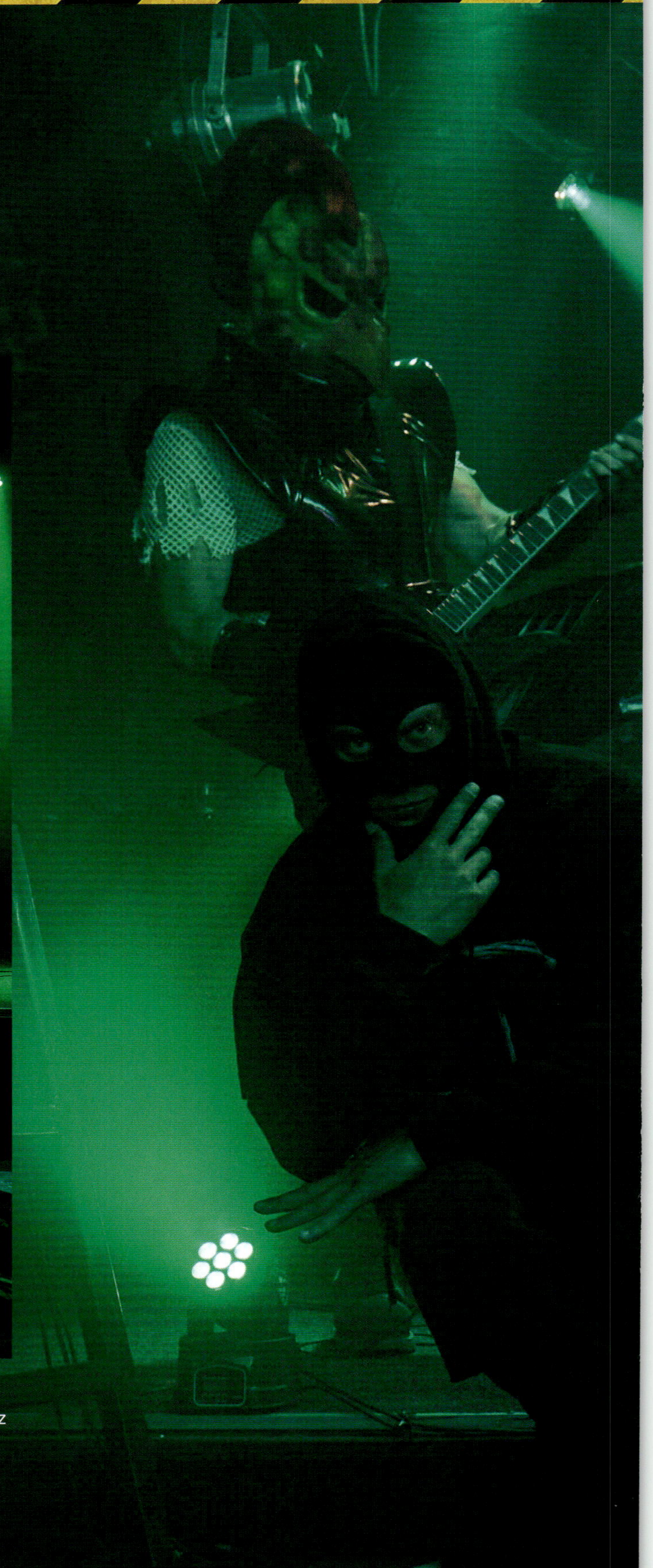

Right The Nutz and Fritz on their grungy home turf: Da Underworld.

"It provides a way to introduce The Nutz as the bad guys of the movie."

– MACON BLAIR,
Director

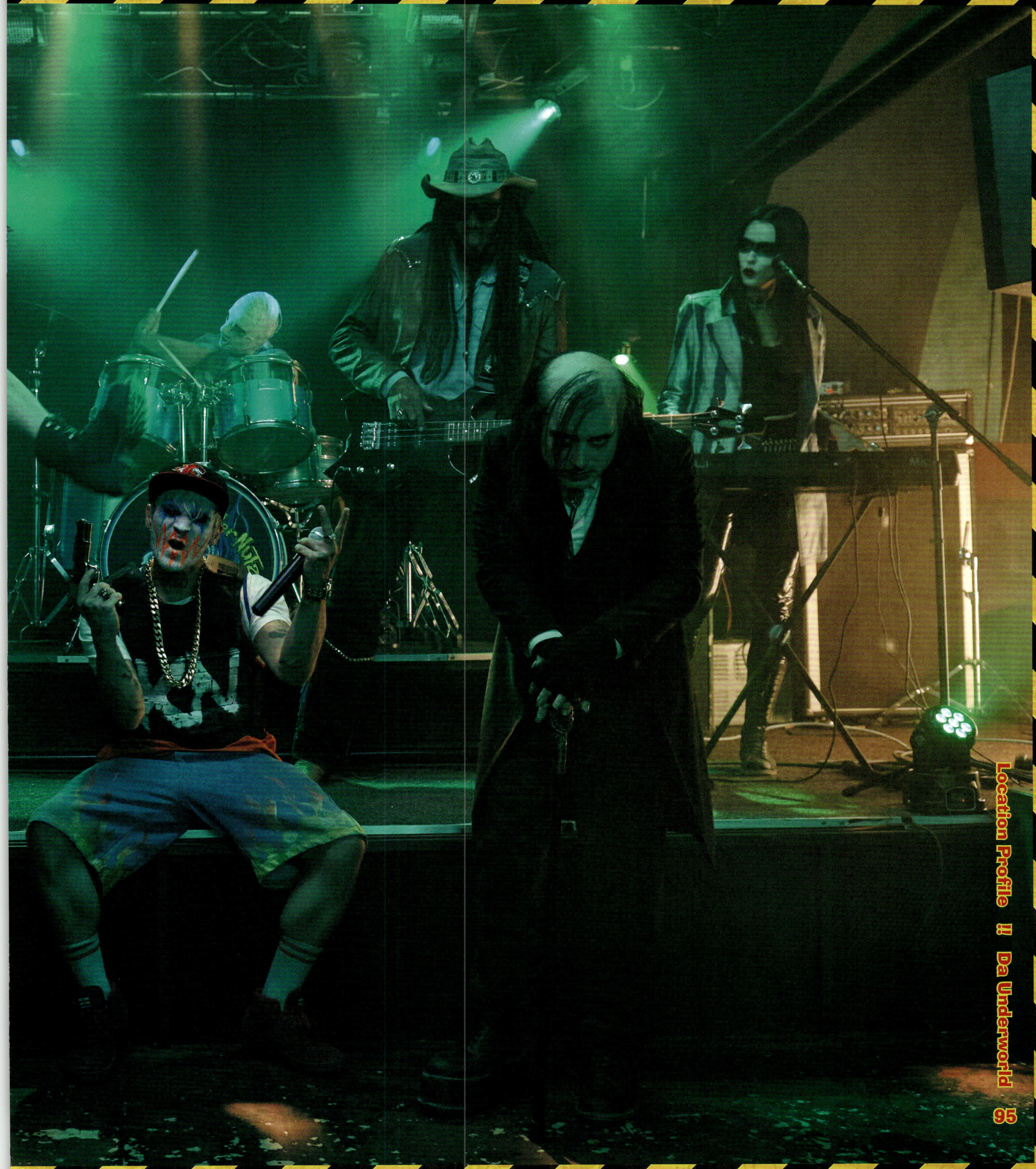

DAISY

PLAYED BY ANNETTE BADLAND

Downstairs from the Gooze apartment lives Daisy, proprietor of the bodega under threat from local criminals the Khaki Klub. This kind and earthy woman is the "grandmother presence" in Winston and Wade's lives, explains Macon Blair. She combines a warm, maternal quality with street smarts and a degree of world-weariness. "We had all these back stories that Daisy still partied pretty hard and likes to stay out late and go on dates and stuff like that," says Blair. "She's not frail."

This backstory chimed well with Porter's main source of inspiration for Daisy's costumes. "There was a lady who's worked at this bar in Queens for, like, 30 years," says the New York-based costume designer. "We came up with a look inspired by her: sort of a salty old lady, with a leopard shirt, leggings, and a lot of make-up."

To play Daisy, Blair found all the qualities he needed in British actor Annette Badland, who appeared in popular UK soap opera *EastEnders* between 2014 and 2017, and more recently took the role of Mae in Apple TV+ hit *Ted Lasso*. "We auditioned a lot of great people, but within the context of the movie Annette seemed the most enjoyable to hang out with; for the audience to spend time with and connect with," says Blair. "It was fun to get her on."

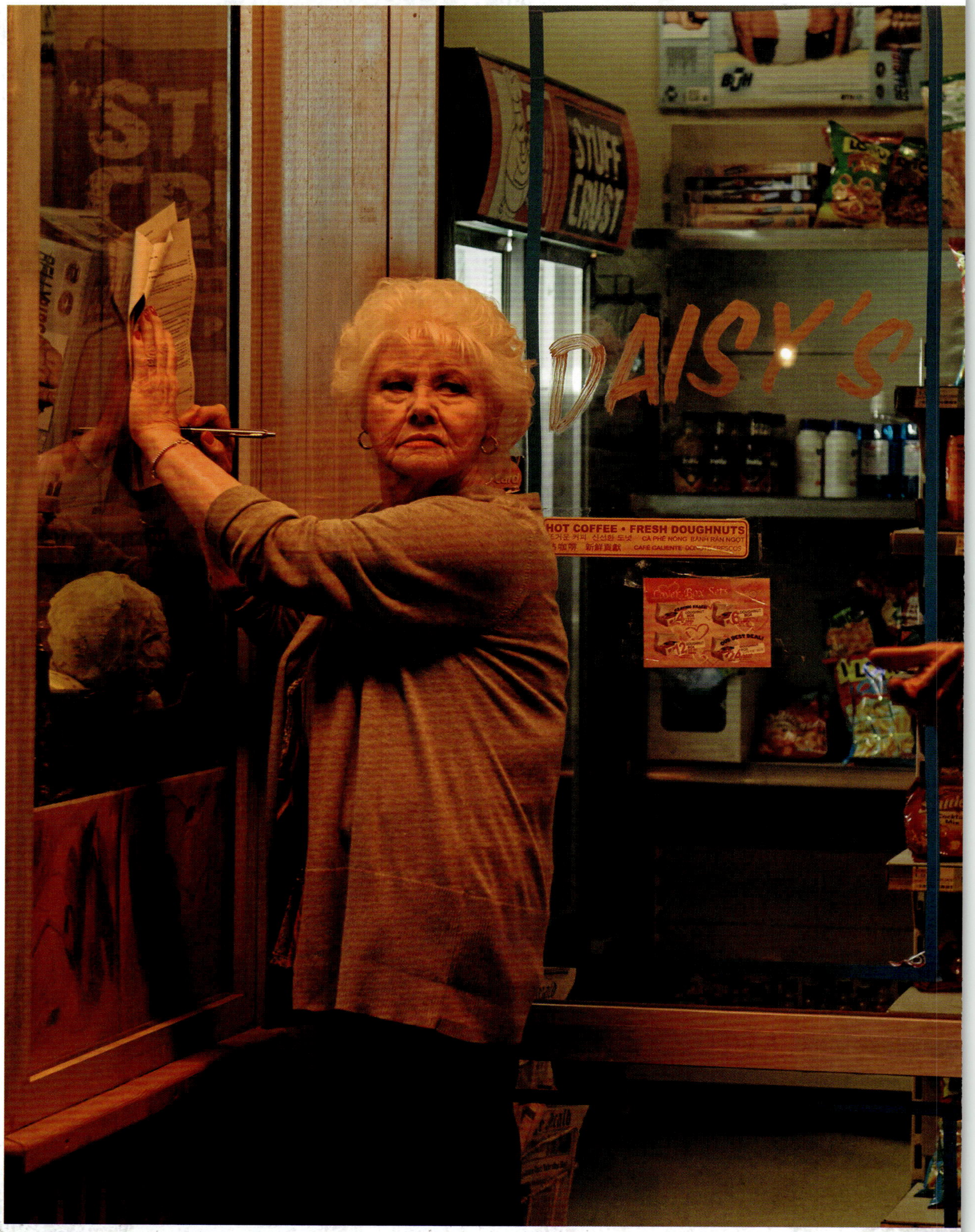

Right Daisy has an unpleasant encounter with preppy gangster Spence.

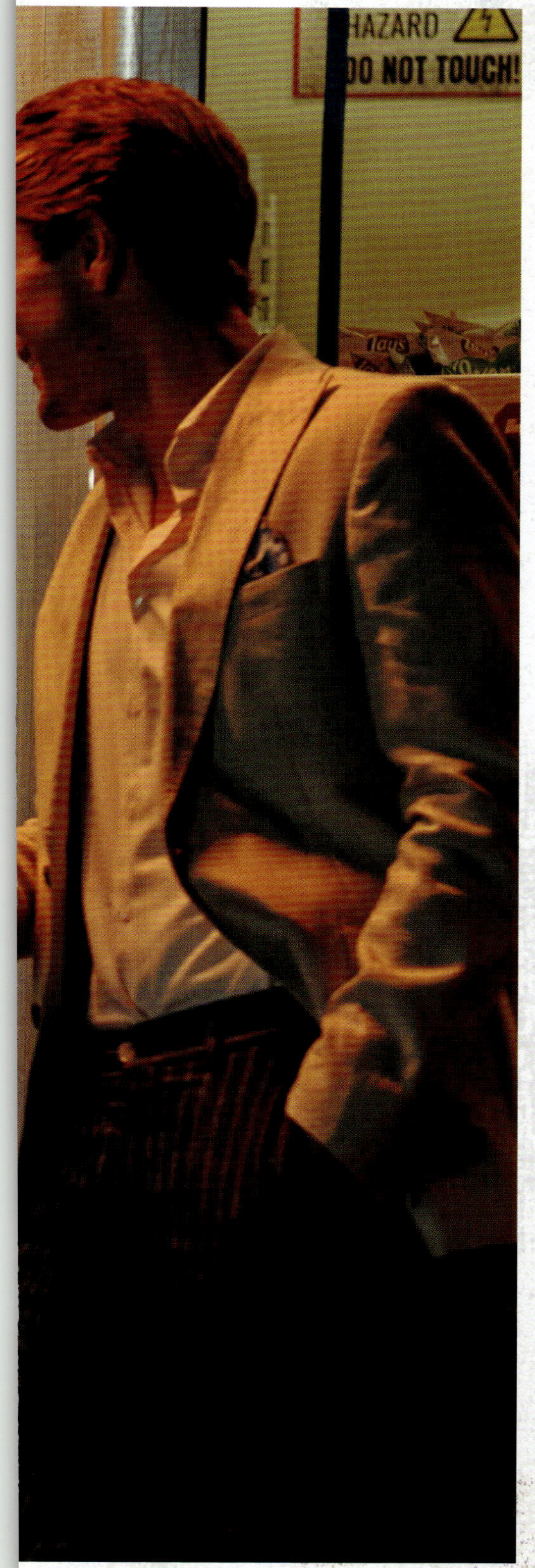

CAT SCRATCH FEVER

Why Mr Treats was the movie's biggest diva

"That cat was a goddamn menace," says Blair. "I tell you, that cat ripped open Annette's arm. That cat ripped open Spence's costume. It would not sit still. It kept running away. Absolute diva!"

When Spence Barkabus (Abraham Lewis) threatens Daisy, he makes his point by holding her dear moggie Mr. Treats hostage, ultimately tossing the poor feline into the Tromaville traffic. Although, from the sounds of it, Mr. Treats was a bigger threat to Spence than vice versa. "We picked him because he looked cute," says Blair, "but it was tricky getting him to do anything. I mean, you don't expect a cat to do any acting, but I kept having to apologize to the actors because it would freak out and scratch the hell out of them."

Originally, Mr. Treats was supposed to return with Daisy during the hospital scenes at the end of the film, but Blair had already seen enough blood (meaning *real* blood). "After that first day, I said, 'That cat is fired.' It never came back."

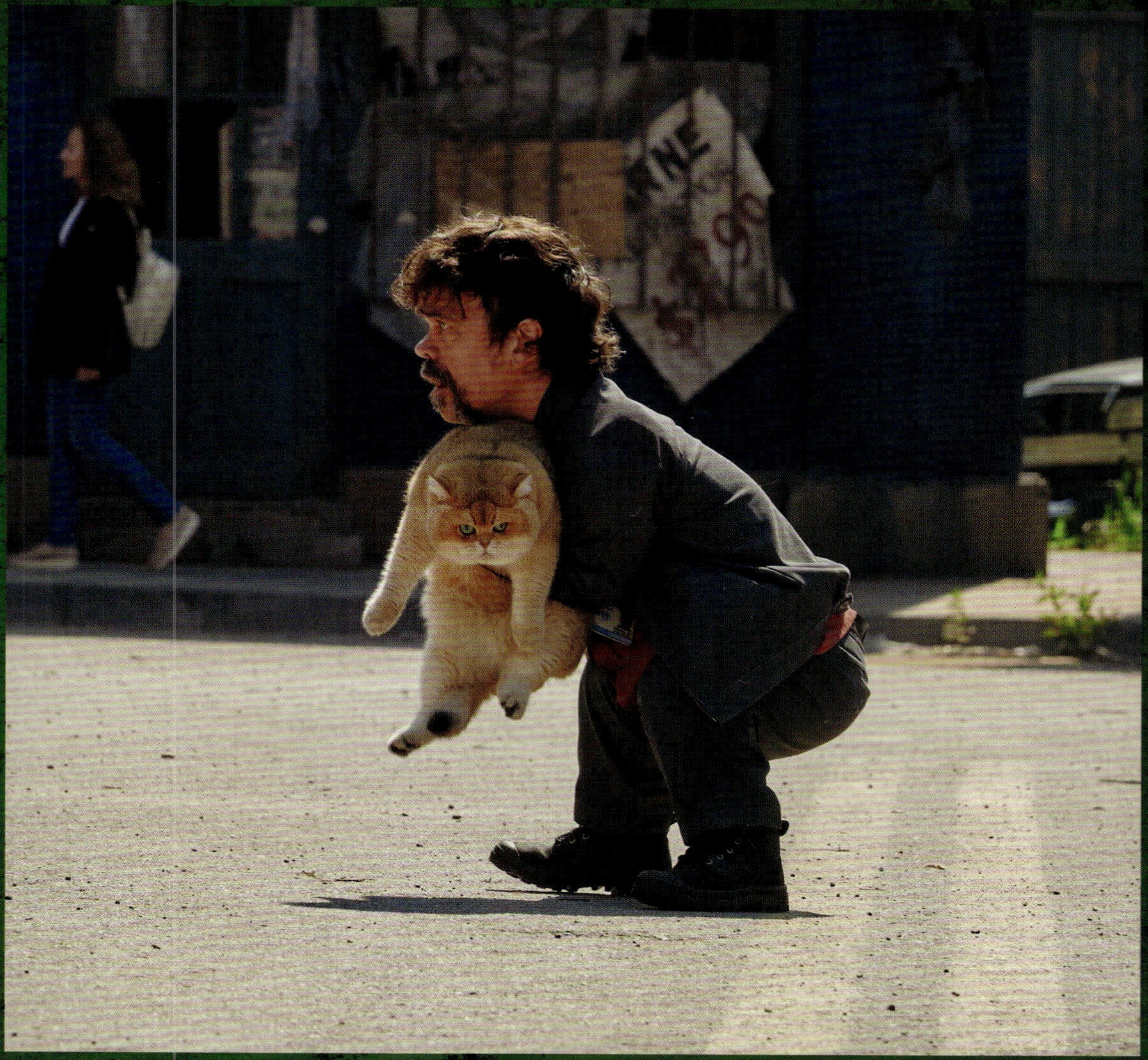

SPENCE

PLAYED BY ABRAHAM LEWIS

Spence Barkabus has the dubious distinction of being the first member of organized crime that we meet in Tromaville. The son of kingpin Thad Barkabus (Jonny Coyne), and a member of preppy sorta-Mafia the Khaki Klub, we find him threatening nice, elderly lady Daisy and tossing her cat into traffic. He certainly lives up to his description in the script as a "WASPy enforcer" and a "smirky prick," while also illustrating Winston's inability to get involved and do the right thing. ("Sometimes it's just better to do nothing," he tells Wade after they witness Spence's shenanigans. "You'll see when you get older.")

To play Spence, Blair settled on upcoming British actor Abraham Lewis. "I remember watching the audition tapes one evening, and he was the one that made me laugh out loud," says Blair. "He really tapped into that smarmy, cheesy, slick shithead vibe that is sort of threatening, but more amusing, in a way."

Spence also has another dubious distinction: he's the first Tromaville villain to encounter Toxie, who makes up for Winston's earlier ineffectualness and rips Spence's arm clean off. "One of the first movies I made with my friends when we were growing up was *Beowulf*," laughs Blair. "So that was me just getting back to my roots, my basics: doing a lo-fi limb-detachment gag for comedy."

Right Spence prepares to throw Mr. Treats out into the street.

Opposite Spence at the function at Mammon Hall.

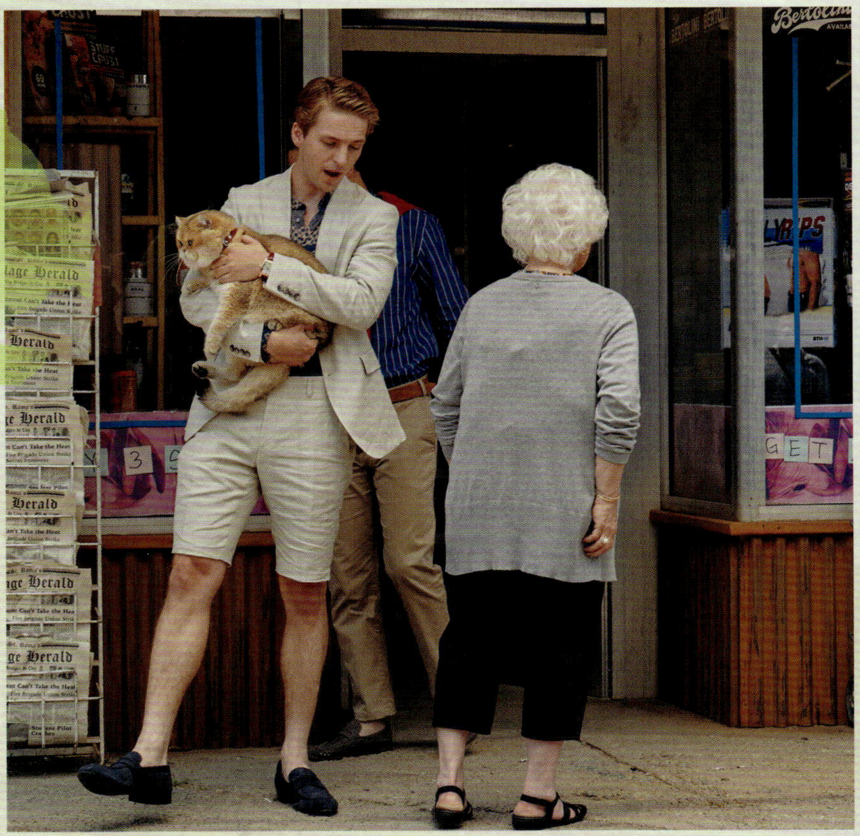

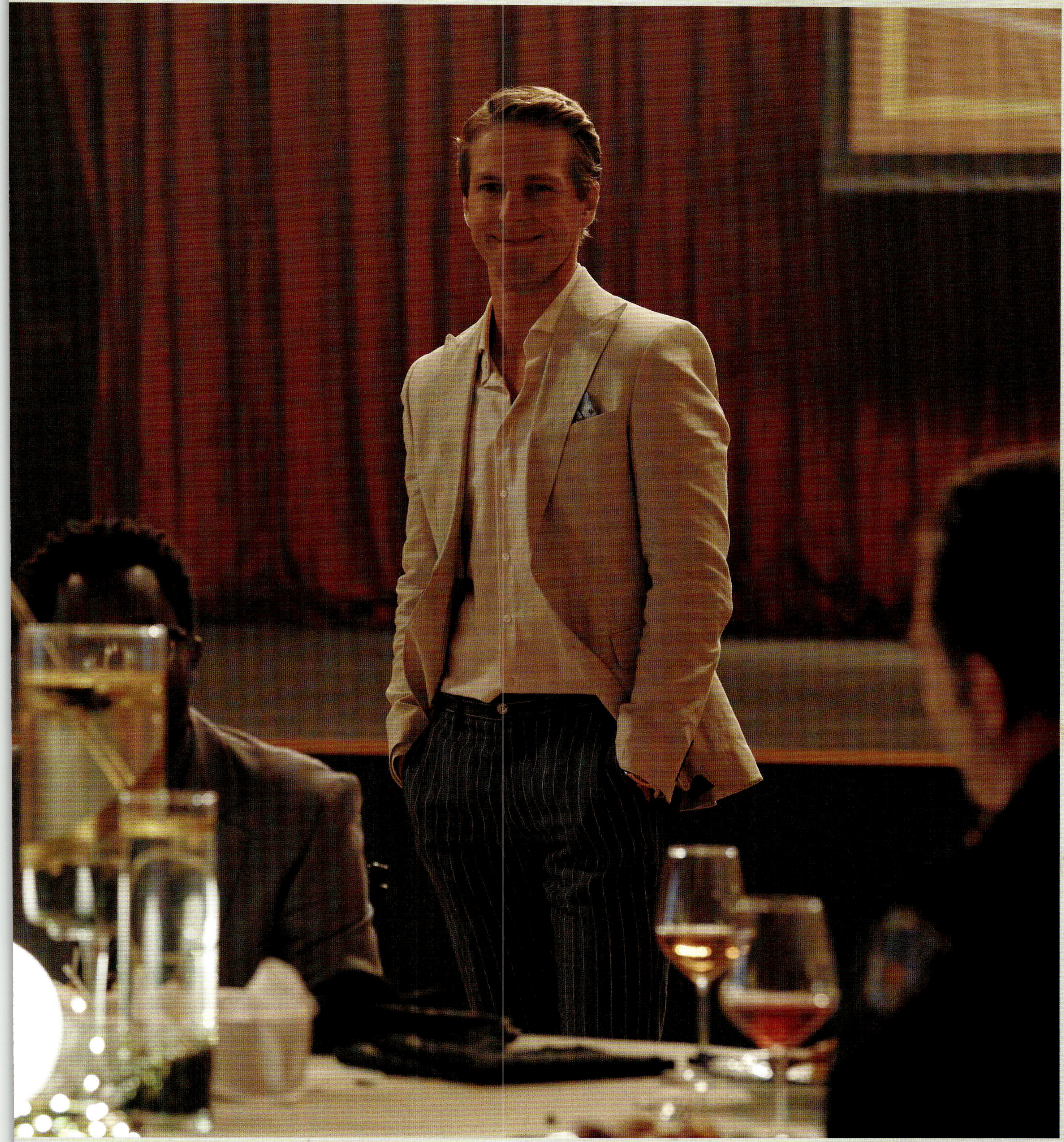

CHÜDHAVEN MANSION

For Bob Garbinger's palatial estate, the *Toxic Avenger* team found a real palace. Namely Vrana Palace on the outskirts of Sofia, which remains the official residence of Bulgaria's former royal family. (Though Simeon II, the country's last tsar, resides in the hunting lodge, leaving the main building free for tourists to visit.) "It's pretty grand, but there were bits and pieces falling off," says Cameron. "That helped with the whole story of Garbinger, who outwardly looks like he's a big boss man, but inwardly his world is falling apart."

Given the building's historical and cultural significance, it took some careful negotiation to establish what the production could and couldn't do in the grounds, where the movie's climactic confrontation kicks off. "They're quite strict," Cameron says. His team were allowed to add their own statues (constructed from polystyrene) to the gardens, including a huge rendering of Garbinger as a Roman emperor, which eventually has a battle axe embedded in its crotch. But there was a limit to what the curators would allow. "They wouldn't let us blow up the outhouse," says Cameron, referring to the shed where Wade is incarcerated by Garbinger and Fritz, "so we actually did that somewhere else, and then we had to comp it in."

Despite the use of digital effects to stitch the shed into the palace grounds during post-production, Ritvo confirms that the

"It's pretty grand, but there were bits and pieces falling off. That helped with the whole story of Garbinger."

– ALEX CAMERON,
Production Designer

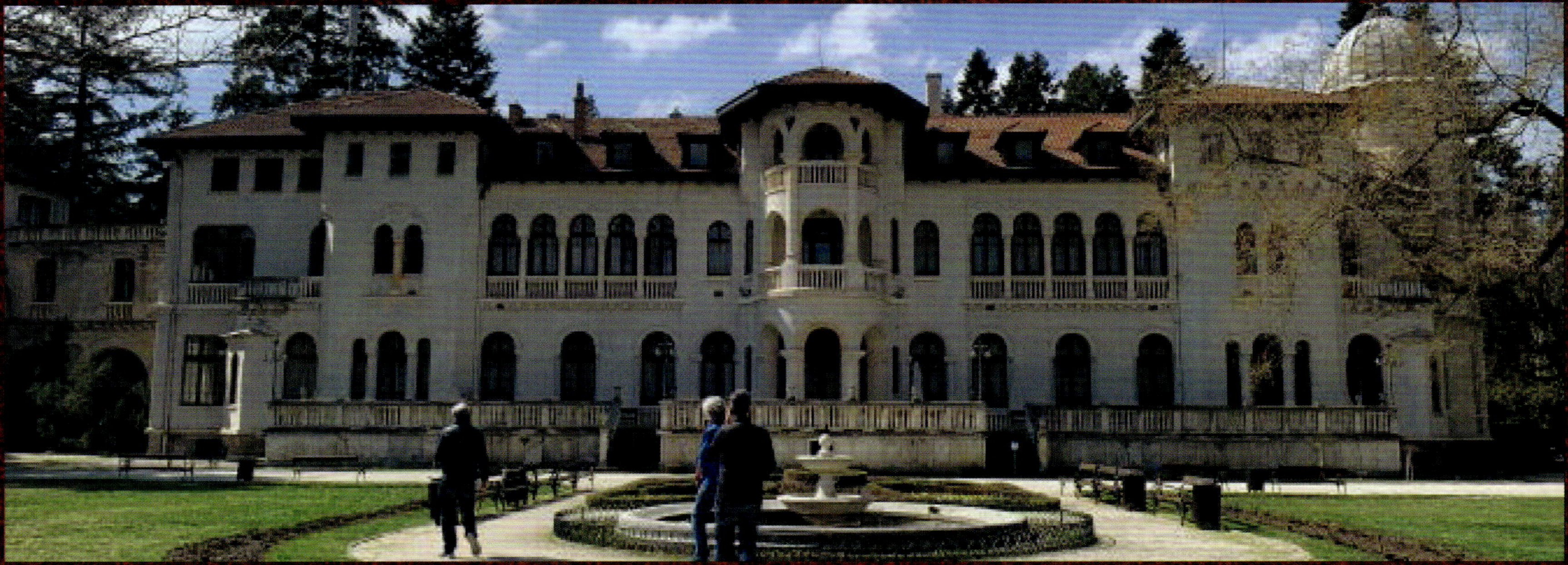

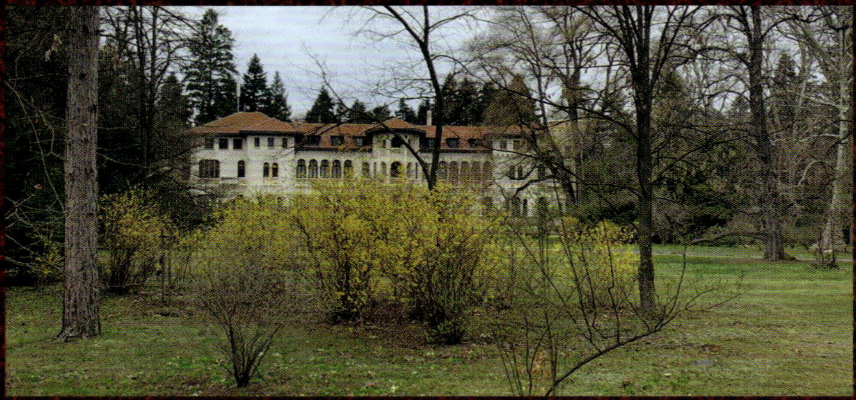

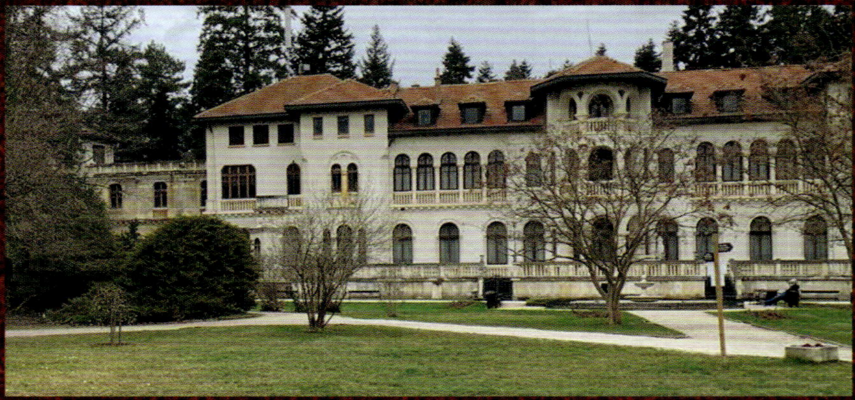

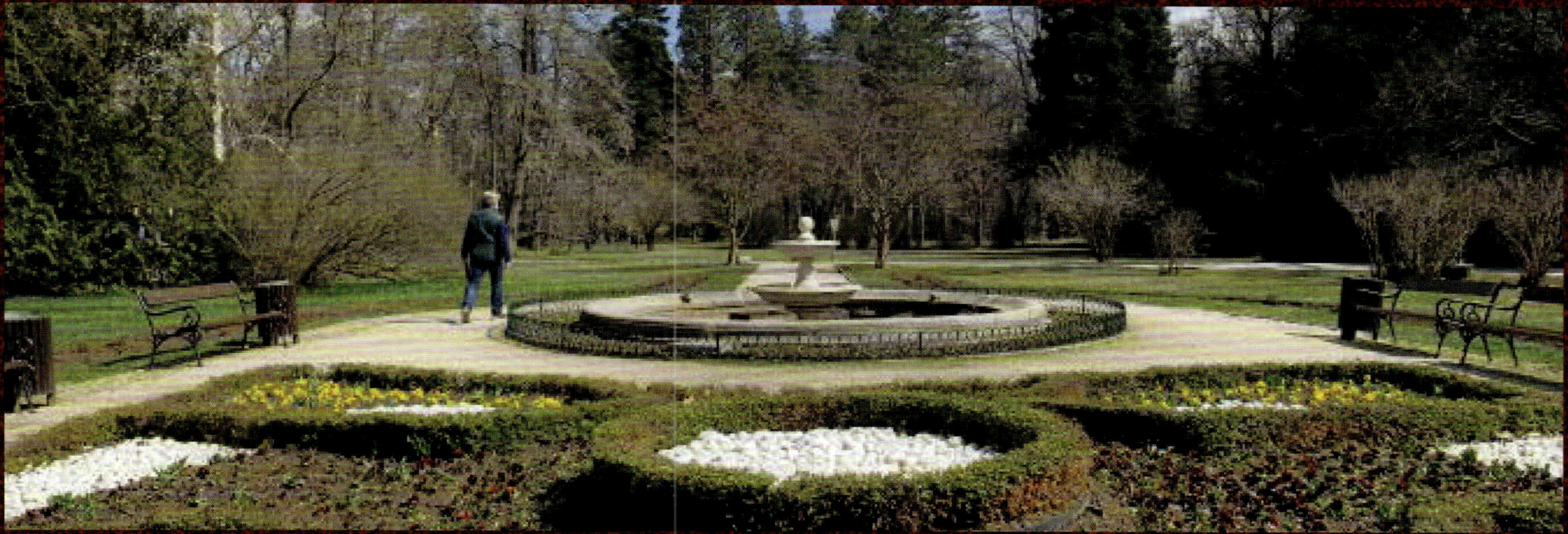

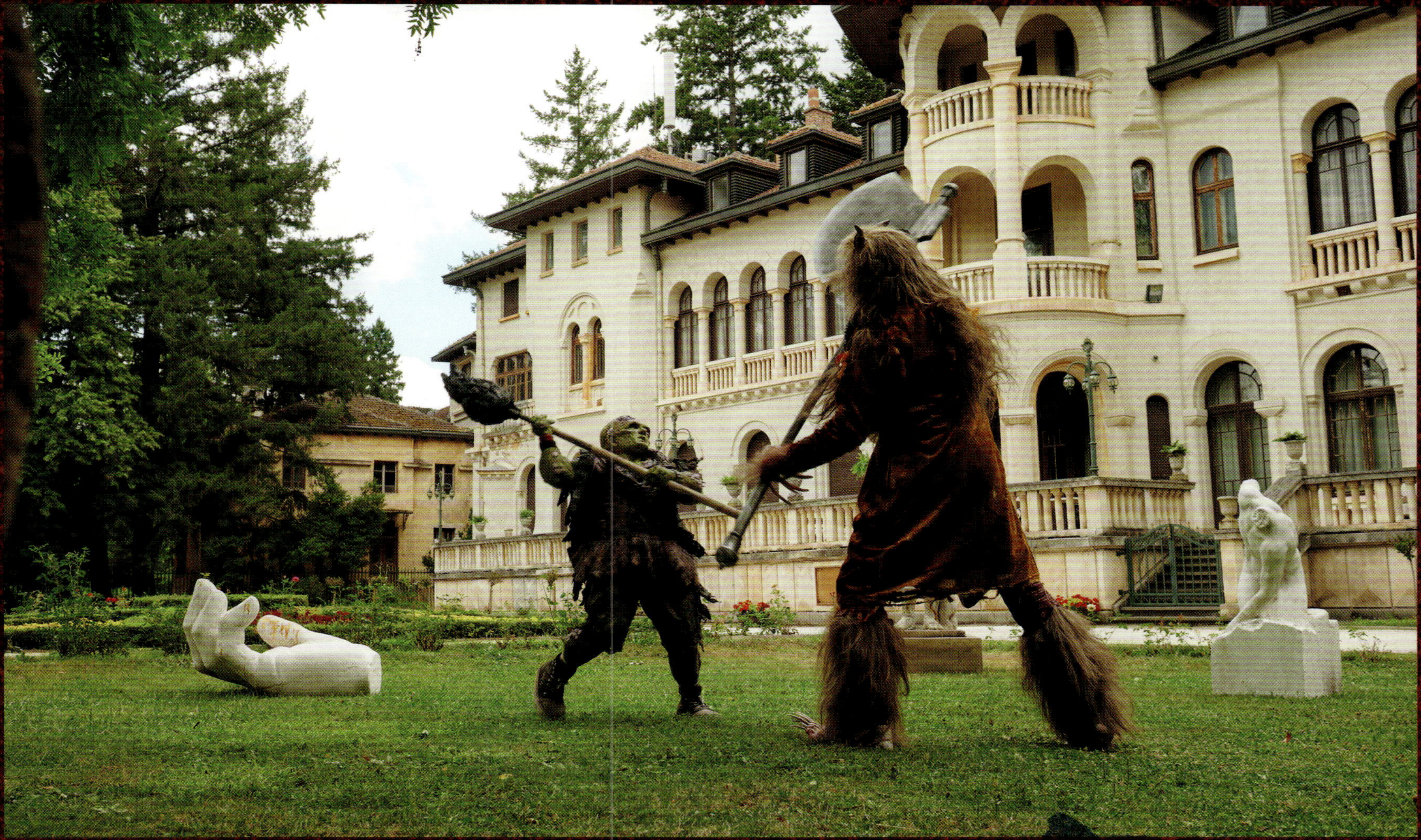

explosion was achieved in-camera. "I would give kudos to the SFX team, because they built one hell of an explosion," he says. "We shot it against a big blue screen on our back lot, but, yeah, the explosion was practical. Macon wanted that kind of black-smoke, gassy explosion that you see in old '70s or '80s movies, and that's exactly what we got. It is one big explosion. It shook every building around us. It was pretty awesome."

This spread Location-scout photography of Vrana Palace in Sofia, which proved the ideal residence for Bob Garbinger.

Above Toxie and Monster Garbinger battle it out in the Chüdhaven grounds.

THE HELLSCAPE

"It was horrible. *Horrible.*" For an area named the Hellscape—the industrial waste ground that forms the hinterland to Garbinger's manor—Cameron's description should come as no surprise. This artificial wasteland was, in reality, a "huge quarry rubbish dump," which only required a minor amount of adapting, primarily the addition of more trash ("Soft rubbish, rather than anything that could hurt anybody," the production designer points out).

During shooting, the Hellscape sure lived up to its name. "The sequence we shot there took three or four days and it was *so* hot," says Gonzales. As the mercury rose to 110 degrees Fahrenheit, "everyone was cooking." Especially Luisa Guerreiro and Spencer Wilding, who, in the roles of Toxie and Monster Garbinger respectively, were performing the final battle in full prosthetic suits. "They come out of Garbinger's house, they start fighting, they roll down a hill and then they're battling through this Hellscape," says Gonzales. "But you can only shoot each gag a couple of times before they overheat. We did have doubles, but their makeup was only good for certain shots; it wasn't good for everything. It was very challenging."

Blair confirms that, with all the rehearsals and complicated choreography required, it was by far the hardest week of filming. "It's literally two actors swinging weapons around and they're both in really heavy prosthetic gear, head to toe, and it's extremely hot out," he says. "There was a lot of stuff to juggle for that particular fight scene. It was pretty remarkable for both of them, in terms of stamina. I was very impressed with them."

Below J.J. and Toxie face each other in the Hellscape.

Right Various reference shots of the Bulgarian rubbish dump, to which the production ironically had to add trash.

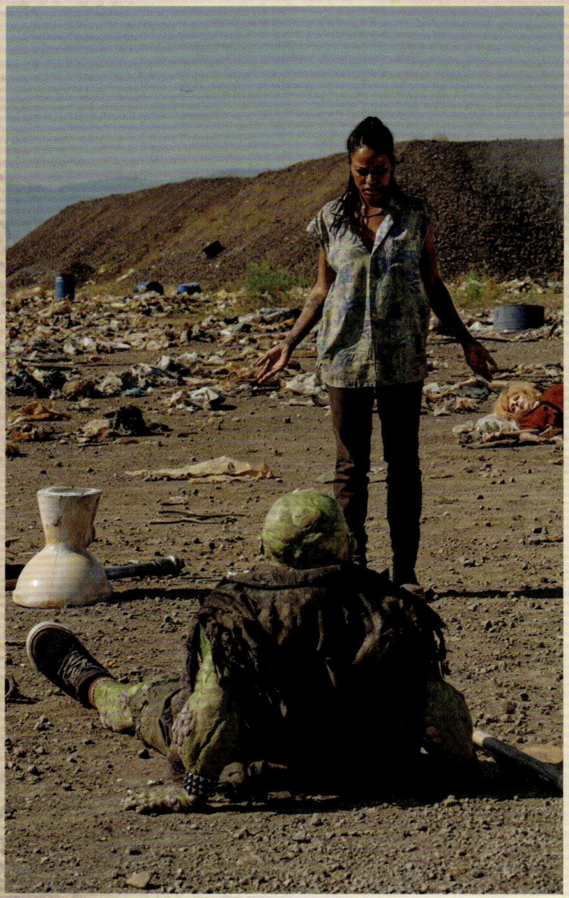

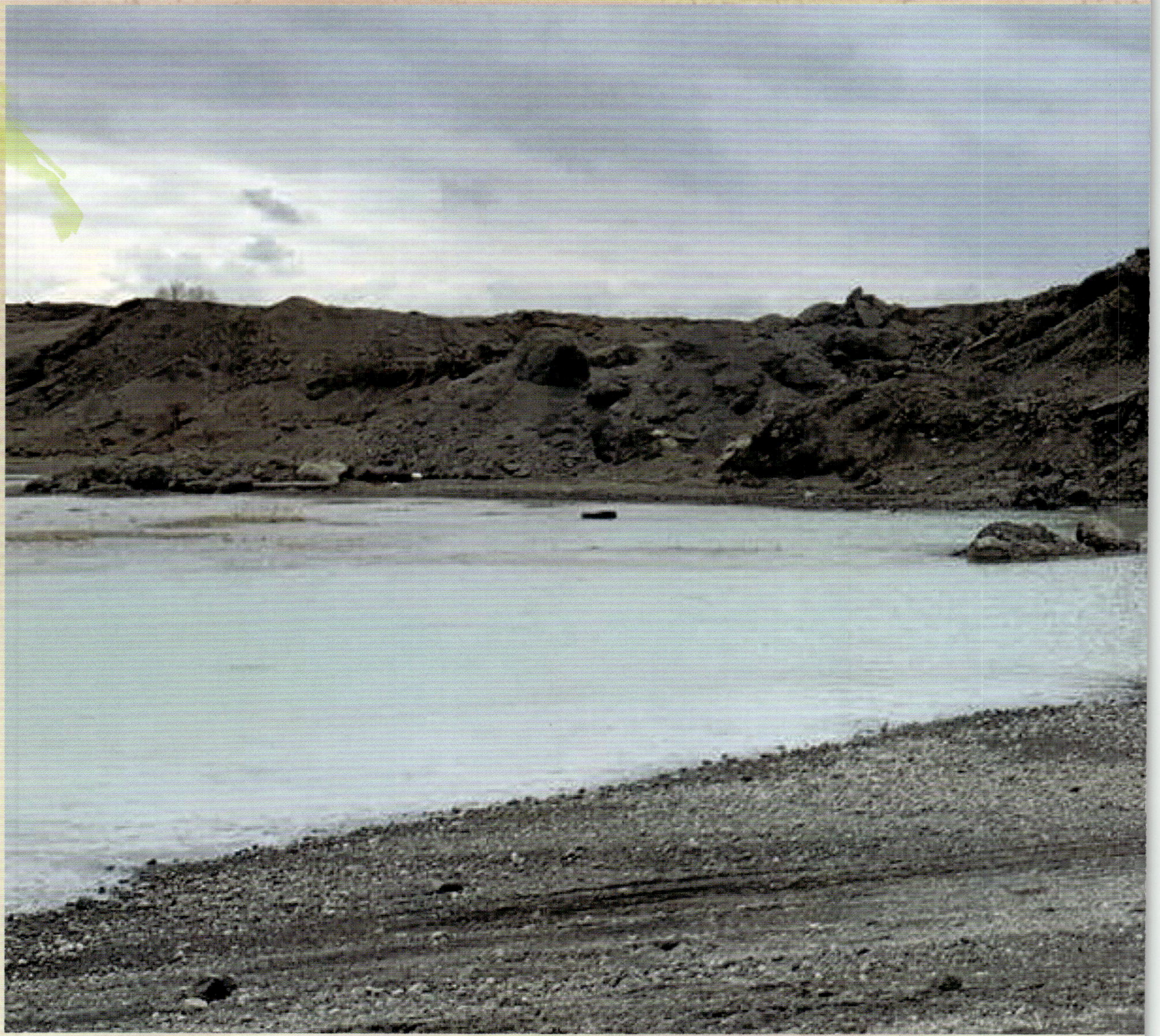

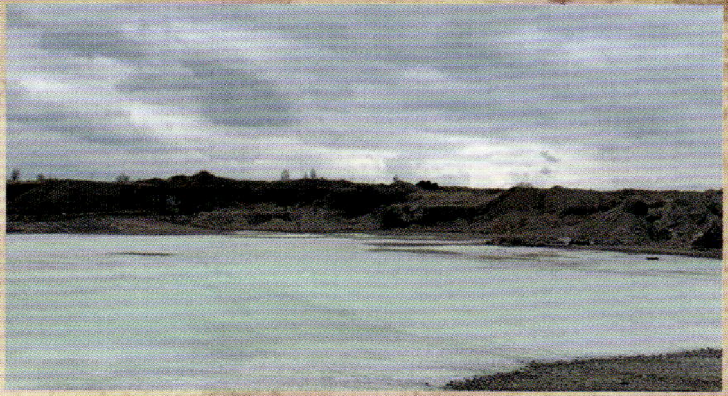

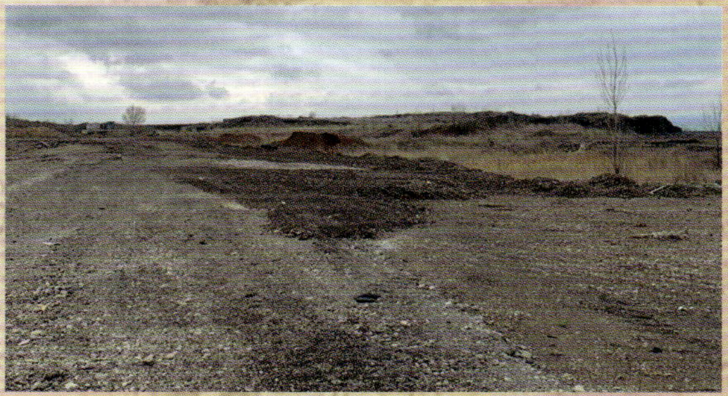

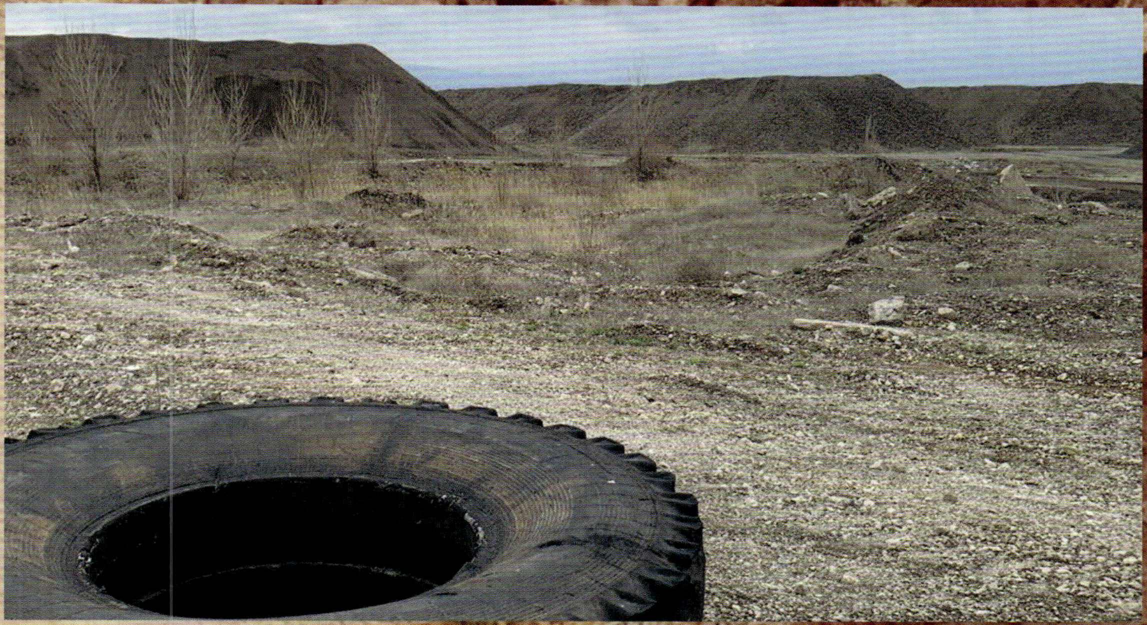

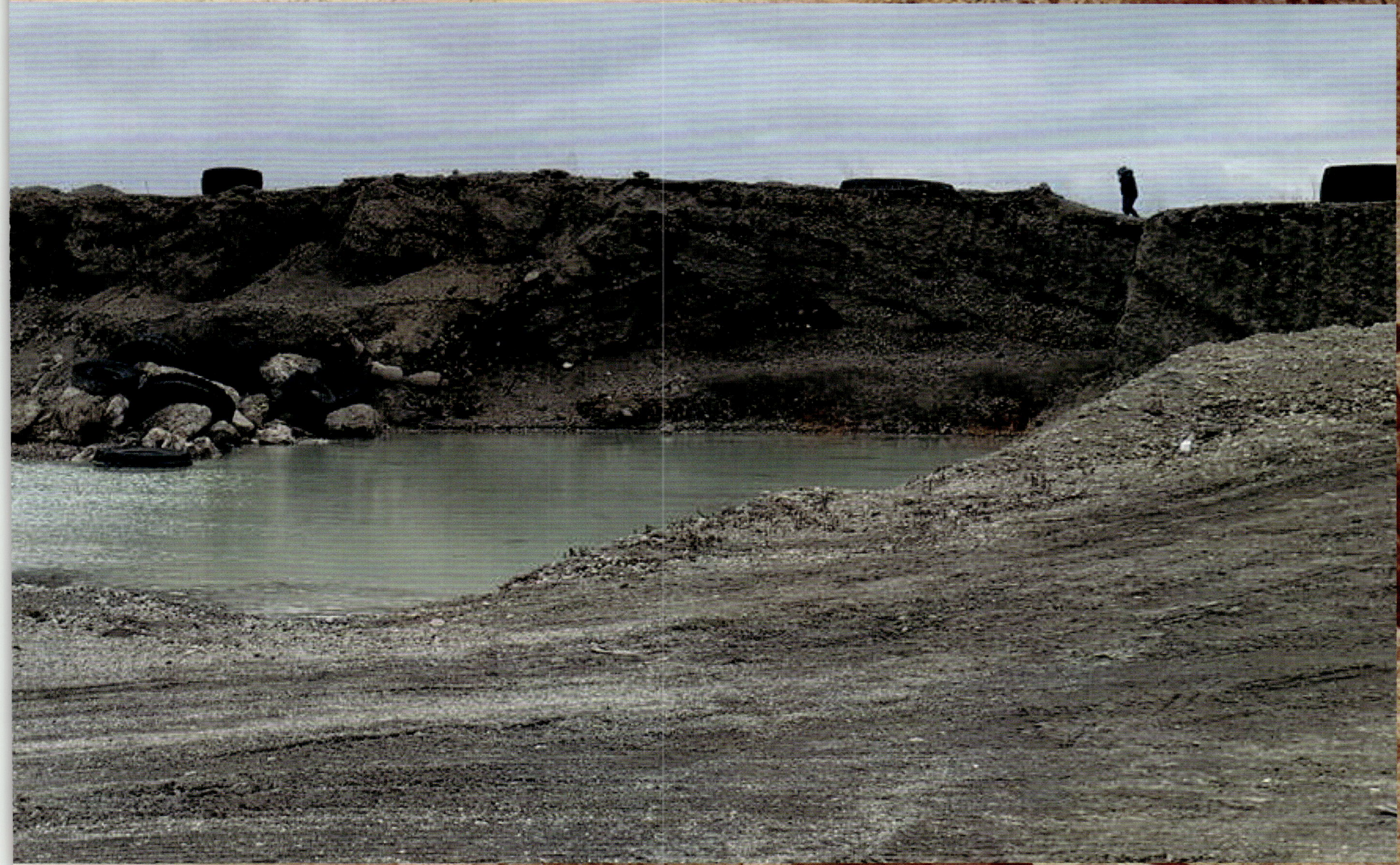

KISSY STURNEVAN

PLAYED BY JULIA DAVIS

During her lauded, 27-year career in British comedy, Julia Davis has never shied away from playing characters who can most charitably be described as 'difficult to like'. In virtually everything from 2004's *Nighty Night* to 2018's BAFTA award-winning *Sally4Ever* (all written, or co-written, by Davis), she's made watchable nastiness her stock-in-trade, something that her fans appreciate as much as her aptitude for semi-improvised pitch-black comedy. So the role of "tightly wound, cold-eyed exec assistant" Kissy Sturnevan, who both works and holds a torch for Bob Garbinger, feels tailor-made for Davis.

"Julia has this refined sensibility, but also a very dark, dry deadpan sense of humour," says Blair, who was blown away by *Nighty Night*. "We did discuss a lot of different actors, but early on Alex (Garcia) brought her up, and she became stuck in my head."

Davis describes Kissy as "quite simpering to Kevin Bacon's character at the beginning, because she's in love with him. But if I was trying to be pretentious, she's slightly Lady Macbeth-ish, in that she also wants power for herself. She is quite evil." Blair was more than happy for Davis to take the character as written and introduce her own tweaks and touches. For example, he gave her free rein with Kissy's accent. "I was going for a sort of mild Australian, but Macon described it as Kiwi," Davis says. "I based it on a beauty therapist I met, who had a very soft way of speaking."

This freedom extended to allowing Davis to improvize while shooting her scenes. "I told her, 'I love that kind of thing and we wouldn't hire you if we weren't going to

Right Kissy meets Winston.

Opposite page Kissy prepares to dine at the Mammon Hall function.

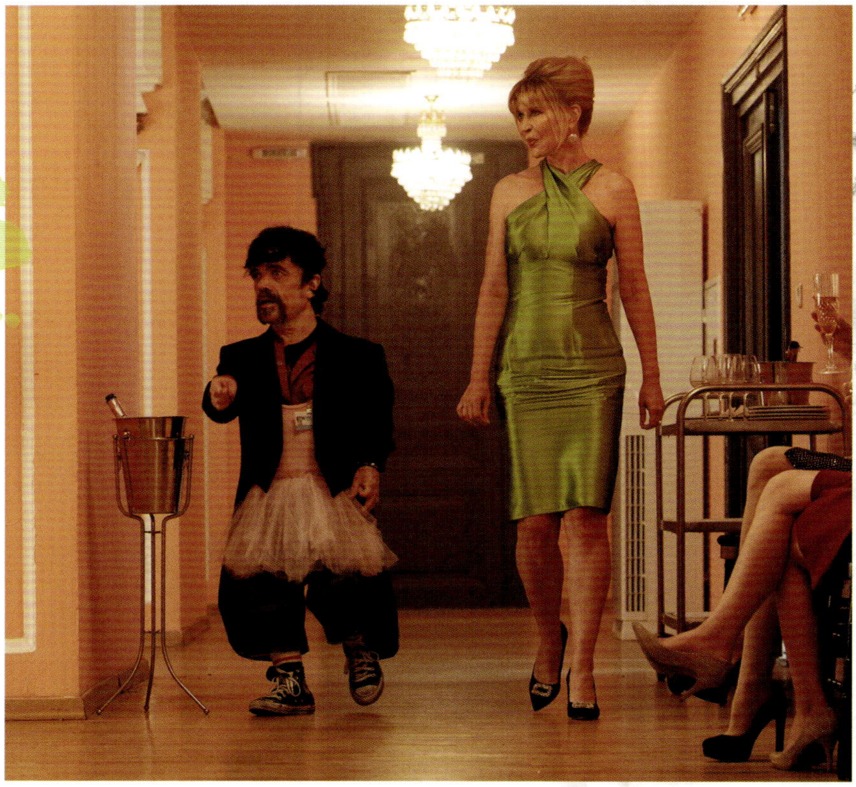

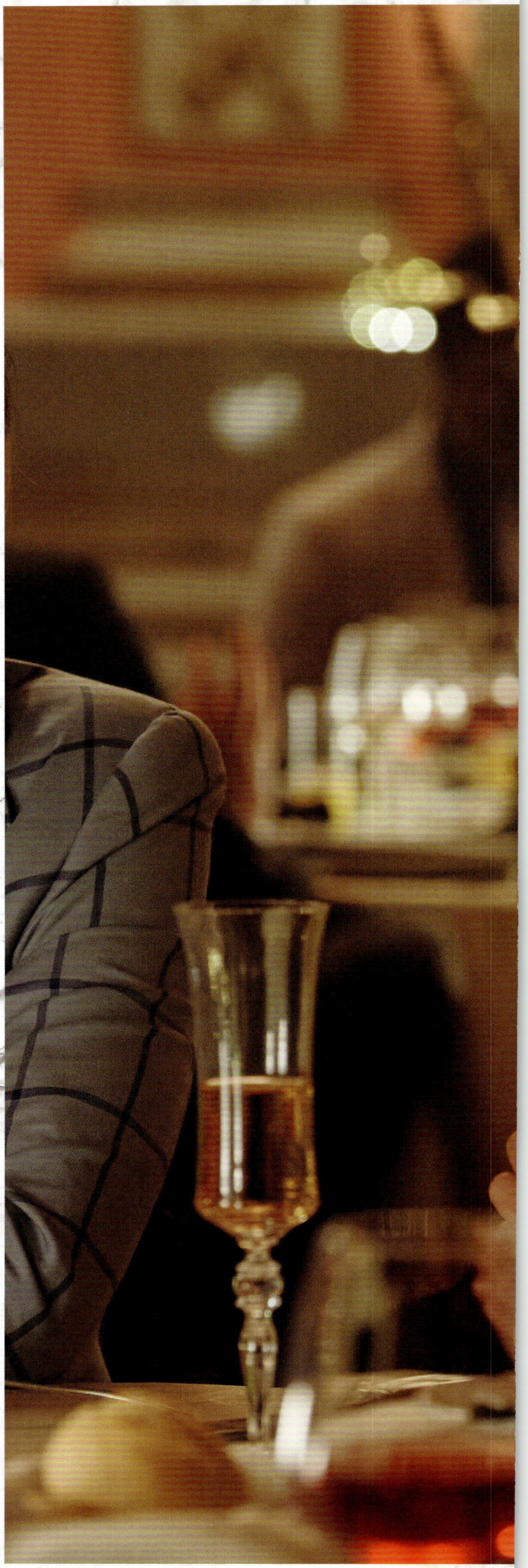

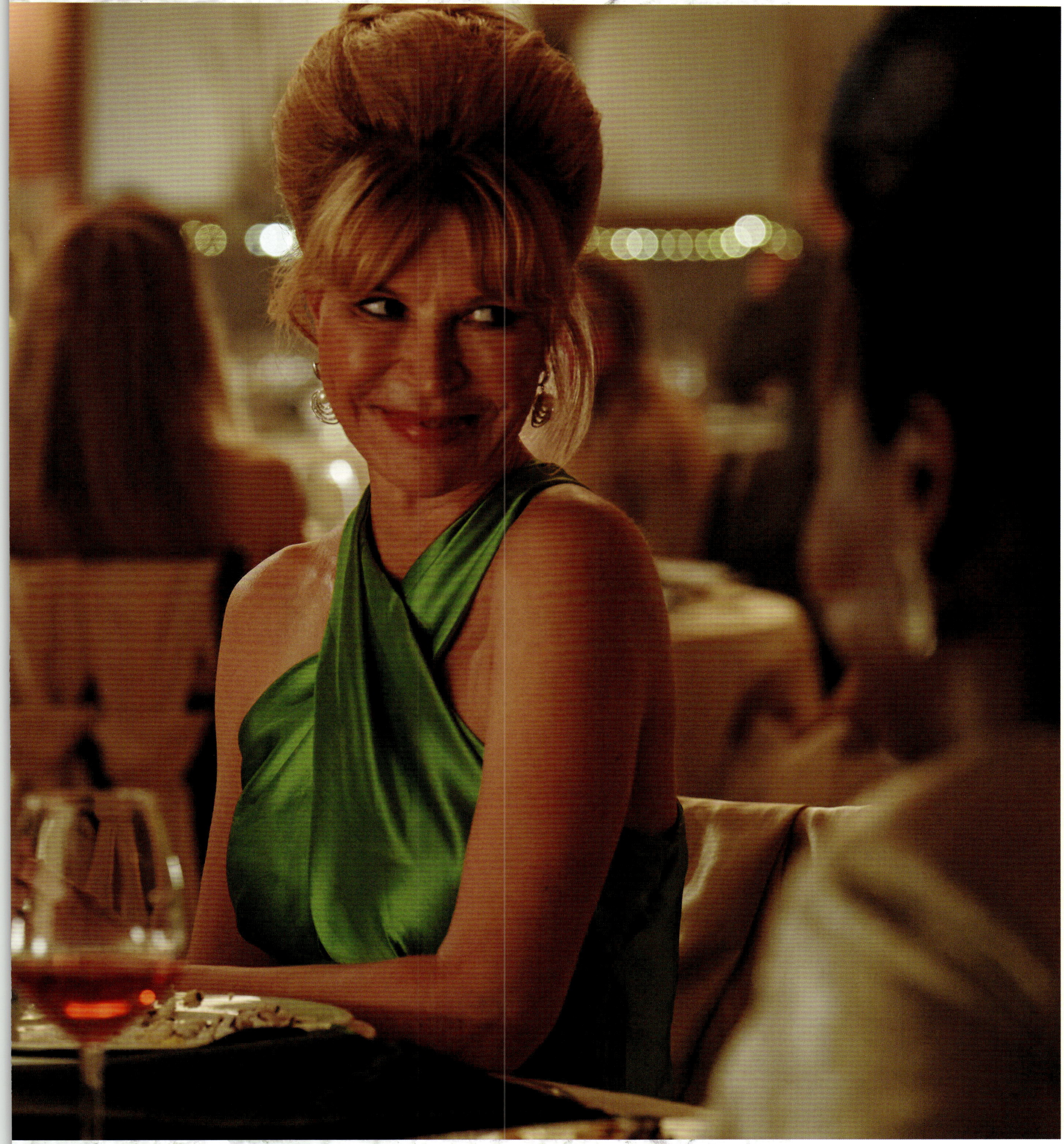

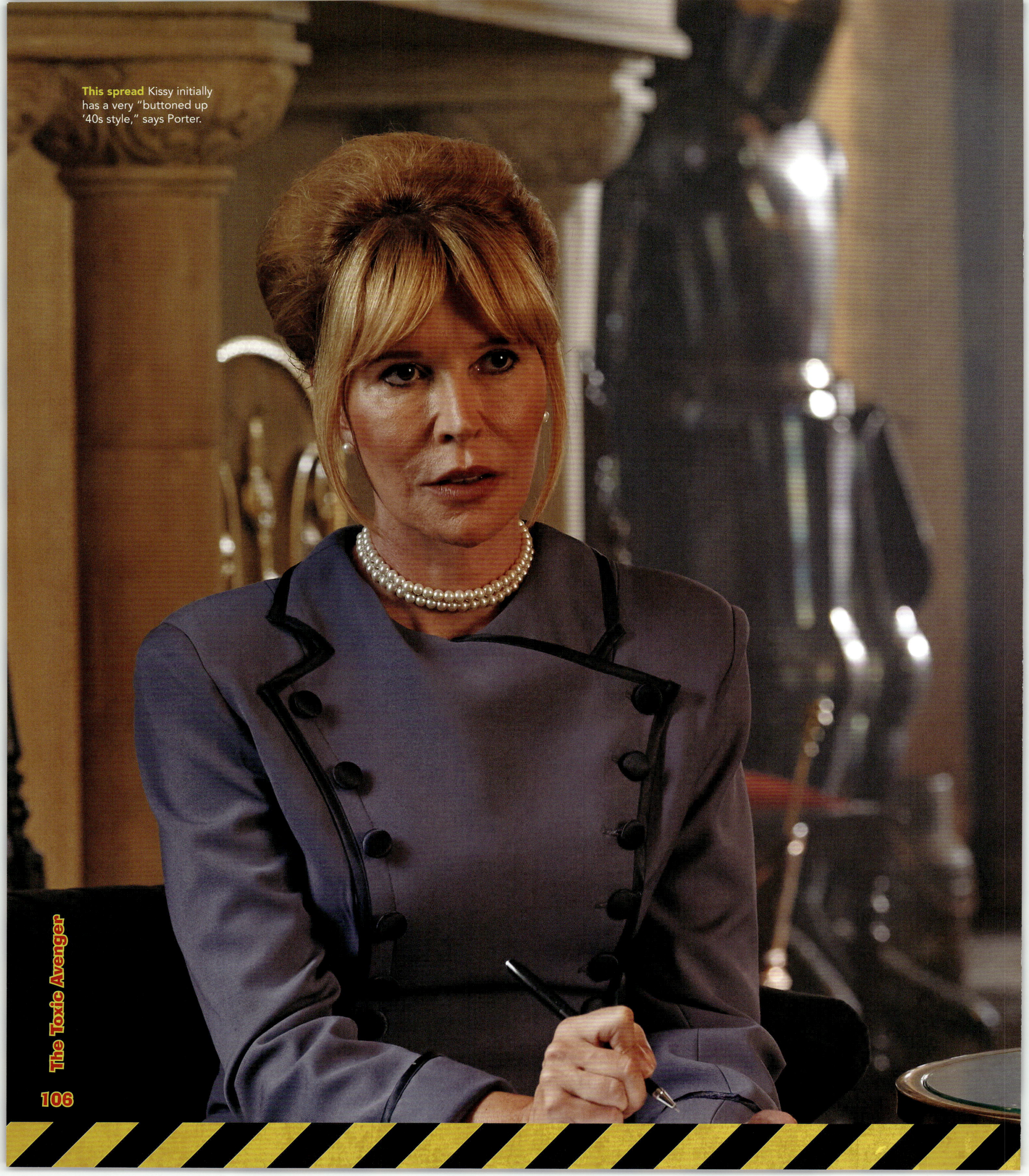

This spread Kissy initially has a very "buttoned up '40s style," says Porter.

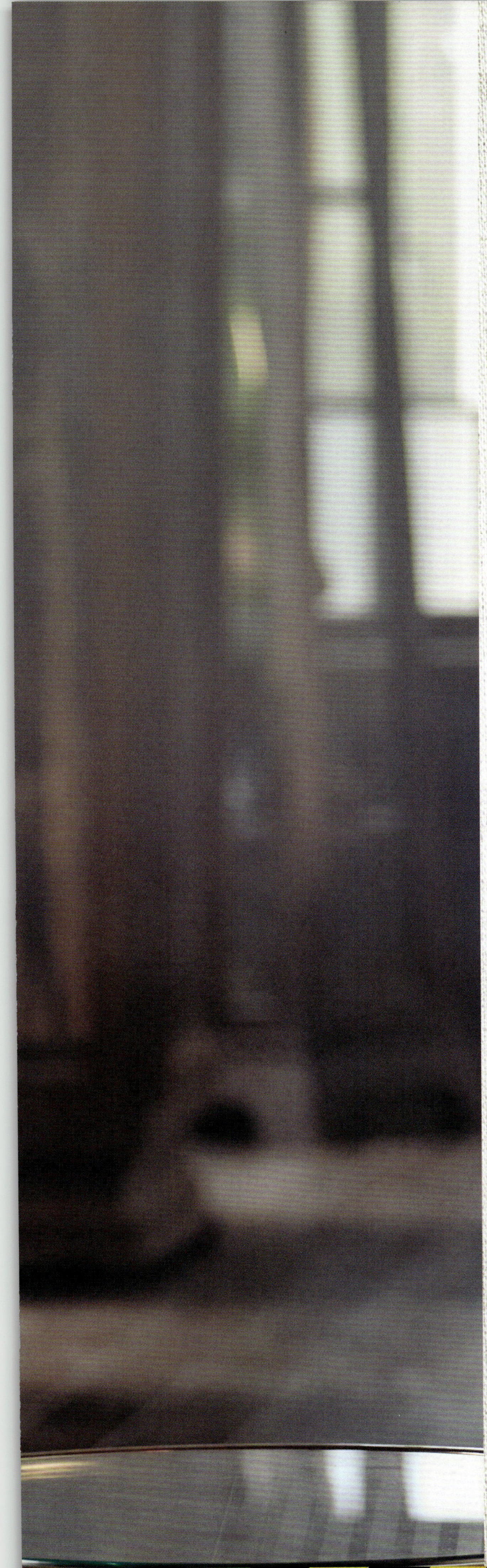

"I start off looking quite held together, with beehivey hair, then I become more and more unhinged. I look absolutely insane by the end."

– JULIA DAVIS,
Actor

ask you to do that," Blair says. "It was fun letting her do her thing and bring that to the role, so there's a lot of stuff in the movie that's just Julia making things up."

Such as the moment where Garbinger orders Kissy to fetch him a smoothie. "I came up with this idea that I'd manoeuvre myself as if I think he's gonna kiss me, and then he doesn't, and I start undoing his dressing gown, just sort of taking it too far," says Davis. "That was fun."

Her approach was embraced by Bacon, too, even though he's an actor who prefers to rehearse and figure things out beforehand. "They both ended up experimenting with scenes and throwing stuff at each other," Blair says. "Even if you don't use most of those takes, you only need one of those unexpected things to really land for it all to have been worthwhile."

Where Kissy took Davis out of her (dis) comfort zone was in her transformation towards the end of the film, after she snatches a few drops of the mutation serum extracted from Toxie, and becomes a demonic warrior woman. "I start off looking quite held together, with beehivey hair, then I become more and more unhinged. I look absolutely insane by the end, with really luminously yellow teeth, veins everywhere, and insane hair. It reminded me a bit of the film *Seven*, where they find that decaying person on the bed."

The makeup process wasn't too onerous ("maybe a couple of hours — nothing as bad as anyone else"), though Davis did draw the line at wearing contact lenses to turn her eyes a diabolical red. "Before I accepted the part I told Macon, 'I'm so squeamish about eyes, I don't think I could do that.' Luckily, he said, 'I'm not employing you for your contact-lens skills. We'll just have to CGI that stuff.' I regret I couldn't do it, but on the other hand all the people who *were* wearing contact lenses were getting horrible eye infections and sand in their eyes and stuff like that. I felt lucky I didn't have to do that."

She also enjoyed getting to do some action for the first time in her career. "I did a few fight things with Luisa, which was quite fun for me, because it's so out of my normal range of stuff. I was nervous, though. I thought, 'I'm not going to be able to remember this sequence that I'm meant to do.' But what I liked about Luisa is she wasn't worried about hurting me. There's a point where she attacks me from behind, and she really went for it. She just grabbed me and whacked me! But I liked it. She didn't really hurt me."

The best thing about getting stuck into the fight work—while wielding a combat chain in one scene, no less—is it finally gives Davis the chance to impress her children. "I've got teenage twin boys who I knew were gonna really love seeing me doing stunts." She pauses and laughs. "Well, they're gonna be very *amused*..."

FRITZ

PLAYED BY ELIJAH WOOD

If B.T.H. overlord Bob Garbinger is a self-made golden god, then his younger sibling Fritz is the creature that lurks in the long shadow Bob casts. "His brother got all the good genes," explains Elijah Wood, who's best known as Frodo Baggins in Peter Jackson's *The Lord of the Rings* saga, but also memorably played shuriken-throwing misfit Tony in Macon Blair's 2017 directorial debut *I Don't Feel at Home in This World Anymore*. "Fritz was essentially born ill. He's sickly, hunchbacked, has unattractive thinning hair. Maybe a product of chemical exposure; we don't know. He very much lives in the shadow of his very successful, *übermensch*, attractive older brother, and that gives him a pretty serious complex. He tries to please his brother at every step and do whatever he needs him to do. Thus he works in the criminal underbelly—although he also has a passion for music and is the manager of The Killer Nutz."

The part, very much in the classic 'cringing villain sidekick' mould, was created by Blair with Wood very specifically in mind. In addition to collaborating on *I Don't Feel at Home in This World Anymore*, the pair had been friends since meeting at genre-movie celebration Fantastic Fest in Blair's hometown of Austin, when Jeremy Saulnier's downbeat revenge thriller *Blue Ruin* (featuring a lead performance by Blair that blew Wood away) screened there in 2013. Blair liked the idea of putting the actor, who's best-known for likeable roles—with some notable exceptions, such as his serial killer in *Sin City*—in a villainous role. "I want this to be a sort of Peter Sellers-type thing where you can really disappear into this makeup and wardrobe," was

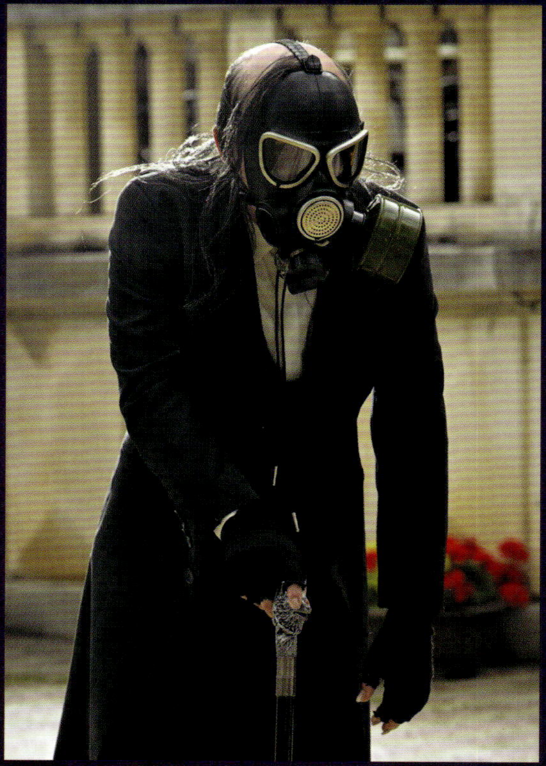

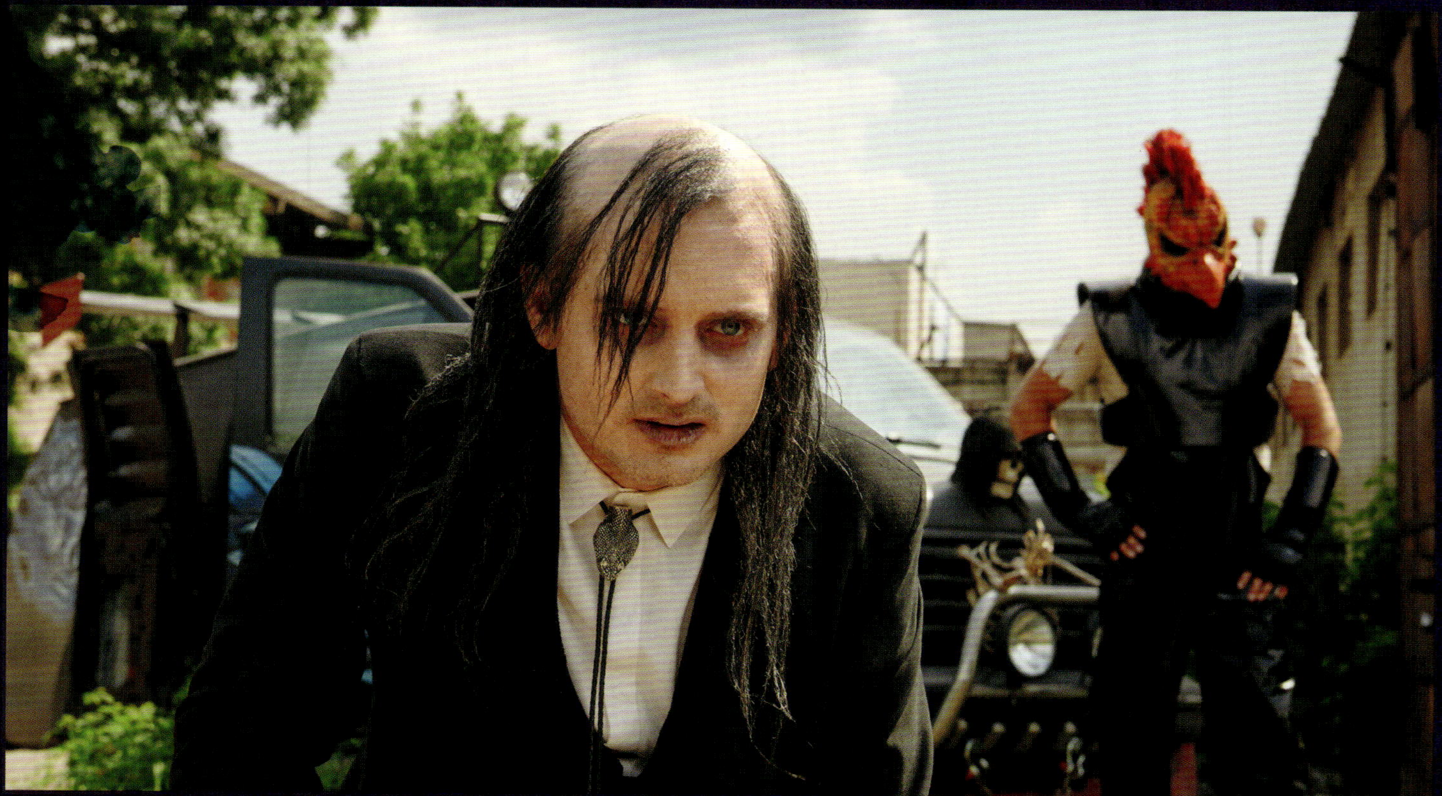

Above right Fritz prepares for a bit of chemical warfare.

Right As well as being Bob's lackey, Fritz also manages The Killer Nutz.

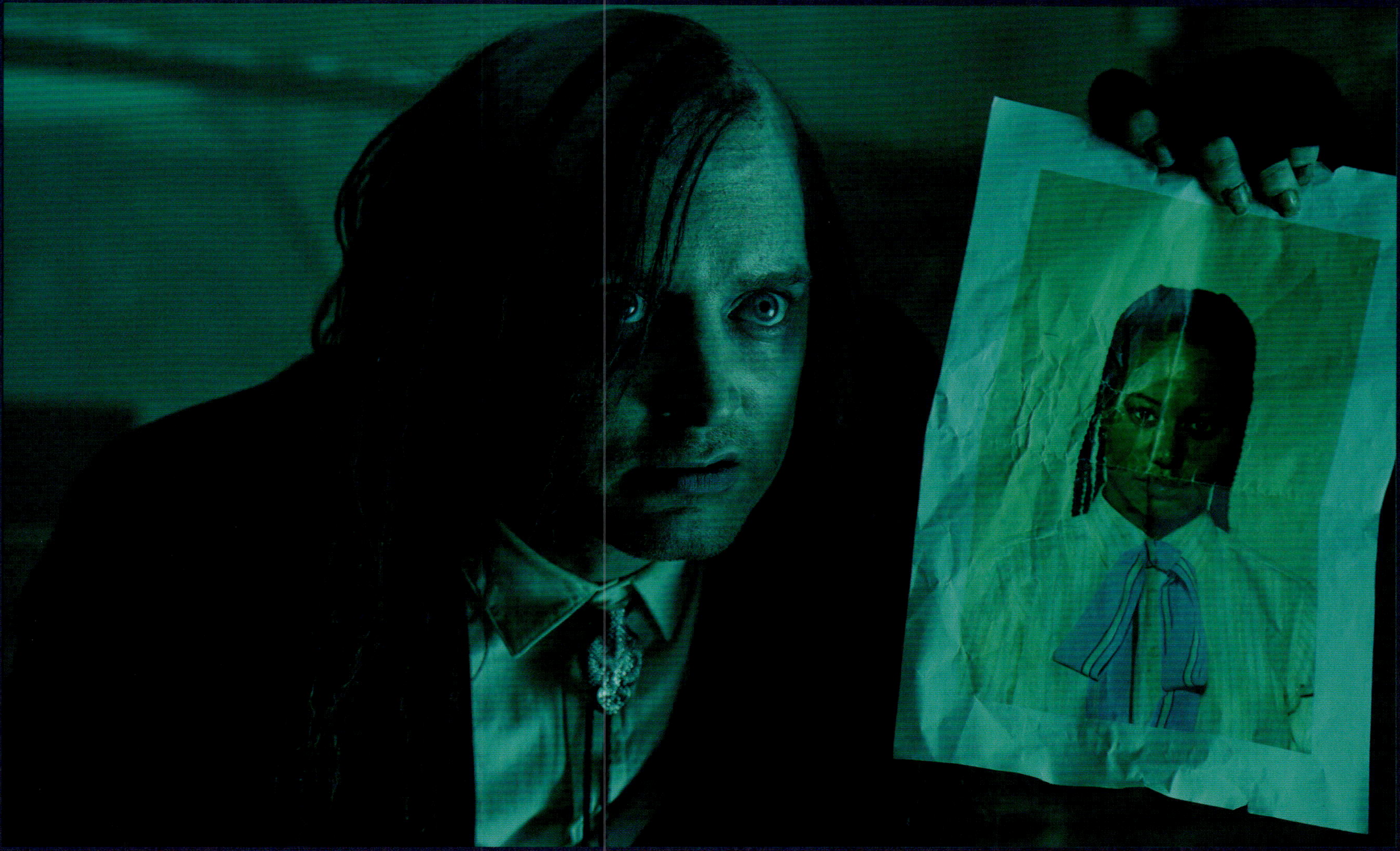

Blair's pitch to Wood. "You will vanish into this character."

Inspired by Riff Raff (Richard O'Brien) in *The Rocky Horror Picture Show*—with a bit of Danny De Vito's Penguin from *Batman Returns* thrown in—Fritz's look, like Toxie's, was anchored in an early concept sketch by character concept artist Vanessa Menendez. "When I was first sent the script by Macon, he included that drawing of Fritz, which we adhered to pretty closely," says Wood. The transformation process took about 90 minutes once it had been refined by the makeup team, with the costume comprising a lank wig, a hump, and long, grimy fingernails. Meanwhile, Fritz's funeral-director-style outfit included a single platform shoe with a false bottom, to represent his mismatched legs.

"It was fun for me," says Wood. "It was the first time I'd sat in a chair and had prosthetics applied. I've not really had that experience before—I mean, outside of putting on Hobbit feet," he laughs. But he was less worried about Fritz's look than getting the voice right. "What does this guy *sound* like?" he wondered. Fortunately, it came together during his costume test, when he became Fritz for the first time. "That was all I needed, to go, 'Oh, okay. He has a wheeze. He has a cough. His voice is going to be gravelly. It's not going to be *my* voice.' I don't often get the opportunity to play a character that looks and sounds so different from me. It was so freeing."

Above Fritz puts J.J. in the firing line.

Right & far right Fritz's look was inspired by Riff-Raff from *The Rocky Horror Picture Show*.

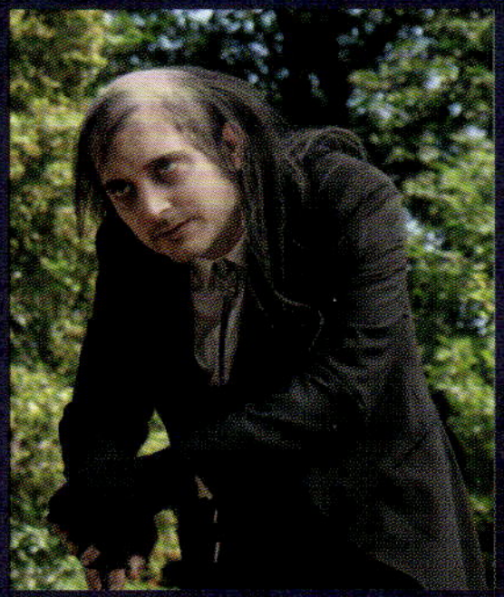

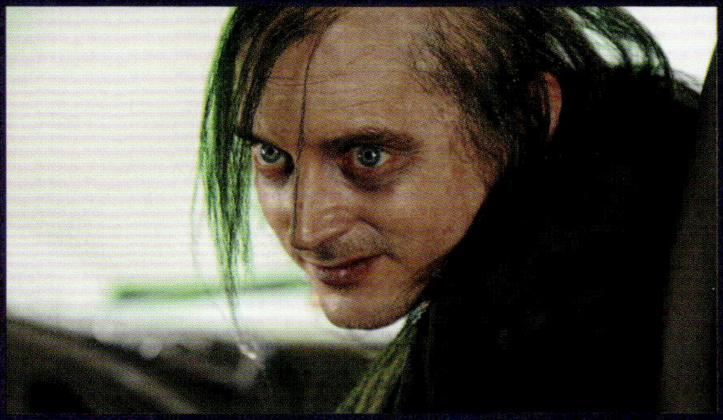

The other challenge of playing Fritz, Wood says, was to make him feel authentic rather than ridiculous. During the film we see him suffering from loneliness, at one point playing a pan flute with tears in his eyes, and he later forms a connection with Wade, which paves his way to redemption.

"He is a human being," says Wood, "not just this caricature of a hunchbacked, creepy man with a cane. So I had to find that in a way that felt like it honoured the character, but also showed a humanity there, too."

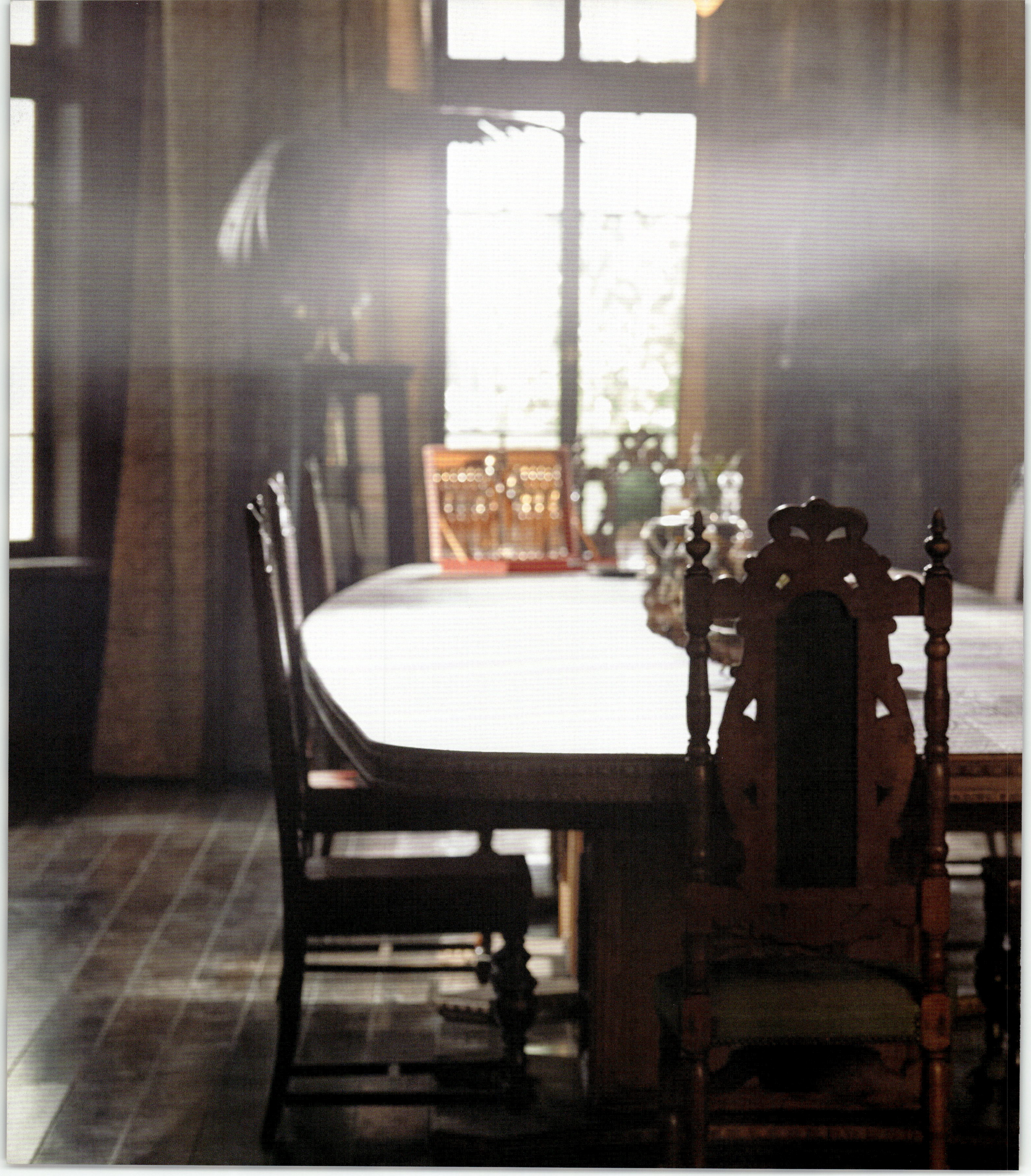

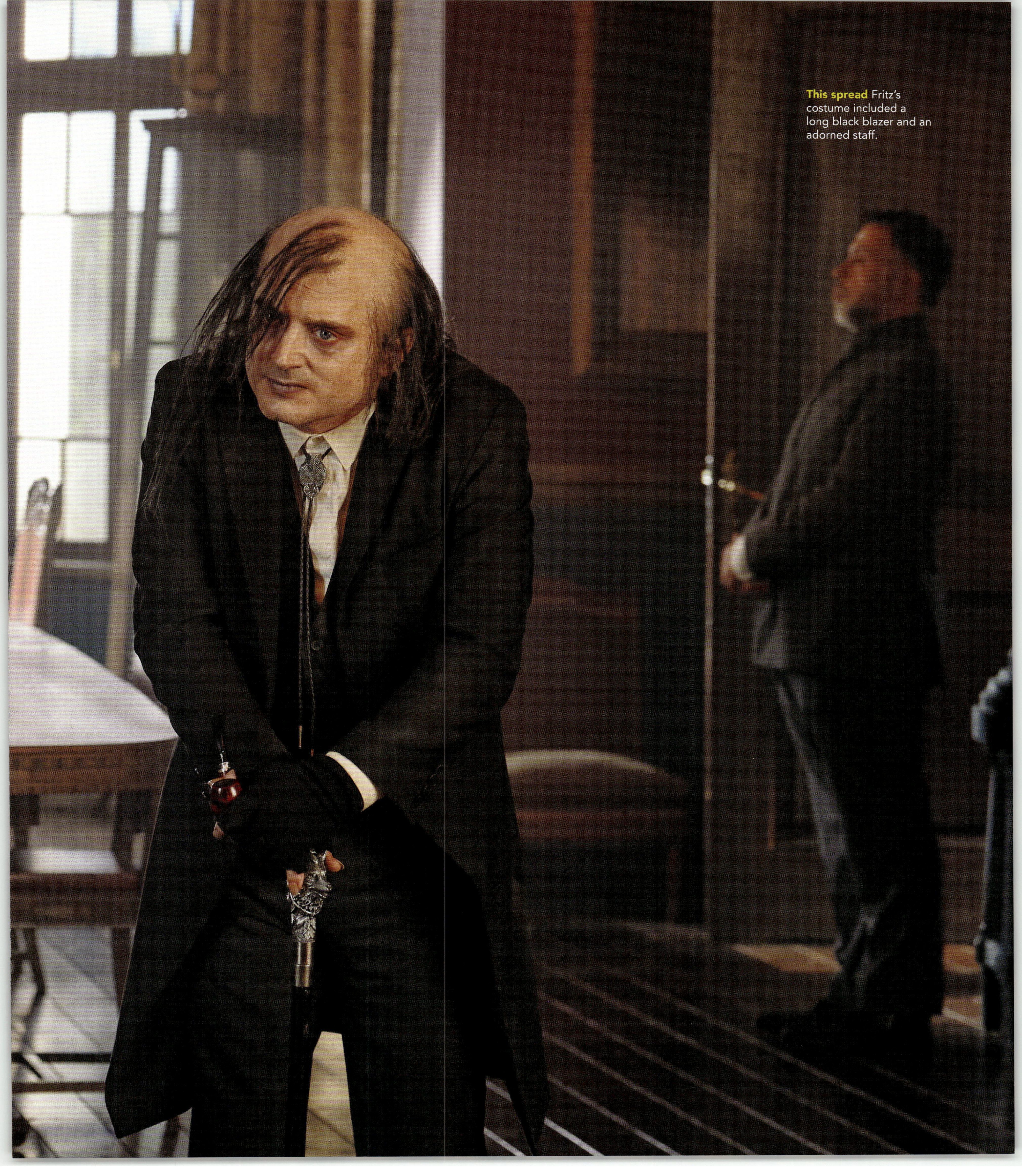

This spread Fritz's costume included a long black blazer and an adorned staff.

DR. WALLA

PLAYED BY SUNIL PATEL

It's a familiar scene: a character with a health concern goes to visit a medical professional, who gives them the worst news possible. Usually, it is a moment of devastation. A darkest hour. An emotional gut-punch. For Macon Blair, however, the scene where Winston visits his doctor to learn he has a potentially terminal brain condition was "a comedic anchor."

The idea was to undercut the intense drama of the moment by making Winston's consultant, Dr. Walla, utterly lacking in self-awareness. Winston's world has stopped spinning since he heard he needed to come in and discuss his test results, and he's desperate to get them. But Walla just "wants to keep shooting the breeze," says Blair. "We wanted to have the answer be as prolonged as it could, and have Dr. Walla keep talking about whatever nonsense he could come up with."

The two-hander scene required someone who could create the required chemistry with Peter Dinklage, and Blair found them in British actor and stand-up comedian Sunil Patel. "He has this style of comedy that is very dry, very low key and deadpan, which made a lot of sense. Winston bites his fingernails off while this guy just drones on and on." It was the first scene shot during principal photography, less due to its catalytic importance to the plot, than Blair simply wanting to do something that presented much opportunity for improvization, and which would elicit a lot of laughter on set.

"I remember that scene very fondly," says Blair. "There was a lot of having to hold the roll and reset, because everyone's cracking up. It was a nice way to set a tone going forward. Obviously, not every day was going to be as fun and jolly as that, but if you can aspire to have fun like that in the course of doing the job, that's a really good thing. There was no fight choreography. There were no special effects. It was just two funny, talented dudes sitting in chairs, hitting the ball back and forth. It was a really great way to kick things off."

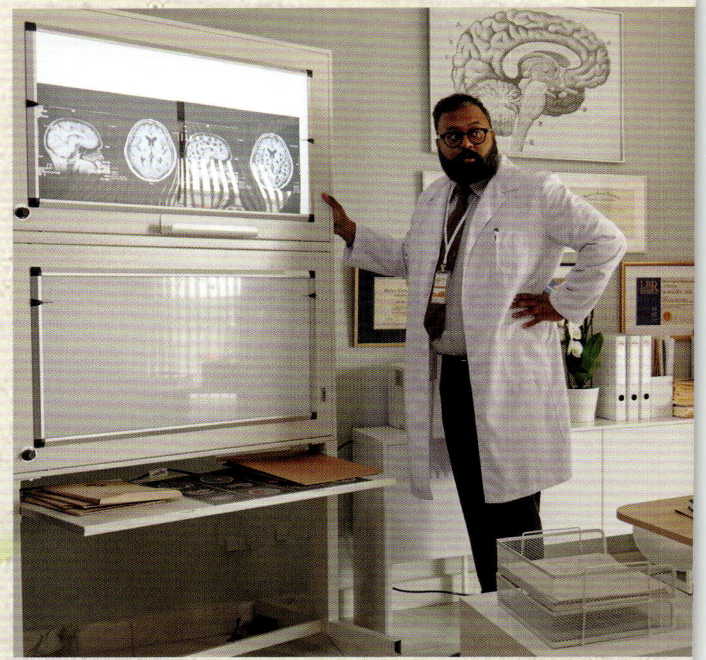

Right Dr. Walla in his office, with some of his "goofy" brain diagrams.

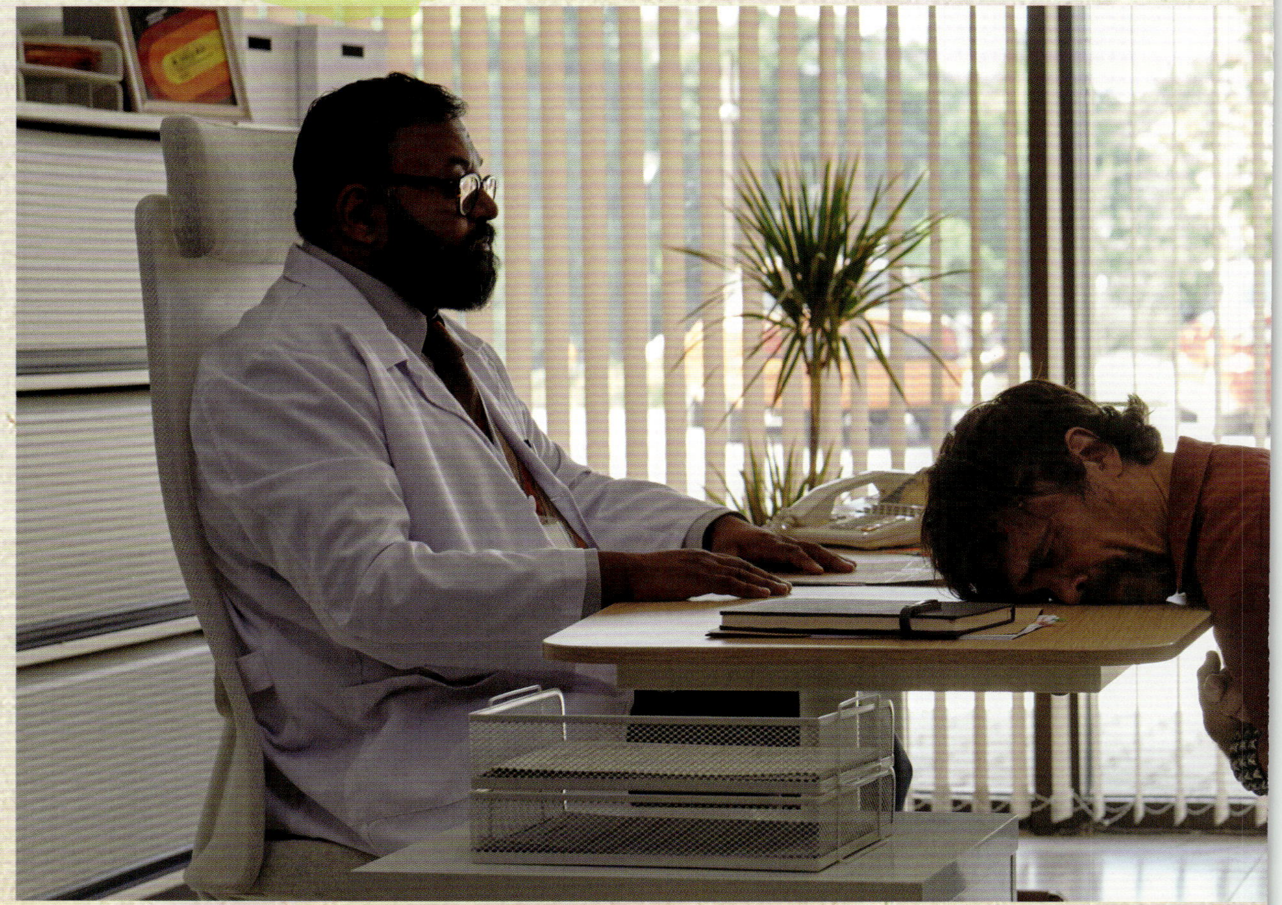

Below Winston does not take the news from Dr. Walla well.

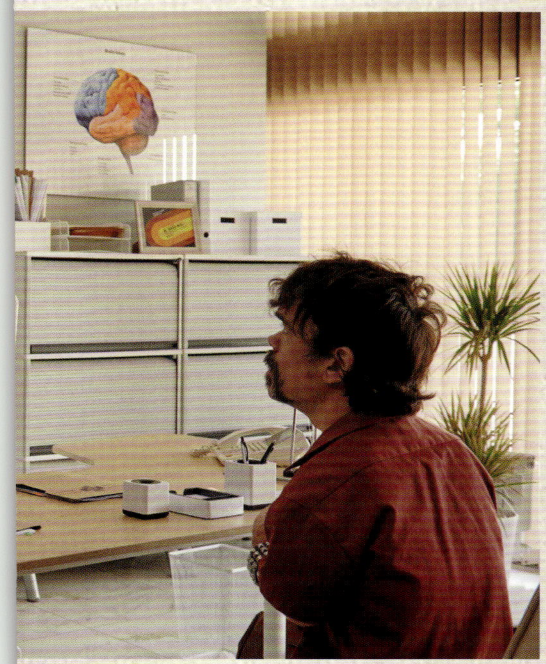

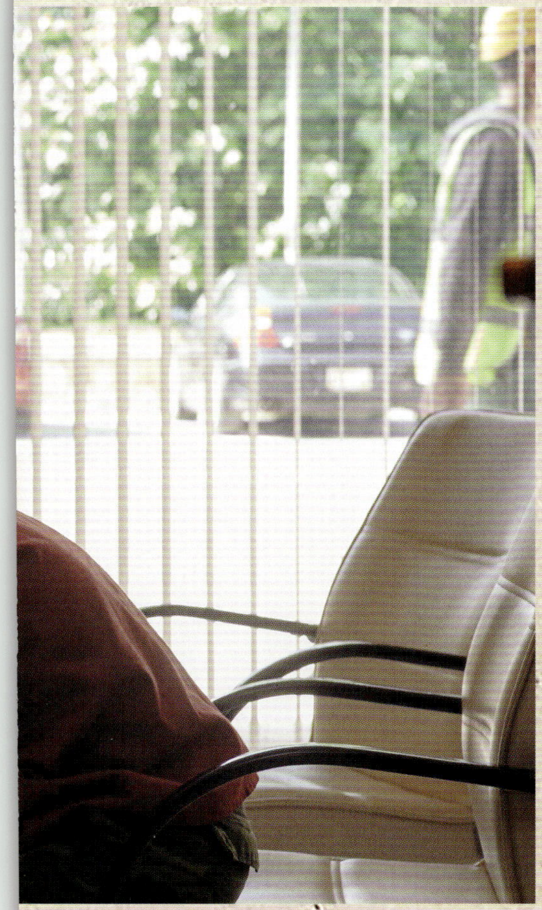

THE OFFICE

Within the four walls of Dr. Walla

In contrast to the comedy sparks flying between the two actors, the aesthetic aim for Dr. Walla's studio-constructed office was, says Blair, "to be deliberately bland, austere and clinical."

However, Cameron was still able to have a bit of fun with it. Dotted around the walls are various posters which depict images of the human brain in the most banal way possible—as if they're meant to offer reassurance to patients that this is definitely a neurologist's office, but they've been created by someone who knows nothing about neurology.

"It's such a stupid design," laughs Cameron. "It says: 'Brain: Front View… Side View'. It's just goofy."

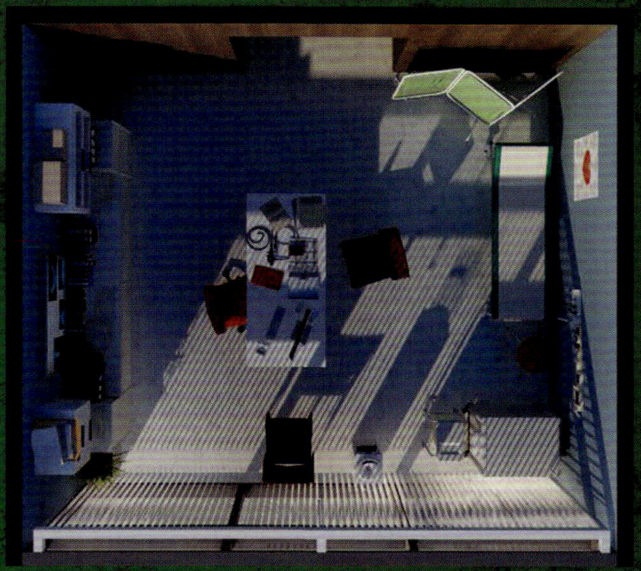

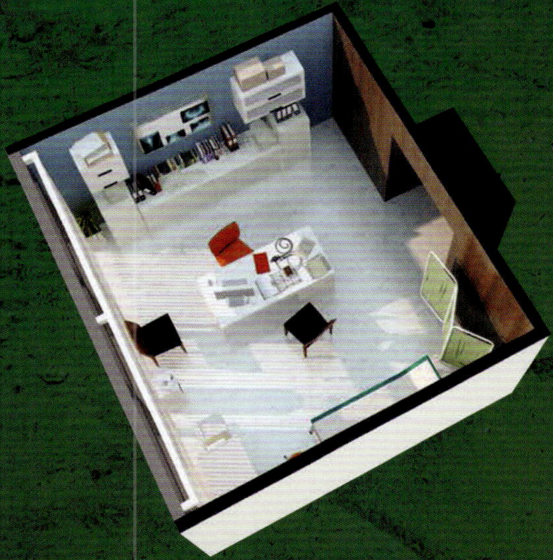

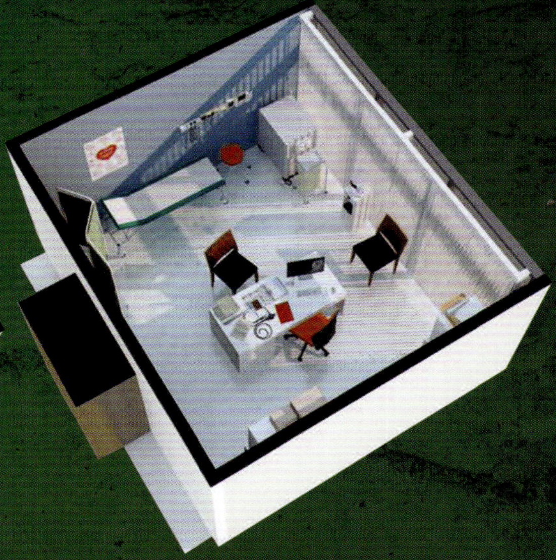

MAMMON HALL

The site of a banquet held in Garbinger's honour (and also of the heartless CEO's only encounter with the pre-Toxie Winston) Mammon Hall harbours Troma's elite, its poisonous crème de la crème, including its venal leaders. "It is supposed to be the centre of decadence and sinister riches," says Blair.

For both the venue's exterior and interior scenes, the production was able to film in and around Sofia's Central Military Club, which is used by the Bulgarian Army, but is also available for weddings and other functions. When he saw scouting photographs of the place, Gonzales was immediately impressed by its opulent yet brutalist design. It recalled one of his visual touch points for the movie: Bernardo Bertolucci's *The Conformist*. "I said, 'Hey, we should really think about shooting these scenes in here!"

Blair was impressed, too. "When you walk in, you're hit by this overwhelming pink-and-gold colour scheme. With its really high ceilings it checked a lot of boxes for us. It was perfect for this scene."

Right The team spaced chairs 2 metres apart to visualise social distancing.

Below Winston infiltrates the banquet as one of the masked waiting staff.

Opposite Behind the scenes during the Mammon Hall sequence.

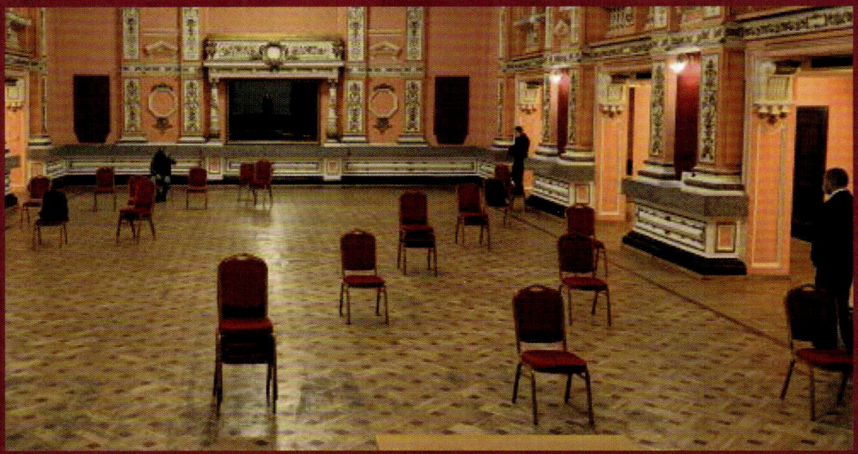

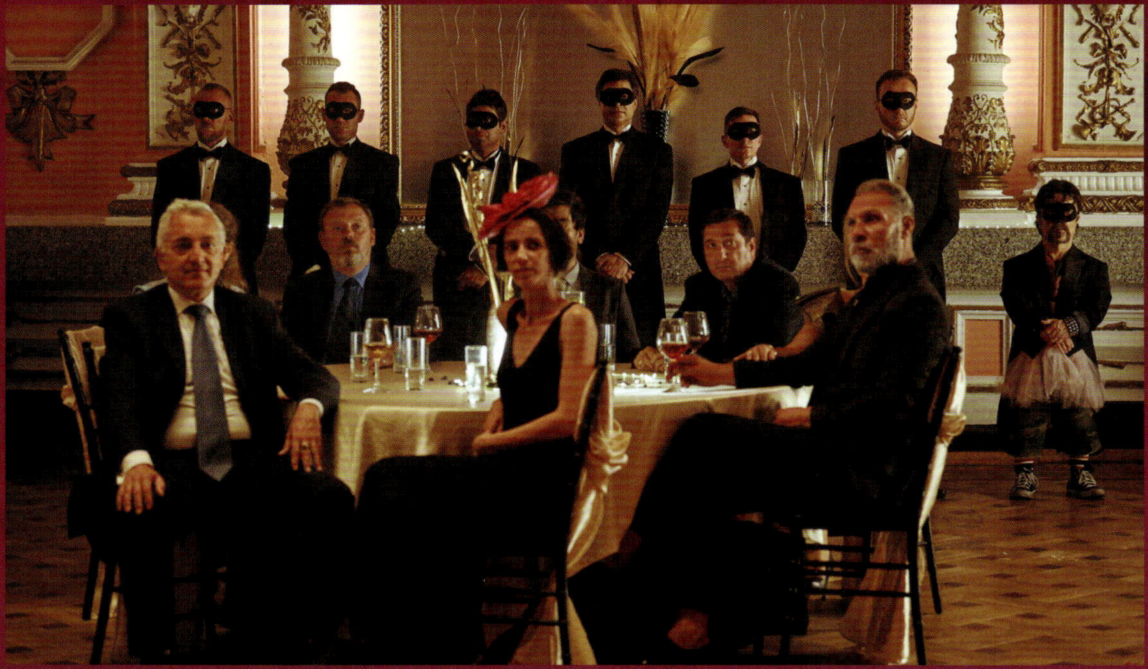

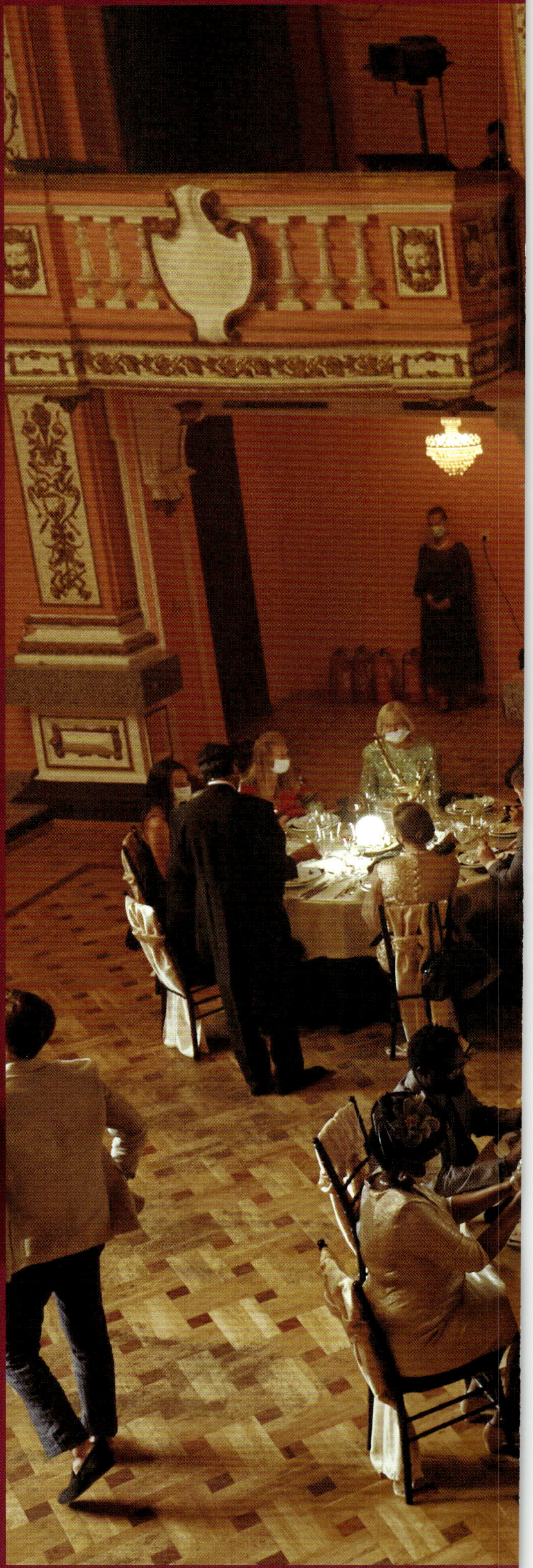

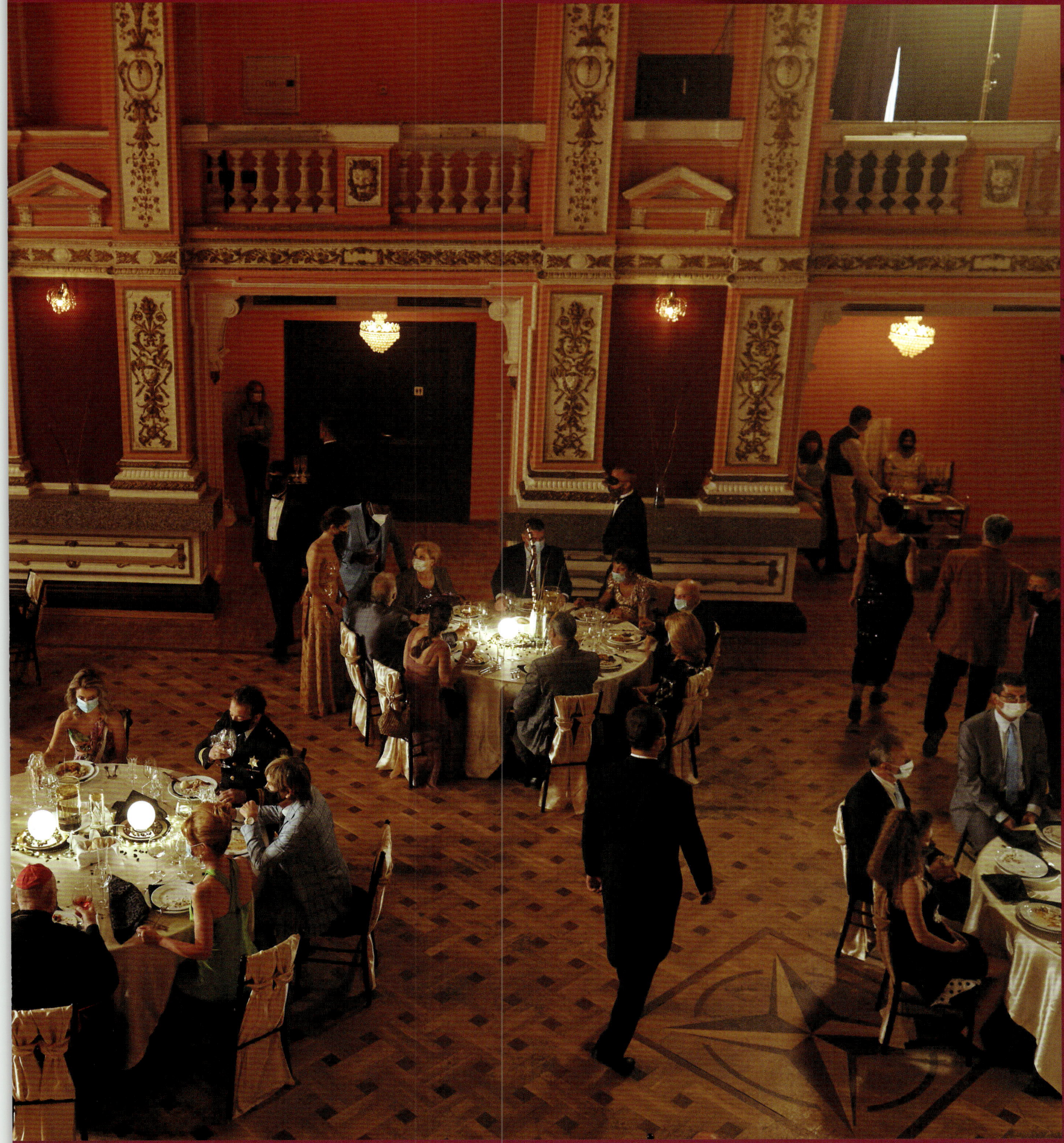

MAYOR TOGAR

PLAYED BY SARAH NILES

Unlike Mayor Belgoody in the original *Toxic Avenger*, Mayor Togar (played by British actor Sarah Niles) is not the town's top villain. However, along with the Police Chief and Cardinal, she does support and enable that top villain. "Garbinger doesn't exist in a vacuum," explains Blair. "He needs the support of the power structure, and they get a little payoff to turn a blind eye to, or help facilitate, what he's doing. There's a whole apparatus of corruption, and a larger machine for Toxie to dismantle."

But there are risks to throwing in one's lot with somebody like Garbinger. "At the beginning of the movie, he's moving onto thin ice—his company is starting to fall apart, which makes him desperate," Blair continues. "So Mayor Togar's on thin ice, too, which makes her very highly strung and anxiety ridden."

He cast Niles before he'd seen her performance as stern sports psychologist Dr. Sharon Fieldstone in Apple TV+ hit *Ted Lasso*. "She just auditioned and did the whole dinner scene in a really funny way," says Blair. "She never stops smiling, even though you can tell it's a very brittle kind of smile and she's about to fly apart at any moment. I just found that hilarious."

Bottom Crime clearly doesn't pay for Togar.

Below Togar in stern press conference mode.

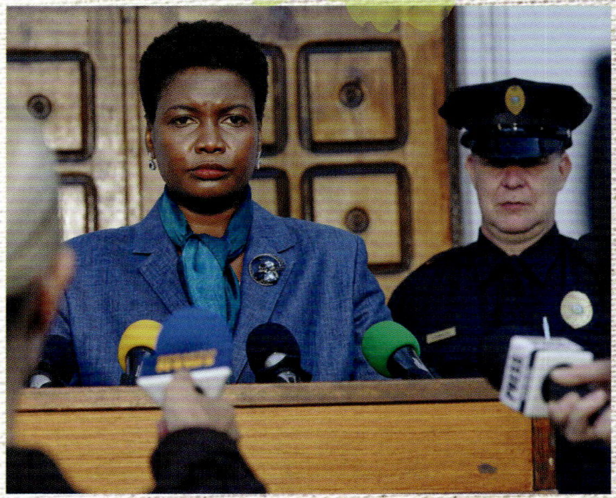

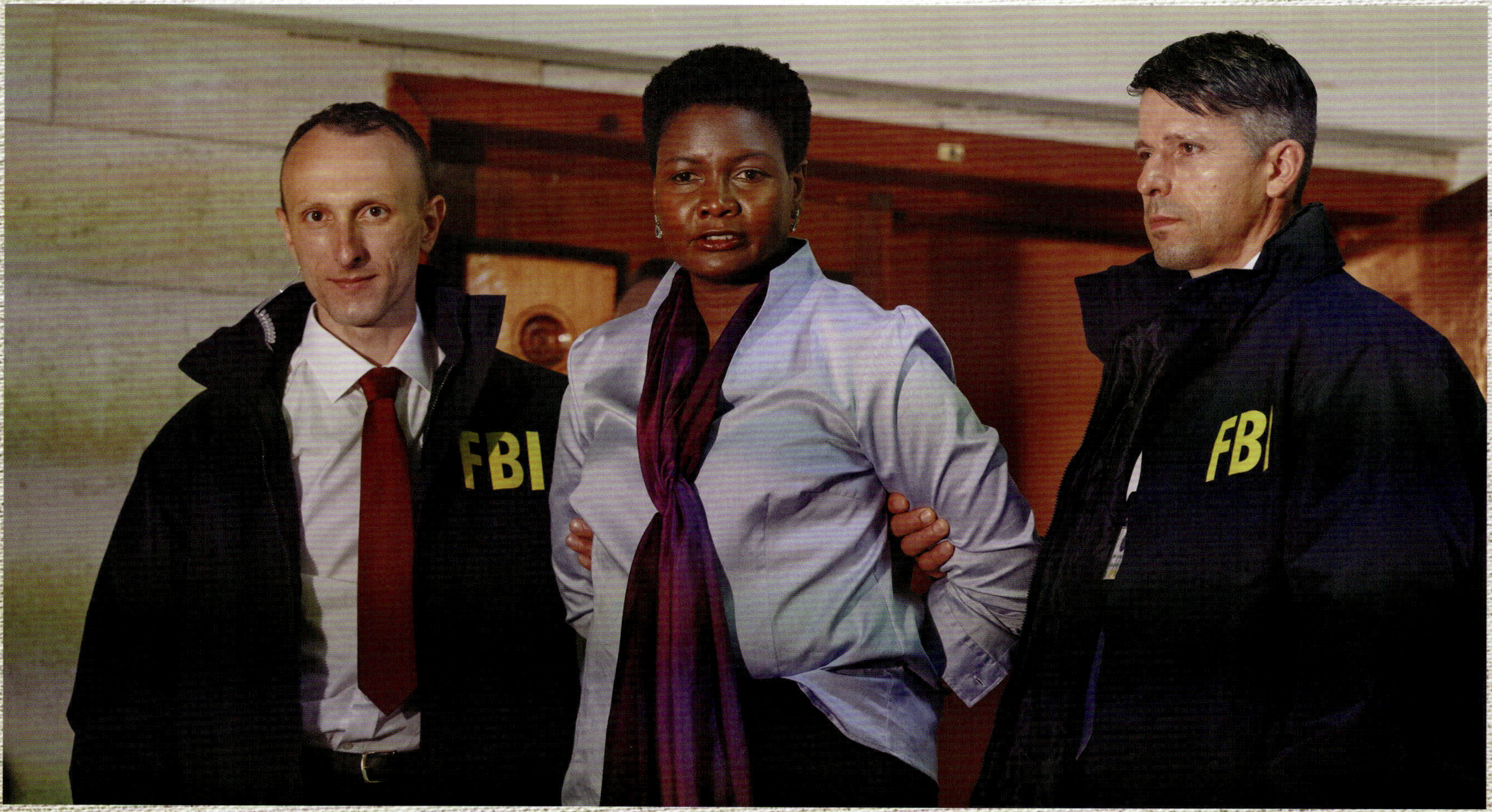

POLICE CHIEF WORMER

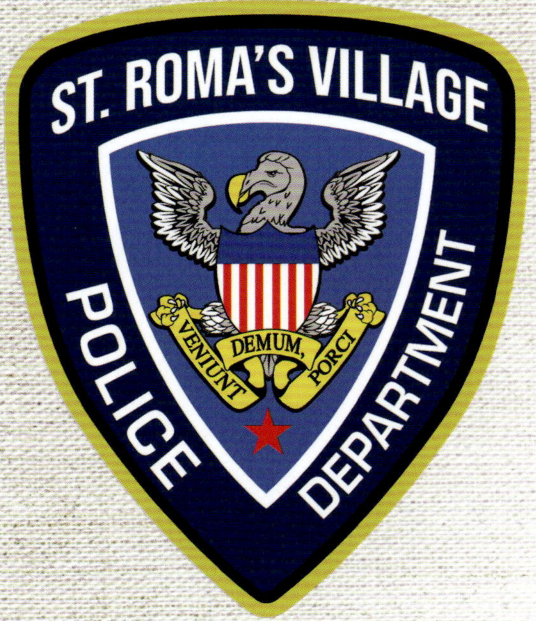

PLAYED BY ATANAS SREBREV

For the medal-festooned, "nakedly fascist" chief of police, Macon Blair enlisted veteran Bulgarian actor Atanas Srebrev, whose hard features and imposing physique have earned him roles in a long list of Hollywood action thrillers, including *300: Rise of an Empire*, 2019's *Hellboy*, and *Rambo: Last Blood*. "He's been working forever," says Blair, "doing a lot of acting in Sofia."

Wormer is Garbinger's "strong arm," the director explains. "He talks about thwarting unionization attempts at Garbinger's factory and deals with any problems Garbinger might have out in the streets. He has a very blustery, macho personality."

Below The venal Chief Wormer, dressed in uniform, attends the Mammon Hall banquet.

Left The St Roma's Village police badge. The motto translates as, 'At last, here come the pigs'.

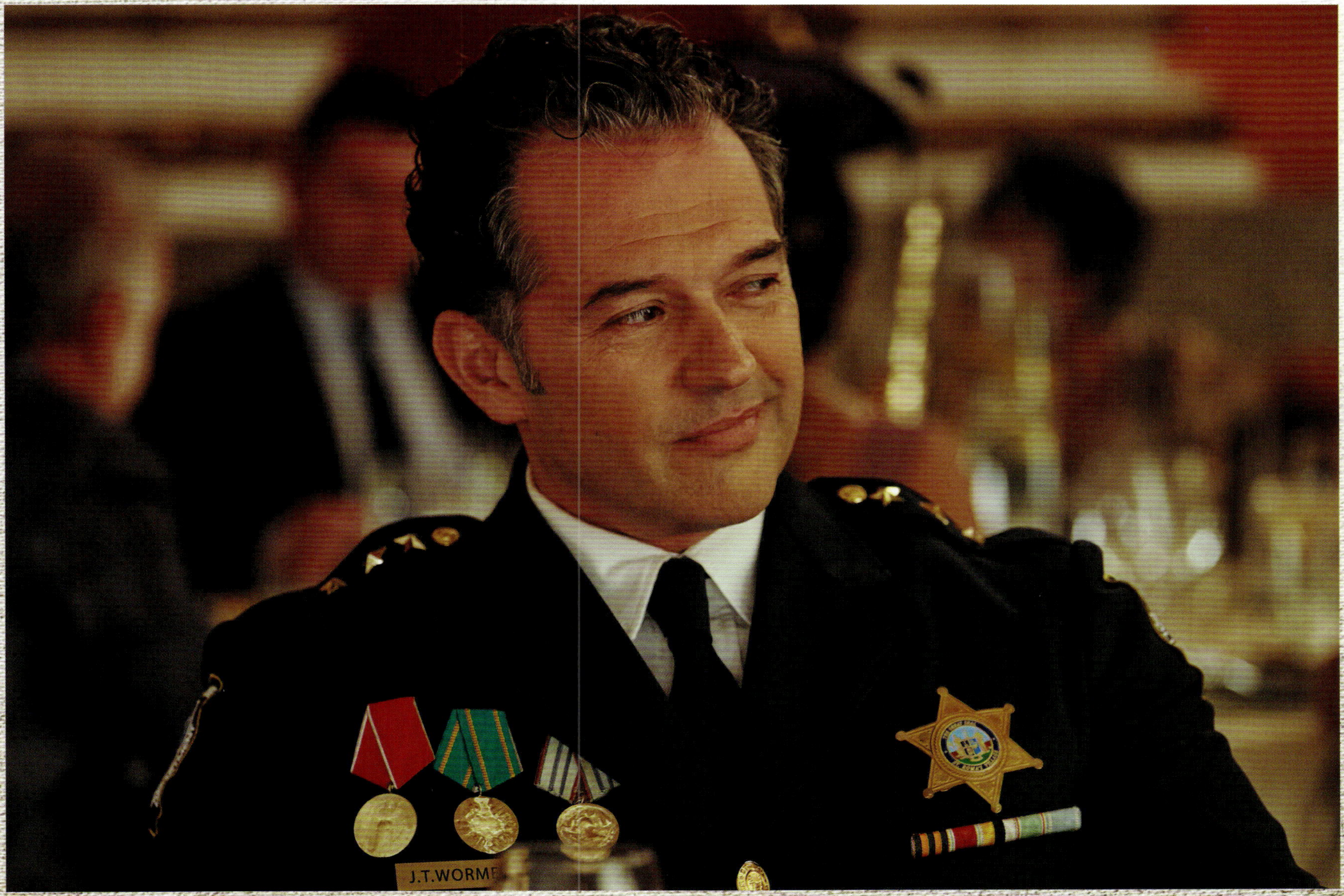

CARDINAL ROONEY

PLAYED BY VALENTIN GANEV

The third person in Tromaville's triumvirate of corruption is the nosebleed-prone religious leader Cardinal Rooney, played by Bulgarian actor Valentin Ganev. Decked out by Porter in full, pushed-towards-the-absurd regalia ("It's more hot-pink and garish than the real thing," she says), the Cardinal is perhaps the least stable of the three town leaders.

"He's meant to be deranged and not altogether there," says Blair. "But he's useful to Garbinger in terms of gathering public support, because he can give sermons that say, 'Garbinger is the best!'"

If this dodgy preacher's name—Rooney—sounds familiar, there's a good reason. "I took all the city power brokers' names from antagonists in teen rebellion-type movies," Blair reveals. "There's Ed Rooney from *Ferris Bueller's Day Off*, Principal Togar from *Rock 'n' Roll High School*, and then Dean Wormer from *Animal House*. I thought that would be cool for film fans, to give them some traditional villainous names."

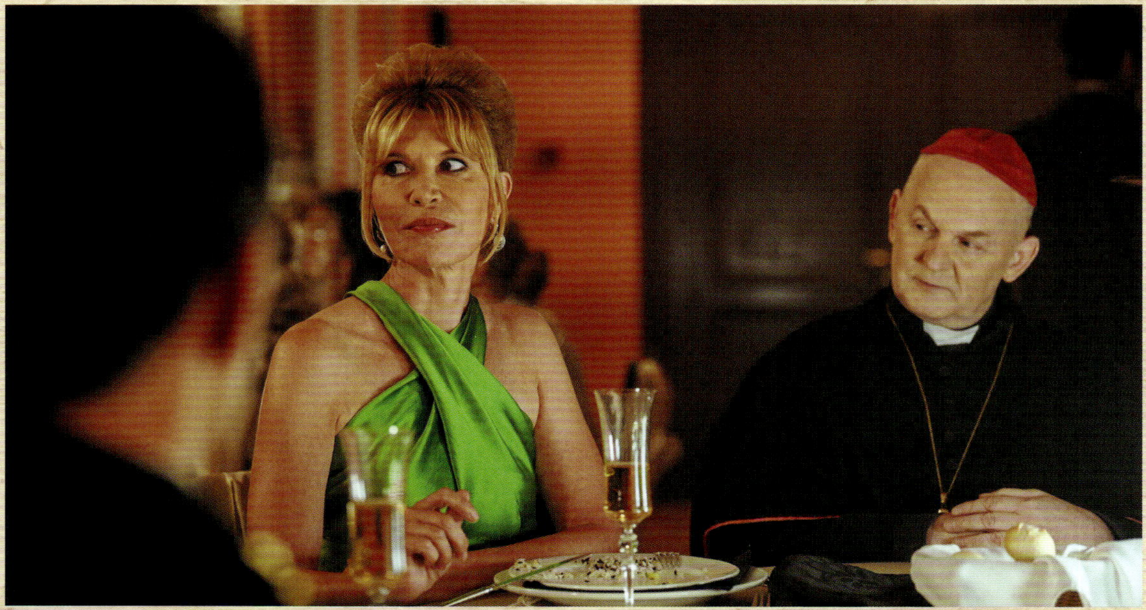

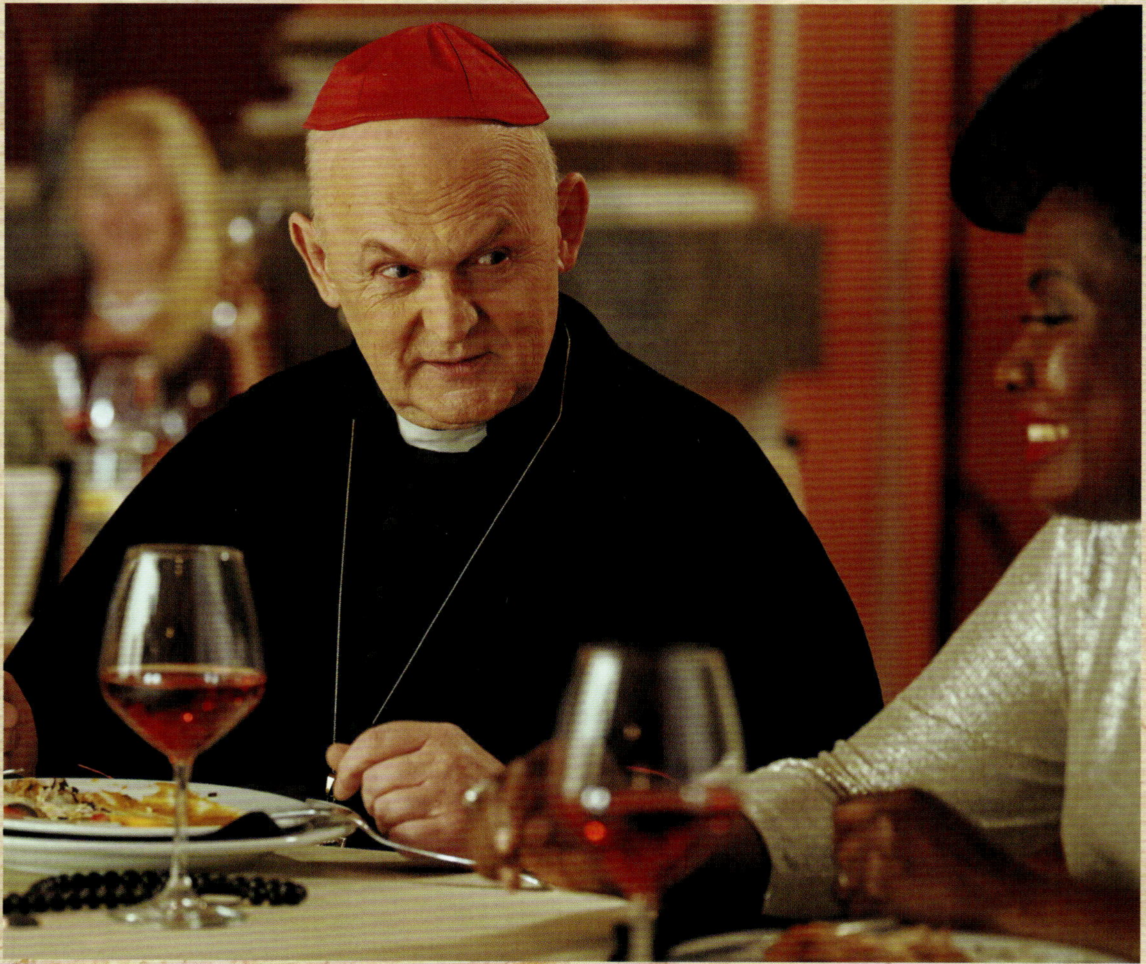

Above Cardinal Rooney attends the Mammon Hall banquet, dressed in robes.

Right Rooney with his partner-in-corruption Mayor Togar.

THE KHAKI KLUB

Knowing he needed to include an organized crime outfit in his narrative, Blair considered his options. He could look at the traditional Sicilian Mafia. Or the Russian mob. But it all felt too familiar, too "real world" for his Tromaville. So, in conceiving the gang godfathered by Thad Barkabus, Blair looked to a very different source of inspiration.

"I dug into '80s-movie rich-kid bad guys," he says. "The kind that James Spader would typically play, or the Socs from *The Outsiders*. But instead of just being rich, WASPy pricks with fancy cars, they'd operate like an organized crime unit, involved in extortion, shakedown rackets, that kind of thing."

For Porter, the costume requirements for these crisply-decked gangsters couldn't have been clearer. "Khaki pants, blue yacht-club blazers, pastel Oxford shirts… We were playing with that '80s prep vibe, although each of the Khaki boys is a different archetype of preppiness," she says. "For example, there's one that feels more contemporary and wears one of those banker bro vests."

"We were playing with that '80s prep vibe, although each of the Khaki boys is a different archetype of preppiness."

– VANESSA PORTER,
Costume Designer

Porter reveals that, above all else, it was Blair's depiction of the film's various gangs—the Killer Nutz, the Khaki Klub, the Nasty Lads—which made her want to work on *The Toxic Avenger*. "They're so defined by what they're wearing," she says. "It's a pretty fun criminal underworld in this movie, that's for sure!"

Below The Khaki Klub features a variety of looks based on '80s rich-kids.

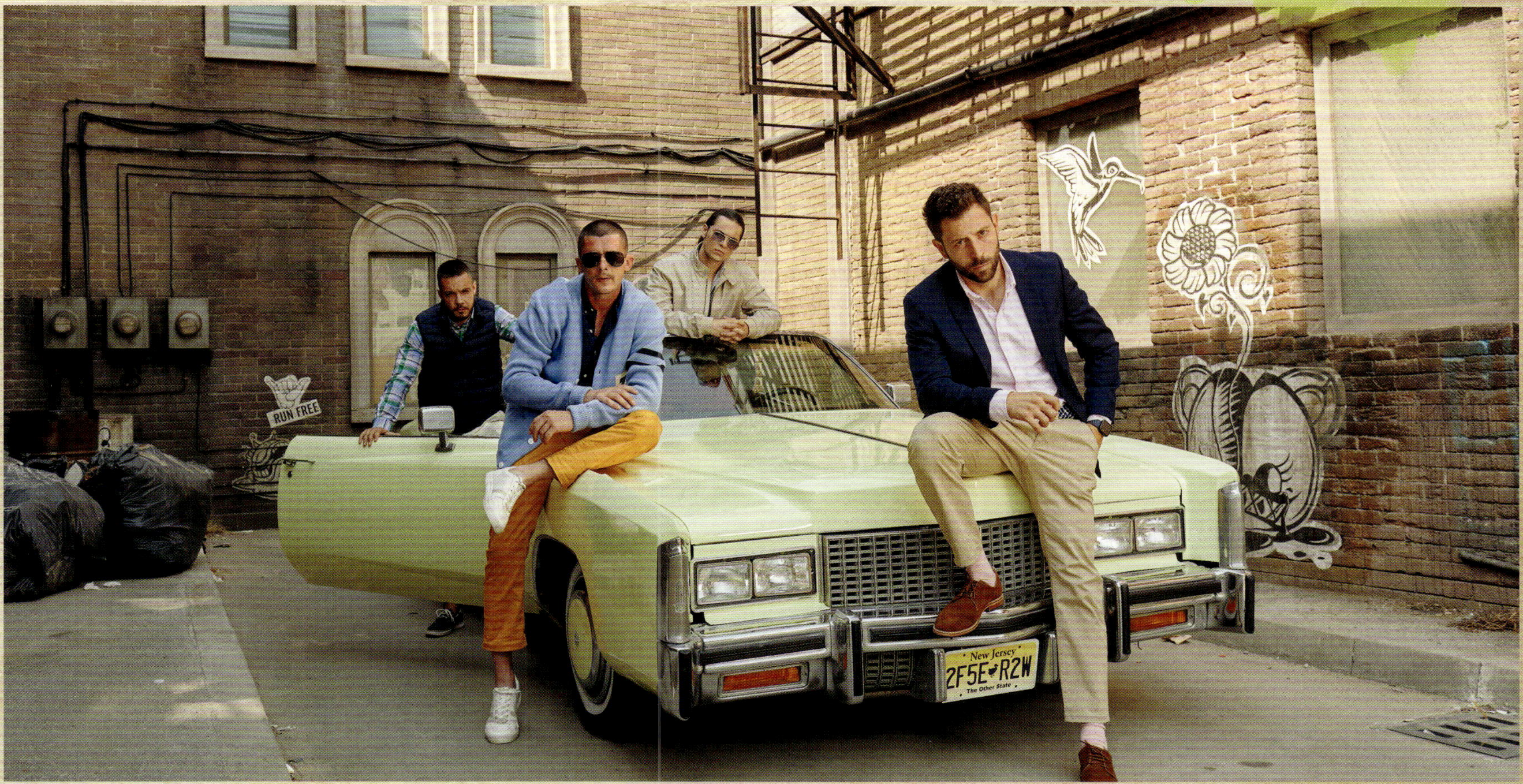

THAD BARKABUS

PLAYED BY JONNY COYNE

Behind the toxic-sludge-producing throne on which Bob Garbinger sits lies the true criminal power in Tromaville: Thad Barkabus, head of the town's preppily dressed Mafia substitute, the Khaki Klub. Described in the script as "a dead-eyed apparition in a yacht club blazer," with a voice that "sounds like boulders grinding together," the role required an actor with a very specific brand of menacing presence.

"This is the one character in the movie that Garbinger is afraid of," explains Blair. "So we needed someone who was quite intimidating and powerful on screen." He and his casting team met with many impressive candidates, but in the end, they decided that British actor Jonny Coyne—who played the mysterious warden in 2012 J.J. Abrams show *Alcatraz*, and more recently appeared in *The Blacklist* and *Preacher*—had the necessary chops to bring Barkabus to fearsome life. It wasn't just that he looks so formidable, with his heavy-set features and bald pate, but also that he offered a striking visual counterpoint to Garbinger's more charismatic and preening vision of evil.

"By that point we knew Kevin Bacon was going to be playing Garbinger," says Blair, "so Jonny felt the best opposite foil for Kevin. He just brought a huge amount of power, ferocity and terrifying energy to that part, that I was really pleased with."

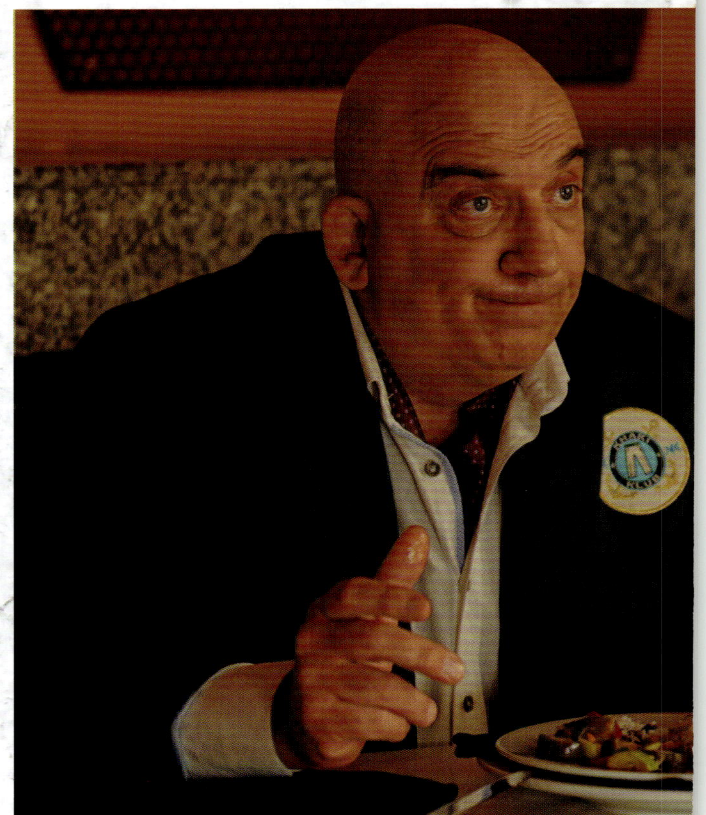

Below Jonny Coyne as Tromaville crime lord Thad Barkabus, flanked by heavies.

Right Barkabus in his signature yacht club blazer (complete with Khaki Klub badge).

Below right Barkabus dealing with his son Spence's limb-related misfortune.

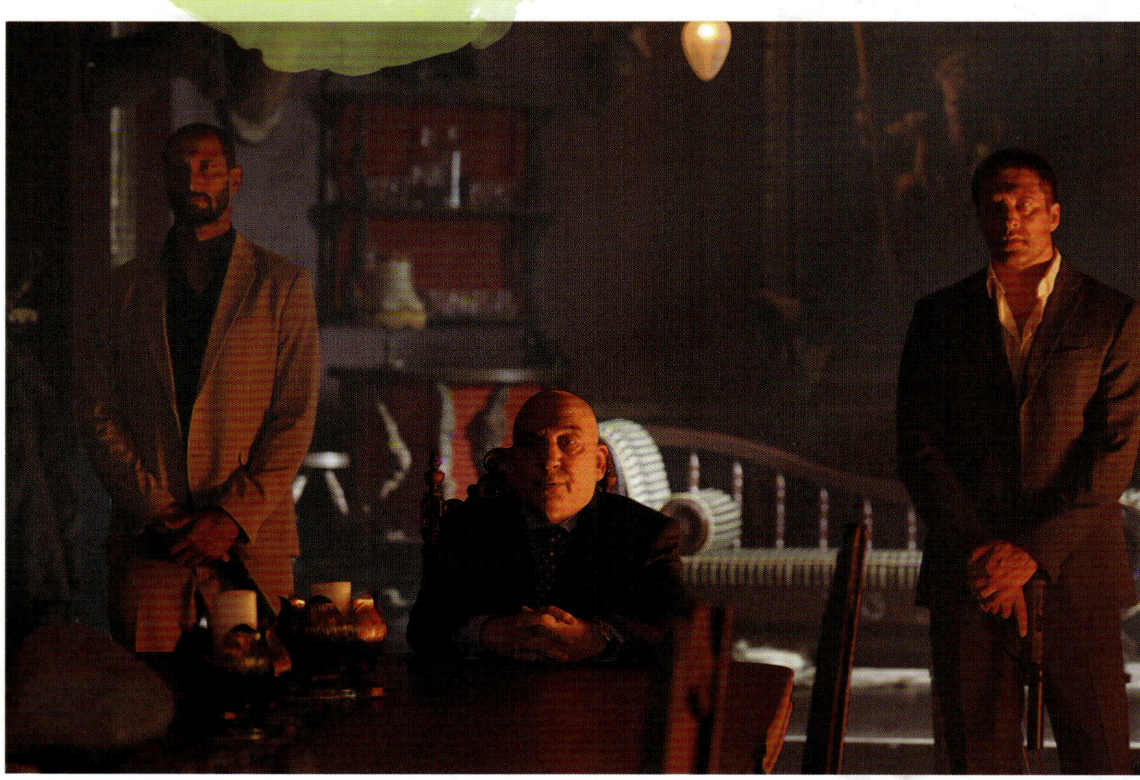

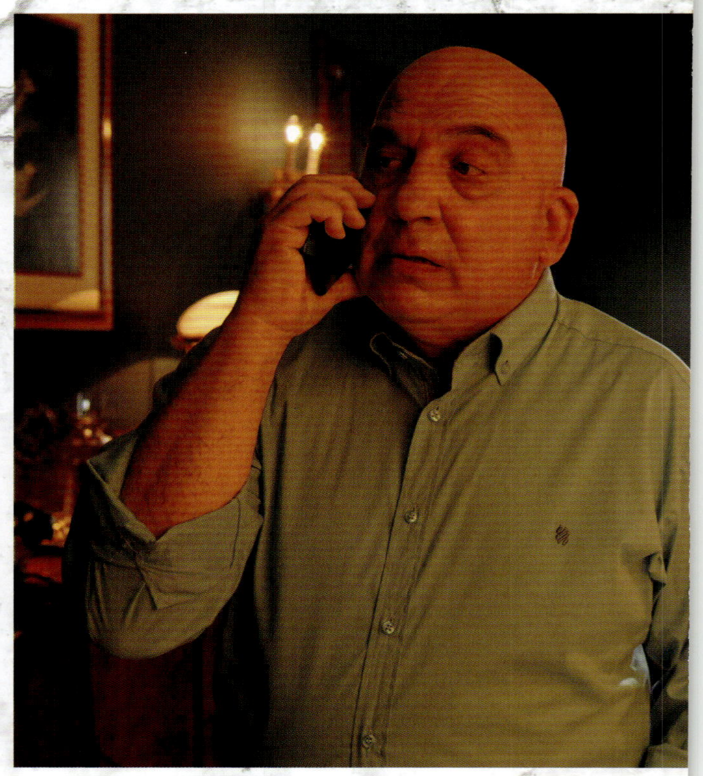

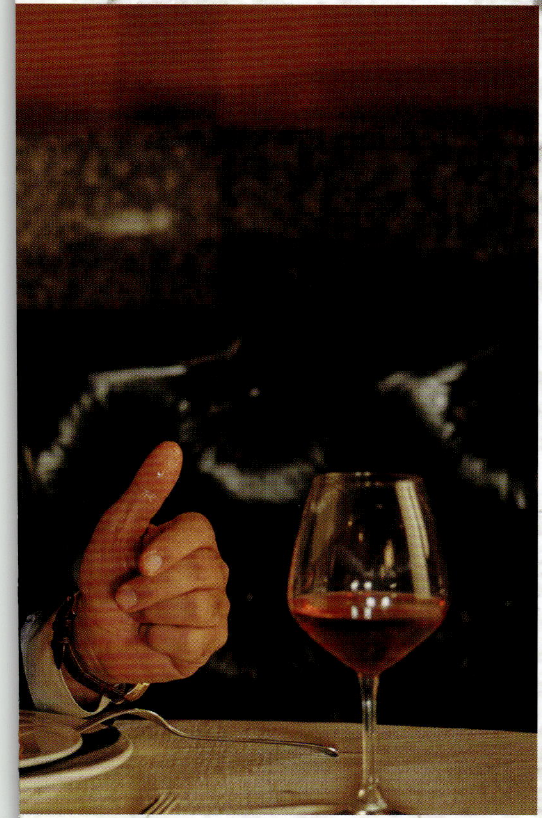

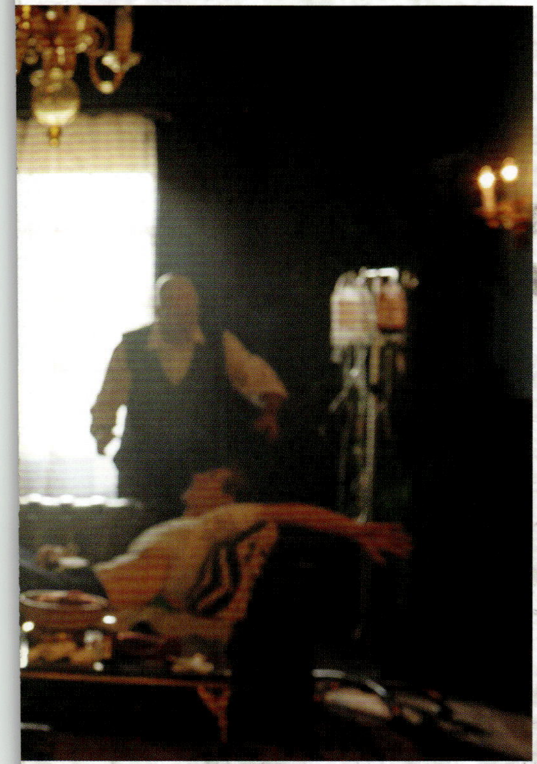

CRIME SCENE

The house that Barkabus built

You can tell a lot about a villain from their home, it seems. "Barkabus' house has a little bit of opulence, but it's not as out of control as Garbinger's," says Blair. "He has a little bit more actual class, as opposed to Garbinger's weird, phoney class." This is borne out by its fine leather chairs, wood-panelled walls and cut-glass tableware, all suggested by Cameron, whose team dressed an existing interior on the German Studios backlot.

"There wasn't a lot of specific description in the script about what was needed," admits Blair. "So this was a set we just turned Alex loose on."

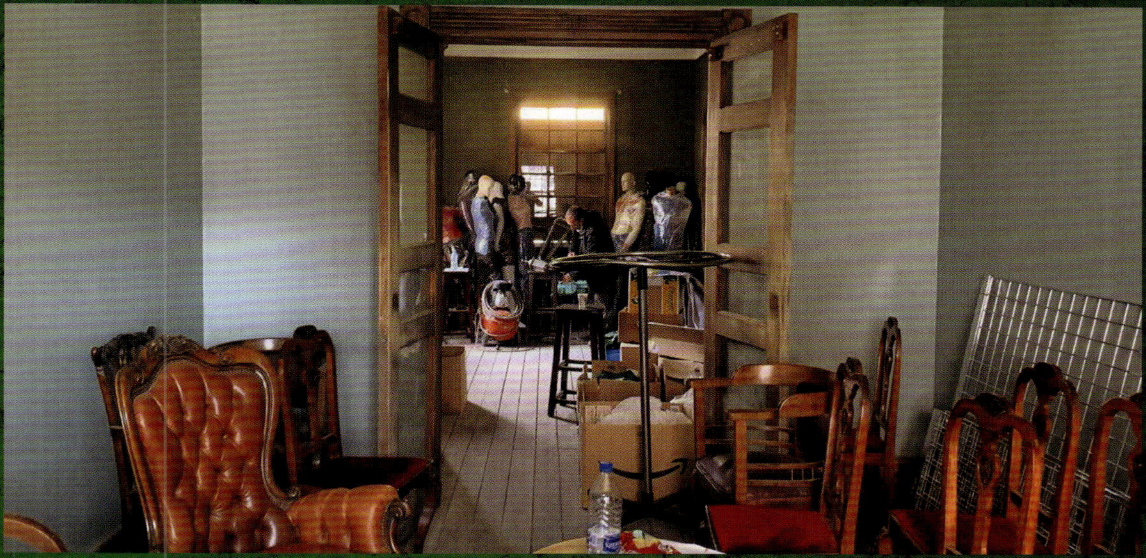

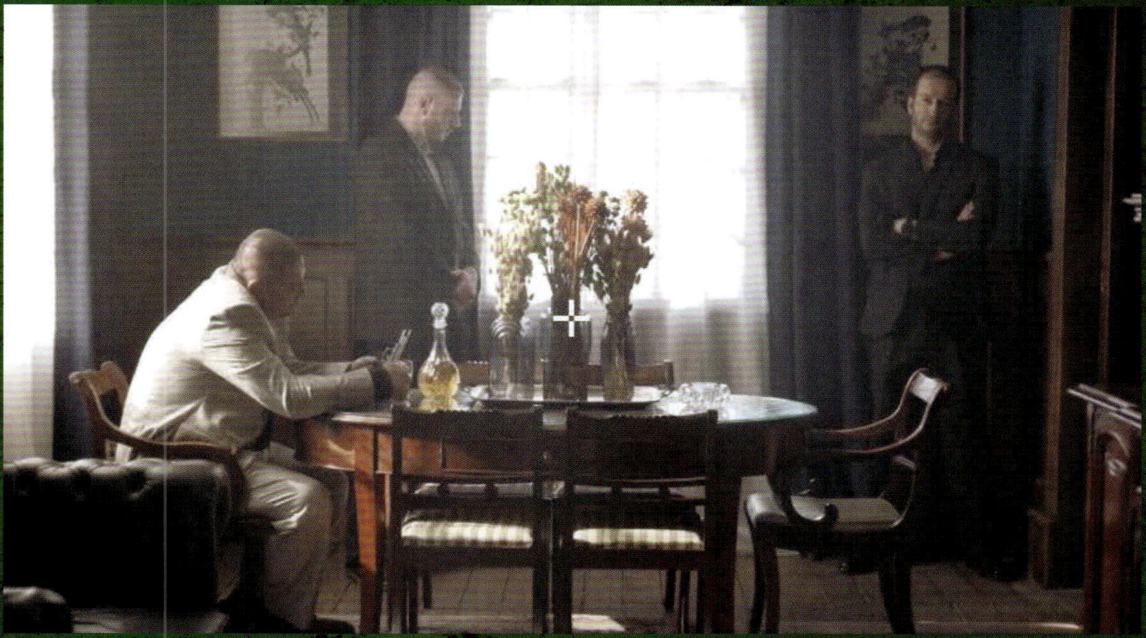

GUTHRIE STOCKINS

PLAYED BY DAVID YOW

Every hero needs a mentor. A sagacious advisor and guide who's lived, lost, and learned from it all. Spider-Man had Uncle Ben. Batman had Alfred. Toxie has Guthrie.

This wise hobo has, we presume, seen much better days, suffering lesions across his face and subsisting on spit-roasted rat in a remote, out-of-town camp. Toxie initially takes refuge here after fleeing from a torch-wielding mob, and later returns to request Guthrie's questionable medical skills after J.J. is shot. Described by Blair as "a demented Obi-Wan Kenobi," and by Garcia as "Macon's twist on the oracle character," he is a dispenser of such wisdom as "Those given much will have much demanded," and "We're all of us dying."

To play Guthrie, Blair had only one person in mind. For his previous film, *I Don't Feel at Home in This World Anymore*, he'd cast noise-rock musician, actor and cat-illustrator David Yow as Marshal, a shady, violent lowlife criminal who memorably meets his end at the fangs of a water moccasin. Having enjoyed that collaboration with the one-time frontman of The Jesus Lizard (a band formed in Blair's hometown of Austin, Texas), Blair was keen for a Toxie-flavored encore.

"We had a really good experience on the last movie, and I felt it would be nice to turn David loose as a good guy—more or less—this time around. He has this unique blend of silliness and menace on

"Macon's twist on the oracle character."

– ALEX GARCIA,
Producer

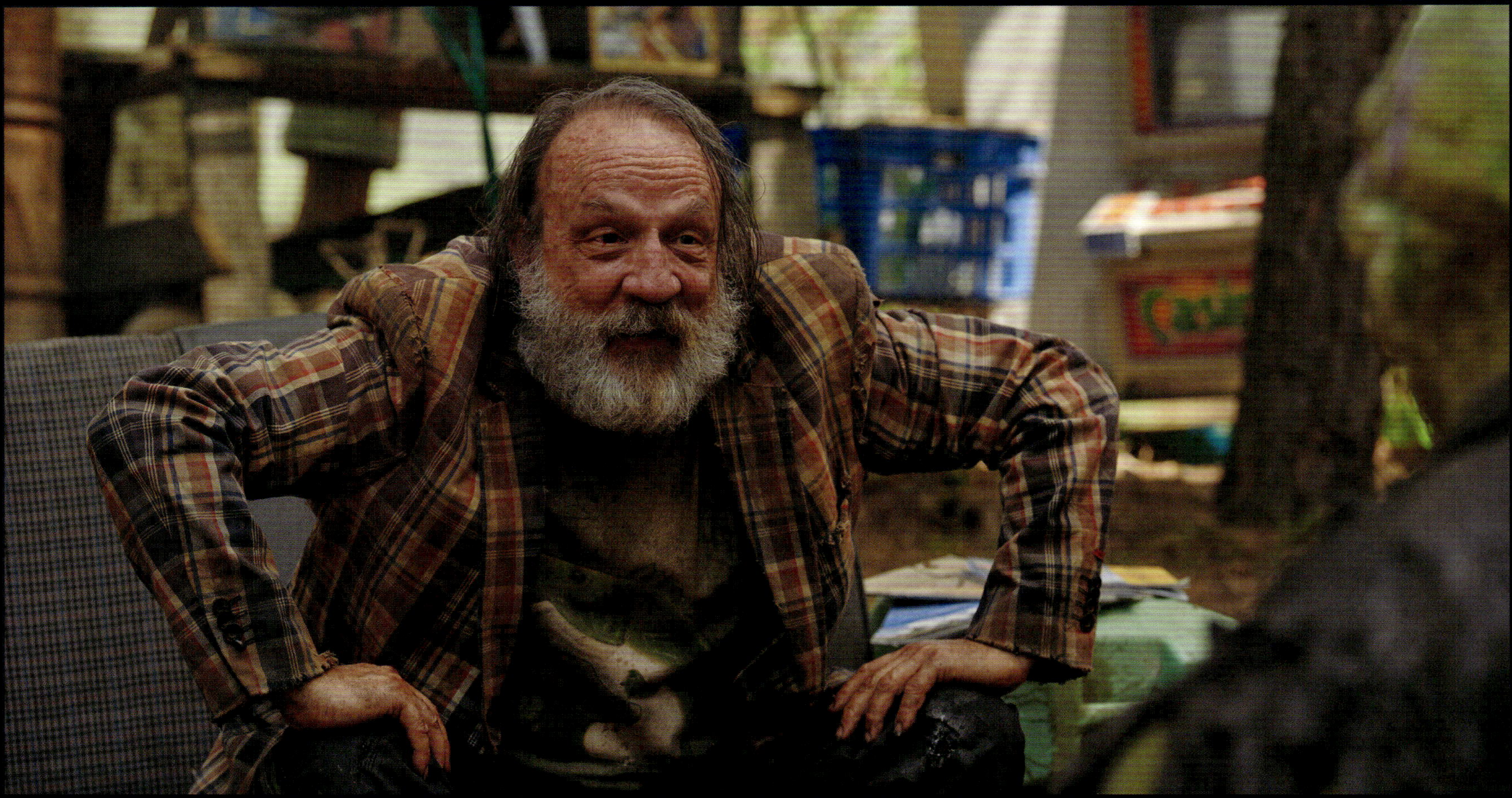

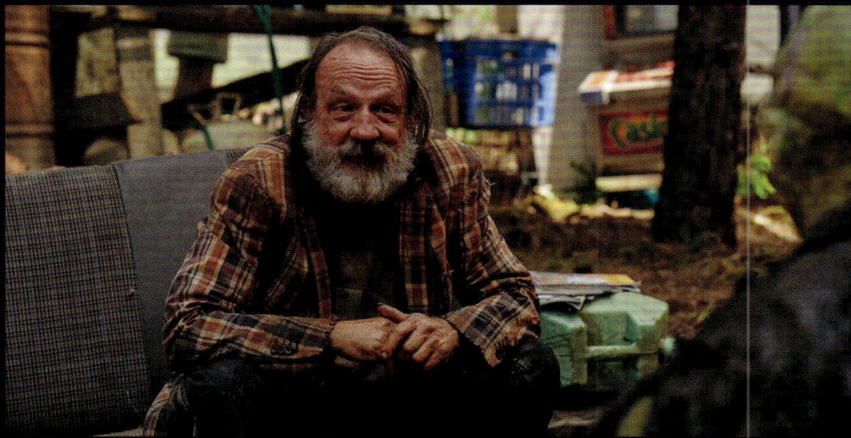

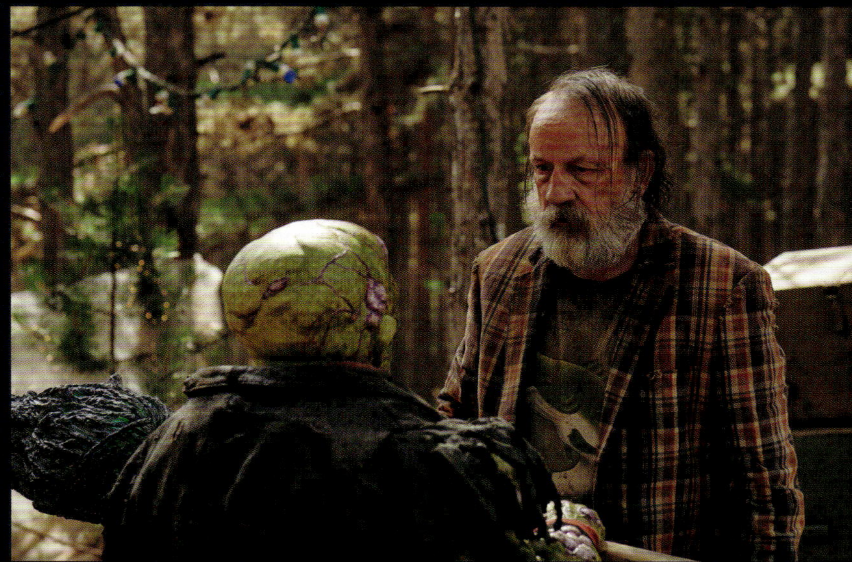

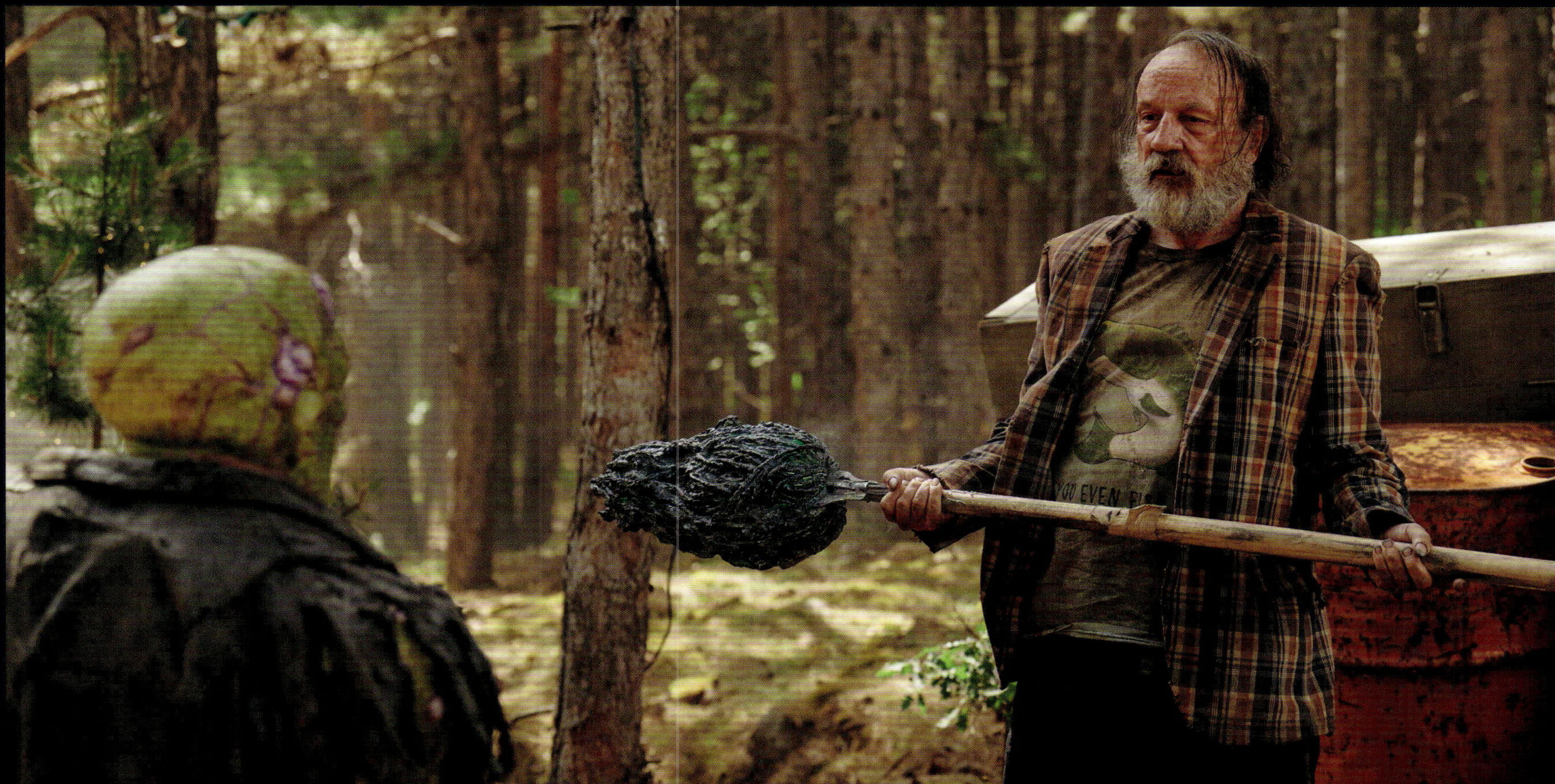

screen that I thought would be fun for this particular character. I don't think he usually does a lot of comedic stuff, but he's very funny in person, so I thought it would be fun to show a previously unseen side of him for this. I'm glad that was able to work out."

To craft Guthrie's look, Porter took inspiration from Cameron's design for his camp. "He lives in this quirky assemblage of different weird stuff he found to make a home out in the woods," says Porter, "so I wanted his clothes to feel like that, too; like he just found pieces in weird places." When we first meet Guthrie, he's decked in a combo of plaid jacket and track pants, but for his later look, he wears one of the biggest sartorial nods to the original *Toxic Avenger* film—after Toxie's iconic tutu, of course. "We gave him a Tromaville health club t-shirt," Porter reveals, referring to the movie's central location, where the first Toxie was born.

Allowing Guthrie to sport such a significant Easter egg costume element indicates just how important he is to the film, despite only appearing in a few scenes. You get the sense, talking to Blair and his behind-the-camera team, that this frazzled vagabond is destined to become an audience favourite. "Yeah," says Blair. "Folks do seem to get a kick out of his appearance."

This spread David Yow as Guthrie, ragged mentor to our mutated hero.

GUTHRIE'S CAMP

On first reading the script's description of Guthrie's self-constructed home in the woods outside Tromaville, Cameron decided he wanted to create something unexpected. Echoing Toxie's chaotic trash-dump home from the original *Toxic Avenger* movies, Macon Blair's screenplay describes the camp as "a remote homestead of trash-as-shelter: a rusty auto husk, tarp tents, shopping-cart furniture." But Cameron was determined to not just make it "some tarpaulins and bedsheets," he says. Instead, his mind cast back to John Carpenter's dystopian sci-fi classic *Escape From New York*, and the yellow taxicab driven in that movie by Ernest Borgnine. "I thought, 'What if something like that was in the woods, and Guthrie converted it into a living space?'"

"Everywhere you look there's something really detailed and interesting."
– MACON BLAIR, Director

Cameron was on a mission: he visited the various prop houses at Nu Boyana Film Studios in Sofia, looking for something that would become the signature piece of his camp set. "I just happened to walk around the back of one place, and there was this shell of a helicopter. I said, 'Let's use that!' So, we put this helicopter in the woods just outside Sofia. I imagined it had crash-landed there and Guthrie had converted it into a living space. It worked really well."

Blair fulsomely praises Cameron, the art department and the set decorators' work on this location. Guthrie's camp is

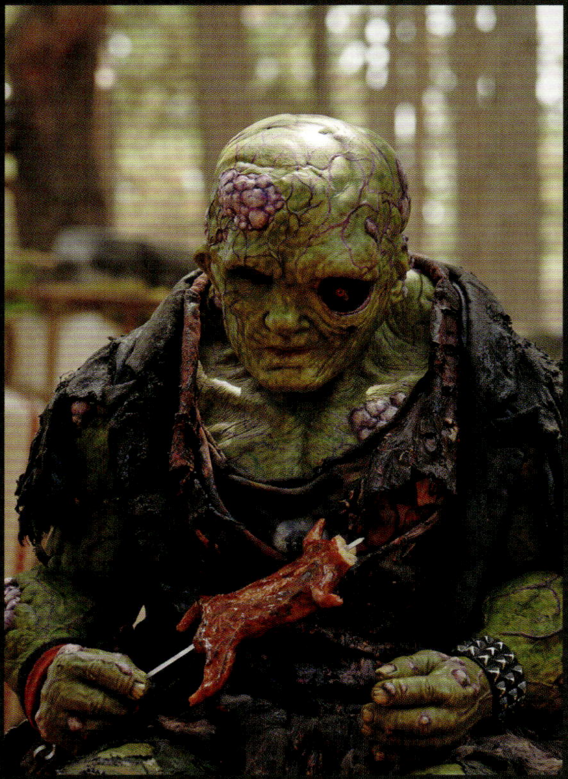

Above Toxie 'enjoys' some barbecued rat.

Below The Bulgarian woods, which played host to Guthrie's camp.

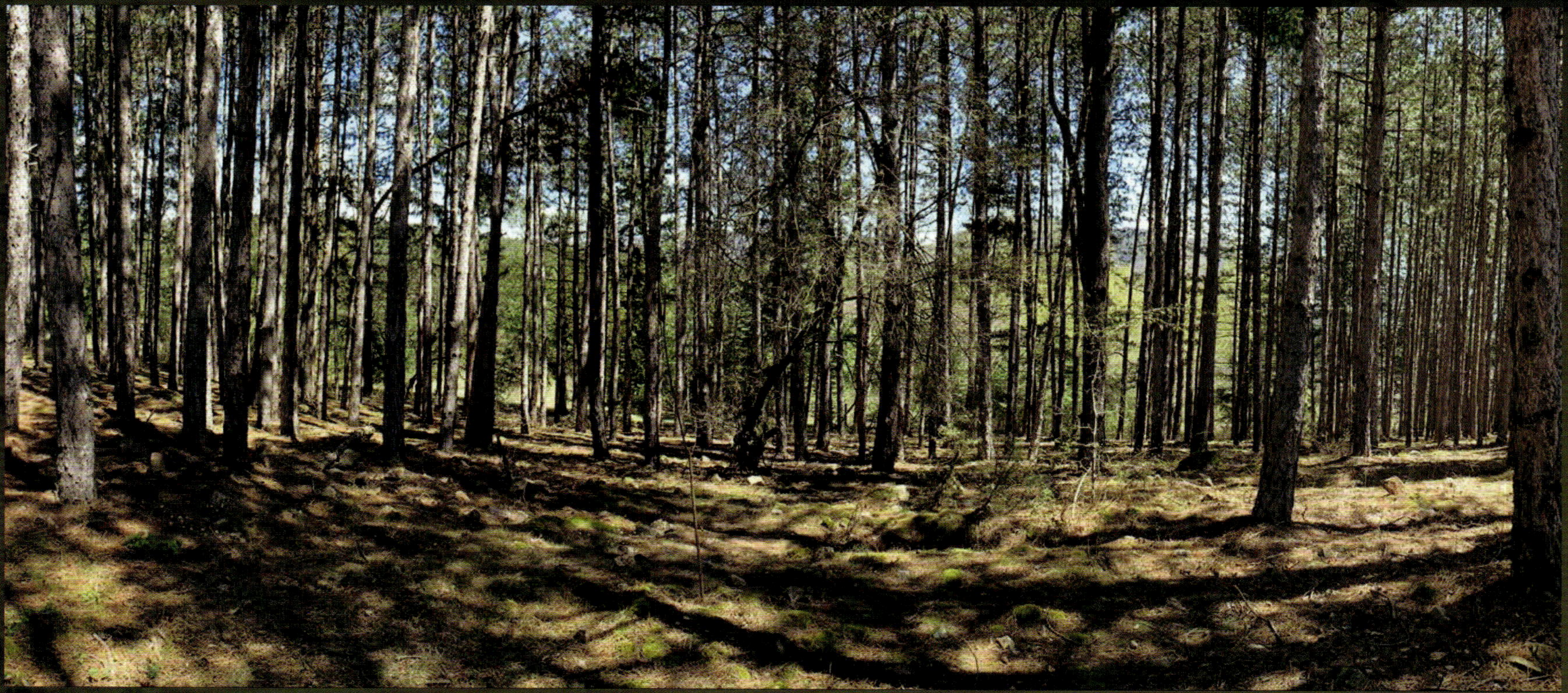

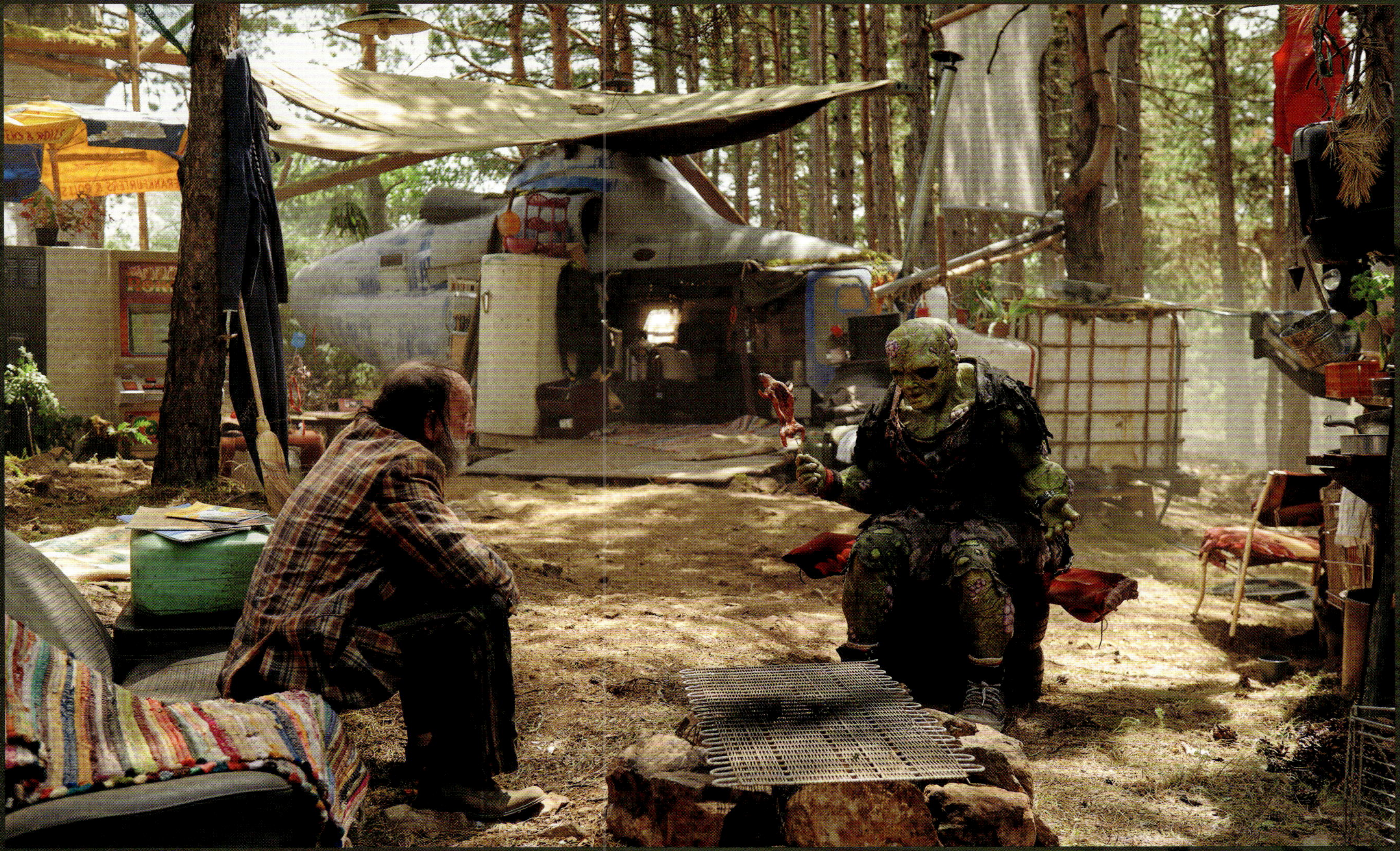

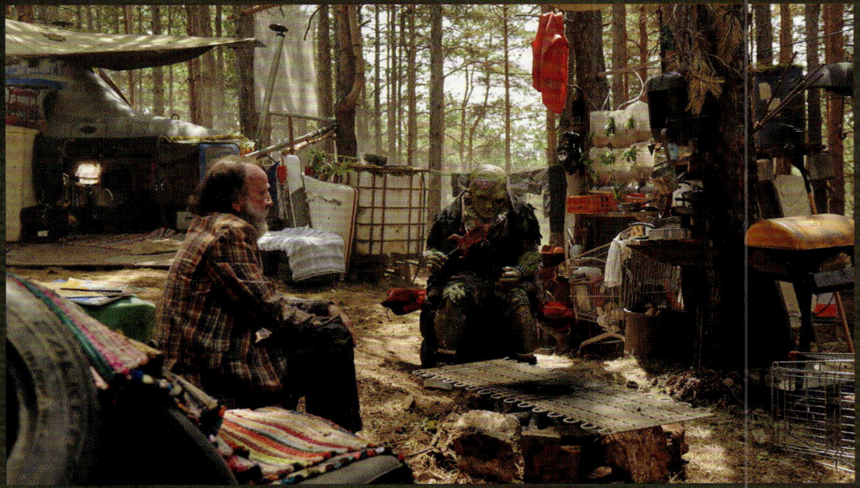

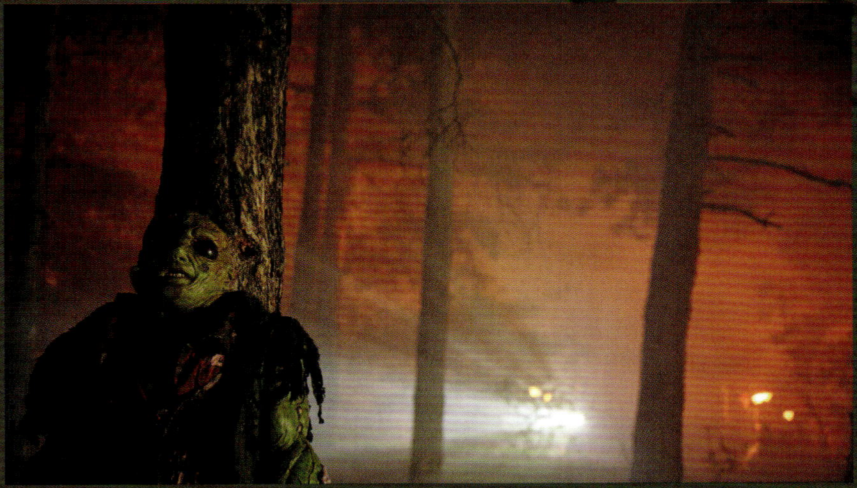

his favourite exterior in the movie. "It was really remarkable. You find all these objects and textures and pieces of junk that had been repurposed to make a functional living space." As well as the downed chopper chassis, he says, "there's this sort of water filtration thing made from all these recycled bottles, and a little garden with an outdoor shower-thing that's been made out from all these pieces of hose. It looks very functional and true, but it also does a lot of lifting for the character. Without Guthrie saying too much, you can glance at this camp and get a sense of what he's about. On the one hand there's this kind of hermit-type insanity thing going on, and on the other hand a very thoughtful, practical self-reliance."

It was all great fun to shoot in, too. "We kept trying to find new angles, because everywhere you look there's something really detailed and interesting. Everything was very thought out."

Top & above left Guthrie and Toxie chat in front of the downed chopper in which the hermit has made his home.

Above Toxie takes cover while running from a hateful mob.

GARBINGER'S OFFICE

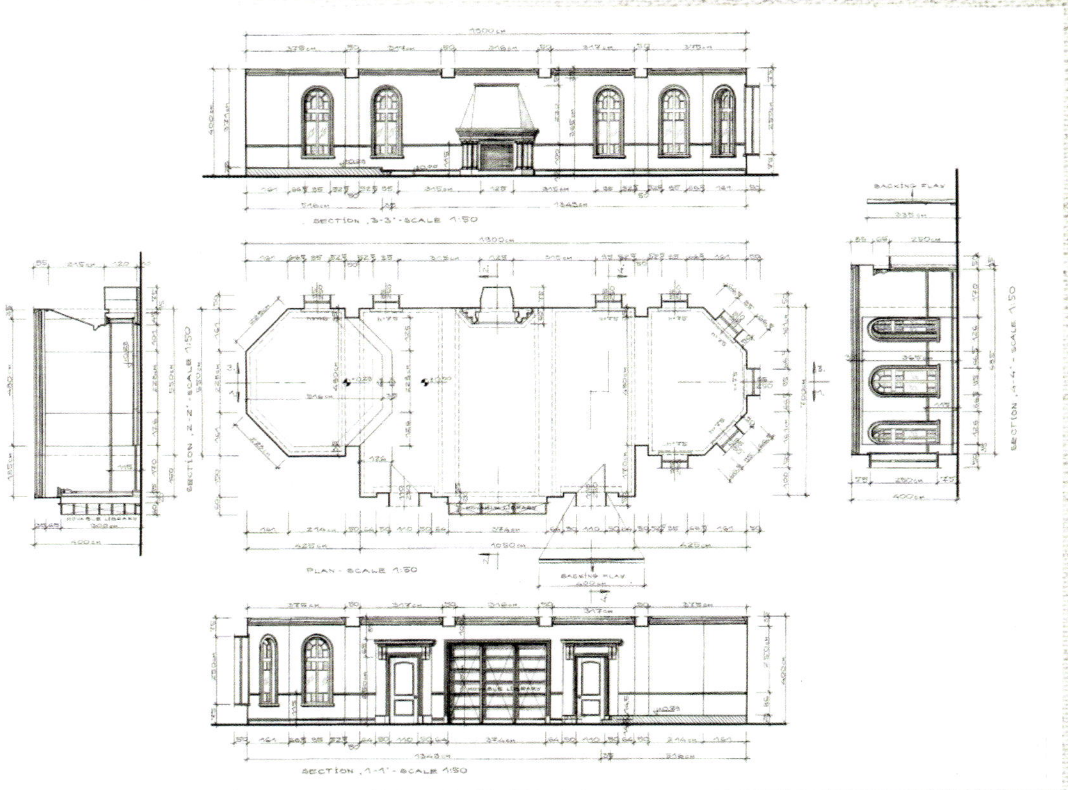

With its grand fireplace, long banquet table and a vast array of medieval weapons on its walls, Bob Garbinger's base of operations feels less like an 'office' than some seat of ancient baronial power. It is far more impressive, one might argue, than its owner deserves.

"The idea was to make Garbinger look like this kind of emperor or statesman," says Cameron. "We placed a raised dais on the left-hand side of the room, with a chaise lounge and animal heads. Our supervising set decorator Elizabeth Boller did a great job. It looked quite grand."

Blair agrees. "Alex did some really remarkable stuff on this movie, in interpreting the realistic yet also fantastical vibe that I did my best to communicate to him," he says. "He was able to take what I was talking about and expand it in a great way. I was consistently blown away by his designs and what his team did, but the one that I really fell head over heels for was Garbinger's office. It looked very credible and impressive on one hand, and then also very tacky and strange on the other. It has all these layers of detail in the set decoration and these little pieces and choices that are not necessarily in the forefront of the frame, but you get a sense of them almost subconsciously. Anywhere you pointed the camera in that room, it looked gorgeous."

One of those strange details is Garbinger's transfusion machine, which he uses to pump apparently power-inducing gorilla blood into his veins while reclining on his chaise lounge. Cameron did work up some designs for this piece of kit, but, he says, "in the end we got a real one." (The gorilla blood, of course, is *not* real.)

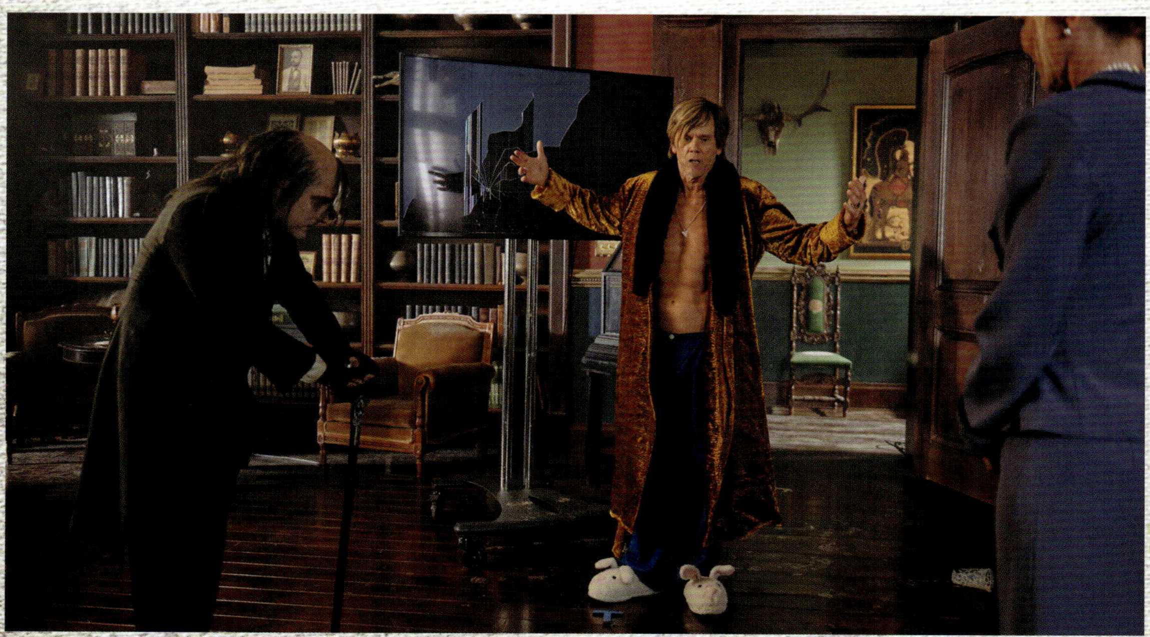

Then there are all those vicious-looking weapons. "Garbinger ends up in an axe fight with Toxie, so we wanted to layer that in a little bit, and give the idea that he collects them," Blair explains. "I grew up playing *Dungeons & Dragons*, so I just wanted a lot of axes and swords and stuff in there; halberds, bastard swords… All the good stuff."

Left Garbinger declaims to Fritz and Kissy.

Above The blueprint for Garbinger's office.

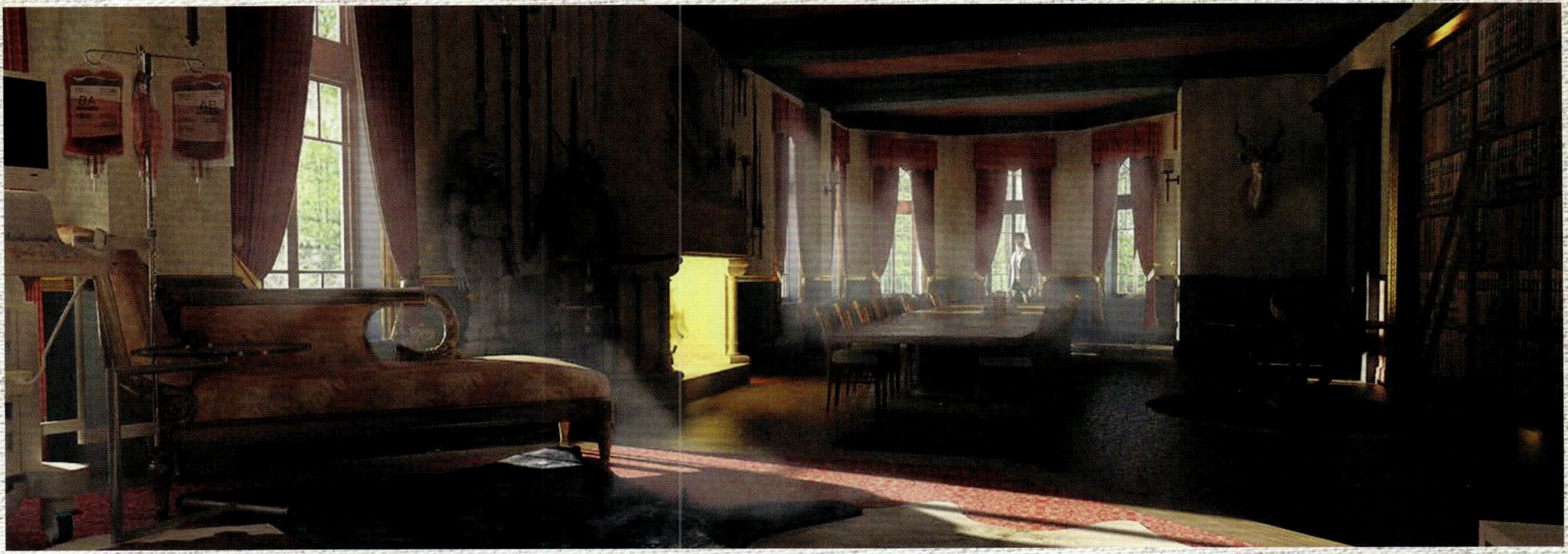

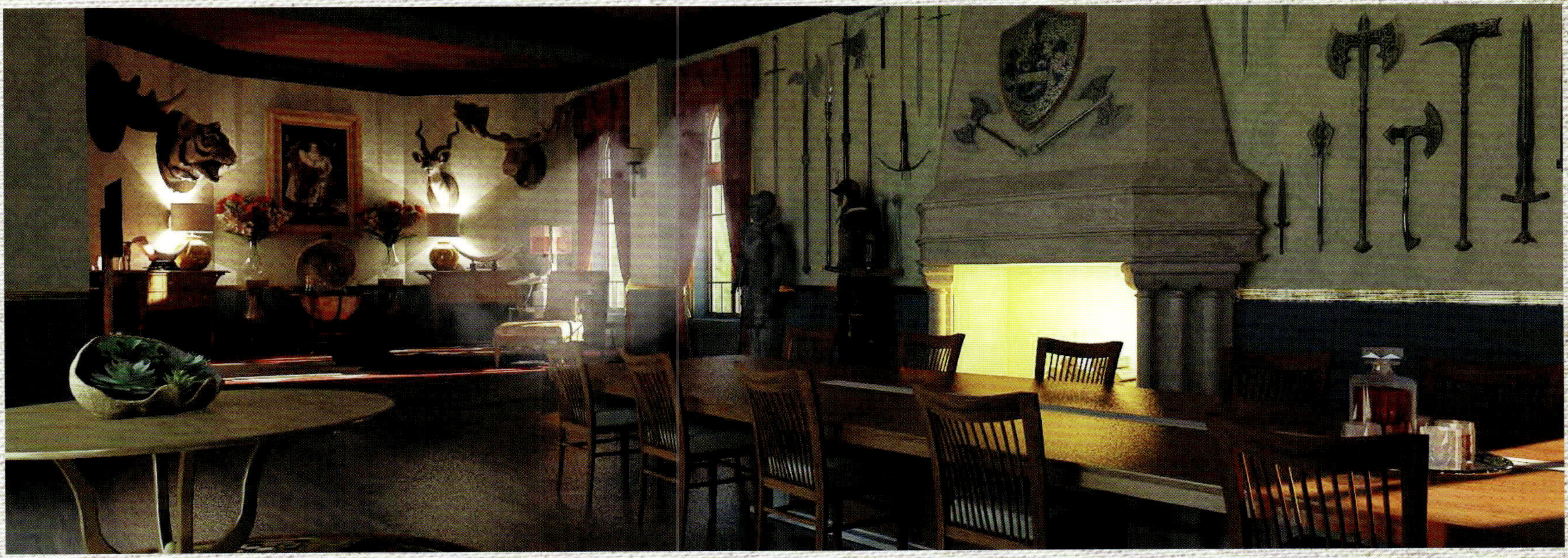

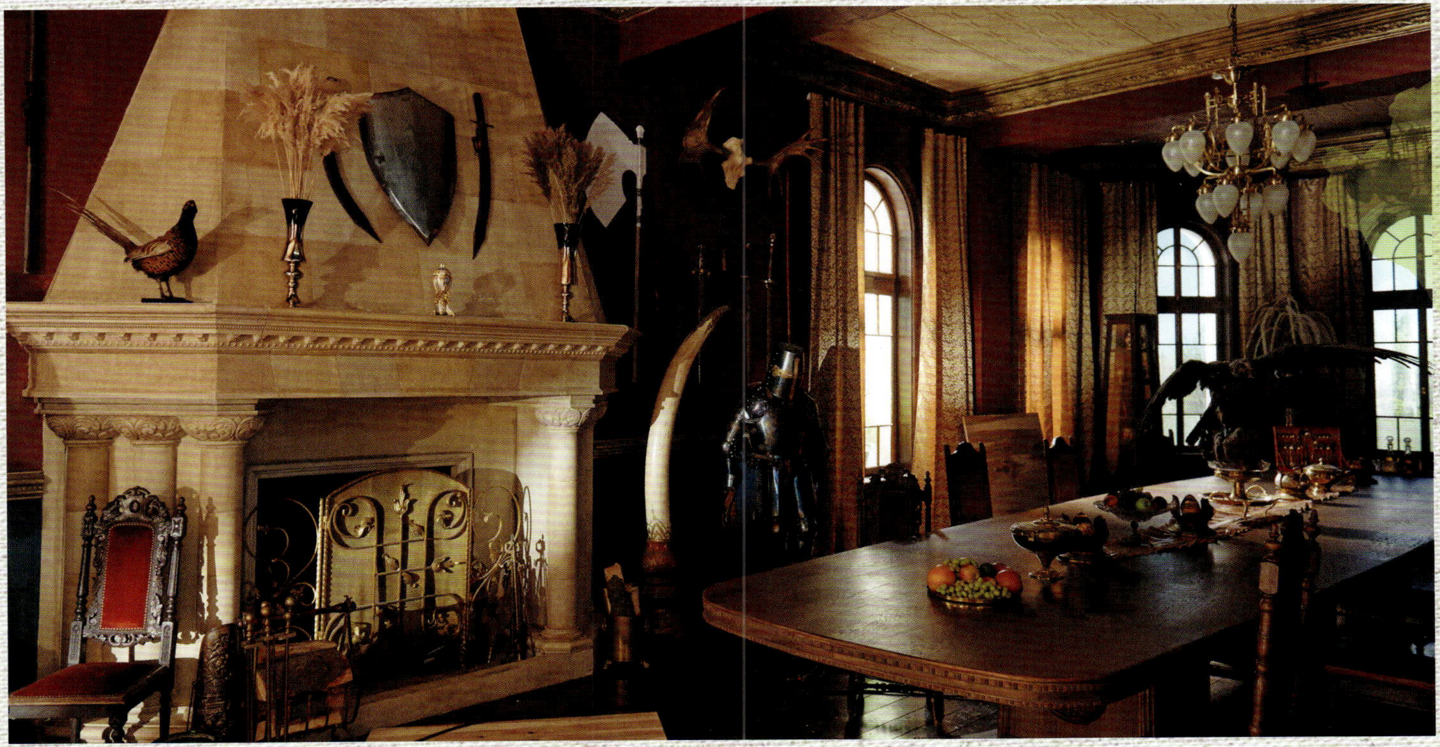

Top & above The original concept designs for the weapon-and-trophy-festooned office.

Left ...And the finished product; the set, in all its tacky opulence.

GARBINGER'S SECRET LAB

James Whale's 1931 Universal horror classic *Frankenstein* and its sequel *Bride of Frankenstein* were a huge inspiration on both Lloyd Kaufman for the original *Toxic Avenger*, and on Macon Blair, too, for his remake. Nowhere is this more evident than in Garbinger's secret lab, tucked away in the gloomy catacombs beneath Chüdhaven Mansion. It is here that Toxie is taken to have fluid agonizingly extracted from his spine via a "Cronenbergian umbilical cord," creating the serum that will eventually transform Garbinger himself into a monster.

Directly inspired by Whale's movies, Cameron fully committed to a look he describes as "over-the-top gothic, low-lit, with heavy stone." He laid out the central lab in a hexagonal shape, with a pair of connected side rooms, in which unspeakable things occur. "We don't go in the room off to the right, but there was a glass wall there, which you could see through into this weird experimentation area, where we built rails and hung blood-spattered shower curtains. And then the room on the left we turned into the torture room, where Toxie and J.J. are tied up."

Blair encouraged Cameron to lean into a "mad scientist's laboratory vibe," for the set, which is filled with a lot of strange, sparking, bubbling machines of no express usefulness. "You're not really sure what they do," says the director. "They just buzz and hum and pump strange liquid around. It's meant to look slightly cartoony, but also kind of dangerous and threatening."

Right & below Concept art for the non-specific mad-science gear found in the lab.

Below left The secret lab's floor plan, built around a hexagonal central chamber.

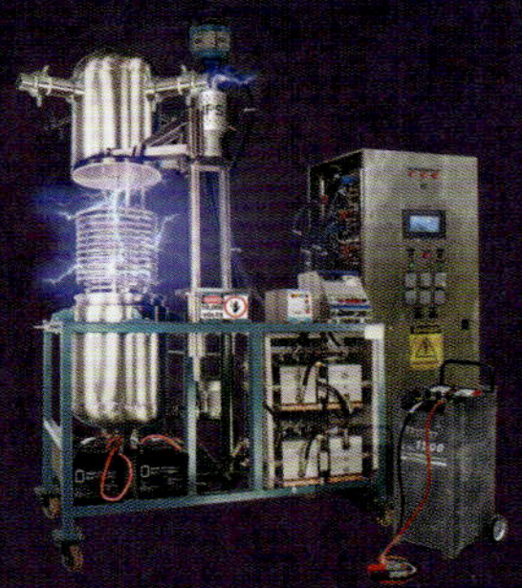

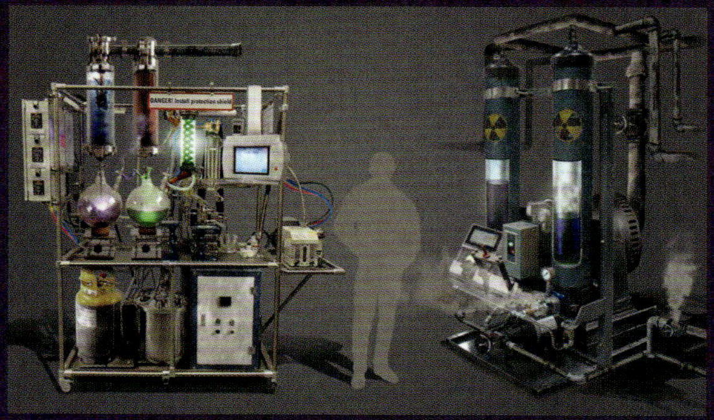

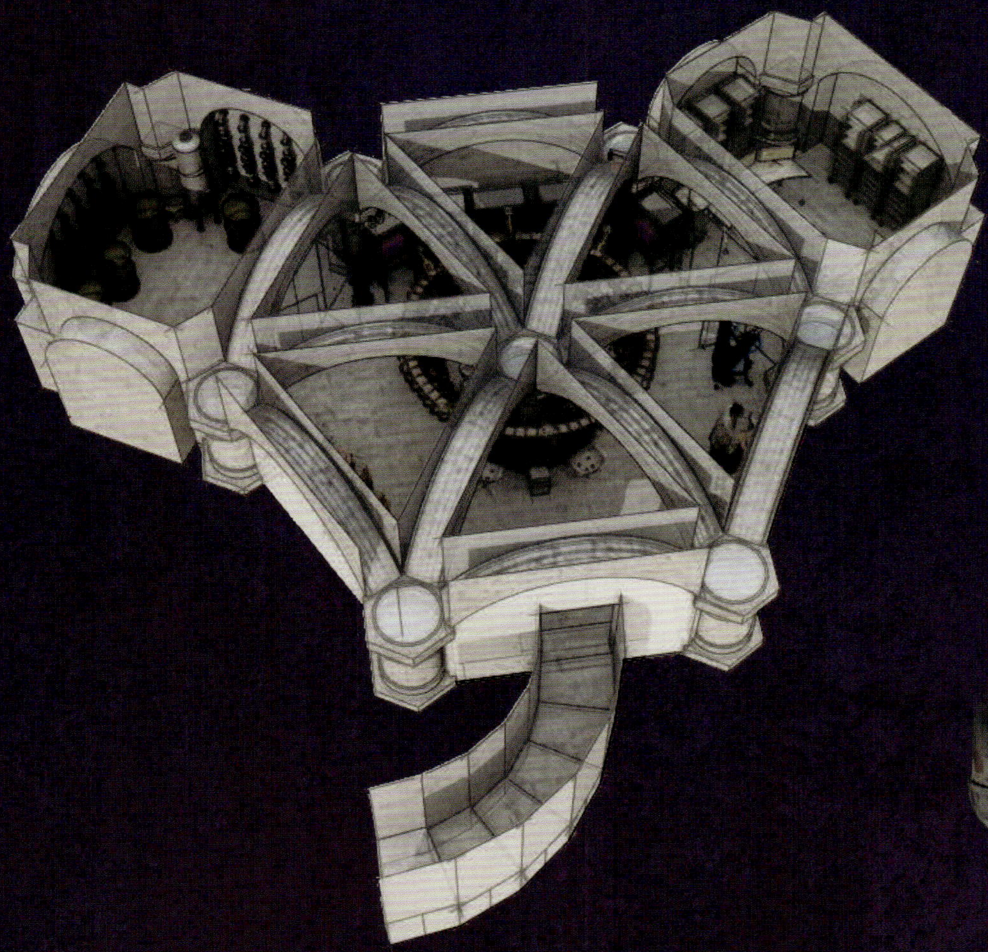

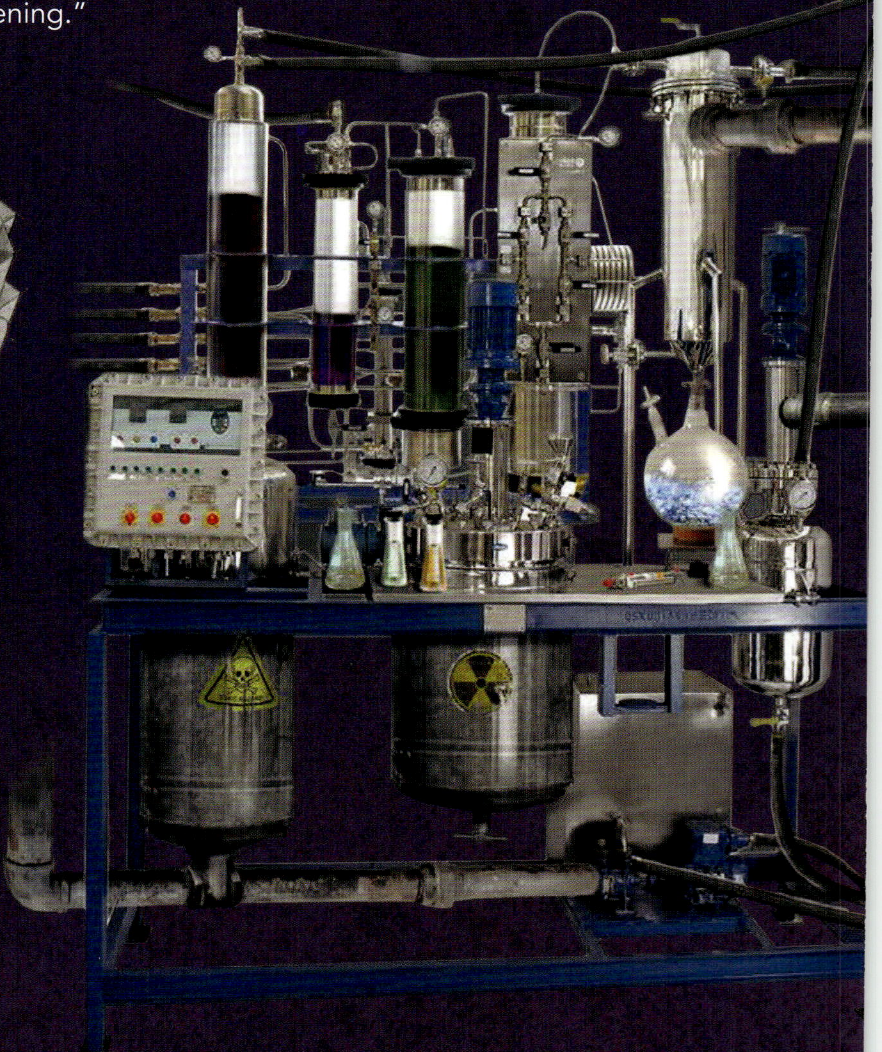

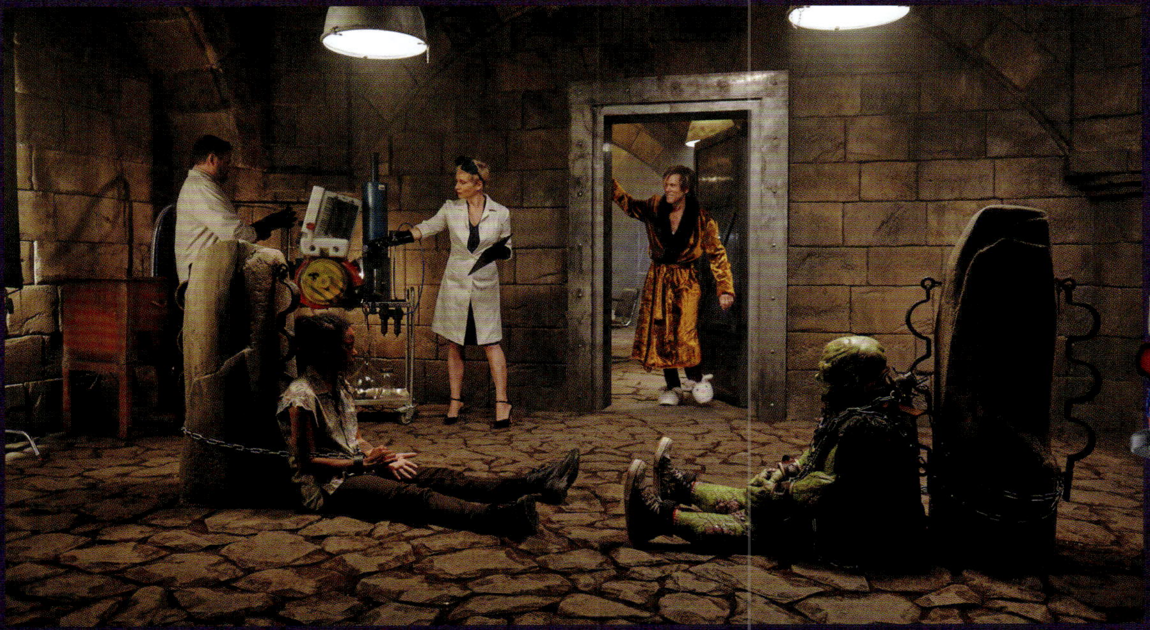

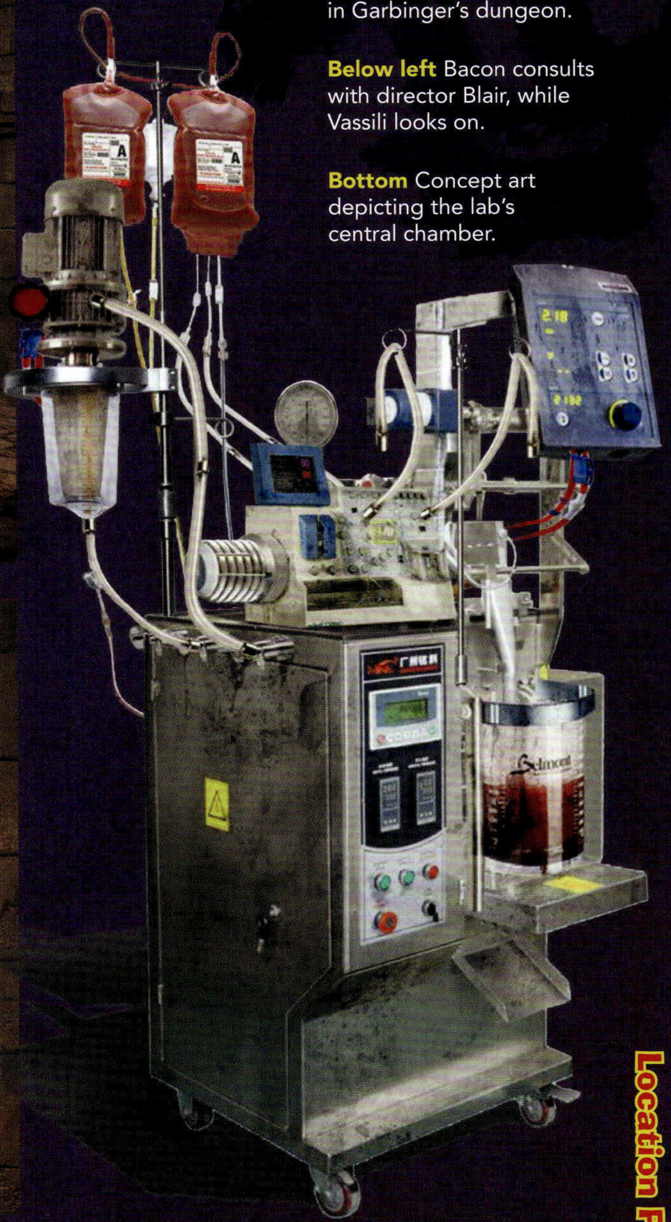

Left J.J. and Toxie find themselves incarcerated in Garbinger's dungeon.

Below left Bacon consults with director Blair, while Vassili looks on.

Bottom Concept art depicting the lab's central chamber.

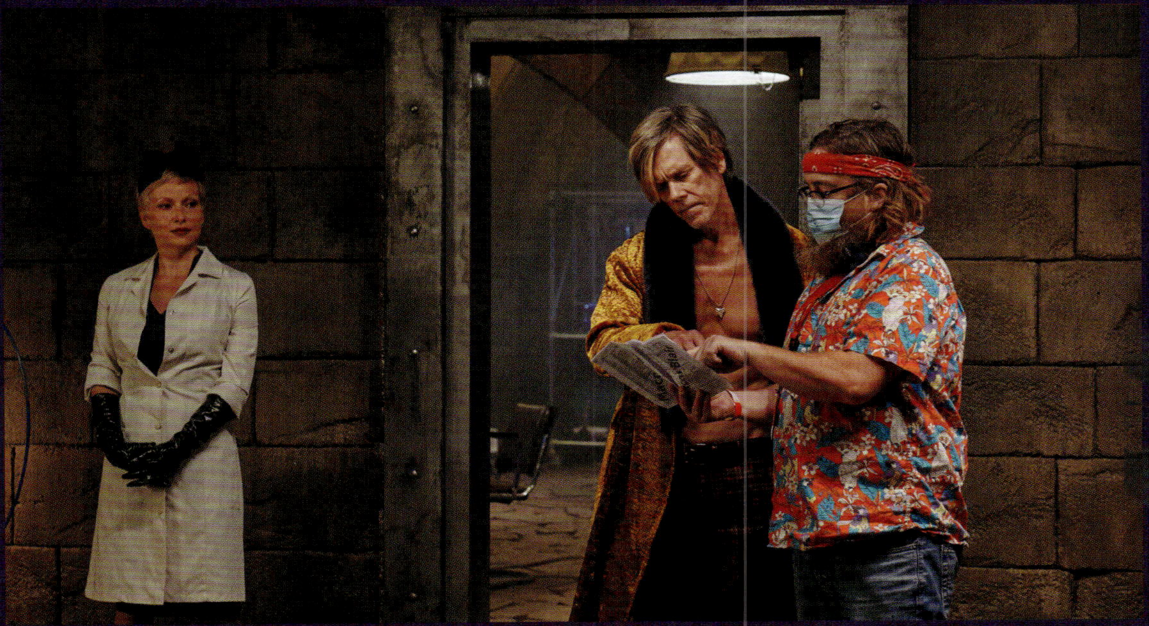

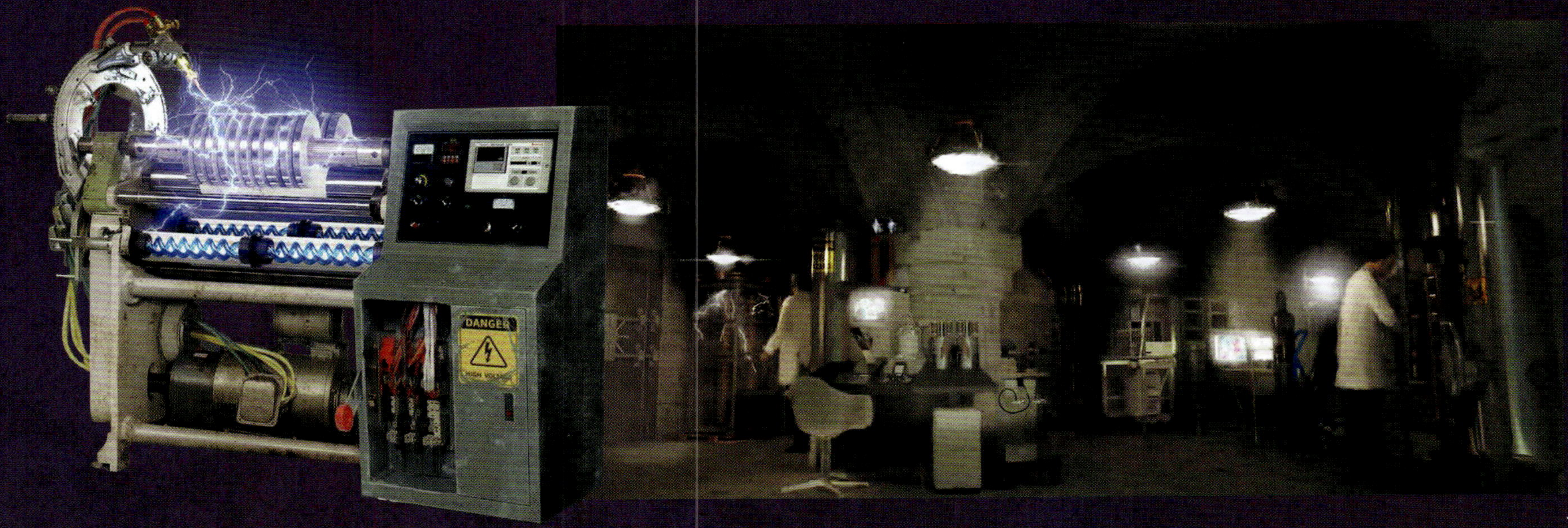

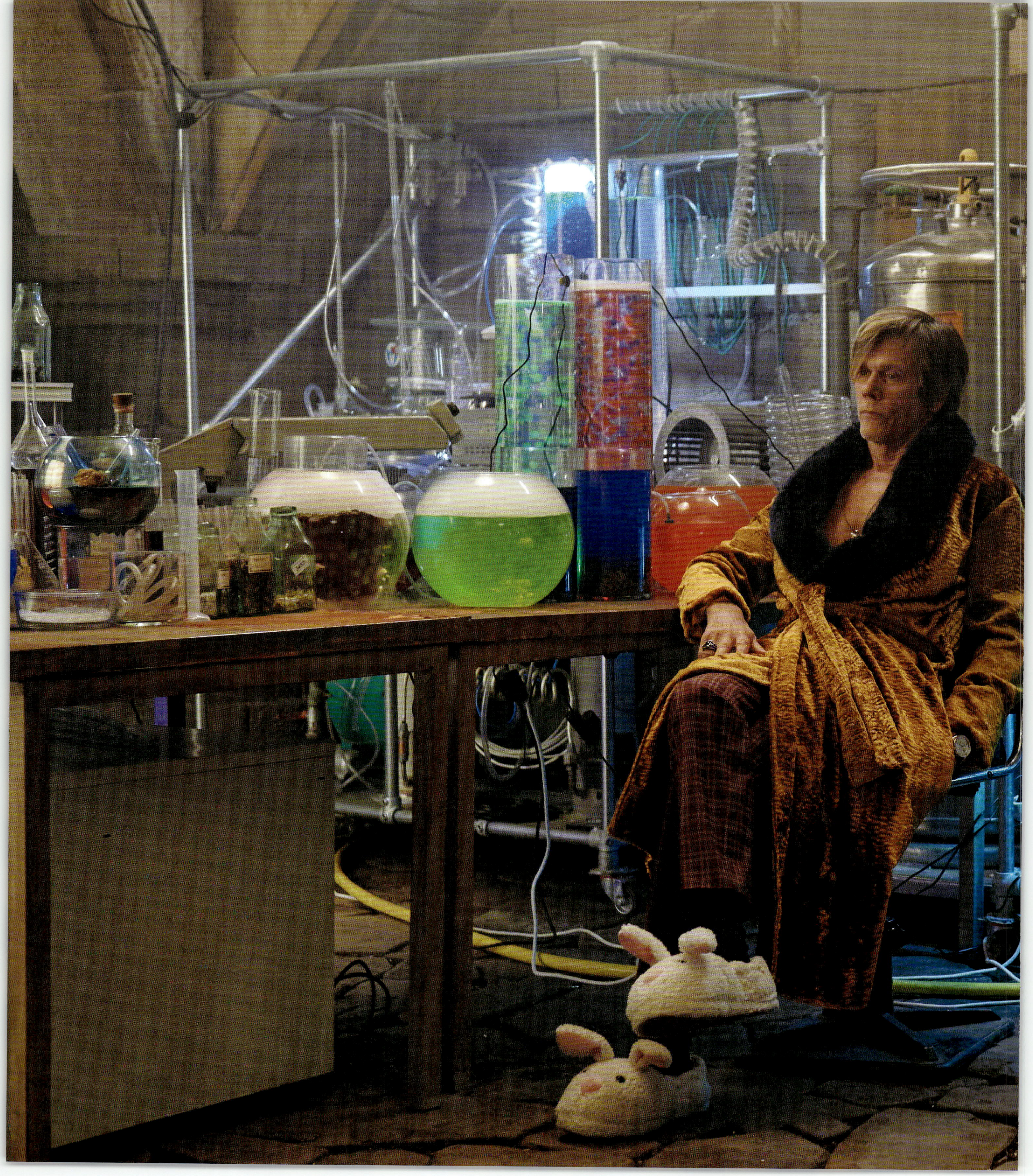

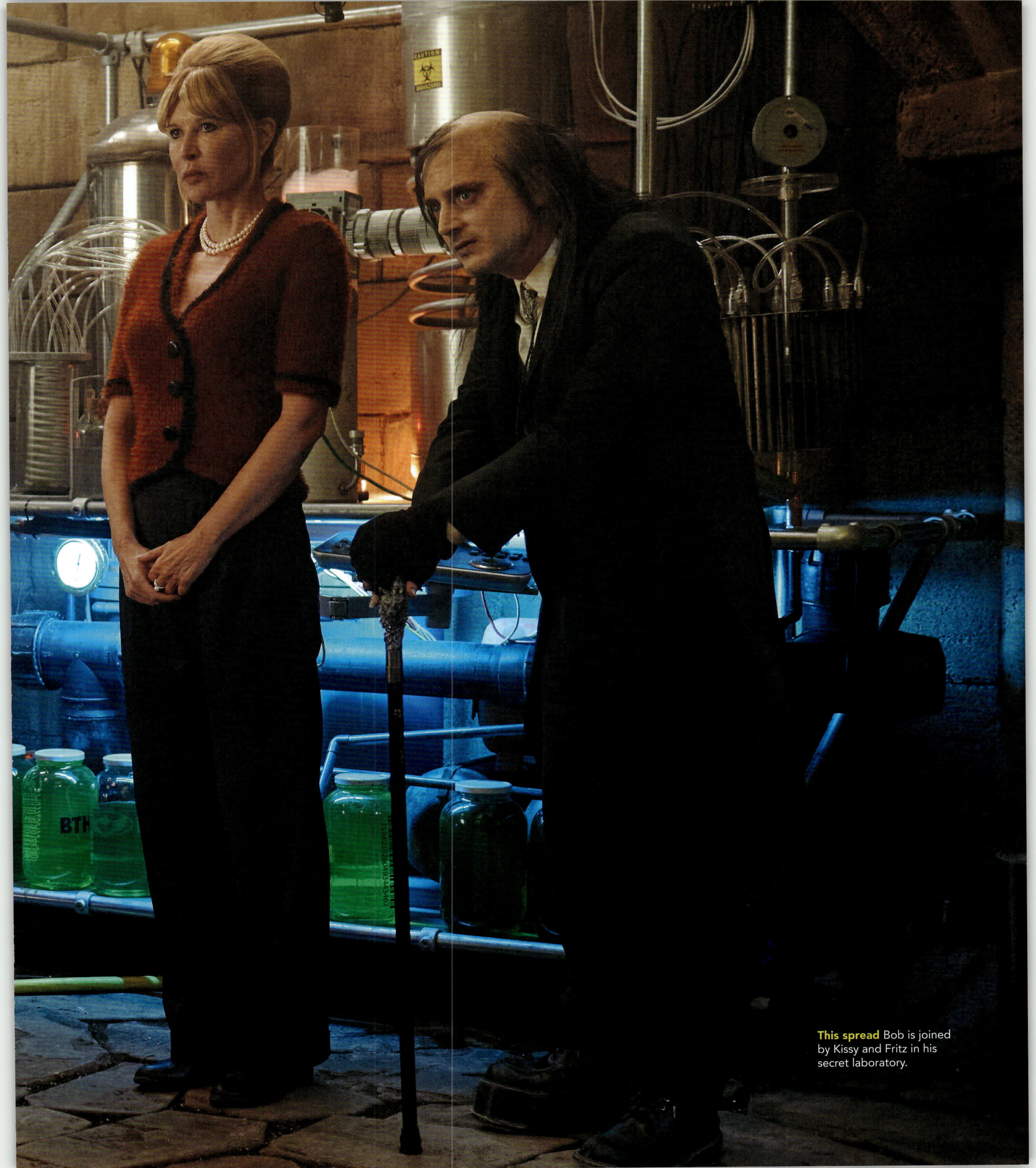

This spread Bob is joined by Kissy and Fritz in his secret laboratory.

KUPP AND SAWSER

PLAYED BY KITODAR TODOROV AND SOPHIA VASSILI

You can't have a mad scientist's laboratory without a mad scientist, and true to over-the-top form, *The Toxic Avenger* has two. Played by Bulgarian actors Kitodar Todorov and Sophia Vassili, Garbinger's resident "science geeks" Kupp and Sawser are on hand to facilitate their boss' unnatural ambitions.

"We needed some evil scientists to help us with the whole mythology of the transformation, and what's going on with Toxie," Blair explains, "so we hired two very funny local actors to form kind of an Abbott and Costello team." However, in one of the film's running gags, any expository moments are punctuated by sudden loud background noises that drown out any specific scientific detail. (This also happens during the earlier scene where Dr. Walla explains the reason for Winston's illness.)

"There's a version of this movie where everything is credible and serious, like in *Batman Begins*, where they have to give a real-world reason for his Batmobile," says Blair. "But it was very clear early on that, with this movie, we didn't want any of that. Like, why did the toxic waste give Winston muscles instead of just killing him? *Who gives a shit*? This is not the movie for that. He fell into the toxic slime and that's all you need to know. The whys of that are not important, so we wanted to highlight that."

Keen to give them a little more to do than simply deliver (incomplete) exposition, Blair imagined Kupp and Sawser as a double act, where "one is nervous and fluttery, and the other is careless, disconnected and not worried about the extent of the evil they're doing." He thought that would be an amusing dynamic, and also allow Todorov and Vassili to create some science-lab sparks of their own. "I wanted to give them a little friction to play with," he says.

Below Garbinger consults with Kupp.

Top right Macon Blair chats with his cast between takes.

Bottom right Kupp and Sawser form an "Abbott and Costello" double act.

"We needed some evil scientists to help us with the whole mythology."

– MACON BLAIR, Director

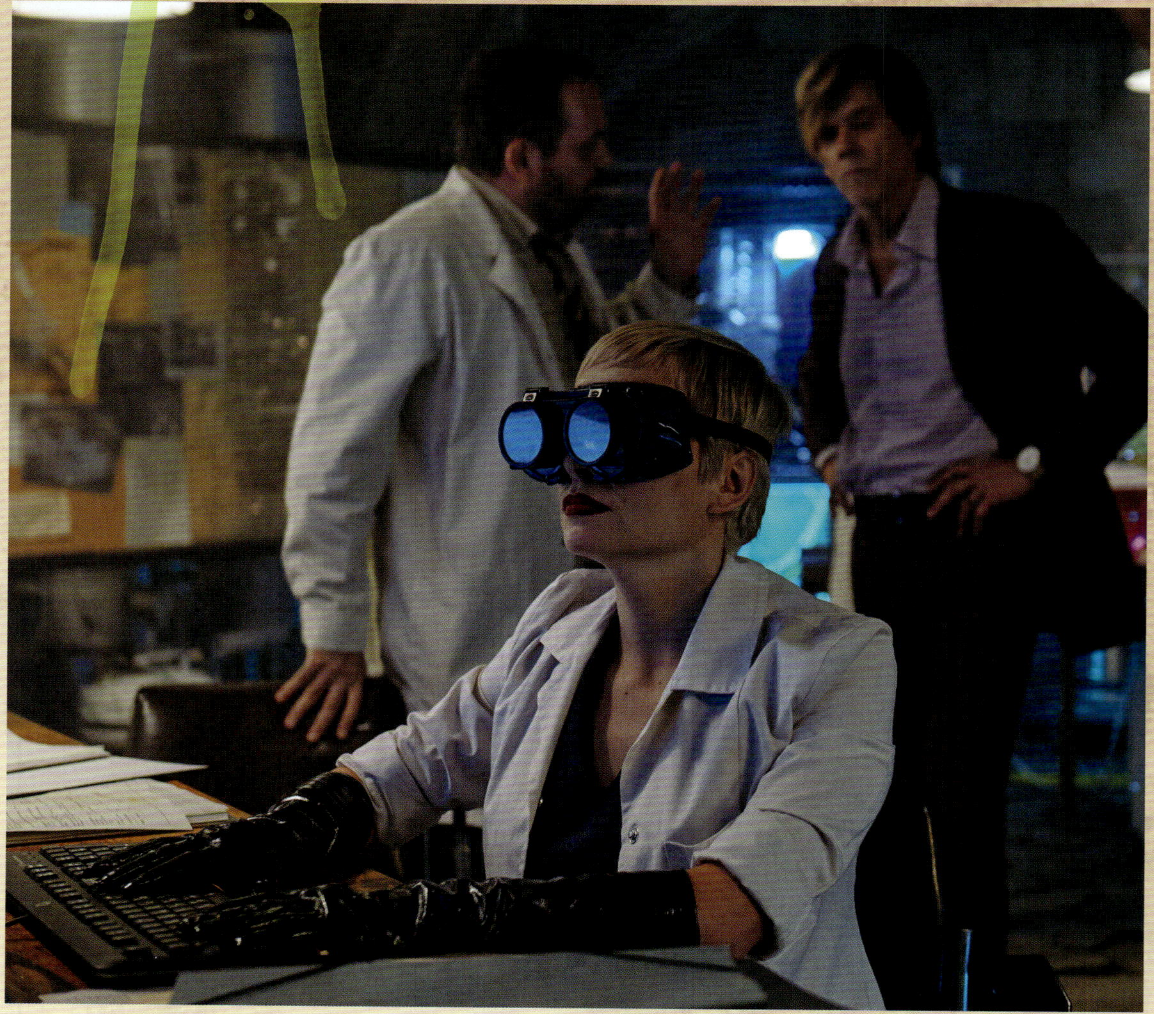

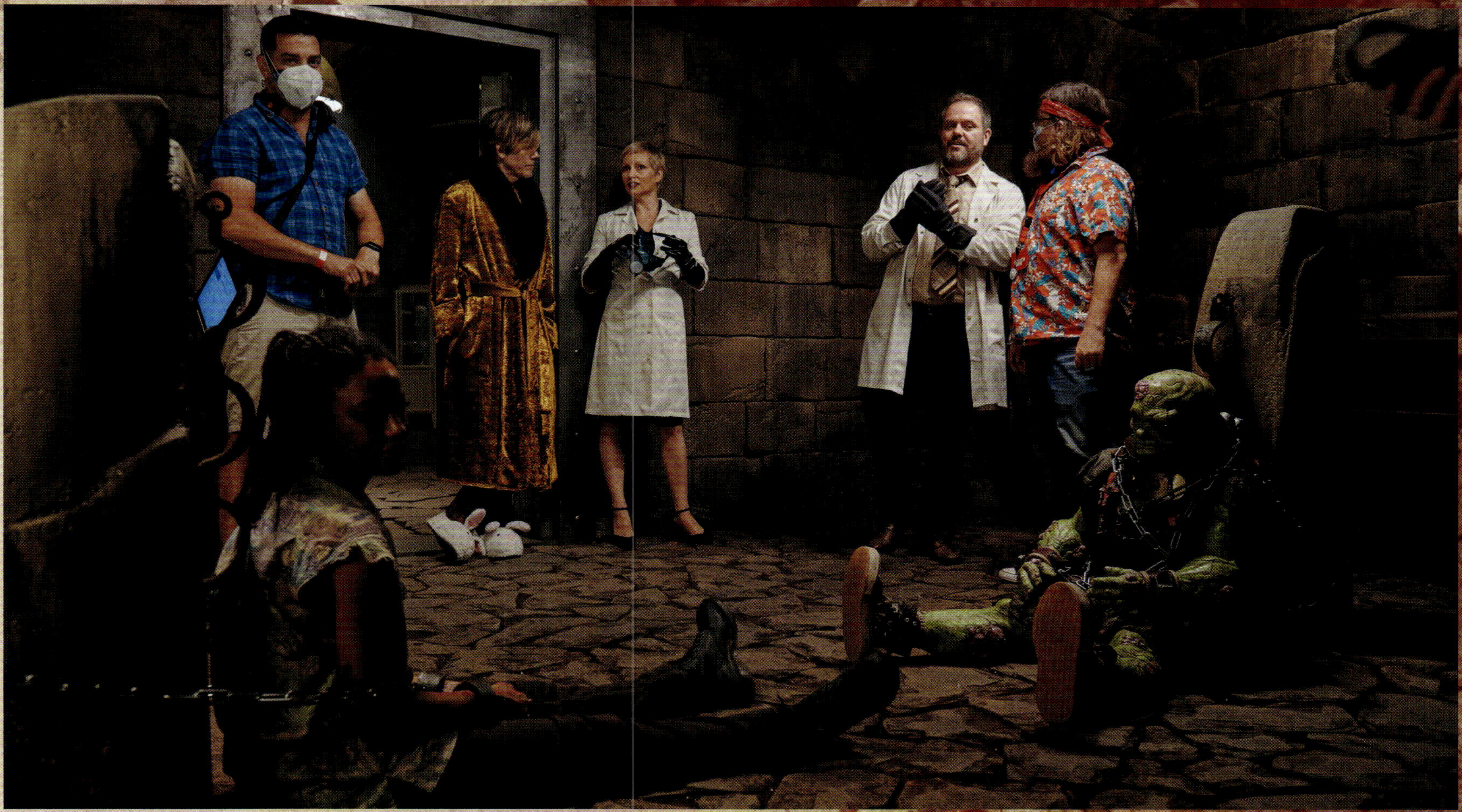

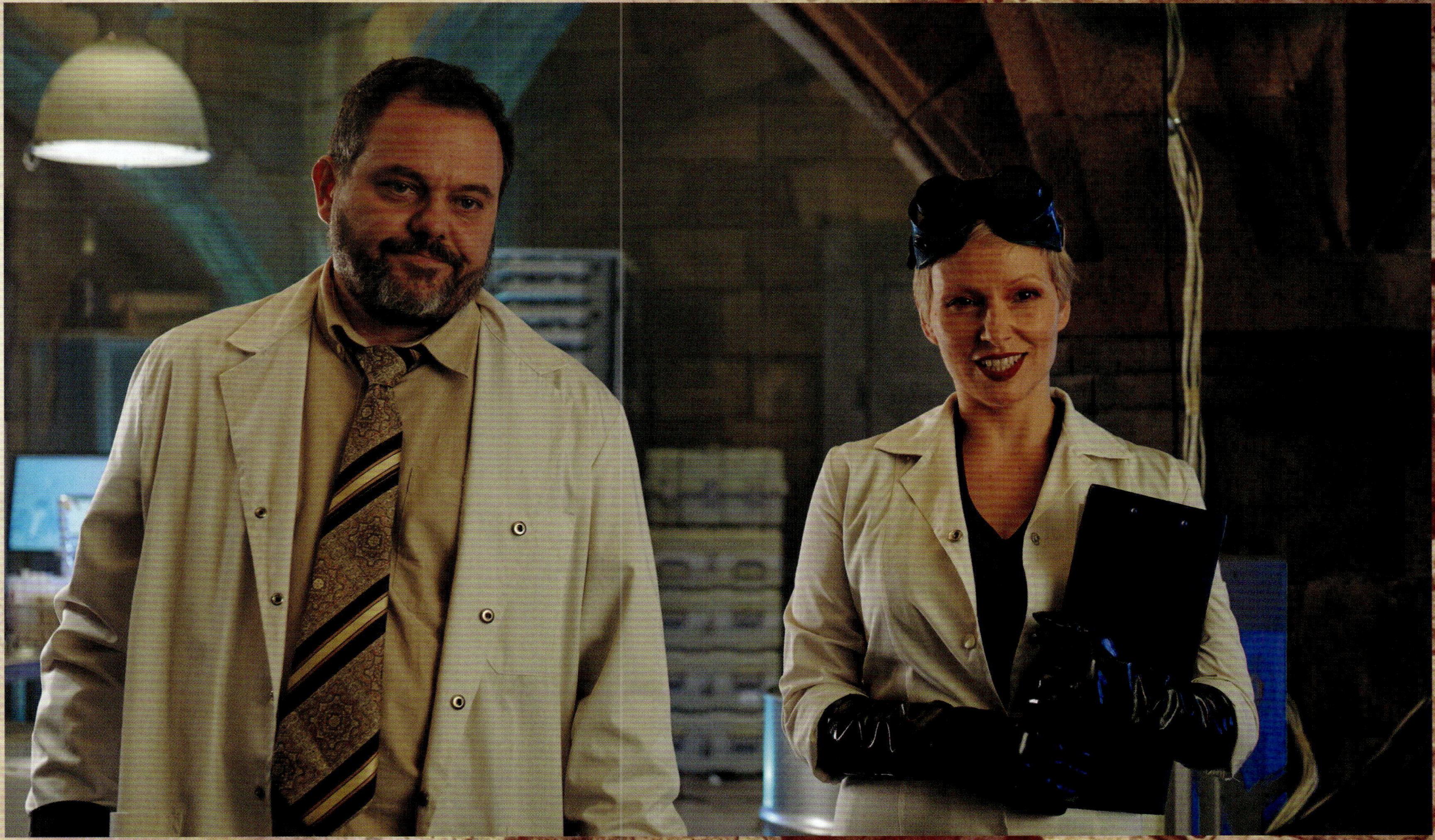

MISS MEAT LUNCHORIUM

In one of the closest parallels with the original *Toxic Avenger*, our monstrous protagonist's first public act of heroism involves rescuing a group of Tromavillian hostages from a gang of violent criminals in a fast-food joint. But rather than the original's taco restaurant, Blair devised his own burger franchise, namely Miss Meat. And like any self-respecting fast-food chain, it needed its own mascot.

"The burger lady was actually the first thing I did on the job," reveals Cameron. Standing atop the restaurant, which Cameron's crew built from scratch beside a roundabout at the far end of the backlot Strip, is a statue of a long-legged woman in a short skirt and crop top, with a huge burger for a head. As he was sketching out his initial concept drawing for this weird, striking icon, Cameron recalls, his wife looked over his shoulder and asked, "What the *hell* are you doing?"

It was just the beginning of a crazed process which led to the set being loaded with idiosyncratic detail. "We were obviously influenced by 1980s McDonald's," says Cameron, "and also '60s diners. It has that black-and-white chequered flooring and bright red seating. But then we have these two columns in the centre that we built these huge lady's legs around."

But his team didn't stop there. "I don't know why, but we took a direction of sexual innuendo, and it got pretty childish, really," he laughs. "John (Pundt), my graphics guy, literally went to McDonald's and got the packaging and very carefully unravelled it to study what shapes it made. If you unravelled the fries packet that we made, it turned into this big phallus. Yeah, I know… But there were so many hidden things like that in there. That set was really detailed. *Ridiculously* detailed."

"That set was really detailed. *Ridiculously* detailed."

– ALEXANDER CAMERON,
Production Designer

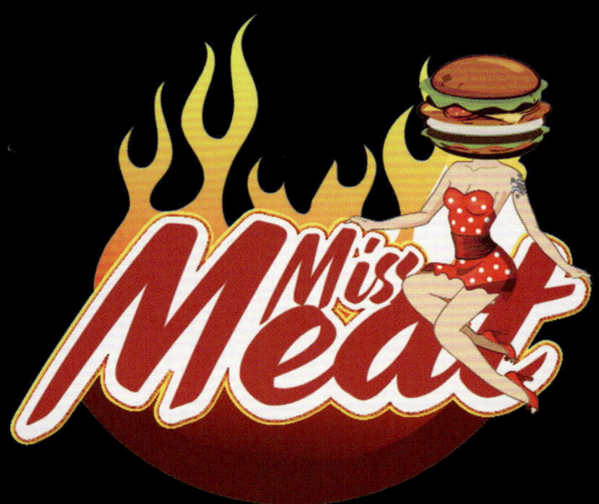

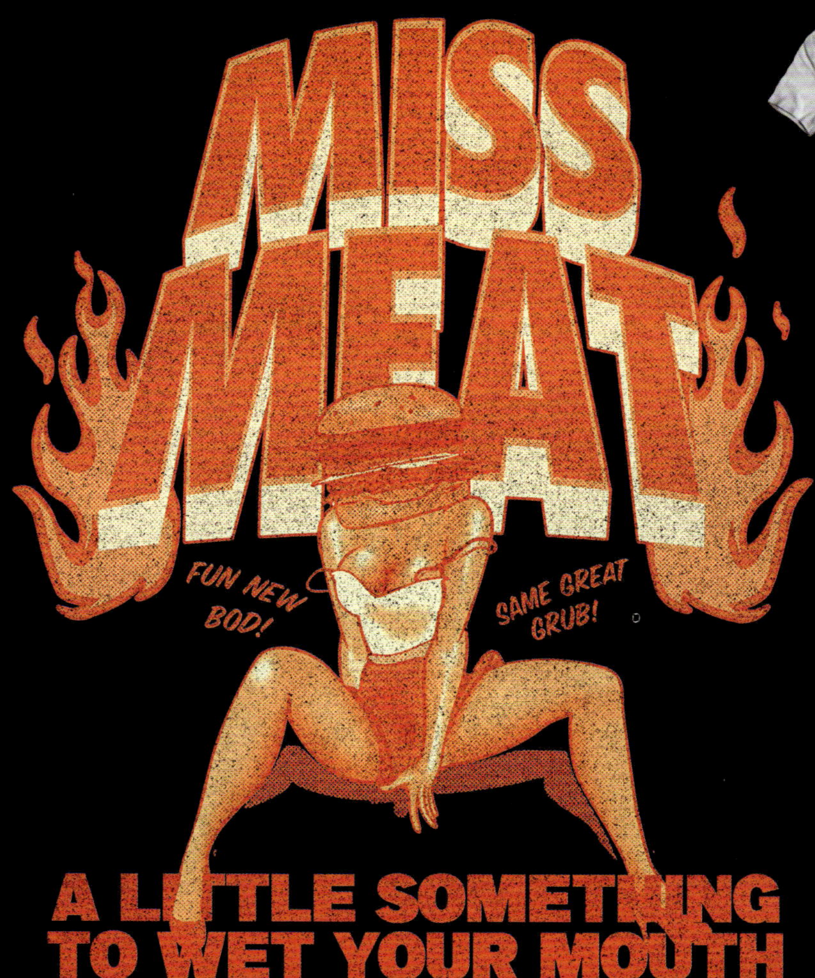

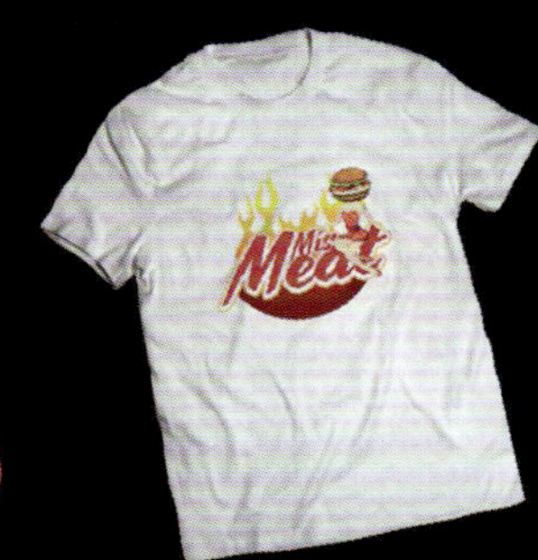

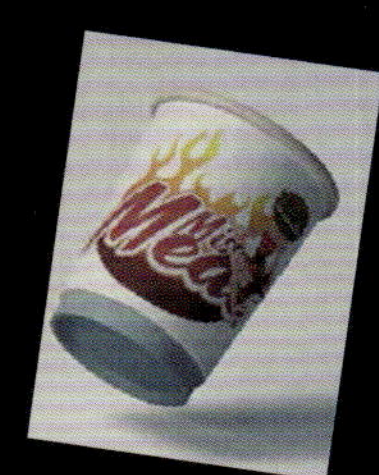

This page Various logo and promotional-material designs for Tromaville's own fast-food joint, including a few logos and cup and T-shirt designs.

Right Toxie emerges from the diner, after having dispensed a little extreme justice to the Nasty Lads.

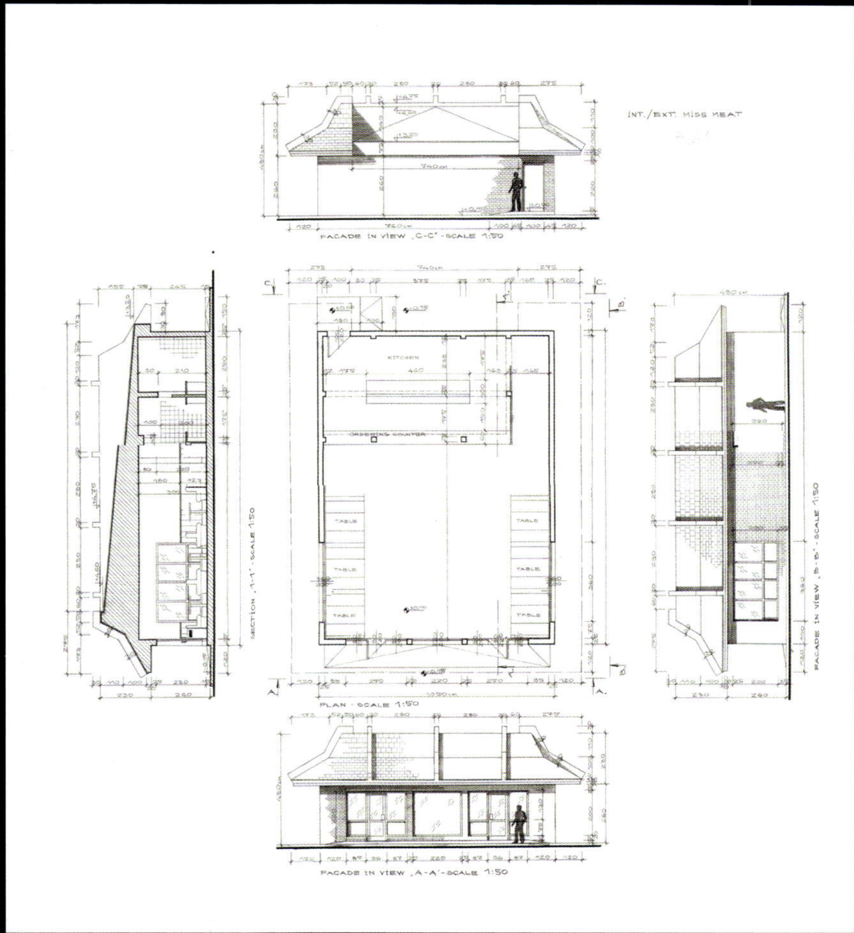

Left The production blueprints for the fast-food restaurant.

Below Further design concepts for Miss Meat iconography.

Below mid The Lunchorium completed, with its roof statue.

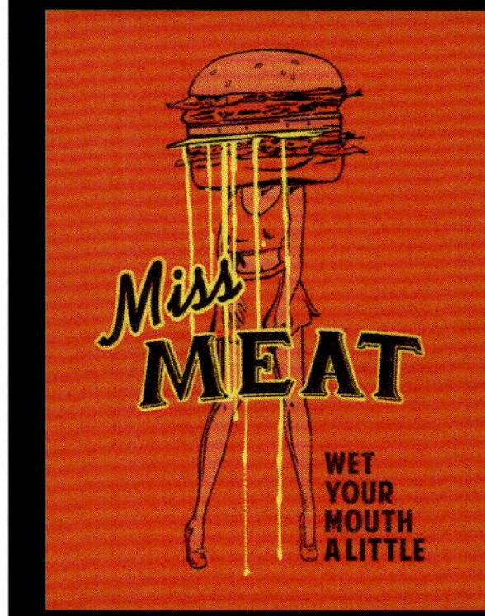

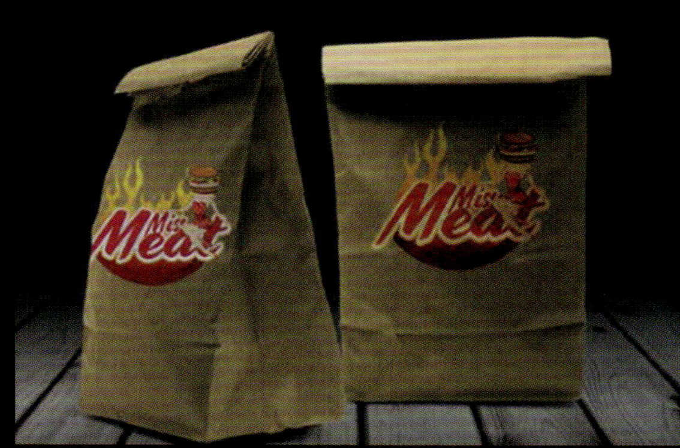

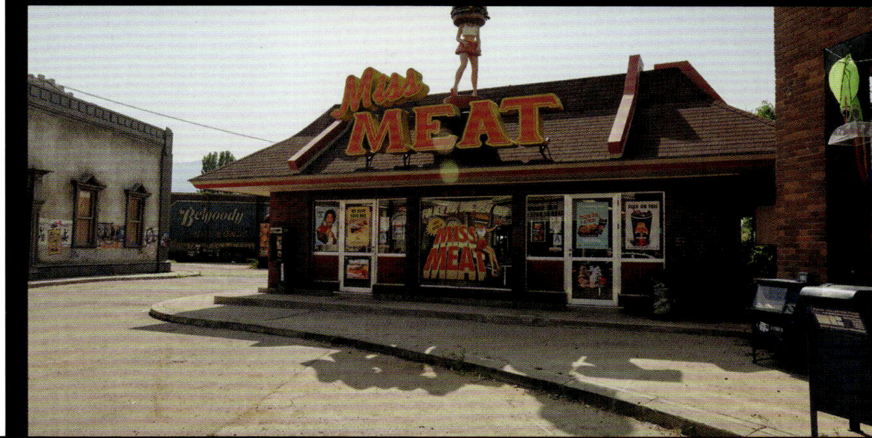

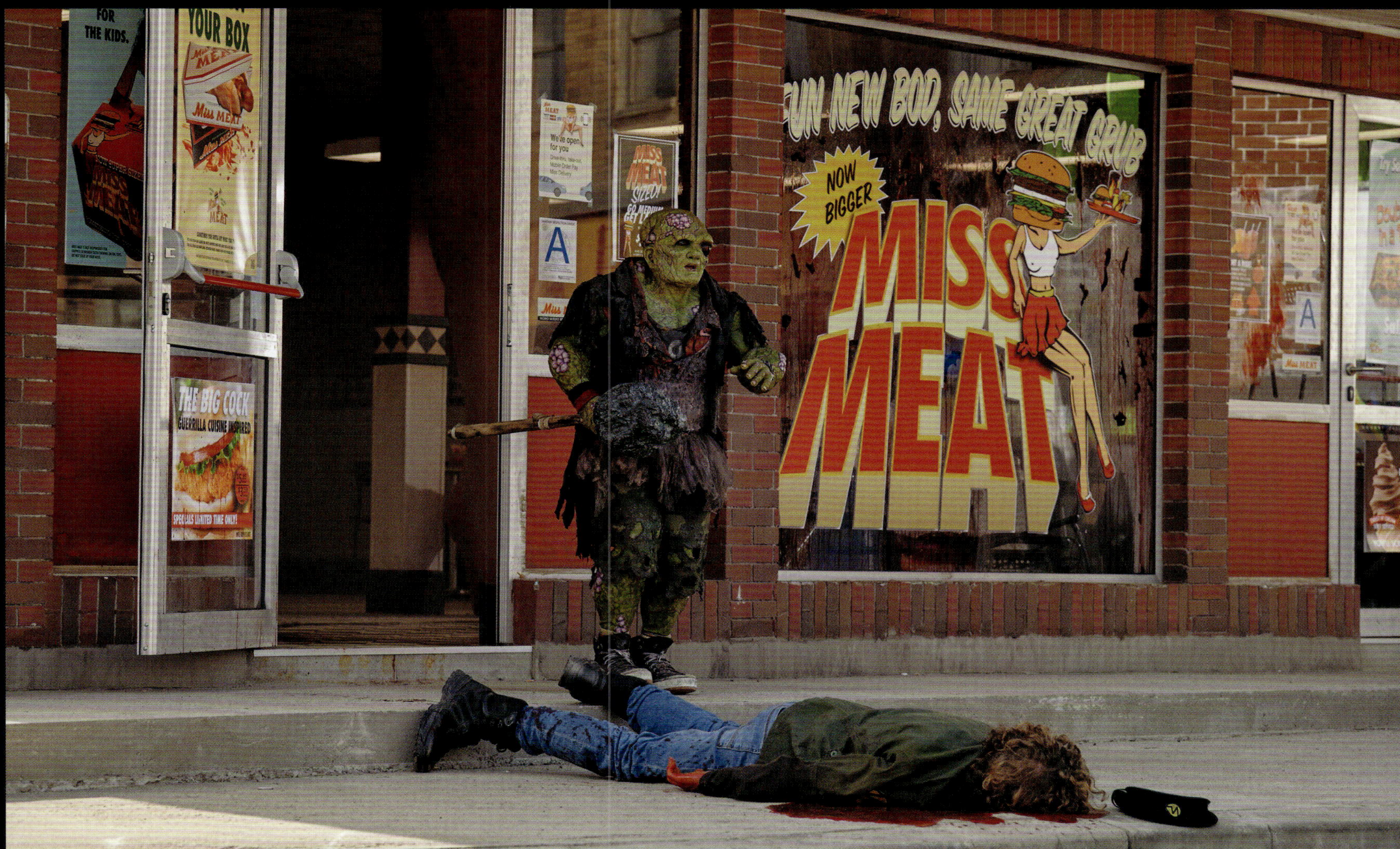

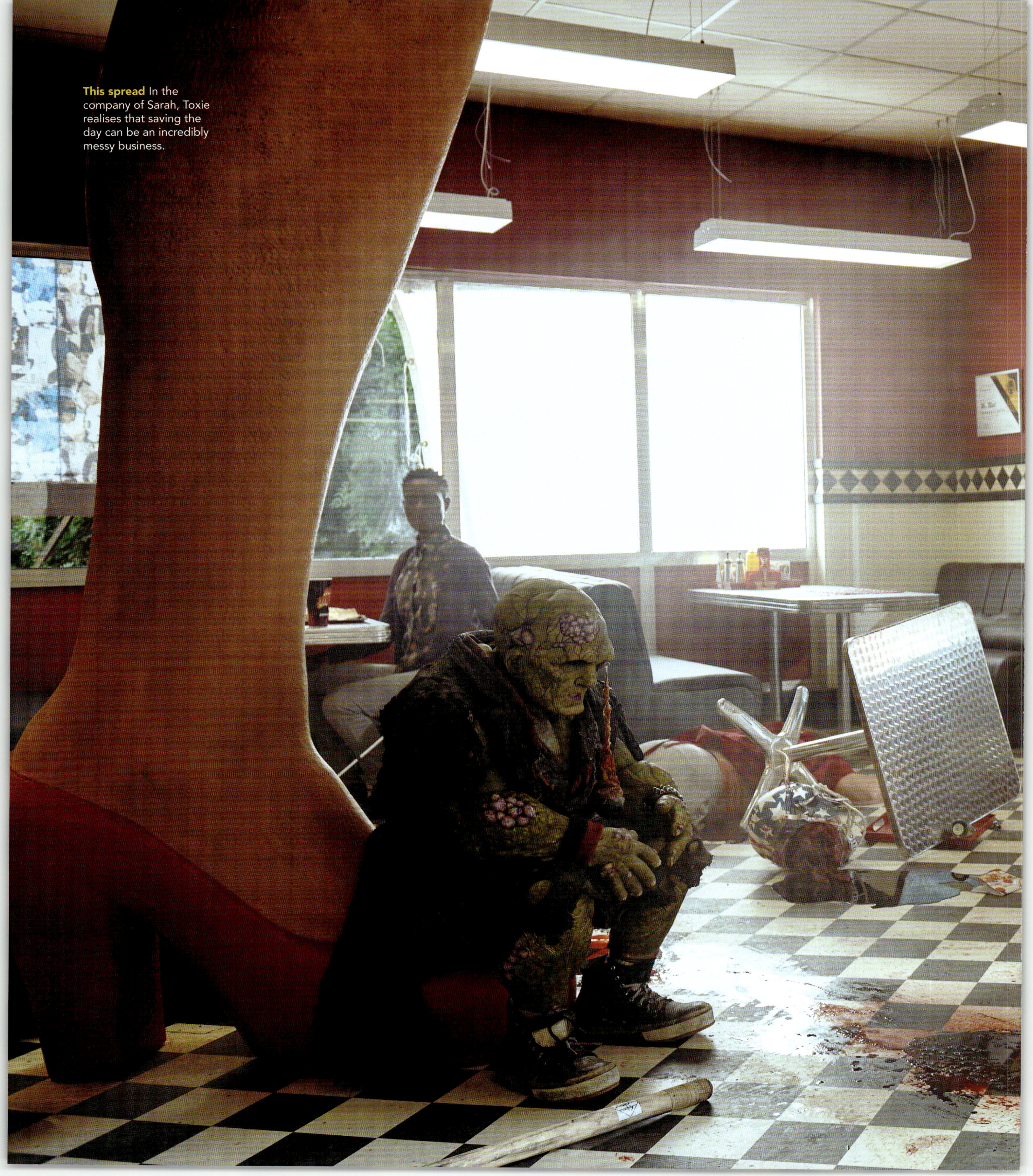

This spread In the company of Sarah, Toxie realises that saving the day can be an incredibly messy business.

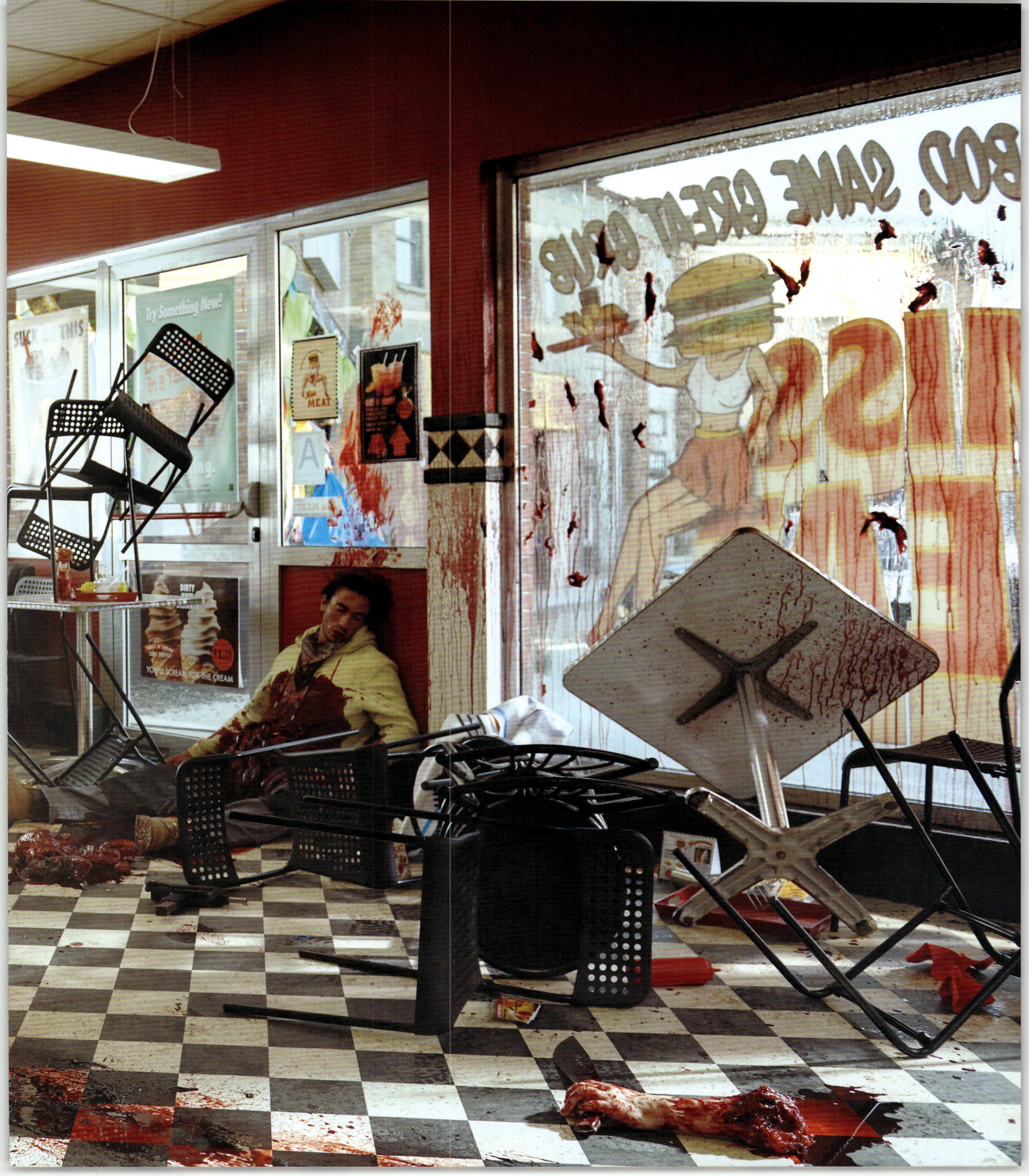
SUCK ON THIS
Try Something New!
MEAT
YOU'LL SCREAM FOR THE CREAM

NASTY LADS

The gang terrorizing the patrons of Miss Meat are a group of "goofball extremists," says Blair. "They're basically violent, aggrieved activist dudes who feel like things are not fair for them."

"Most of the Nasty Lads are subtly referencing casual militia-type styles," Porter says, "but some of them are a little more over-the-top. We have one guy who's wearing an American-flag football helmet, with a red cape and no shirt and sweatpants."

Blair insists that *The Toxic Avenger* is not supposed to be "a statement type movie." It's more a question of giving the bad guys some characterization and a degree of groundedness. "In the original movie, I'm not sure exactly what those guys were after," he says, referring to the garish miscreants in the taco joint. "They seemed to be some sort of overlap between the Satanic Panic of the '80s, weird rock 'n' rollers, and crazy druggies. So I just looked at what is available to us today; making them crazy druggies doesn't make a lot of sense in 2020s. Whereas a bunch of dudes who have a list of grievances against society and want to take it out on a hamburger restaurant felt like it did apply."

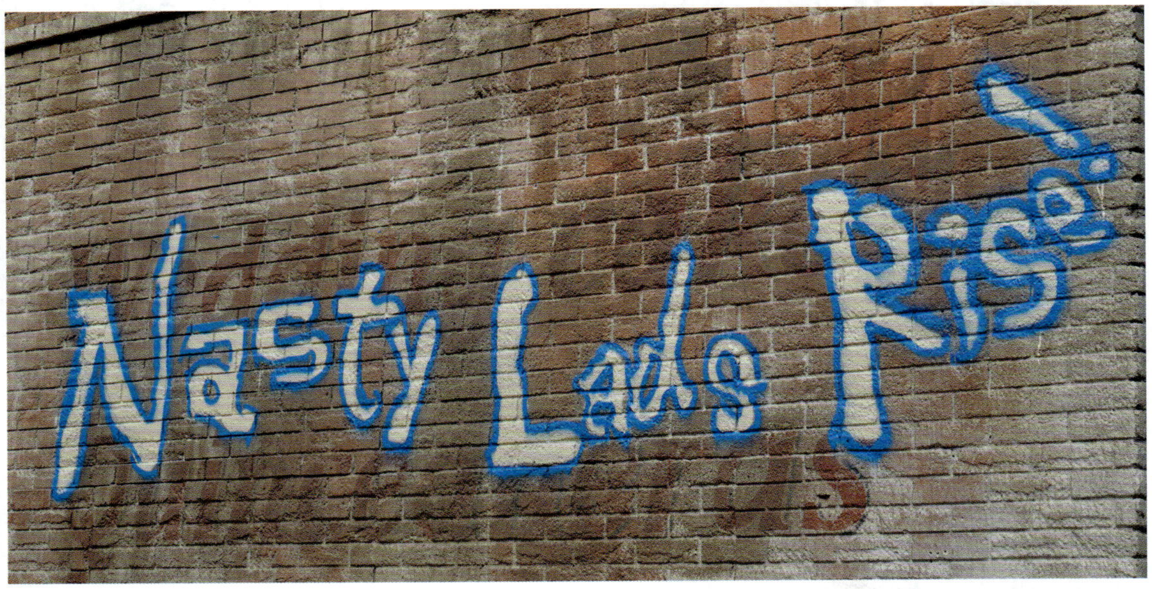

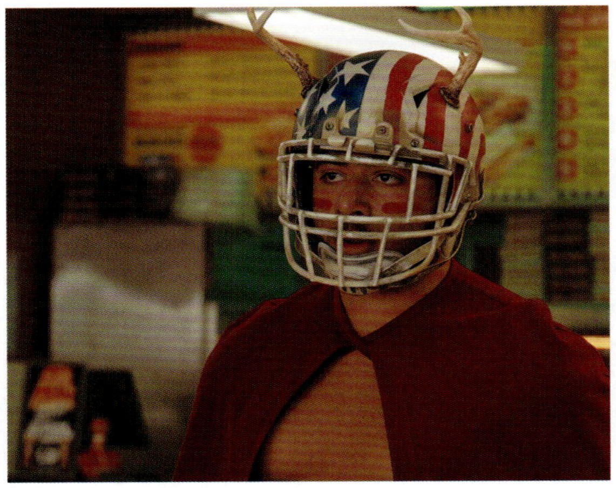

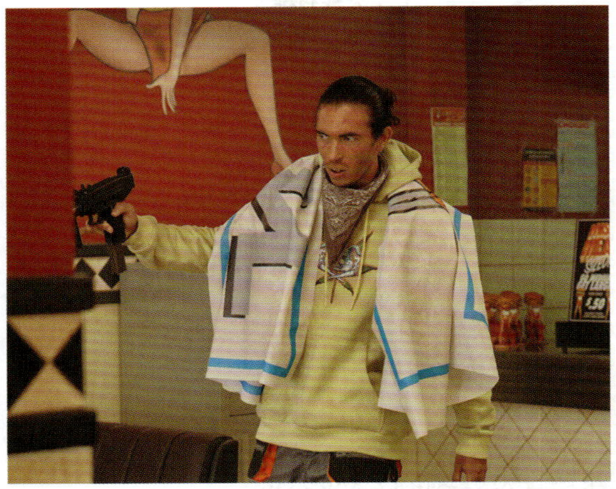

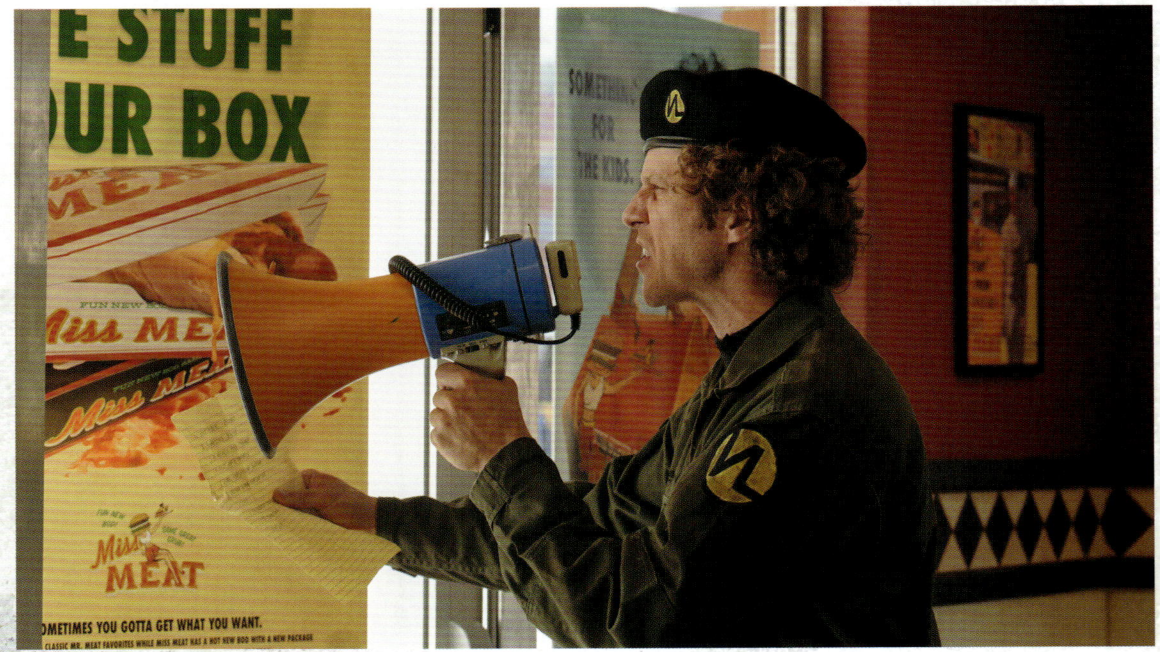

Top A little Nasty Lad graffiti on The Strip.

Right The Nasty Lads terrorize the Miss Meat Lunchorium.

AGENT SARAH WEATHERWAX

PLAYED BY MARGO CARGILL

No character imported from the original film has undergone more of a transformation than Sarah. Played in the '84 *Toxic Avenger* by Andree Maranda, the kind-hearted, visually impaired Sarah was one of the hostages rescued by Toxie during the taco restaurant hold-up (but not before her guide dog was shot and she suffered an attempted sexual assault), and soon became his love interest. After all, the joke went, who else could love a "hideously deformed" monster, other than someone who can't see? However, in the 2025 *The Toxic Avenger*, Sarah is no ditzy piece of arm candy for our hero. While she's introduced in similar circumstances, she has no romantic connection to Toxie, and it is later revealed that she is in fact the undercover agent known as Sneaky Cheetah.

"This story was not going to be about a young guy who's trying to get a date," says Blair, referring to the set-up for Toxie in the original. "In that kind of scenario, him connecting romantically with Sarah makes sense. But for this one, that was never in the recipe." Instead, the idea was to preserve the character in such a way that she provides a wink to the '84 original, while also neatly seeding the unexpected reveal later on.

"I wanted to give Sarah something different to do and have her purpose in this story be a little bit of a surprise at the end," says Blair. "She's now this secret character that people have been referring to as the one driving the investigation and prosecution of Garbinger."

Another significant difference between the new Sarah and the old is the fact that she's played by someone—British actor Margo Cargill—who is visually impaired, rather than a sighted actor who, in many scenes, played Sarah's blindness for laughs. "That was important," says Blair. "We only read visually impaired actresses for that part. It made sense and there wasn't a lot of discussion around it."

Cargill struck Blair as having all the required qualities for the role. "She was able to project a stern quality that seemed right for a federal agent and investigator, in a way that we could have fun with; when you have that reveal at the end, it retroactively makes sense. Her demeanour clicks with some sort of investigative outfit."

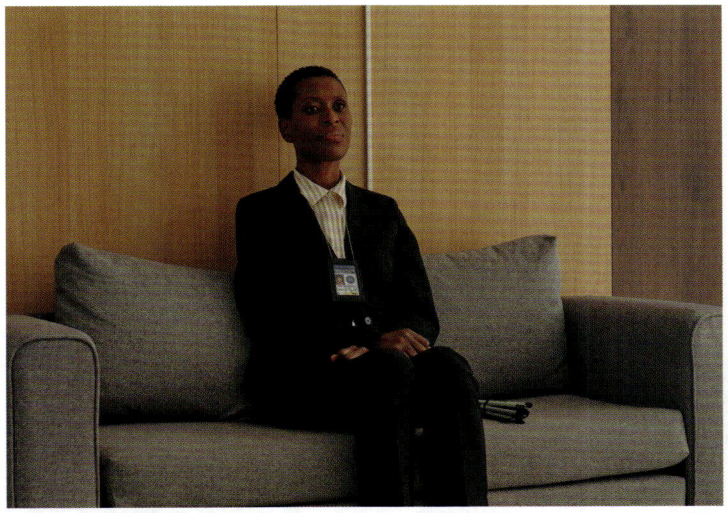

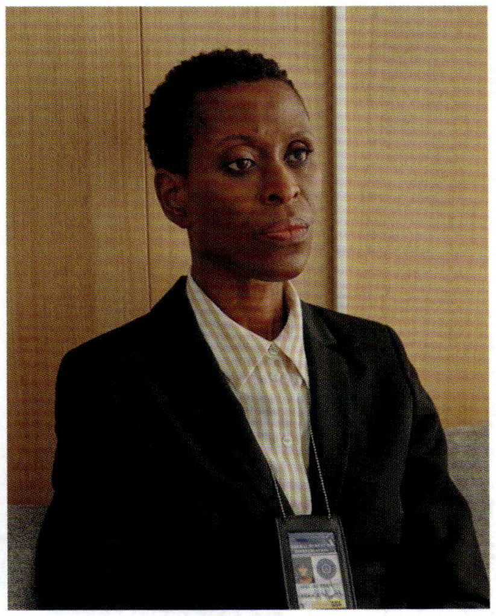

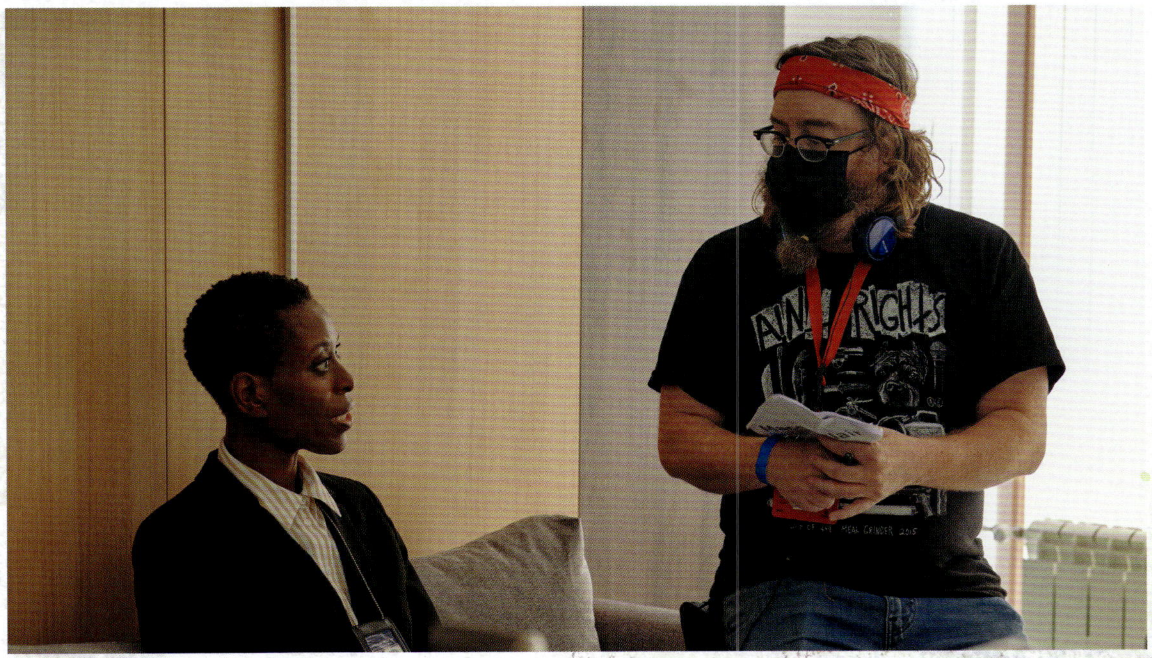

Top secret agent Sarah Weatherwax waits patiently.

Bottom Cargill and Blair discuss the scene.

TROMA FEST

St. Roma's Festival—which with a few letters scratched out becomes "Troma Fest"—is both the site of The Killer Nutz's big performance and of their final reckoning, at the hands (and mop) of Toxie. In true Troma style, there is loud rock music, a bit of gratuitous nudity and a big splash of extreme violence. Although, says Cameron, the event also reveals that the band isn't as drop-dead cool as they make out.

"The idea was that the Nutz thought they were much better than they actually are," he laughs, "so rather than having a huge sound system and stuff, there's these crappy little speakers. It shows they're not as big as they imagine."

Porter says it was an enjoyable sequence, with her department dressing around 150 background performers, "in a mix of different kinds of alternative looks." However, she adds, "it was the height of summer, so it was very hot those days."

The location team found their Fest at Borisova Gradina park in the centre of Sofia, which has a clamshell-style open air stage that was easy to adapt for their Tromavillian purposes. But working in a public place presented significant logistical difficulties, says Cameron, while "from a shooting point of view, it was three action-heavy days, and the sun was just beating down. I mean, there were people fainting."

At the heart of it all was Luisa Guerreiro, creating Toxie's big hero moment on stage, firstly performing Motörhead's 'Overkill', and then violently dispatching the Nutz—all the while suffering that sunshine in a full-body prosthetic.

"Luisa is so unbelievably good," marvels Gonzales. "She dealt with the heat, and her physicality was amazing." But his favourite Toxie moment was neither the rocking out, nor the Nutz-cracking. "After she kicks all the band's asses, Toxie pleads with the crowd, revealing to them how Garbinger's big corporation is trying to fuck them," he says. "The scene switches from combat to this kind of grassroots action, which grounds it so quickly in a really cool way."

"Luisa is so unbelievably good."
– DANA GONZALES, Cinematographer

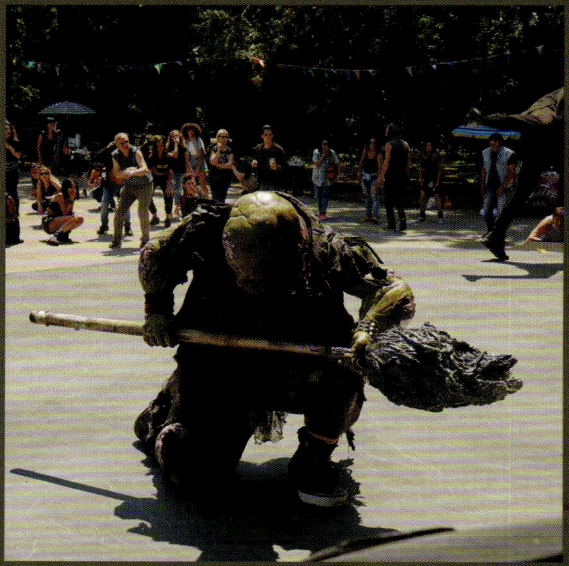

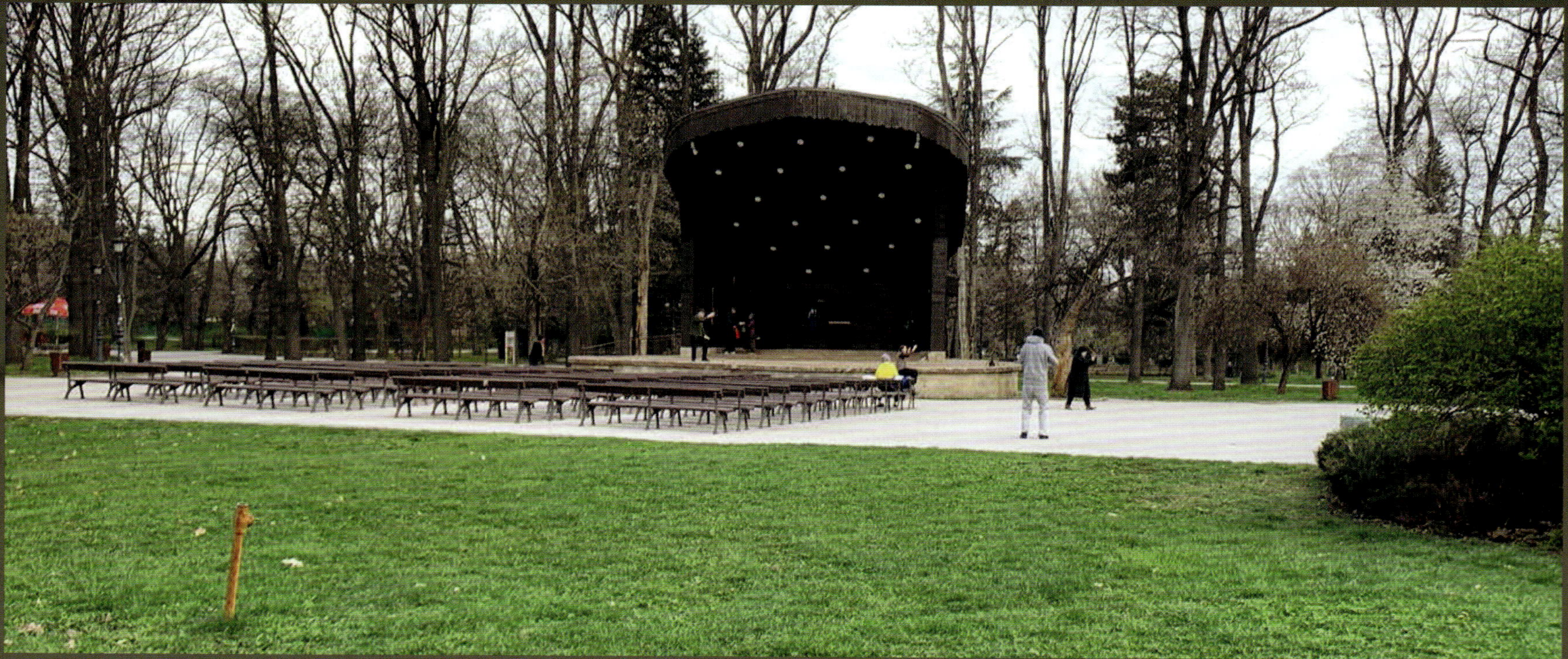

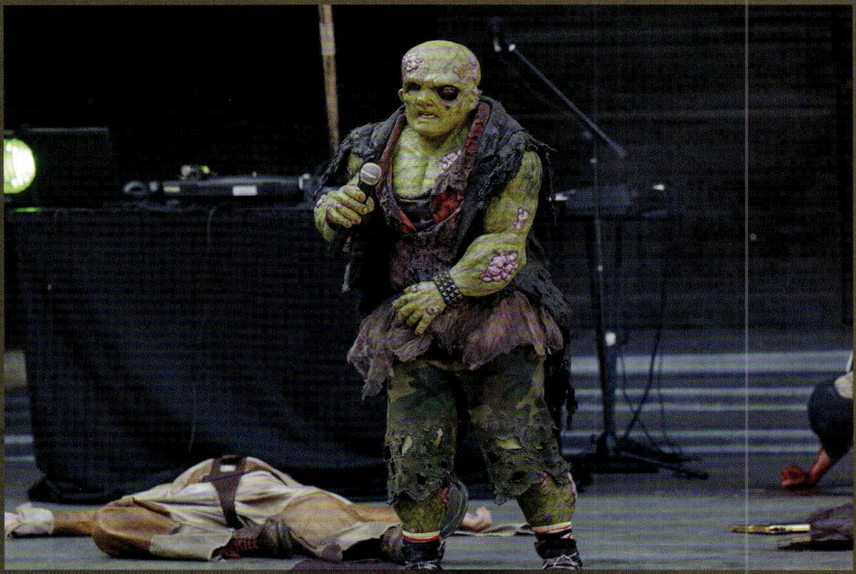

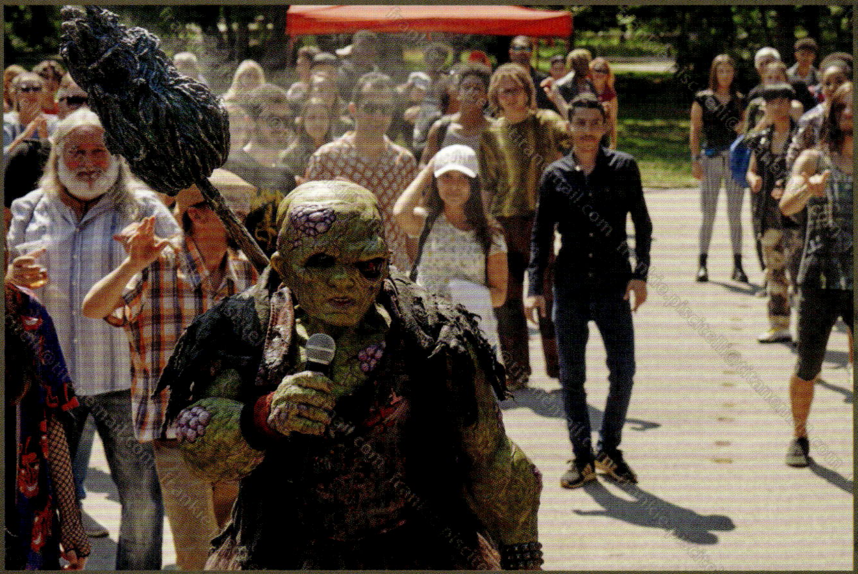

Left Toxie in mop-wielding mode.

Below left & right Location photos of Borisova Gradina park in Sofia, where Troma Fest would be created.

Above Toxie takes the mic and whips up some anti-Garbinger fervour among the crowd.

Below Toxie confronts the Killer Nutz during their big performance.

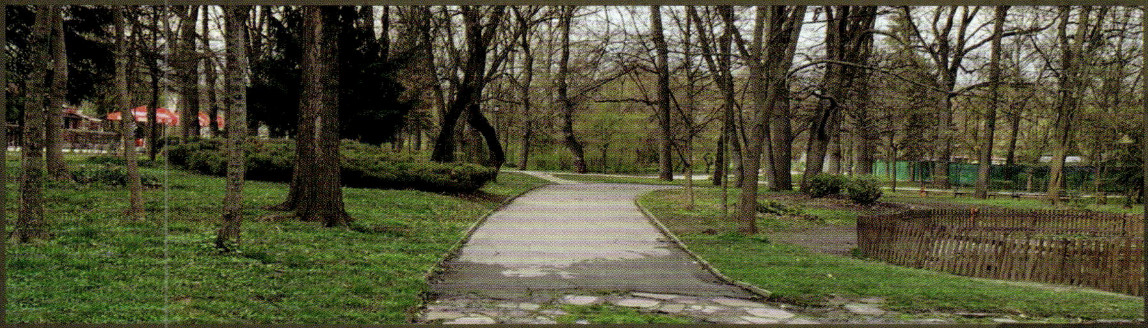

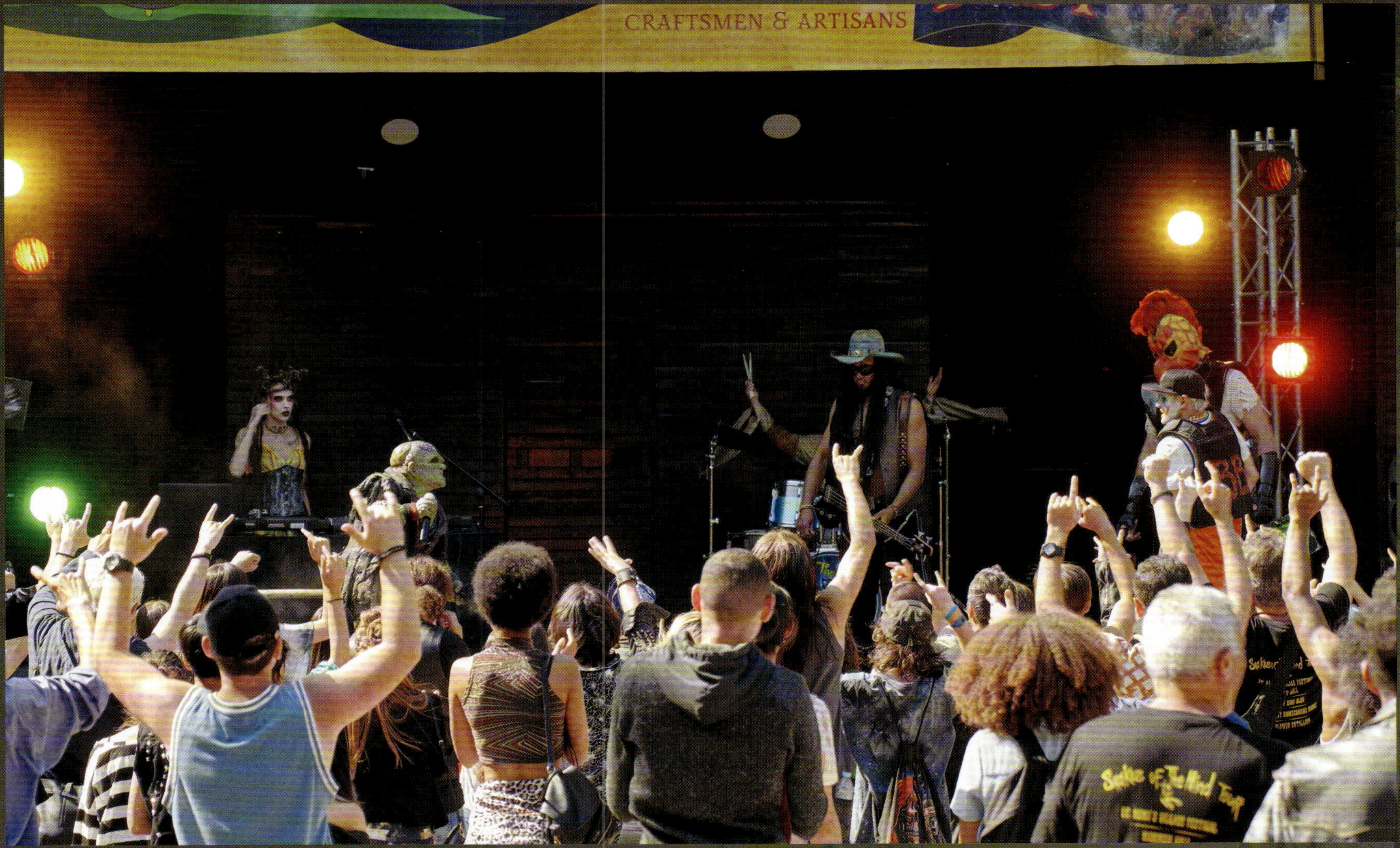

MONSTER GARBINGER

PLAYED BY SPENCER WILDING

When Bob Garbinger quaffs a dose of Toxie elixir, concocted from our green-skinned hero's spinal fluid, he undergoes his own incredible transformation. But the resulting creature is a hideously deformed monstrosity of a very different stripe.

Having originally used Frankenstein's monster as a visual starting point for Toxie, Blair and Menendez sought inspiration for Monster Garbinger elsewhere in the classic Universal horror canon. "Originally he was much more in a Dracula zone," reveals Blair, "with a Nosferatu vampire-type look. But then we started thinking, 'If Toxie is hairless and sleek, it might be cool for Monster-Garbinger to be furry and hairy as a way to offset that.' So we took a left turn and started thinking of him more in terms of a werewolf-type look."

For a while, Monster Garbinger was closer to Lon Chaney, Jr.'s iconic Wolf Man, but over time he mutated into the more distinct troll-like appearance he has now, featuring horns which, Blair says, "are meant to be his skull growing in a misshapen way."

Similar to Toxie's evolution, Blair and Menendez's original drawings were taken by Millennium FX in Buckinghamshire, England and developed as 3D digital models, before the prosthetic elements were physically produced and shipped to Sofia. "Originally Monster Garbinger had much thicker hair on his face, but we were

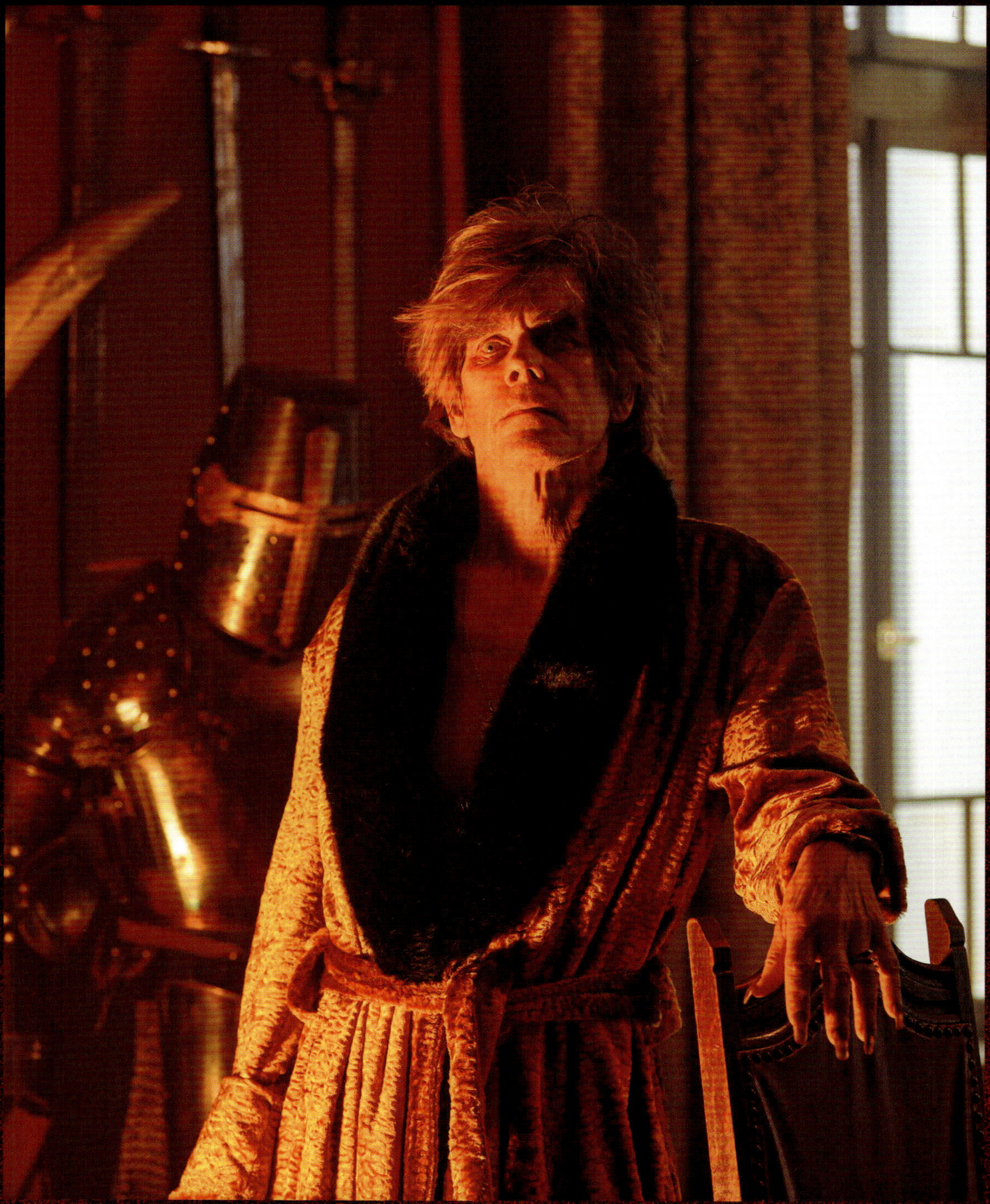

Below & right As the serum starts to take hold, the villain doesn't immediately transform, requiring only minor makeup effects to be applied to Bacon.

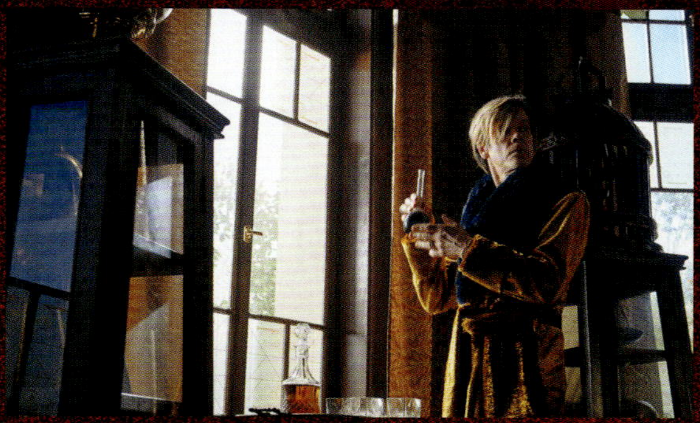

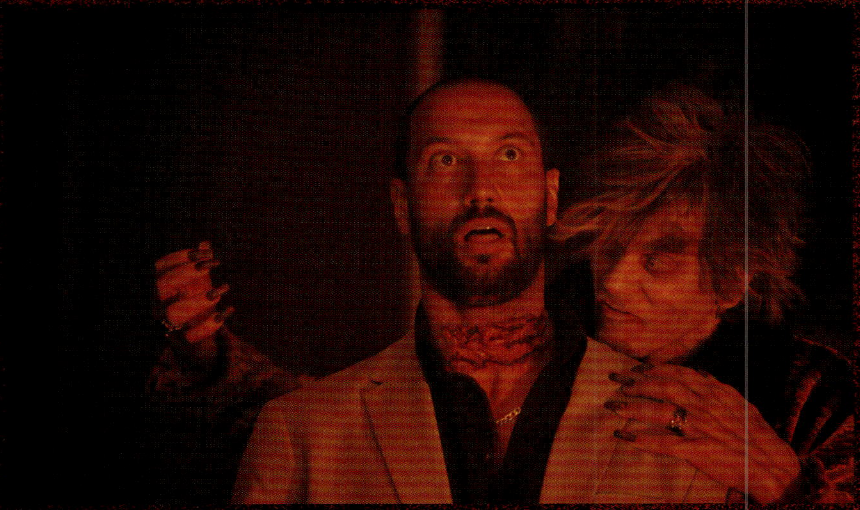

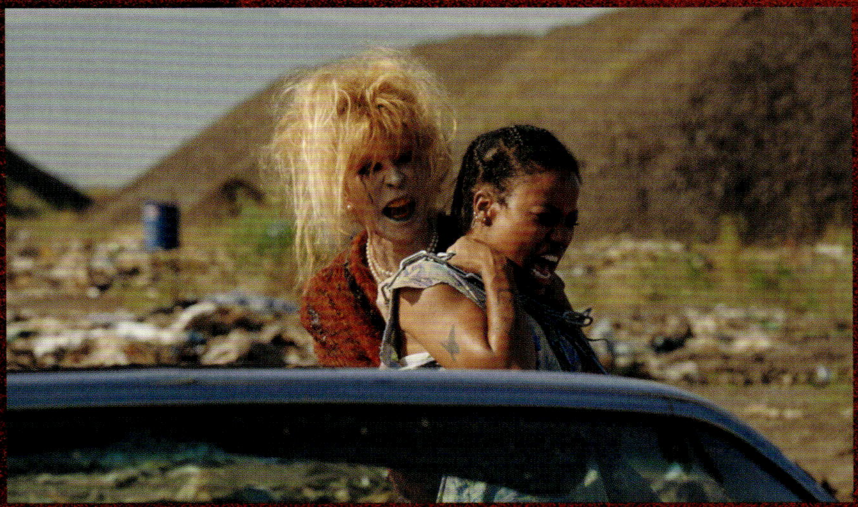

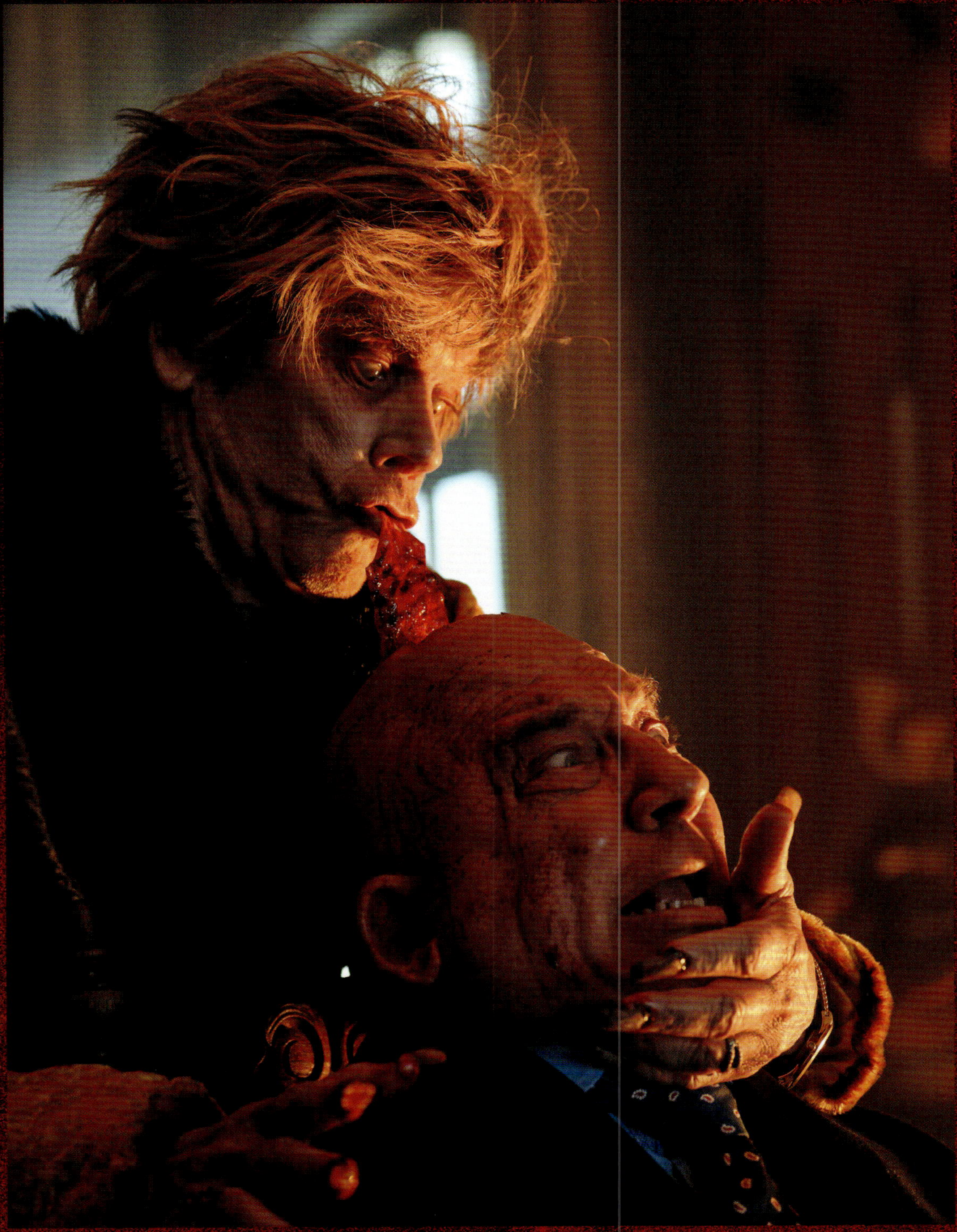

trying to avoid him looking too much like the Wolf Man," explains creature effects lead Christopher Goodman. "Or even the Beast from Disney's *Beauty and the Beast*, because he has this gaudy dressing gown and a big fluffy collar that reminded me of the Beast. The way we tackled that was by making the hair a little sparser, revealing patches of blotchy skin, making him veer more towards the grotesque."

To wear this unsightly mask and suit, which was covered in a mix of acrylic fibre and human hair, Blair enlisted Spencer Wilding (who portrayed Darth Vader in *Rogue One: A Star Wars Story*), the actor already on board as Him Under The Hood. "We felt, if he's going to come all the way to Bulgaria, we might as well use him as much as we can," says Blair. "He was such an asset." However, while it was Wilding wearing the costume, the monster had to convince the audience it could have sprouted from the very different features of Kevin Bacon. A tough task for the team at Millennium FX.

"It was really tricky to get this Welsh boxer's face inside of Kevin's longer, more delicate features," says creature effects supervisor Kate Walshe. "You have to create

Top left Monster Garbinger's new claws enable him to dispatch a Khaki Klub goon.

Left Garbinger uses his new power to rid himself of the troublesome Thad Barkabus.

Top right Kissy gets her own transformative shot of serum, as J.J. painfully finds out.

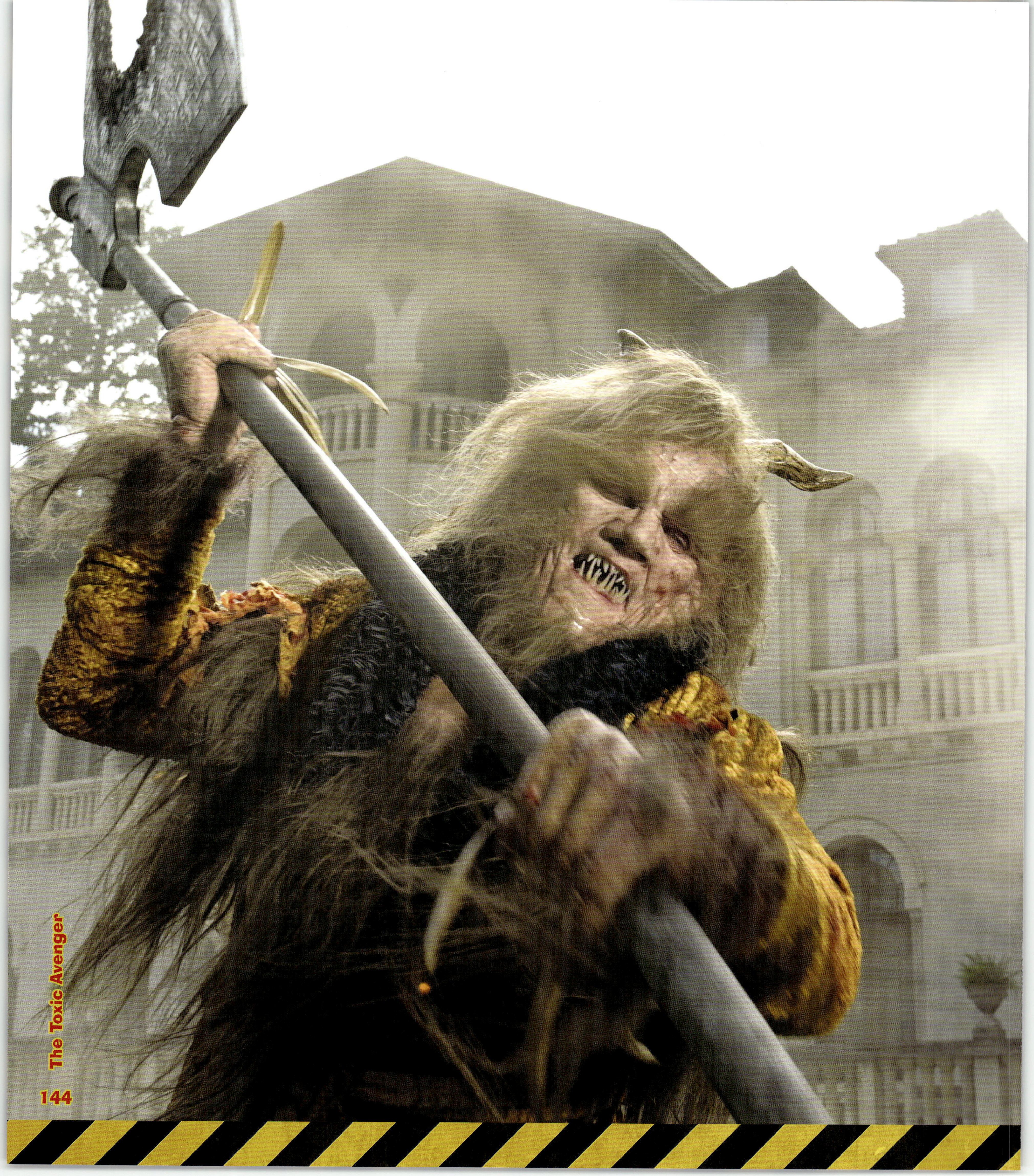

a happy medium, where you're getting these hints of Kevin in the design. But as a performer, Spencer is really powerful and just mad as a brush, and he really embodied Monster Garbinger."

Although both this character and Him Under The Hood are of a similar physical size, Blair points out that each required a markedly different acting approach. "Him Under The Hood is more of a silent, hulking sort of presence, whereas Monster Garbinger has more of a comedic physical type of presence. There's more fighting and performative stuff that I think Spencer enjoyed getting into."

At one point during Toxie and Monster Garbinger's climactic melee, Toxie sears his foe's face with his mop—a gag which Chris Ritvo reveals required no CG assistance. "It's a really nice gore-score moment, where his skin peels off and there's pieces coming off. It looked amazing; Millennium did a really cool paint job with a prosthetic. So that's all practical. We didn't touch that!"

But worse is yet to come for the trollish businessman, who sends the movie's gore score geysering through the ceiling with a spectacularly bloody death. "By this time in the movie you've seen a lot of ridiculous things," laughs Gonzales, "and then there's this over-the-top, far-fetched moment where he's thrown into a car engine and starts spinning around, getting ground up like he's in a woodchipper."

Using the memorable death of Johnny Depp's character in *A Nightmare on Elm Street* as a reference, Bulgarian SFX team Illusion Industries created a practical rig for the scene, with a pair of spinning legs and jets of stage blood. The spraying gore, digitally augmented in post-production, was shot by Gonzales in super slow-motion. "It's like 150, 200 frames per second," he says. This allowed him to capture it spattering the nearby characters, including Toxie, Wade and J.J., in minute detail.

"It's really fun," grins Gonzales. "A ridiculous demise in a ridiculous world."

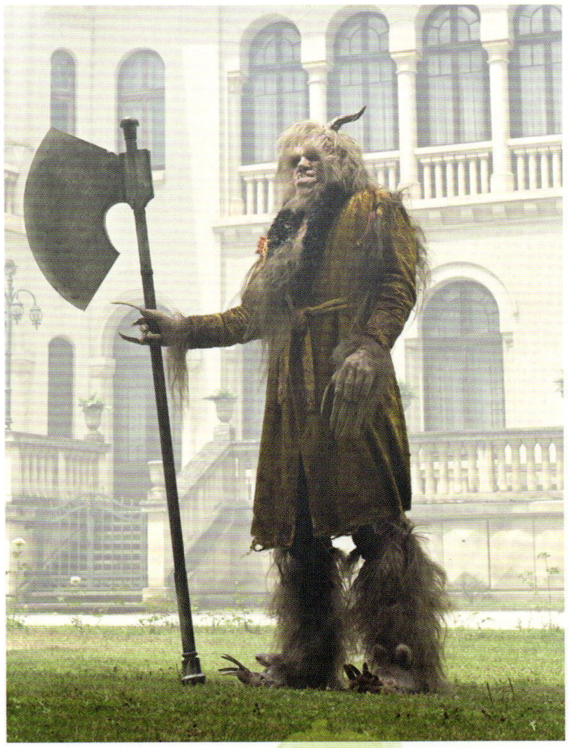

Above, opposite & below left Wilding as the fully transformed Monster Garbinger, with his mop-damaged axe.

Below Monster Garbinger's facial mop wound was acheived entirely with practical effects and makeup..

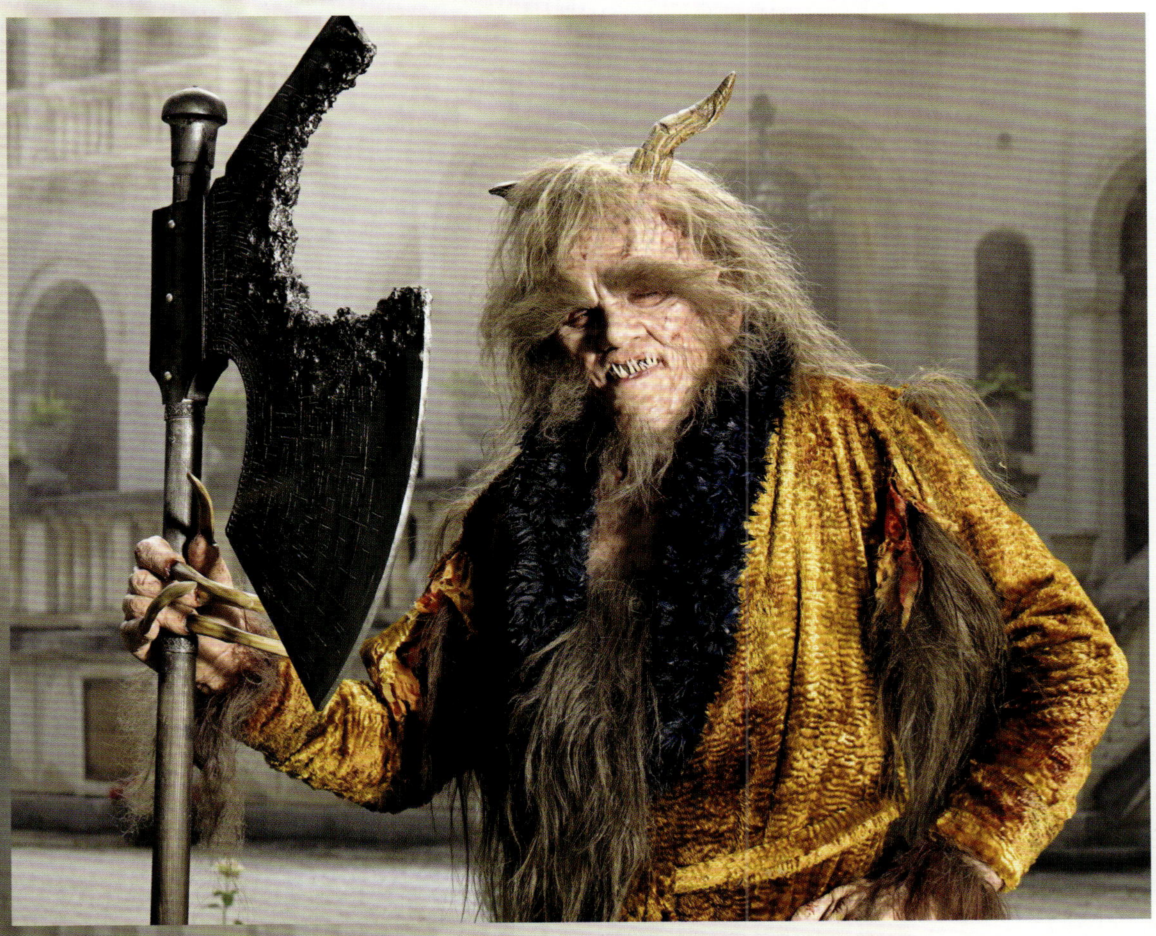

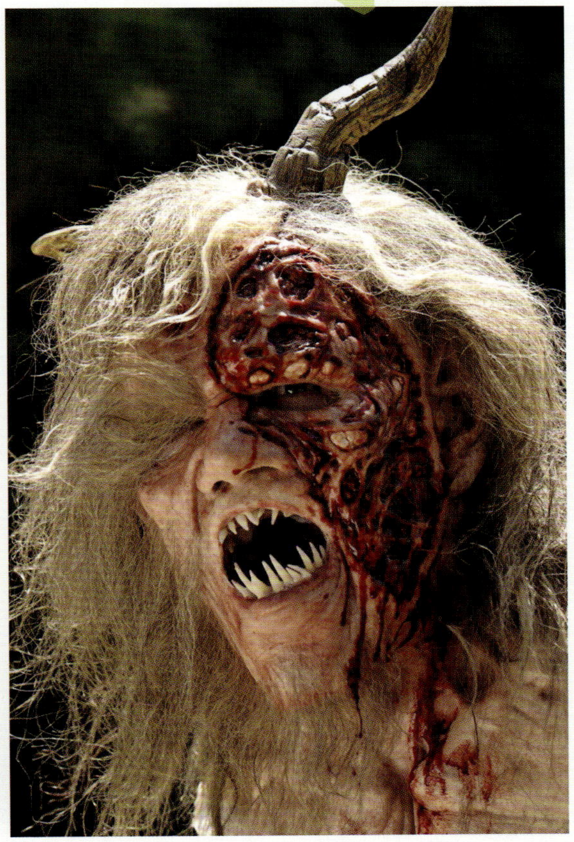

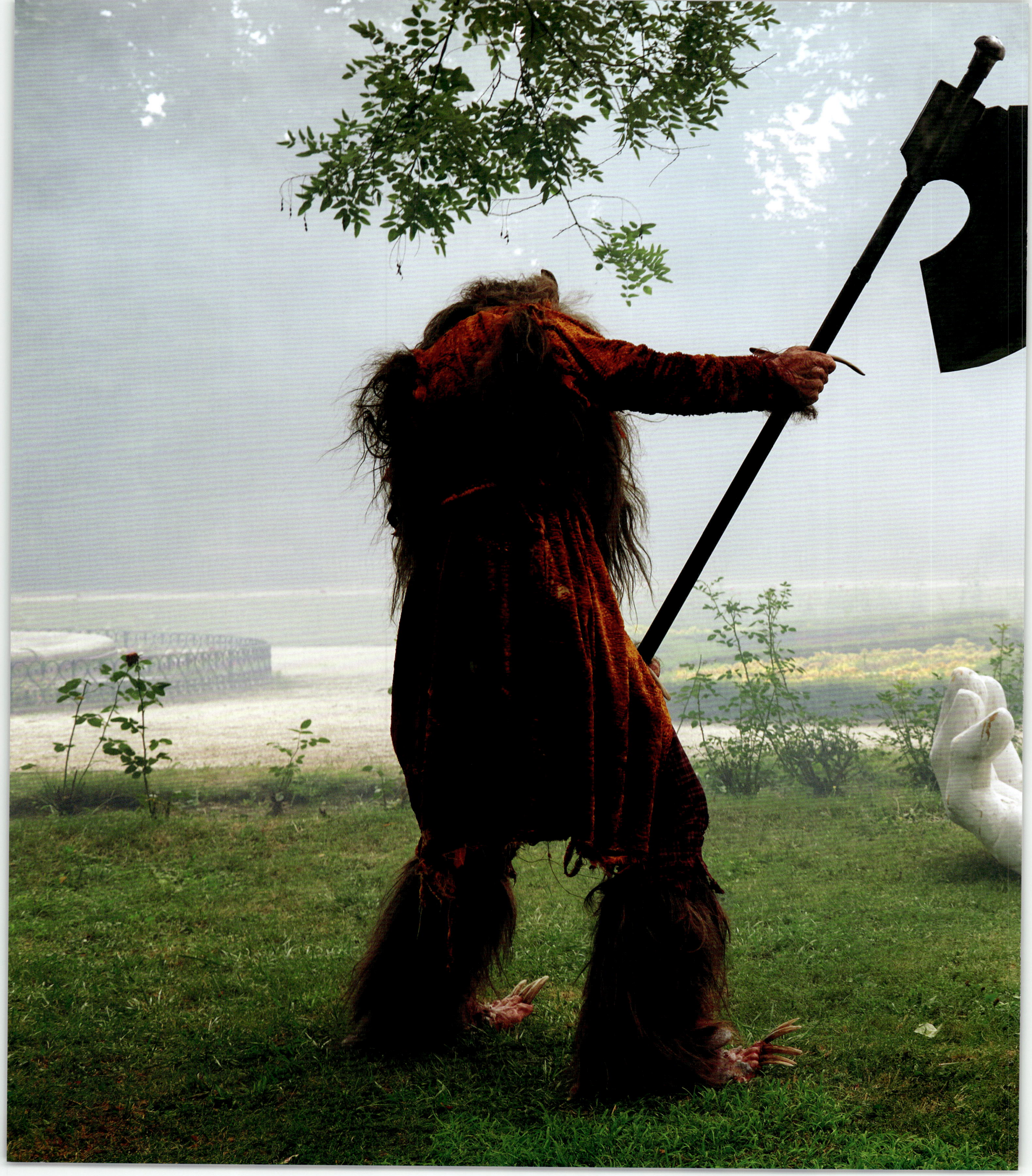

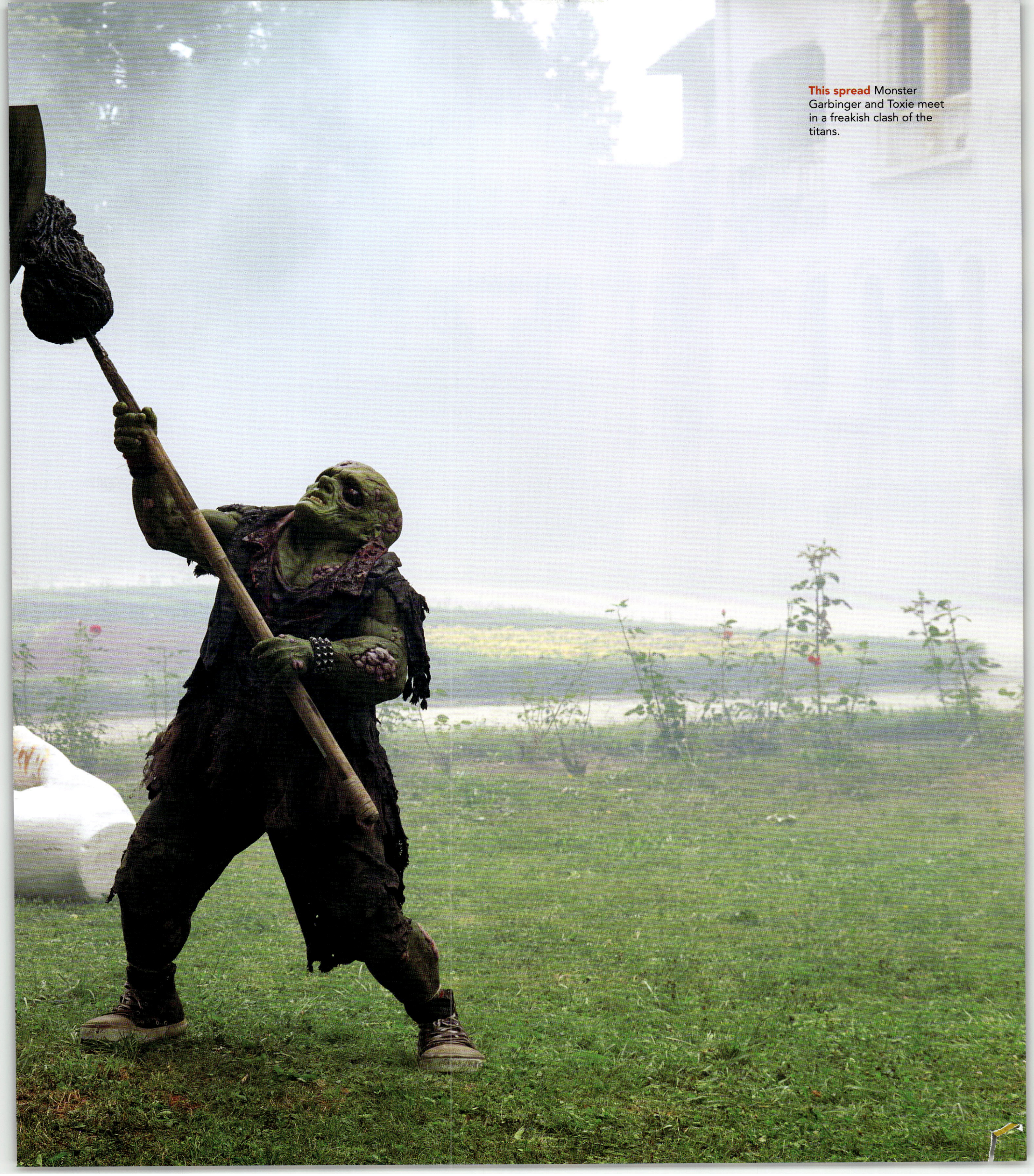

This spread Monster Garbinger and Toxie meet in a freakish clash of the titans.

VISUAL EFFECTS

While shooting *The Toxic Avenger*, one of the words Macon Blair repeated the most to his creative team was "analog". Though it is not a period movie—there are laptops and websites—the world of Tromaville is consciously positioned a little outside our heavily digital age, with a distinctive retro feel that came to suffuse every aspect of the production.

"We never wanted to do anything with the camera where it's flying through spaces and making impossible moves, which maybe is really dynamic and very cool, but on some subconscious level, you know a camera can't really do that," says Blair. "We were deliberately putting limitations on things so it all stays within this certain zone, giving the movie a particular vibe that suits this type of story."

The origin point for this approach was Toxie himself, and the decision to have him performed by an actor in a suit, rather than using the kind of motion-capture techniques that conjured the Na'vi of James Cameron's *Avatar*, or the apes of the most recent *Planet of the Apes* movies. Of course, to some degree this choice was motivated by financial reality. For a "super hard-R movie" like *The Toxic Avenger*, Blair points out, a heavy and hugely expensive CGI component is going to be much harder to justify. But first and foremost, suit-over-CG was an aesthetic decision.

"I'm not a purist. I think the technology is truly incredible on the *Planet of the Apes* movies. But it's a choice. Like: do you want to play the song on an acoustic or an electric guitar? They're both valid. They're just going to sound different, and they're going to have different positives and negatives. So, it was a question of what fits the material better. And for me, what I said at the beginning, before we had even figured out the story, was I wanted to rely on prosthetics and puppets. It just feels different than when you use the slicker digital type of tools that are available now. I even had aspirations to really get into model miniatures, but we ended up not going in that direction."

Blair's analog intentions became immediately clear to Ritvo during their very first meeting. "We jumped right in," Ritvo says. "There was a lot of onus on making

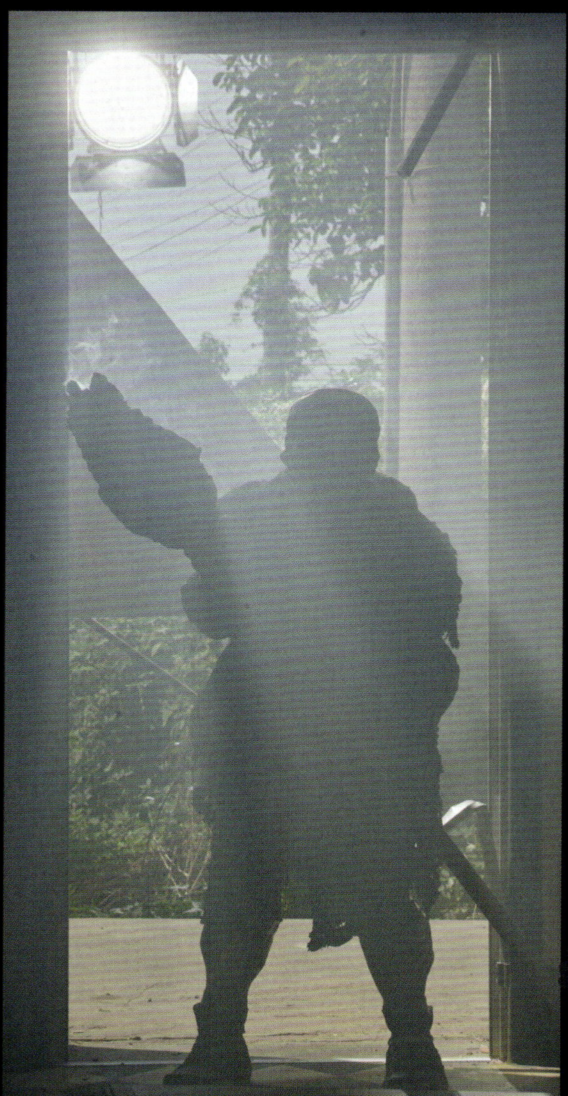

Left Toxie makes a dramatic entrance.

Right Blair in full-on directing mode.

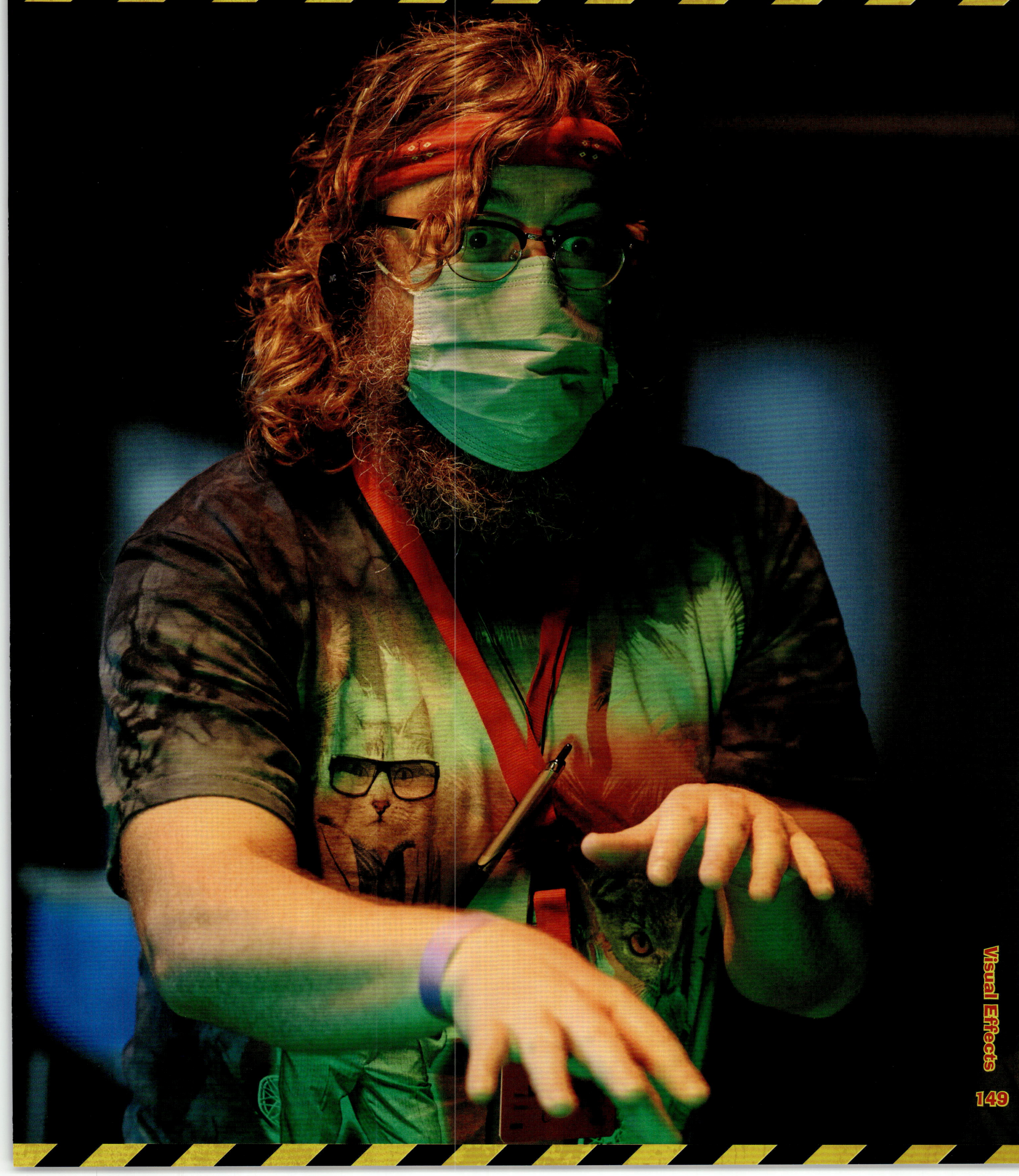

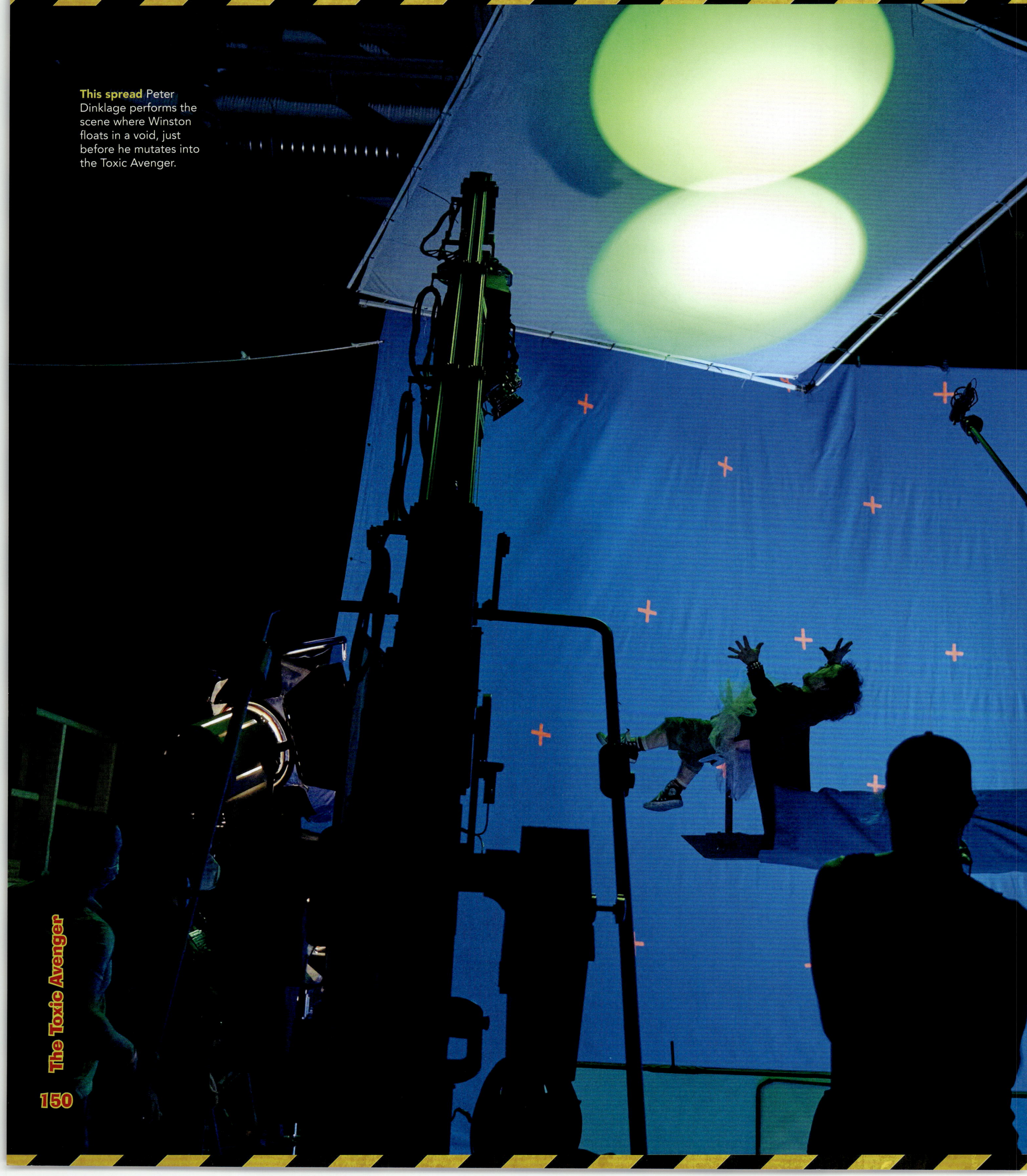

This spread Peter Dinklage performs the scene where Winston floats in a void, just before he mutates into the Toxic Avenger.

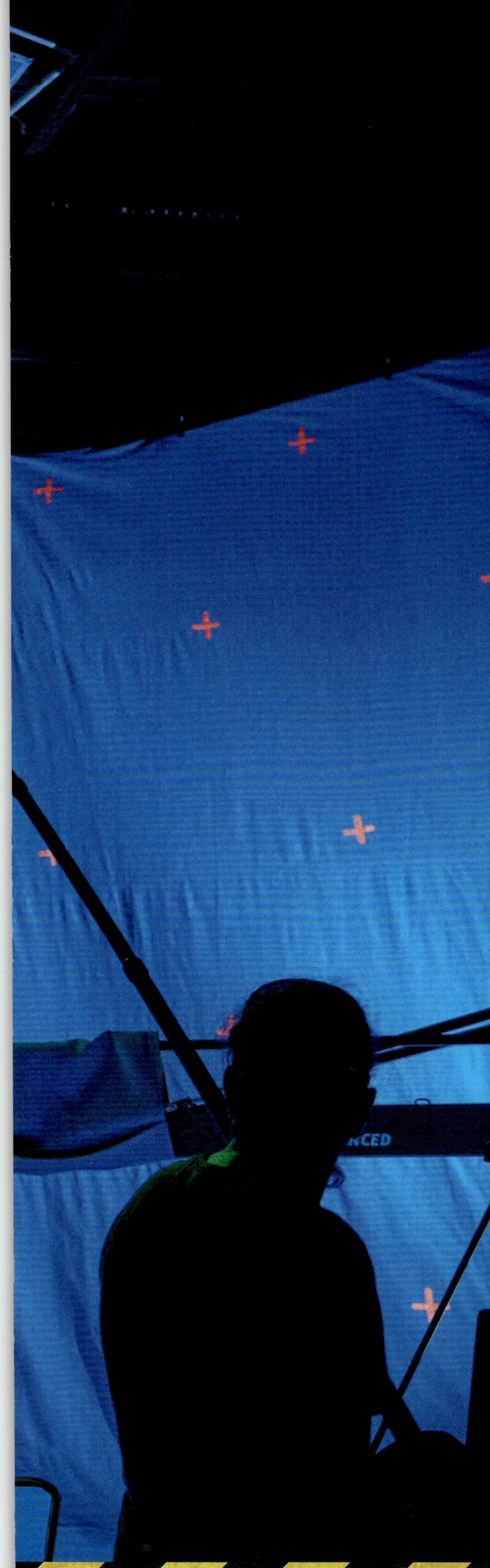

stuff practical, which is great. *Toxie* is all about making it tangible, and avoiding too many shiny looking visual effects." One major example of this prevailing approach is the sequence where Winston transforms into Toxie, which eschewed CGI for a literally organic approach.

Blair and Gonzales spent the first two days of principal photography shooting macro photography of green-dyed soap bubbles and meat being ripped apart. "It was all kinds of crazy substances and chemical reactions," says Gonzales, "like you're seeing the molecules transform. It's all photographed, which is always pleasing to me."

Meanwhile, to represent Winston's skeleton thickening to Toxie proportions, Illusion Industries crafted special-effects bones covered in wax, which were heated up and shot in reverse as they melted. This gave the impression, Ritvo says, of "recombining and becoming really thick."

All these elements were used to form a psychedelic backdrop—"Almost like the Star Gate sequence in *2001: A Space Odyssey*, or a '70s music video," according to Ritvo—against which we see Peter Dinklage as Winston, who is seemingly floating in a void (or rather toxic waste), but in reality mounted on a teeter-totter rig in the studio, in front of a blue screen.

"I was up 30 feet in the air, on wires, flailing about on this weird, tiny seat," recalls Dinklage. "I was flying around in eternity, basically. If I had vertigo I would have been in trouble!"

Nothing in the sequence is computer-generated, Ritvo confirms. "We're just compositing it all together. It's a very abstract

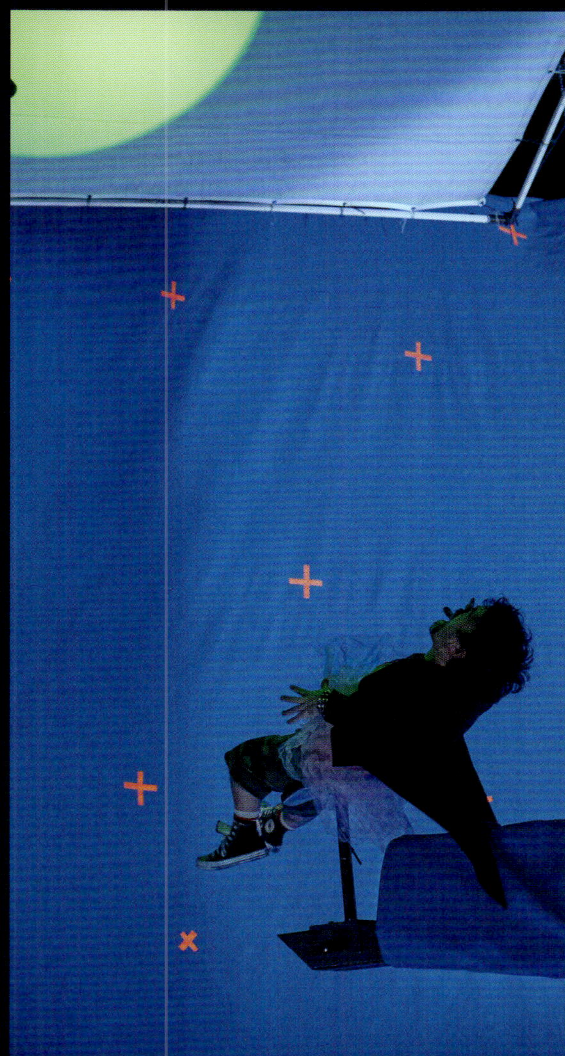

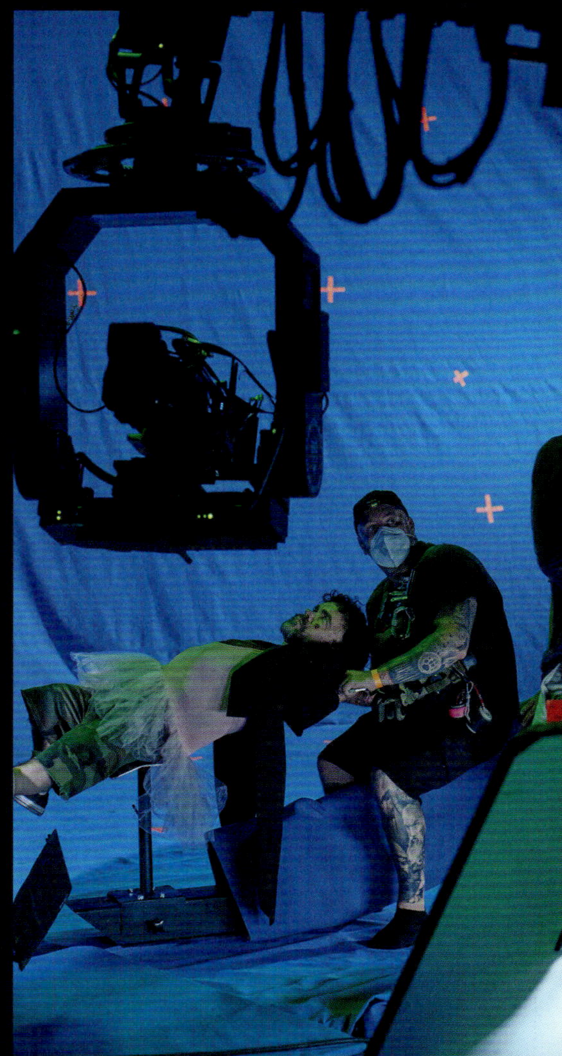

idea, pretty unique and interesting."

However, *The Toxic Avenger* isn't entirely analog. There are, Ritvo says, around 200 digital VFX shots in the film, although he points out this is "definitely low" for a movie of this genre. As we have seen in the previous pages, these primarily involved the augmentation of environments such as the B.T.H. Factory and the city surrounding Toxie during his 'hero rooftop' scene, as well as adding to elements such as the gore which splatters everywhere during Monster Garbinger's death. However, one place where the movie does go "full CG", as Ritvo puts it, is the flying mop shot during the Troma Fest segment, where Toxie hurls his weapon clean through Nightmare Josh's head and skewers DJ Cool Cthulu against her turntables.

"That's one of our biggest visual effects in the movie," says Ritvo. "Because of the very dynamic camera move that Dana created, every element in there is CGI, except the stage and the characters. Well, Nightmare Josh is real up to a point. But it's a CG mop, and a CG prosthetic that we're adding to his face to explode it. It was a lot of fun."

In the days of the original *Toxic Avenger*, and with Troma's shoestring budgets, it's not hard to imagine Lloyd Kaufman and Michael Herz achieving the same gag with a few squibs and a packet of beef mince. But, even to a pro like Ritvo, that was all part of the original's appeal. "I think the fun of the original *Toxie* is the low-budget practicalness of it," he says. "It doesn't have to be hyper-real. Its low-budgetness is its tone, you could say. The audience is in on the joke. And I think it's very important that we don't lose that."

Below Toxie goes out on a limb; specifically, Spence's right arm.

Right The bloody practical FX includes this field-surgery scene, where Guthrie saves J.J.'s life.

Bottom left Blair and his crew, hard at work on location.

Bottom right The crew captures a little more Toxie mayhem.

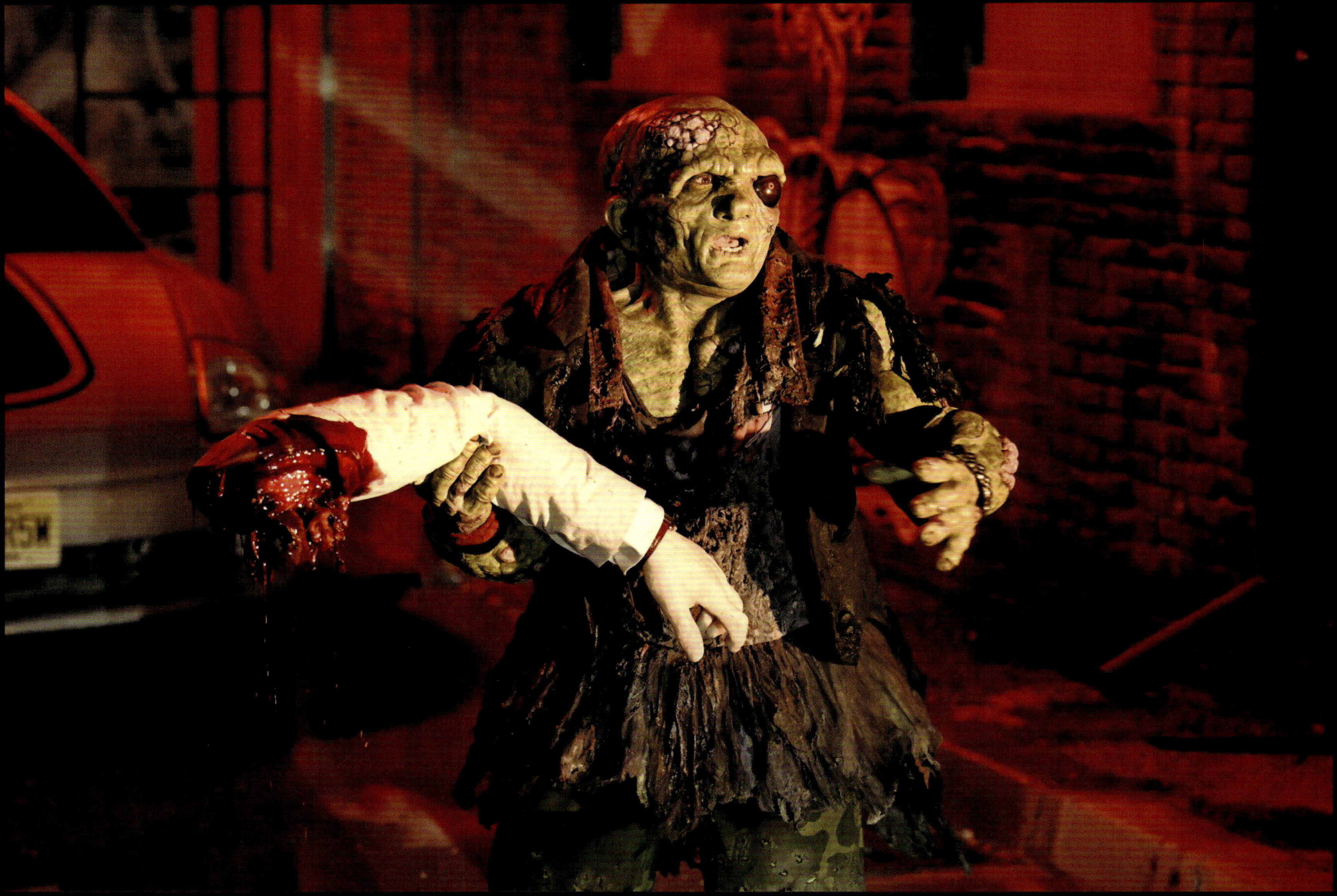

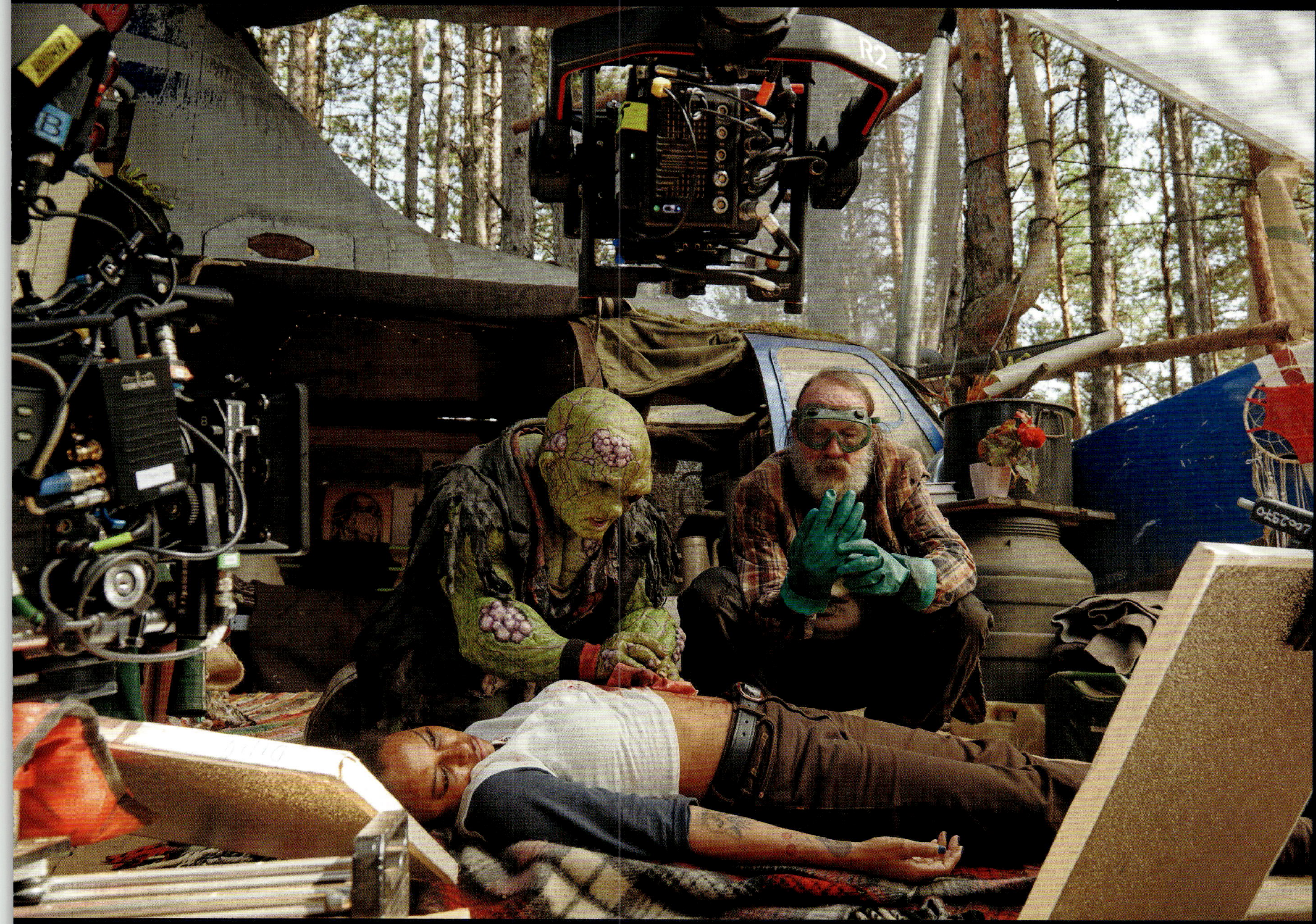

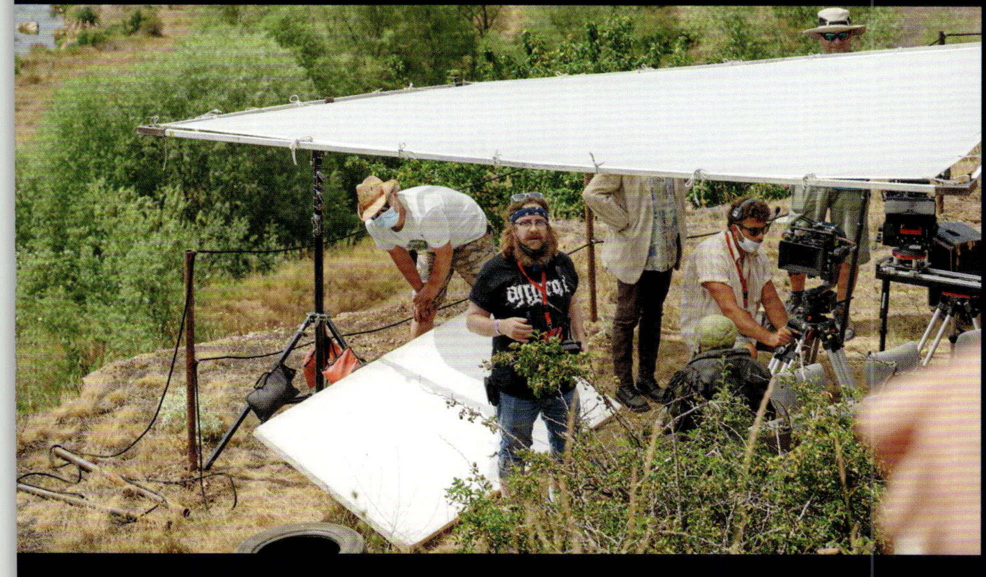

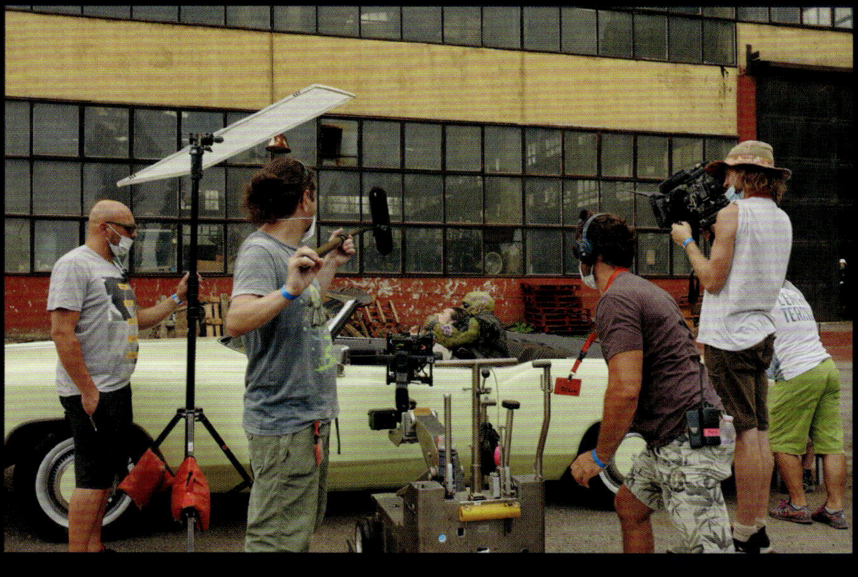

LLOYD

PLAYED BY LLOYD KAUFMAN

"Michael Herz wanted to get rid of me for a while," says Lloyd Kaufman, referring to his Troma co-founder and producing partner of 51 years. "So I forced Macon to give me a cameo, and he was gracious enough to do it."

Kaufman is joking, of course (he does that a lot). In truth, it was important to Blair that the creator of the original Toxie should make an appearance somewhere in his movie, and that he should make that appearance alongside Blair himself, already established in his role of the "loudmouth" stoner Dennis. This meeting of directors occurs in one of the film's final scenes, where a crowd at the hospital is cheering the wounded but triumphant Toxie, with Dennis cheering louder than most.

"Then the camera pulls a little wider and you realise that Lloyd is standing next to Dennis," says Blair. "And Lloyd says, 'Can you keep your voice down? You're being ridiculous.' The gist is that Lloyd is saying, 'This movie sucks. My movie was better!' He's basically shitting on this movie, and I thought the best version of that would be to have him directing that commentary to me. Lloyd loved the idea, and we had a great time."

Kaufman has some stories to tell about his brief time visiting the set of *The Toxic Avenger* to play the character named in the script as "Lloyd, the hospital grump." And, as is often the case with Lloyd Kaufman, they're best served raw. So, enjoy...

"I went over there to Bulgaria, which is a beautiful country. The food is great. I'm a vegetarian, and the food they had on set included a vegetarian option. That was terrific!

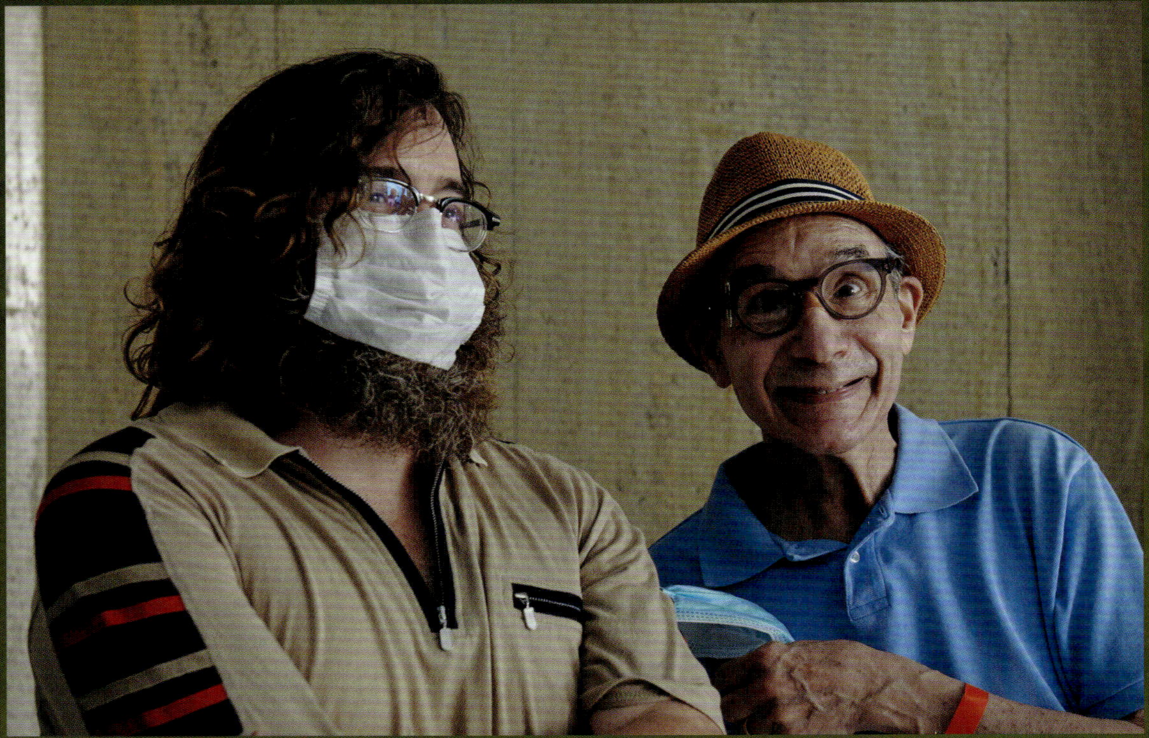

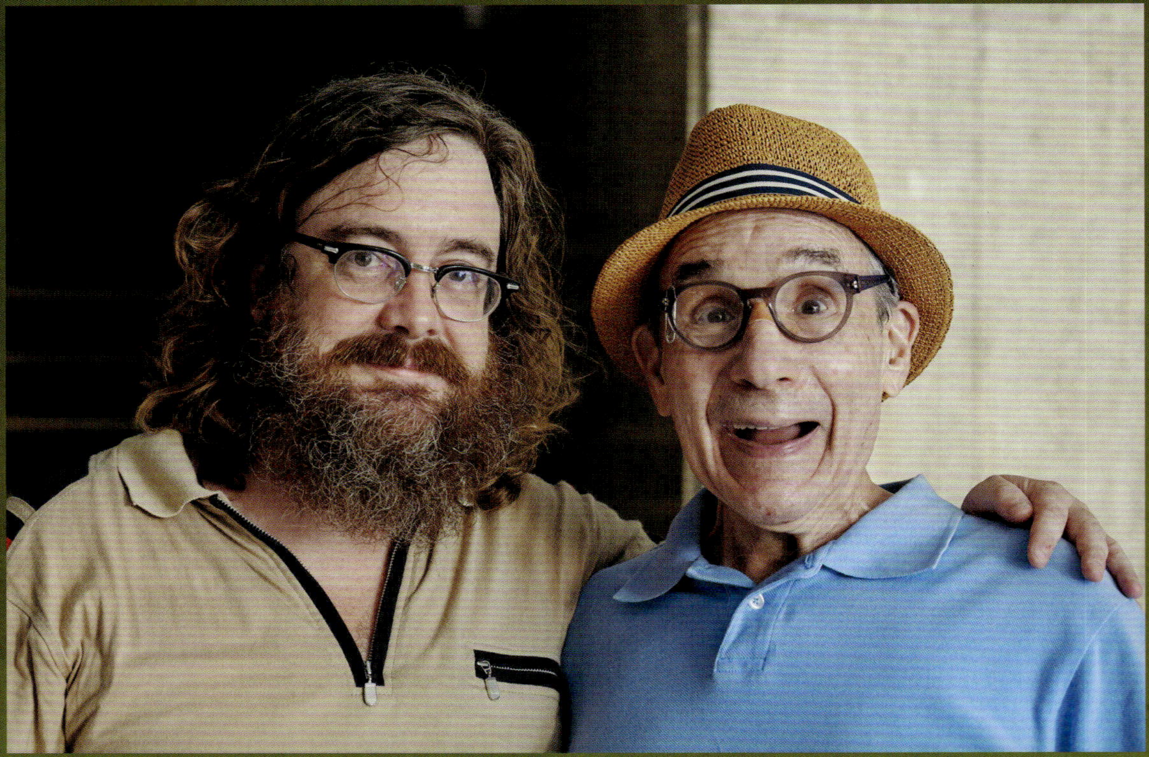

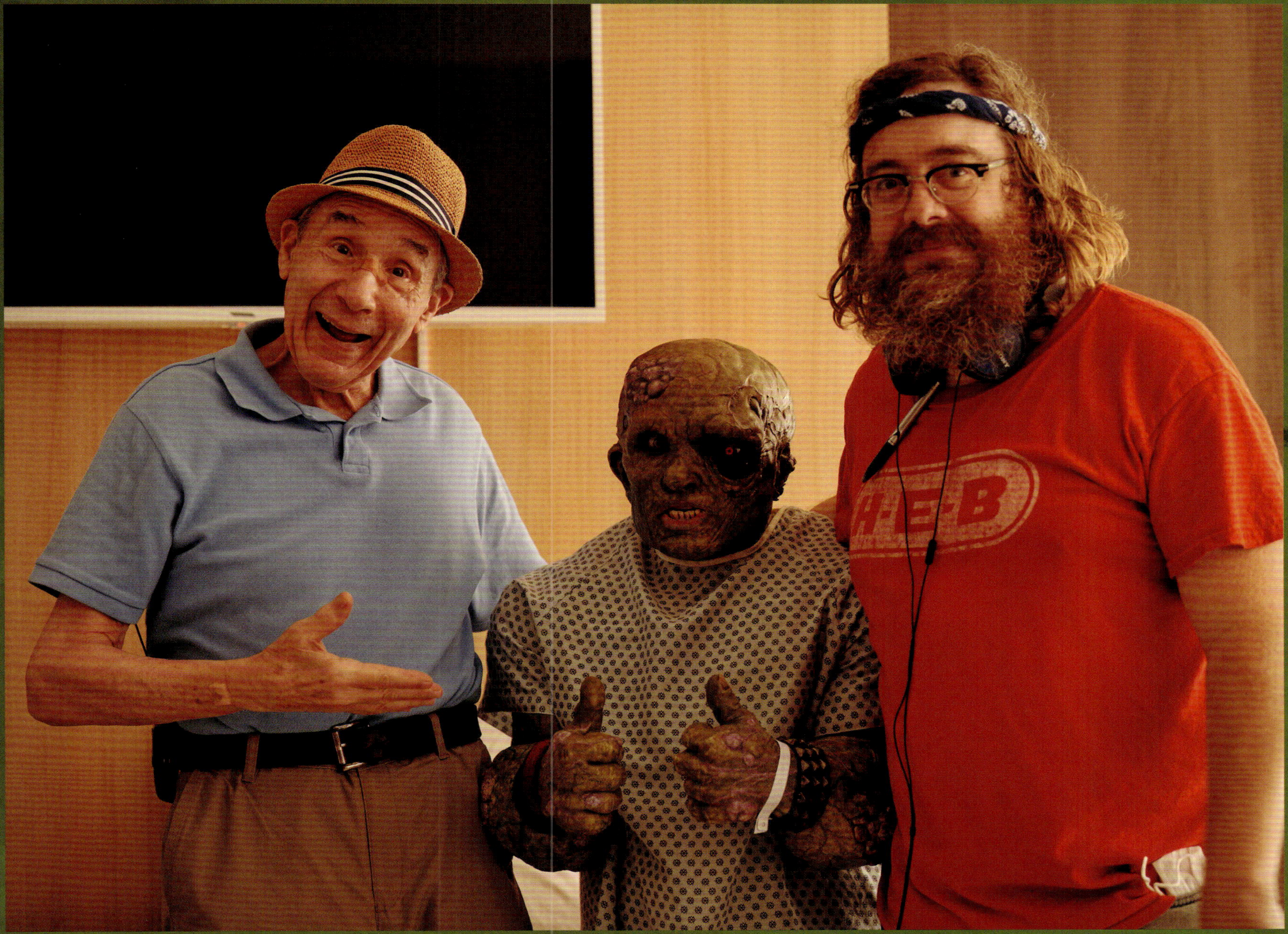

"And the crew was terrific. It was great, well-run. Legendary did a great job. Great people. Wonderful cast.

"One day, I saw Peter Dinklage sitting alone, so I go up to him and I start kissing his ass. You know: 'Oh Peter, this is so wonderful. I love you. I can't wait to see *Cyrano*. Did you see *The Toxic Avenger*, Peter, when you were younger? What did you think?' Then a Bulgarian on the crew comes up and says, 'He doesn't speak English! He doesn't speak English!' So, that was Peter's double. His stand-in.

"The next day, they wanted to introduce me to some people on the set, and there was Toxie in bed, in the hospital room. I assumed it was Peter, because it wasn't like he was doing any stunts. So I did the same thing again and it was a British woman [Luisa Guerreiro] inside the costume and the mask. She was extremely pleasant, she asked for a hug, and it all worked out great. Although I looked pretty stupid..."

Opposite Page Blair and Kaufman pose for some shots during Kaufman's cameo on set.

Above Original *Toxic Avenger* director and creator Lloyd Kaufman with Guerreiro as Toxie and new *Toxic Avenger* director Blair.

BONUS CONTENT!

A TOXIC FLASHBACK

It all began, like some of the best fairy tales, with a frog.

Indie filmmaker Lloyd Kaufman and his wife Pat were on a camping trip in the United States during the summer of 1981. Wherever they travelled they noticed, with some disgust, Styrofoam fast-food containers and cups littered everywhere. One day, Kaufman found a frog struggling along with a plastic beer-can pack ring tangled around one of its hind legs. "It was clearly not going to get very far," he says now. "So, after I laughed at it for quite a while, I freed it from captivity…

"No, I did not laugh at it! I'm a big animal-rights person. That's very important, as well as the environment."

This amphibian encounter, and the environmental concern it awoke in Kaufman, were just the first ingredient of a heady cocktail that resulted in 1984's *The Toxic Avenger*. There was also his and his Troma Entertainment partner Michael Herz's contrary desire to make a horror movie, just as *Variety* announced the horror movie was dead. Plus, the compulsion to set it in a gym, which came from Kaufman's stint as a location manager on *Rocky* ("the training scenes in *Rocky* presented some good satire and also some very good violence"). And his love of *Frankenstein*, of course—not to mention the concept of the monster being a good guy, which went back to an unmade script Kaufman had written with Stan Lee (yes, *that* Stan Lee) in 1971, titled *Night of the Witch*.

"The witch only killed bad people," Kaufman explains. "The people who got killed made the bombs for Vietnam or manipulated the stock market. So actually, the witch at the end of the movie turns out to be a good person. And she turns out to be a man."

With a budget of only around $500,000, the movie—then called *Health Club Horror* — went into production in New Jersey, with the shoot focusing on Jersey City. "In those days it literally was a dump," says Kaufman. "The whole waterfront was totally derelict, so that *was* Tromaville! Now that whole area's been cleaned up. They kicked out all the original community: elderly people and people of colour. All the yuppies moved in to where we were filming."

To play bullied nerd Melvin, who becomes the "monster hero", Kaufman and Herz roped in the film's script supervisor Mark Torgl, who'd also script-supervised and appeared in previous Troma production *The First Turn-On!* "Mark's, uh… *unusual* acting added a lot to the insanity of the film,"[1] Kaufman once wrote, referring to the fact that, thanks to Torgl's performance, some viewers took Melvin as being less awkward than developmentally disabled.

For Toxie, meanwhile, they found the 6'4" tall Mitchell Cohen, who Kaufman credits with bringing a lot of kindness and "comedic grace"[2] to the character. He also suffered through four hours of makeup each day, despite being paid "very little," Kaufman admits. (This might explain why he didn't return for any of the sequels.) Still, it could have been worse.

"My original concept for Toxie was to be very disgusting, to have pus coming out of his face, and worms and maggots. Really horrible," says Kaufman. "But our special-effects makeup artist Jenny Aspinall — who has become very successful, from *Saturday*

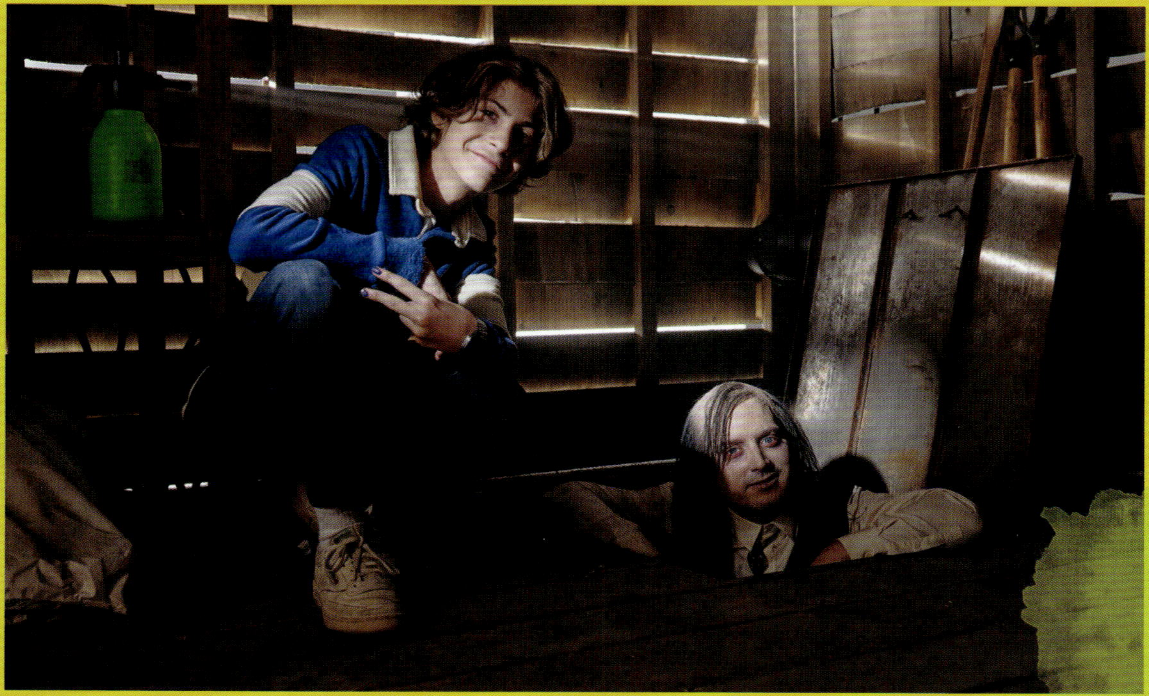

Left Tremblay and Wood pose between takes.

Opposite page A gallery of behind-the-scenes snaps during production in Sofia, Bulgaria.

---

1 *All I Need to Know About Filmmaking I Learned From The Toxic Avenger*, Lloyd Kaufman and James Gunn, p. 173

2 ibid. p. 172

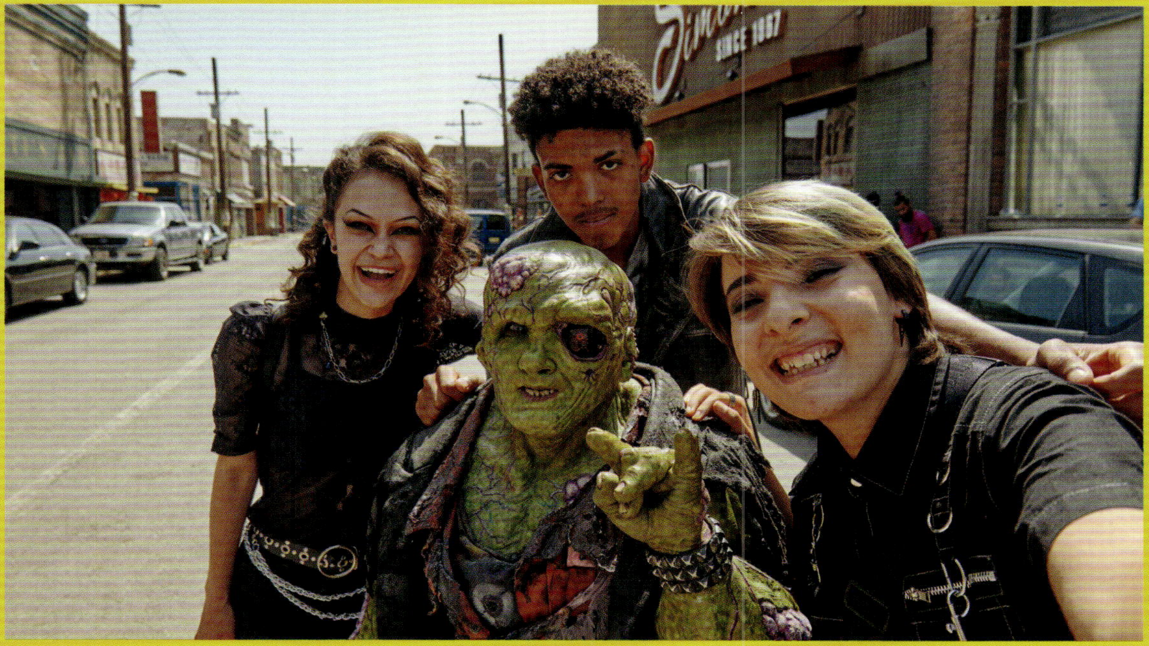
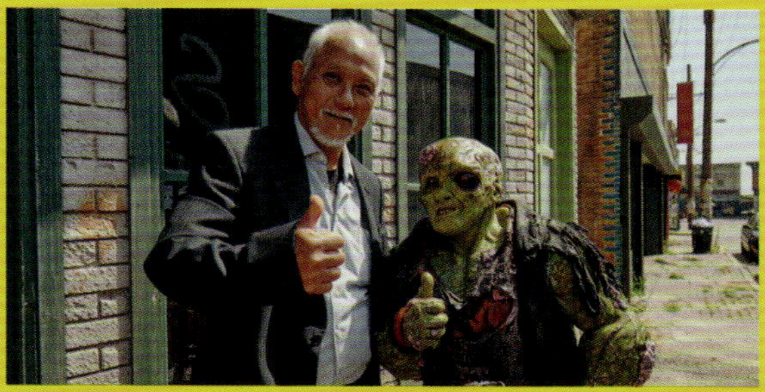
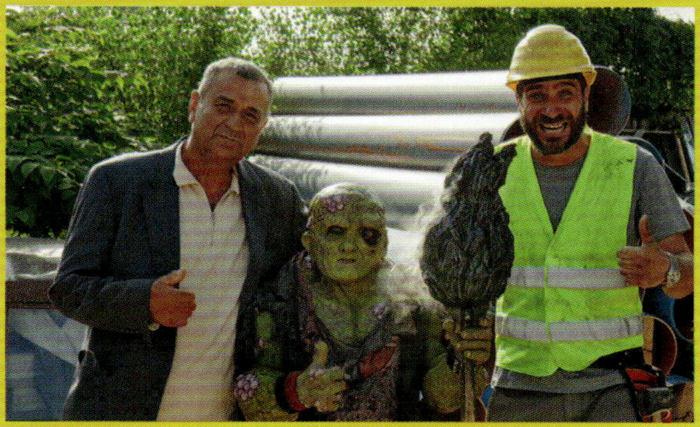
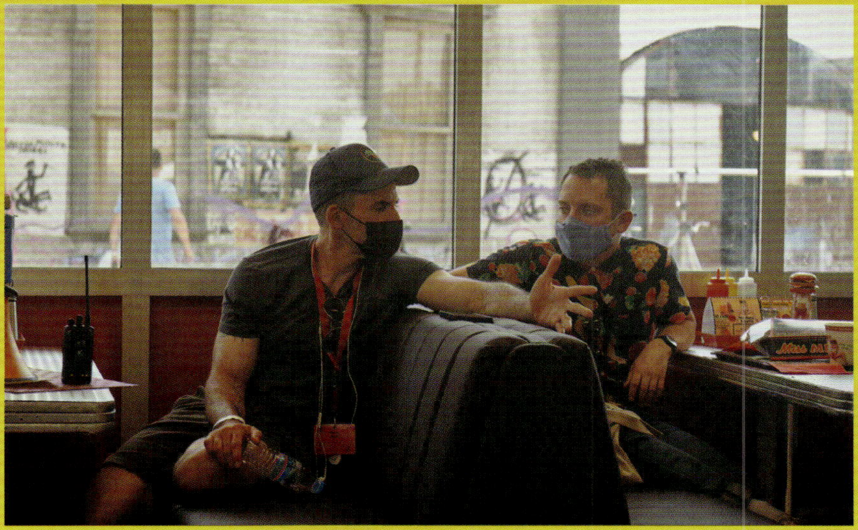
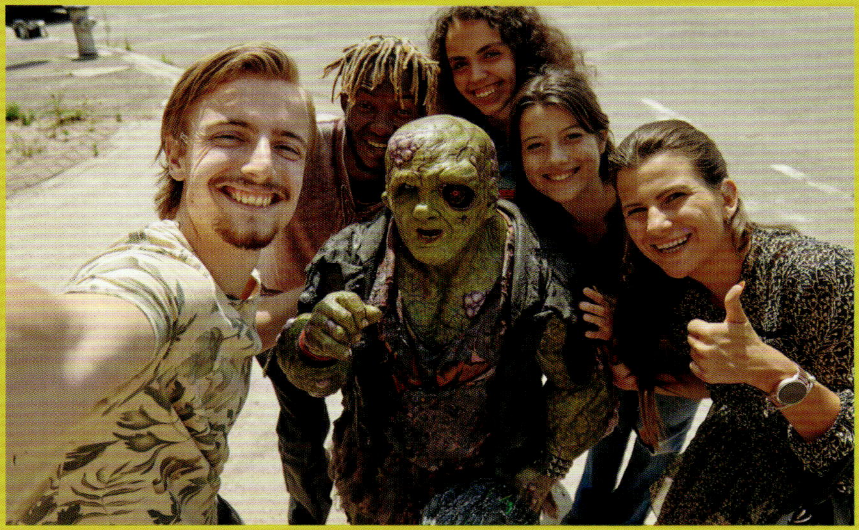
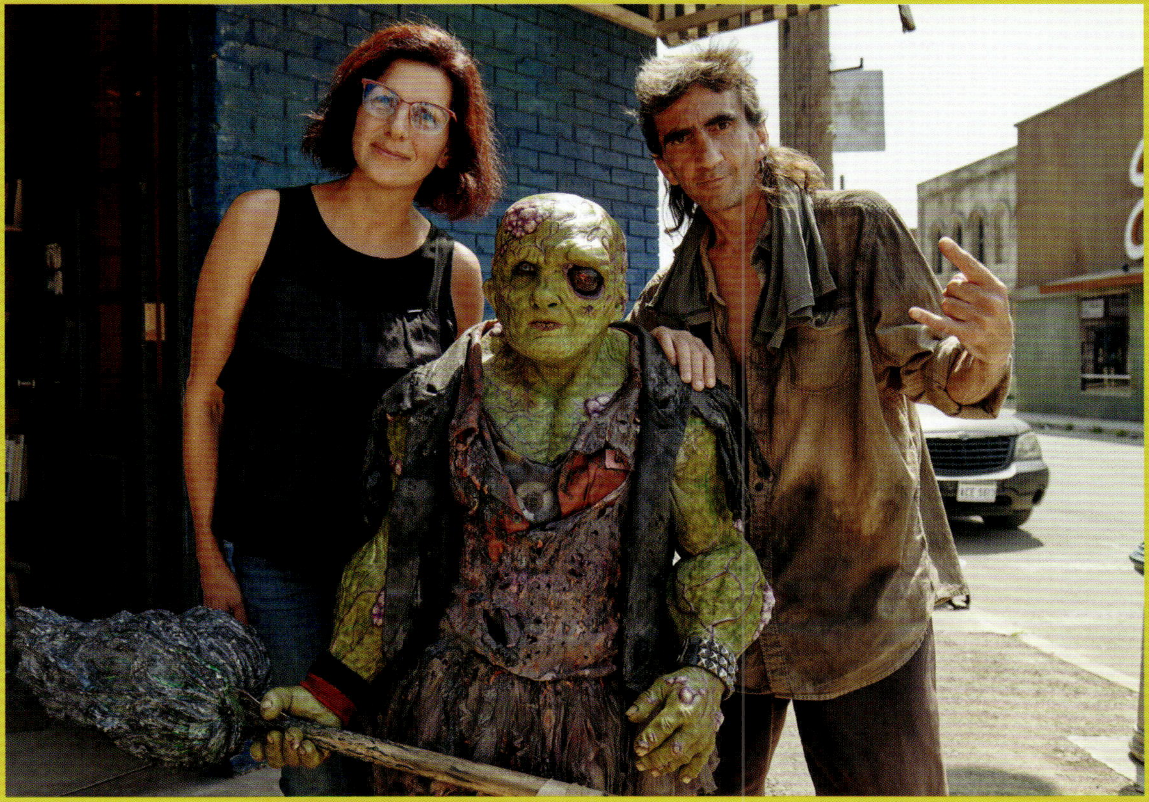
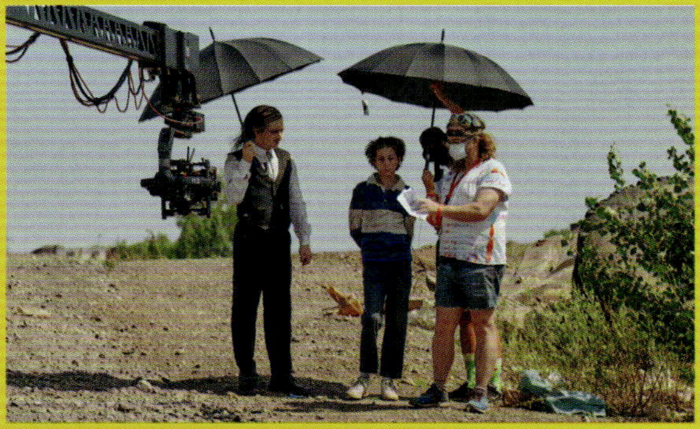
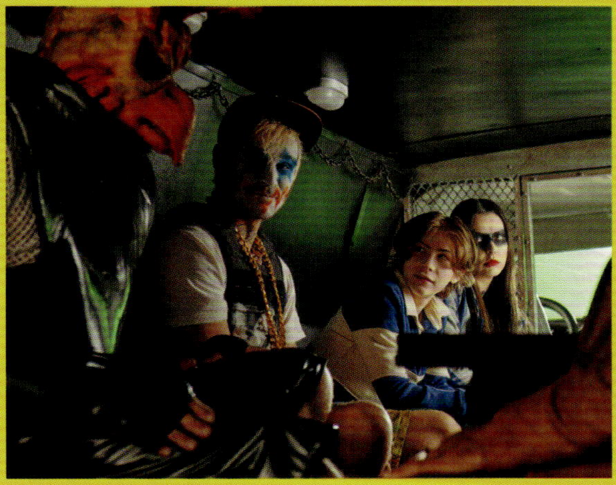

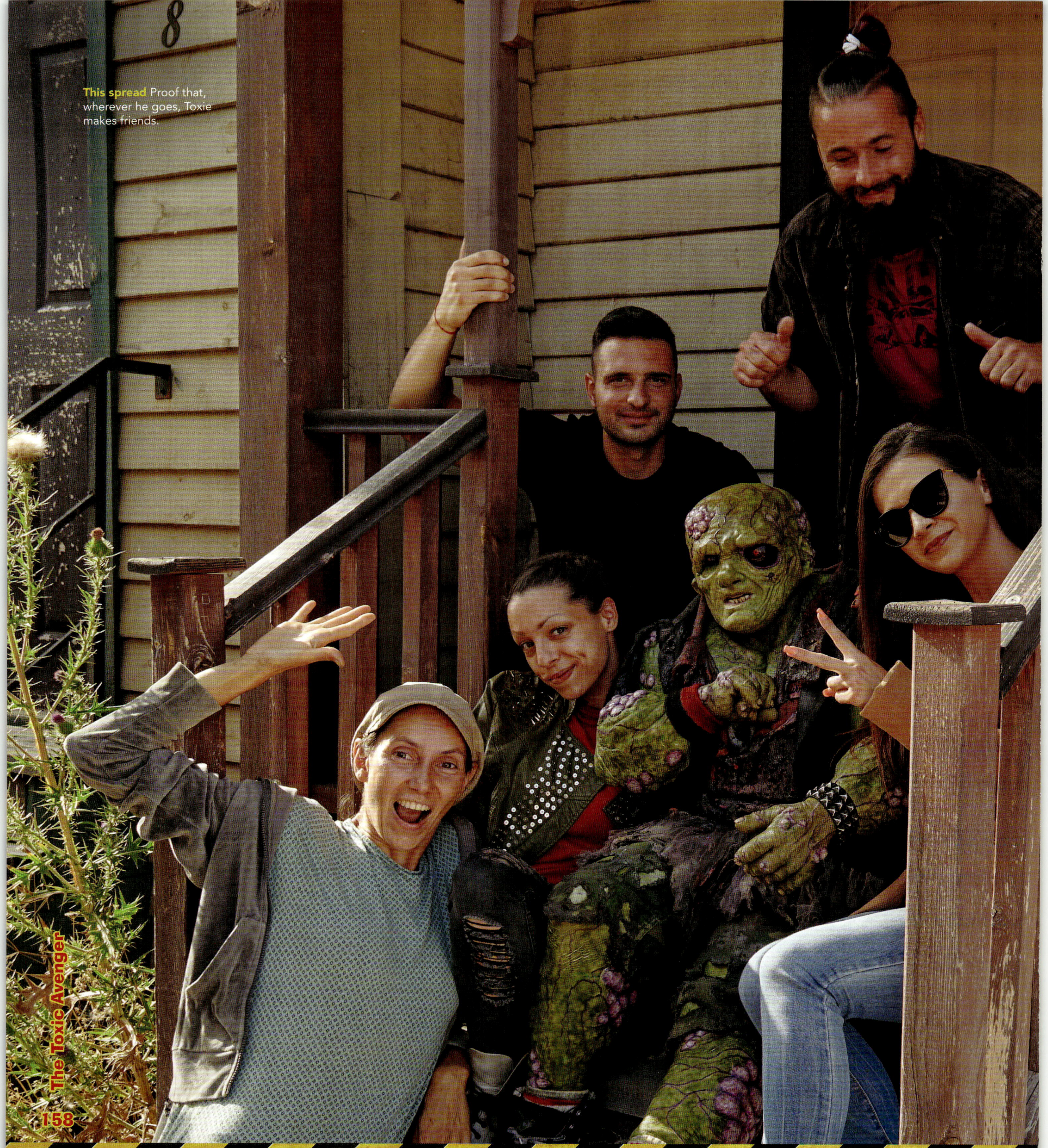

This spread Proof that, wherever he goes, Toxie makes friends.

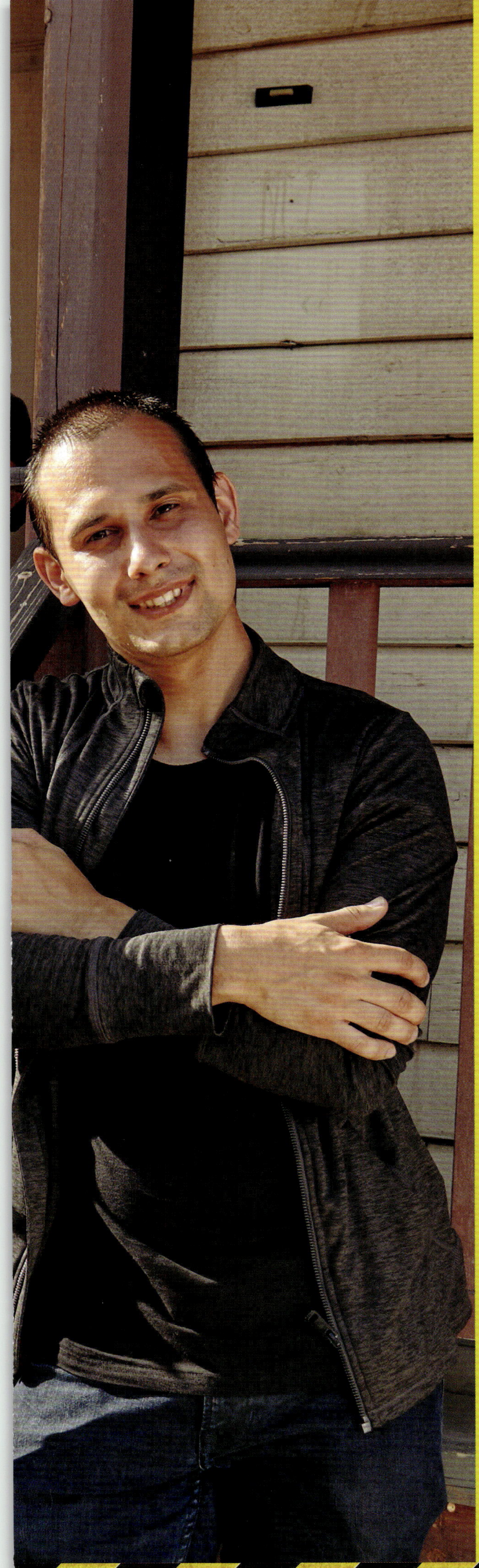

Night Live to the Metropolitan Opera—kept sending me back sketches of this sympathetic-looking guy with a wonderful set of teeth and a very sweet face. I kept sending them back, saying, 'No, I want snot coming out of its nose!' And she just politely kept ignoring me."

Eventually, Kaufman had to start shooting, so he gave up sending Aspinall notes to make Toxie more repulsive and just resignedly accepted her design. Soon after, he realized Aspinall was right all along. "While we were filming in the streets, I noticed that children would run after Toxie. Little kids. They weren't scared of him. They loved him!"

It wasn't always the smoothest of productions. The scene where Melvin is dressed in a polka-dot tutu and stumbles around in the street, screaming as toxic waste burns his skin while a crowd looks on and laughs, became too much for Torgl. "I'm being exploited!"[3] he complained to Kaufman, who chose not to push him any further and wrapped the scene with the footage they had.

More serious was the car stunt that went wrong. Inspired by *Mad Max: The Road Warrior*, Kaufman craved some vehicular mayhem in his movie, and concocted a stunt that would see a car hit a ramp and flip over onto its roof. To achieve this, he had a roll bar fitted into a car, to prevent the roof being flattened and crushing the driver. But when he and Herz filmed the sequence, the flipped vehicle "flattened like an accordion"[4], as Kaufman described it. This was the result of the roll bar not being installed correctly; it had simply been bolted to the floor of the car and was pushed through its underside on impact. Miraculously, the stunt driver survived, relatively unscathed.

One of the last things to fall into place was, surprisingly, the film's title. This is why its monster hero is only rarely referred to as "the Toxic Avenger" during the movie; it required some 11th-hour dubbing to get in those mentions. By the time he was editing, Kaufman was sure *Health Club Horror* needed to change, and decided the title had to involve the word "Toxic". As he recounts in his book *All I Need to Know About Filmmaking I Learned From The Toxic Avenger*, he spent weeks trying to find the right noun to go with it: "Toxic Cereal Box. Toxic Pit Bull. Toxic Pencil. Toxic My Leg."[5] In the end, he credits his friend Walter Manley (producer of 1968 sci-fi horror *The Green Slime*) with suggesting "Avenger". Mainly because, Manley told Kaufman, movies containing that word in their title performed well abroad.

And true enough, the film did go down very well in Japan (one of the reasons why the sequel is largely set there), while, as previously mentioned, it became a midnight-movie hit in the United States, while establishing Troma as a trash-cinema powerhouse. But the most important thing to realize about the original *Toxic Avenger*—apart from it having that bit where the kid gets his head squished—is that for Kaufman, really, it's always been personal.

"My wife says that the Toxic Avenger is *me*," he says. She makes a good point. While Kaufman is by no means "hideously deformed," he (and by extension Troma) has always been an outsider, doing things his own way beyond the confines of the Hollywood system, and often receiving opprobrium for the usually offensive results. Yet the purity of his intentions is hard to question.

As *The Toxic Avenger* shows to anyone who pays attention, beneath all its slime, gore, violence and titillation, you can feel the steady beat of a good heart. A heart belonging to somebody who cares about the environment and community in the face of corporate malpractice and indifference. Somebody who also, at the end of the day, just wants you to have a bloody good time.

3 ibid. p. 173

4 ibid. p. 217

5 ibid. p. 176

ACKNOWLEDGMENTS

FROM DAN JOLIN

At Titan Books, I'd like to thank Frankie Piscitelli, my editor of superhuman size and strength (who is in no way hideously deformed), along with ace designer Kerry Lewis, who made my words look punkily fabulous. I'm also grateful to non-fiction managing editor Jo Boylett and the all-round lovely bunch at Titan, who are a pleasure to work with.

At Legendary, big thanks to Robert Napton, whose assistance in gathering together all the Toxie talent proved invaluable, and Zak Kline for sharing a wealth of cool and fascinating visual reference materials. Speaking of talent, I remain stunned by the sheer generosity and geniality of writer-director Macon Blair, who gave up many hours of his very precious time to chat with me during the crazy throes of post-production, even Zooming from his sickbed one week. I'd also like to thank producer Alex Garcia (with whom I've had the pleasure of chatting about many movie monsters over the years), production designer Alex Cameron for going above and beyond in his world-building illumination, and the idiosyncratic icon that is Lloyd Kaufman for his sometimes not entirely printable insights and often hilarious stories. I would also like to give special thanks to Michael Herz, Romy Schneider, everyone at Cineverse, and the Legendary Creative Marketing team.

Then, of course, there are all the other interviewees who carved time out of their busy schedules to talk to me: Julia Davis (great to natter with over a Soho cuppa), Peter Dinklage (who kindly offered to send help when he thought I might be lost in a cave — don't ask), Dana Gonzales, Chris Goodman, Luisa Guerreiro (yes, she said "coccyx"), Taylour Paige, Vanessa Porter, Chris Ritvo, Jacob Tremblay, Kate Walshe and one-time Ringbearer Elijah Wood (nobody else uses the word "rad" with such panache).

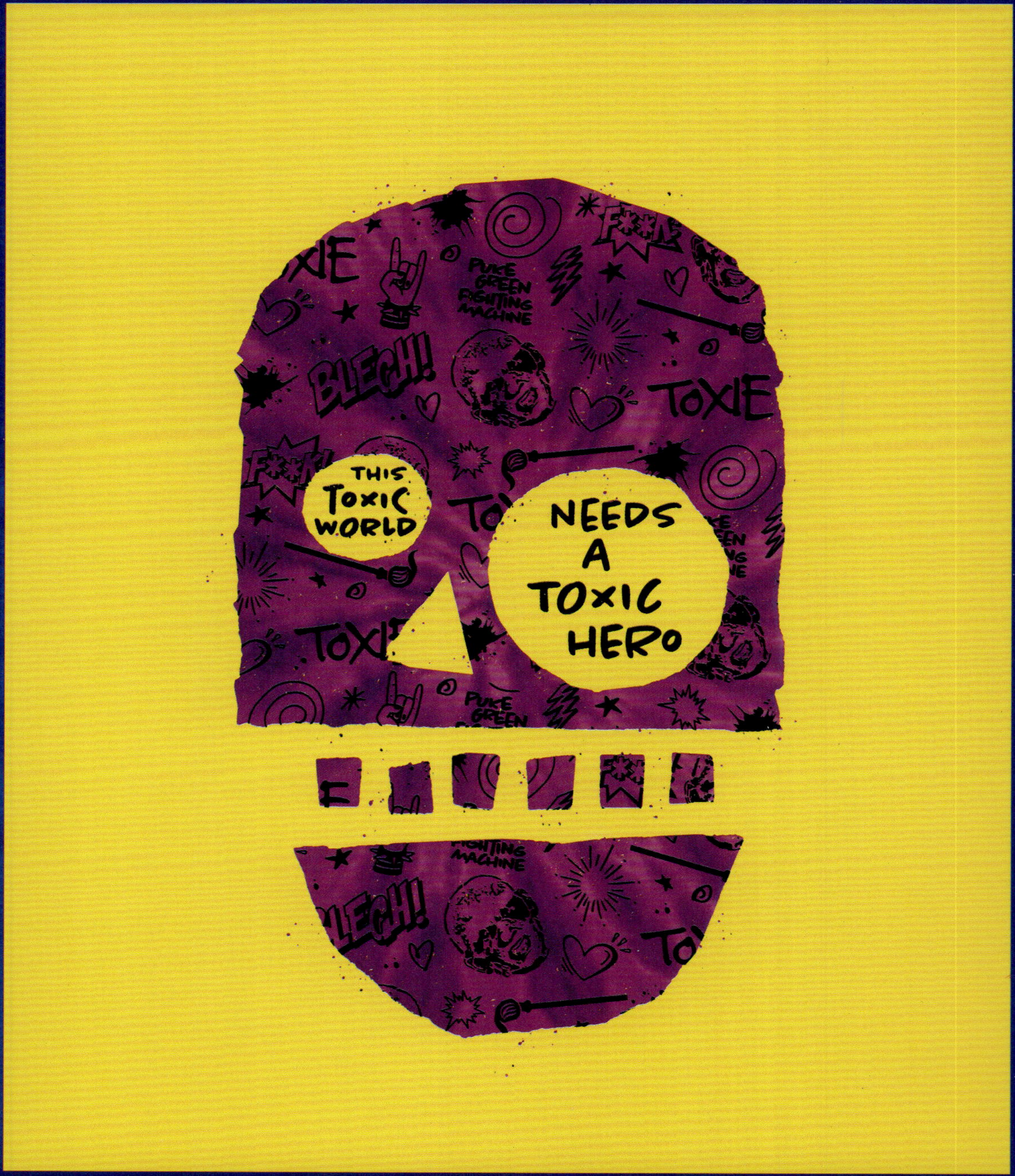

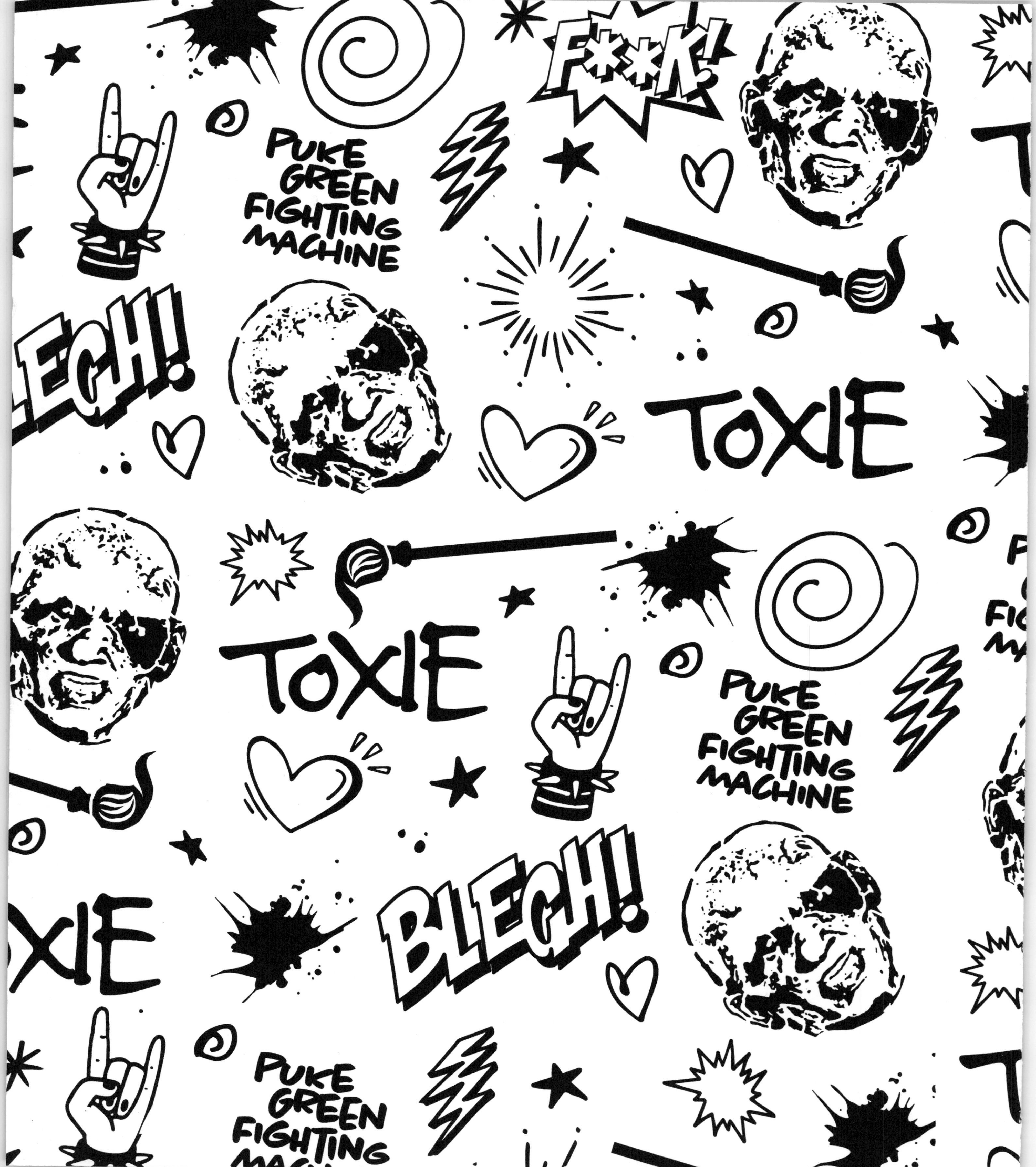
F**K!
PUKE GREEN FIGHTING MACHINE
BLECH!
TOXIE
TOXIE
PUKE GREEN FIGHTING MACHINE
BLECH!
PUKE GREEN FIGHTING